The Work of Words

The Work of Words

Literature, Craft, and the Labour of
Mind in Britain, 1830–1940

Marcus Waithe

EDINBURGH
University Press

Edinburgh University Press is one of the leading university presses in the UK. We publish academic books and journals in our selected subject areas across the humanities and social sciences, combining cutting-edge scholarship with high editorial and production values to produce academic works of lasting importance. For more information visit our website: edinburghuniversitypress.com

Edinburgh University Press Ltd
13 Infirmary Street
Edinburgh EH1 1LT

First published in hardback by Edinburgh University Press 2023

Typeset in 10.5/13 Adobe Sabon by
IDSUK (DataConnection) Ltd

A CIP record for this book is available from the British Library

ISBN 978 1 3995 1229 9 (hardback)
ISBN 978 1 3995 1230 5 (paperback)
ISBN 978 1 3995 1231 2 (webready PDF)
ISBN 978 1 3995 1232 9 (epub)

Contents

Figures

Acknowledgements

I wish to thank the Leverhulme Trust for the award of the Research Fellowship that enabled me to complete this book. Additionally, I am grateful to the Master and Fellows of Magdalene College, Cambridge, and to the Faculty of English at the University of Cambridge, for supporting my research.

I have received assistance from librarians at a number of institutions, including The Ruskin: Library, Museum and Research Centre (Lancaster University), Gladstone's Library (Hawarden), the Huntington Library (San Marino, CA), the John Rylands Library (University of Manchester), Cambridge University Library, the British Library, and the Bodleian Library (University of Oxford).

This book has benefited from the help of many people over the long period of its inception and composition. I want to thank Ruth Abbott, Matthew Bevis, Dinah Birch, Joe Bray, Matthew Campbell, Lida Lopes Cardozo Kindersley, Helen Cooper, Rita Dózsai, Jonathan Ellis, Georgina Evans, Daniel Gabelman, Josephine Gabelman, John Gardner, James Grellier, Ingrid Hanson, Alex Houen, Jane Hughes, Michael Hurley, Duncan Kelly, Fern Leathers, Joel Love, Elizabeth Carolyn Miller, Sarah Mollart, Kathryn Murphy, Francis O'Gorman, Jane Partner, Péti Miklós, Richard Salmon, Jan-Melissa Schramm, Goran Stanivukovic, David Trotter, Carl Watkins, John Whale, Claire White, Claire Wilkinson, and Clive Wilmer. I am especially grateful for the care, collegiality, and intellectual generosity, of the two anonymous Readers appointed by the Press.

My greatest debt is to my parents, for the way they have encouraged my own work of words.

Preface

Basil Bunting's short poem 'What the Chairman Told Tom' (1965) stages a one-sided exchange between a self-styled authority figure and a poet. 'Poetry?' the Chairman exclaims, 'It's a hobby': 'It's not work. You dont sweat' [*sic*].[1] The pompous tone and shifting argument lend the sense of a voice designed to bring suspicion of the arts into disrepute.[2] At the same time, the poem puts up an uneasy sort of resistance. While the indignant query 'How could I look a bus conductor | in the face | if I paid you twelve pounds?' is transparently cynical, it also hangs awkwardly in the air. Tom might argue that poetry has been mischaracterised, that poetry is 'work' after all. But it isn't obvious what counterclaims would convince the Chairman. Should Tom advance an alternative conception of work, one suited to the poet's labour? Or should poetic effort be reshaped to fit an existing definition? If the first option sounds overly ambitious, the second gives too much away. Tom might defend poetry on its own terms, as something other than work; but he would do so at the risk of reducing it to a distraction, akin to the 'model trains' the Chairman recommends as a more wholesome hobby.

The poem addresses the vexed relationship between the value accorded to work in modern British society and the unstable basis for valuing literary endeavour. Such problems are not new: the spectre of the idle artist has haunted the terms of public debate for centuries. In 1904, W. B. Yeats wrote that 'to articulate sweet sounds together | Is to work harder' than to 'scrub a kitchen pavement, or break stones', 'and yet | Be thought an idler by the noisy set | of bankers, school masters, and clergymen'.[3] The speaker in Vladimir Mayakovsky's 'The Poet Worker' (1918) complains that 'They shout at a poet: "Why aren't you doing a real job, working a lathe, bolt and nuts? [. . .]"'.[4] Yeats and Mayakovsky were writing at the end of a period during which writers sought solutions to problems of cultural self-definition. And yet, anything like Mayakovsky's answer that 'We smooth brains with the file of our tongue' seems out of reach for Bunting's Tom. Instead, it is the lack of novelty in his predicament – its belatedness – that defines a sense of disappointment, offering mute testimony to the falling away of more confident methods of self-justification.

This book examines the life cycle of one such defence of artistic effort. Arising in the literary and philosophical culture of early Victorian Britain, its impetus was felt among writers who needed to believe – and yet doubted – that their primary occupation qualified as work. In this context, comparisons with manual labour are understood less as slights than as a self-invited challenge. The work of the hands had the advantage of being demonstrable, visibly strenuous, and purportedly honest. If writing, too, could be invested with manual or craft connotation, and its practical characteristics revealed, its working credentials might then be assured. The precise form of this strategy varies between individuals, and across generations. It is complicated by differing class and gender positions, and it means different things at different times. Instead of an unbroken arc, a recurrence of related approaches emerges across the date span of this book. The links between cases nevertheless reveal explicable, if sometimes counterintuitive, chains of influence and inheritance.

As will become clear, these Victorian and early twentieth-century solutions fall short in several respects. They accord insufficient attention to the distinctive nature of manual process and physical craftsmanship; and they suppress the intangible aspects of written composition in ways that are self-defeating. Equally, an investment in the author as the sole agent of production obscures the breadth of a book's material genesis, ranging from the work of typesetting and binding to that of proofing and editing.[5] What remains of value is the effort to propose a *working* model of literature at all. Today's service economy is distant from the Victorian 'workshop of the world'; but it feels remote, too, from the manufacturing society of Bunting's 1960s poem. The paradox endures, all the same, that the further modern society departs from processes of material production, the more its unofficial conceptions of value evince longing for the intrinsic and the visible. The Chairman's work is bureaucratic, but he commends 'sweat' all the same. The contortions of 'management speak' frequently employ metaphors drawn from mechanical processes. Meanwhile, government funding models instrumentalise books and articles as 'outputs', as if emerging from a production line established by a Taylorian caste of experts. Writers today face versions of the same charge that 'It's not work'. The difference is that they are comparatively unprepared to defend themselves. The conditions of the present are complex and singular, but our continuing hesitation over matters of value and vocation in intellectual life confers special interest on past attempts to provide a credible answer.

Introduction

In a revised edition of his influential compendium *The Literary Character* (1818), Isaac D'Israeli observes that it was Jean de La Bruyère who 'discovered the world's erroneous estimate of literary labour'.[1] 'There requires', he reports, 'a better name to be bestowed on the leisure (the idleness he calls it) of the literary character', so 'that to meditate, to compose, to read and to be tranquil, should be called *working*.' Though translated from a seventeenth-century source, these words propound a distinctly nineteenth-century approach to the problem of writerly identity, one that foregrounds work by renaming and redefining disputed territory. D'Israeli begs the question in the process: he refers to 'literary labour' as if it were a settled category, and his easy movement between thinking, composing, and reading goes unexplained. But even these cross-currents are pertinent. They express enduring uncertainty about whether literary effort dwells in the mind, on the page, or elsewhere. And they evince a corrective focus on language, a medium susceptible to reform because coined and reissued by writers themselves.

Understanding such claims requires an appreciation of what authors thought the world was erroneously estimating. In *Absent Minds* (2006), Stefan Collini distinguishes the ways that intellectuals talk about themselves – notably, the various 'Fall' narratives unwittingly or deliberately perpetuated – from the historical record.[2] This, it turns out, reveals a less tortured social experience than we tend to expect. The history of legislation governing literary reward substantiates this analysis. Discussing Talfourd's second reform to the Copyright Act 1814, Martha Woodmansee notes the scale of its success in 'confer[ring] dignity on the profession of authorship'.[3] Brad Sherman and Lionel Bently, likewise, document the 'privilege' in law accorded to 'the labour of mind over that of the body'.[4] In particular, they show that a legal window opened briefly in the mid-nineteenth century, when mental labour was not just recognised by the courts but regarded as a test of ownership. This study is influenced by such revisionist accounts, but it focuses on the action of writing (and therefore 'the writer') rather than on the figure of the 'intellectual'. And it proceeds on the assumption that anxieties about the life of the mind are revealing – and indeed subtly causative – even where they are misplaced. Equally, it is clear that writers' legal advantages conferred limited reputational benefit. As Deirdre David observes, artistic and intellectual roles were consistently 'associated by the Victorian middle class with unprofitably utilised leisure'.[5] The timing of D'Israeli's complaint is significant in this respect. By the first half of the nineteenth century, the system of aristocratic patronage – previously the chief support for writers – had fallen into disuse. This situation coincided unhappily with increased emphasis on the social value of demonstrable effort, an overdetermined, and broadly ethical, influence that would later be dubbed the 'Gospel of Work'.

Scholarly interest in this popular phenomenon first stirred in the 1950s, with publications on the subject by Asa Briggs and Walter Houghton.[6] While Briggs concentrated on Samuel Smiles and self-reliance, Houghton discussed the mystical absolutism of Thomas Carlyle and the post-Romantic 'dignity of labour'. Both are notable for tracing the Gospel through the period's material culture.[7] Late twentieth-century historians and critics continued to address these manifestations.[8] Raymond Williams and Catherine Gallagher explored the ways in which work comes to the surface of literature, a medium ostensibly devoted to the reader's leisure.[9] A more recent iteration of this approach – Carolyn Lesjak's *Working Fictions* (2006) – concentrates on 'labor's less visible presence in Victorian novels and nonfiction', 'its imprint in unexpected places'.[10] By contrast, it is the field of authorial labour that concerns me here. Rather than approaching labour as a literary topic, I consider its bearing on writers and the writing process. Indeed, it is only relatively recently that critics have turned attention to the way that the Gospel conditioned occupational anxiety among writers. Two strands of scholarship stand out. The first focuses on comparisons with manual labour; only, it understands the literary version of the Gospel less as a moment in the long history of modern work ethics than as a crisis in the history of masculinity. In broad terms, the contention is that male authors revered manual labour because they feared that letters had become feminised, with the literary working environment of the home exacerbating that feminisation. Examples of this approach include Herbert Sussman's *Victorian Masculinities* (1995), Martin Danahay's *Gender at Work in Victorian Culture* (2005), and Tim Barringer's art-historical study, *Men at Work* (2005).[11] These studies contain much that is compelling and persuasive, but their version of the Victorian home implies the constrained roles of a 1950s suburban household. This initially convinces, because advocates of the 'separate spheres' were already seeking to code the domestic realm as female. But that process was far from complete, and even in the notorious case of Ruskin's *Sesame and Lilies* (1865), the oft-quoted allusion to 'man's work in open world' sits alongside calls for women's 'physical training' and a broader philosophy that understands 'House-law' (*Oikonomia*) (17:19) as a secure root for political economy.[12] Equally, the factory system and the daily commute had yet to efface the memory of cottage industry: at least, not so radically that an idea of the home as workplace could not be sustained. The landed classes, for their part, were sufficiently confident in their sense of settlement not to feel that working in their study damaged their standing. As discussed in Chapter 4, scenes in the illustrated news of famous writers labouring at home revive, if anything, the dignity of the medieval scriptorium. An emphasis on masculinity also fails to catch a crucial feature of the phenomenon in question: namely, its selective appeal to women. Rather than understand physical exertion as a metaphor for work, this study concentrates on the definitional matter of what counts, and is allowed to count, as skilled labour. As such, it moves from an idea of compensatory heft to consider a more processual picture based in the traditions of craftsmanship, and an associated aspiration towards unalienated working conditions.

A second strand concentrates on a professional method of enfranchising writers: 'professional', that is, in the sense of those liberal occupations regulated by bodies such as the Law Society. Studies by Daniel Hack and Richard Salmon reveal how mid-Victorian writers constructed a new authorial professionalism from the ruins of patronage, in that way propounding an idea of literature based in agreed standards and networks of mutual support.[13] While Hack addresses the controversy around mendicant authorship sparked by William Thackeray's *Pendennis* (1848–50),[14] Salmon applies Pierre Bourdieu's term '*disenchantment*' in accounting for a move away from literary priests to literary professionals.[15] Clare Pettitt applies a related focus to the interface between professional life and the mechanical realm. Inspired by emergent professions, such as engineering, she argues that writers were 'borrowing their claim for the utility of their work' from those 'who could make a far clearer case for the use-value of their ideas'.[16] As such, she focuses less on the pre-industrial examples that concern me here – where routine process and incremental skill are paramount – than on leaps of invention connected to professional recognition and intellectual property.

The present book recognises an open field in which several tactics could flourish. Some were indeed modelled on the professional bodies that structure middle-class life.[17] Others ruled out ideas of exchange or earnings altogether, either through a reversion to aristocratic leisure, or by casting literature as a form of prophecy. William Blake's claim that

Milton (1804–11) was 'all producd without Labour or Study' epitomises the last approach.[18] Among Victorian writers, a related conception
of the '*vates* poet' runs through Carlyle's 'Man-of-Letters Hero',[19] and
Elizabeth Barrett Browning's reading of Shelley.[20] Only, in these cases
the opposition between vaticism and conscious labour begins to break
down. This proves a significant development – as I shall discuss – in
that it restores and renews the relationship between ordinary bourgeois
materialism and theology. But my own concern is neither with the prophetic nor the professional, and the cases in question strain less towards
social respectability or proprietorial relations than towards physical
prowess and manual dexterity. As such, these chapters consider a relationship with manual labour that shakes off, rather than deflects, class
shame and status anxiety. While most existing works are differently
focused in this regard, several contain passages that bear on my enquiry.
Though not addressed to craftsmanship, Danahay articulates the wider
transferred ideal that preoccupies me here: 'the uneasy class position',
as he puts it, 'of writers who professed admiration for the "Gospel of
Work", but chose the working classes as their ideal rather than the
middle classes'.[21] Barringer likewise queries 'The relationship of intellectual to manual labour' across a range of connected sources.[22] Through
her attention to the marginal case of 'artisan-mechanics', Pettitt helpfully
tests the boundary between the 'inventor-heroes' and a wider world of
technical skill.[23] Most relevantly, she demonstrates how aspirant professions bolstered their claims by 'protecting the "mysteries" of their
trades' in a fashion reminiscent of the guild system.[24] Salmon offers the
most concerted treatment of this convergence. He notes, for instance,
'the adoption of seemingly "anachronistic forms" of social production',
including the 'paraphernalia of archaic guild structures'.[25] And he demonstrates the role of Carlyle's Goethe translation – *Wilhelm Meister's
Apprenticeship* [*Wilhelm Meisters Lehrjahre*] (1794) – in conceiving a
novelistic debt to the shape of working lives.[26]

   While these examples hint tantalisingly at the reach of artisanal
premises, they also suggest the need for a dedicated – and chronologi-
cally expansive – view of their progress and success. This would take
us beyond notions of nostalgic or romantic revival, and equally of a
craftsmanship that signifies obsolete methods. Like the equally mis-
understood medievalism which it closely tracks, the craft revival
revolves around futures as well as pasts, and its qualitative emphasis eludes reductive historical placing. So, while Christopher Frayling
notes the paradox that it is in the industrial age that the crafts become
'*visible* for the first time', and as such 'admirable',[27] my findings incline
towards Jean Baudrillard's counter-claim that it is 'not enough' to define

'artisanal work' as 'a process of concrete labour, in opposition to industrial life'.[28] He conceives it, rather, as *something other than labor* in the industrial sense, since the artisan's work resists 'the transformation of his materials into use value or exchange value'.[29] Some sense of this radical otherness – this sense of re-thinking rather than simply reverting – inspires my treatment of the writerly interchange of 'concrete' and intellectual effects. In impetus, the authorial turn towards craft could be vocational, generational, class-inflected, or politically driven. By accounting for these valences, this book fills a gap in the intellectual history of literary labour. But authorial gestures of this kind were just as likely to be informed by technical aspiration: rising to the challenge, that is, of the work in hand. In this regard, vocational claims are also tested at the level of writerly texture. Clifford Siskin's portrait of eighteenth-century writing entering material states hints at where this processual emphasis might lead;[30] as does Hack's view of the mid-century novel's 'multifaceted materiality'.[31] Only, I concentrate less on materiality *per se*, or on raw productivity, than on ideas of constructedness and making. These depend, fundamentally, on the human trace, on a coincidence between conception or design and the real-time impression of chisel marks. And rather than representing the dead-end of an archaic working process, such textures activate fundamental questions concerning, among other things, the connection between new and ancient forms of value, the role of chance in relation to creative intention, ideas of reverence and creative overreach, the border between freehand work and machine work, and convergences between practical and social discipline. In short, an emphasis on craftsmanship opens a rich vein of speculation that situates occupational self-description amid aesthetic, theological, political, and philosophical issues that extend well beyond the criterion of 'hard work'.

* * *

The remainder of this introduction asks what prompted authors to redescribe themselves in the first place. As William Hogarth's famous image of *The Distrest Poet* (c. 1736) amply demonstrates, reports of impoverished and embattled artistry were hardly new.[32] But while images of dishevelment remained in circulation across the following century – and to some extent persist today – they did not escape modification. Drawing on its vocal multiplicity and powers of contrast, the Victorian novel replaced mystified hardship with ironical distance. These narrative versions of the theme present flawed characters who confuse their actual prospects with the folk memory of artistic patronage. Dickens's *Bleak*

House (1852–3), most notably, resolves the myth of poetic leisure – as exemplified by Harold Skimpole's assaults on the cant of the 'busy bee' – directly into the question of debt and dependency.[33] George Eliot dramatises similar concerns in *The Mill on the Floss* (1860). When Tom Tulliver asks his mercantile uncle why Latin should hinder him getting on, he is told that 'There's heaps of your sort, like so many pebbles made to fit in nowhere'.[34] 'Fitting in', it transpires, is continuous with being fit to contribute.

These notions find their ideological source in Adam Smith's barbed commentary on 'That unprosperous race of men commonly called men of letters': a class whose education 'at the publick expense', and whose numbers, cause their wages to be depressed by oversupply.[35] Relatedly, Smith distinguishes the 'labour of the manufacturer' – which 'fixes and realises itself in some particular subject or vendible commodity' – from the labour of those whose 'services generally perish in the very instant of their performance'.[36] Among the latter, he includes the 'menial servant', and the writer. On one level this anticipates the modern 'invisible' economy, where service roles are praised for generating wealth.[37] Only, Smith's emphasis on unfixable value suggests a closer resemblance to the perishability of agricultural produce, understood not as a service but as a waning product. We glimpse, accordingly, a critique of the French physiocrats, for whom agriculture, not manufacturing, represented the true source of national prosperity.[38]

In her seminal account of this differentiation, Hannah Arendt discusses the demise of the *vita contemplativa* – a version of the contemplative life that might recall D'Israeli's being 'tranquil' – and its associated standard, 'fame'. She understands the latter as a traditional method of fixing value, of preserving what naturally perishes.[39] Its modern abolition, in favour of transactional and commodity value, witnesses a division of all activities 'into manual and intellectual labor'.[40] Thinking, here, is not simply downgraded but despised as 'parasitical, actually a kind of perversion of labor'.[41] Recent critics have been kinder to Smith: Gallagher, among them, regards his distinction as 'a neutral analytical tool', one that was 'never intended to separate valid from invalid, or useful from useless occupations'.[42] Smith himself disclaims any dividing line based in morality or status: 'The labour of the most respectable orders in the society is,' he insists, 'like that of menial servants, unproductive of any value'.[43] For present purposes, though, the point dwells less in what Smith intends than in the occupational slight intuited by so many of his literary readers. Not without provocation, he lists among those whose labours do not fix value 'churchmen, lawyers, physicians, men of letters of all kinds; players, buffoons, musicians, opera-singers, opera-dancers,

&c.'[44] The presence of 'lawyers' and 'physicians' might reassure the suspicious, but 'men of letters of all kinds' are still found perilously close to 'buffoons', secured only by the polite fiction of a semi-colon. Spurred by such terms, D'Israeli retorts that 'jargonists' and 'arithmetical seers' have sunk 'the intellectual tasks of the library and the studio [. . .] into the class of what they term "unproductive labour"'.[45] Shelley, likewise, refers chidingly to 'the unmitigated exercise of the calculating faculty'.[46] William Hazlitt, for his part, reverses the terms of Smith's distinction: contrasting the perishable, yet skilful, mechanical labour of the Indian juggler with the lasting and more demanding work of the writer.[47]

Jeremy Bentham's infamous caricature of literature as a game of 'push-pin' ensured that similar arguments were replayed amidst the controversy surrounding utilitarianism.[48] Fought out initially between Benthamite mechanists and Coleridgean metaphysicians, the lines of argument would eventually shift to cut across that opposition. In this way, argues John Whale, 'imagination' takes its origin from 'the threat of utility', and as such is 'collusive with it'.[49] This is both an historical argument, and a poststructuralist account of mutually sustaining binary terms. In common with Collini's questioning of oppositional stances and supposed declines, it is also counterintuitive, making as it does a distinction between declared grievances and the actual state of things. The chapters of this book address a retreat from the imaginative high ground that relies on a comparable synthesis of opposing elements. Instead of attacking Smith's categorisations, the writers in question reject defences based in literary exceptionalism. They do not quibble with his distinction between manufactures and perishable thoughts. Rather, they internalise it. Having done so, they seek exemption by reassigning, re-describing, and re-categorising literary activity. Instead of a waning service or mouldering crop, authorship emerges as a process that fixes value permanently in an enduring product.

The turn from fame to manufactured value prompts a reformation of literary identity, but its foundations are not just economic. They also reflect medical, social, and theological, determinants of what counts as work. The first such influence arises from a gathering perception that compositional processes are damaging to health, a connection exacerbated by the emergence of what Salmon calls 'the "living author"': a move from conceiving literature as a matter of the ancient, and therefore dead, to imagining authors as visible, breathing entities.[50] Though he addresses the taxonomic and consecratory function of biographic 'galleries', one might equally note the susceptibility of all this living flesh and the ways in which the mind itself proves perishable under the conditions of intellectual work.[51] As Carolyn Steedman shows, it was in this period that physicians began prescribing remedies for the wasting and feverish effects of 'brain work', or 'labour of mind'.[52] This, in turn, conditioned a demand for demonstrably physical – one might say 'life-like' – alternatives to the world of books.

In his study of scholarship and the 'popular imagination', A. D. Nuttall identifies a related tendency: an early nineteenth-century 'movement away from electric danger, Faustian glamour, commerce with the devil, towards sexless deathliness',[53] a change epitomised by Robert Browning's 'A Grammarian's Funeral' – whose hero 'decided not to Live but Know' (139) – and by George Eliot's portrait of Edward Casaubon in *Middlemarch* (1871–2).[54] Dinah Birch rightly wonders whether Eliot preferred an 'inclusively imagined approach' to literature over 'the high tradition which had produced Mr Casaubon'.[55] Indeed, the work as a whole models a novelistic elasticity that defies reduction to the musty and dusty. Casaubon remains all the same a model for what can go wrong, and as such a basis for authorial self-scrutiny.[56] His dim-sightedness and emaciation reflect Lamarckian errors of usage – typical of scholars and symbolic of scholarship – that grow ever more concentrated through the generations. *Middlemarch* draws in this way on the tokens of a non-specific scholarly malaise, epitomised by Robert Burton's warning in the epigraph to Chapter 5 that the 'gowts, catarrhs, rheums, cachexia, bradypepsia, bad eyes' of 'Hard students' are brought on by 'over-much sitting'.[57] However, Eliot's special interest lies in combining these customary associations with modern description and diagnosis. Thus Casaubon's condition comes to a head in Chapter 29 when he suffers the more immediate and physical shock of a heart attack. As the 'library-steps' are transformed into a scaffold, his fallen book suggests a resignation of work under pressure from the same.[58] Casaubon has suffered a kind of bibliographic seizure. In this respect, he falls victim less to the weight of learning – or some other figurative hazard that turns physical – than to a defined set of environmental risks associated with the library as a scene of labour. To understand his demise in this way is to identify Eliot's unlikely hero as a victim of occupational disease.

Eliot was well-placed to pursue this line of enquiry: G. H. Lewes would later publish a book on *The Physical Basis of Mind* (1877),[59] and the collection of books he shared with her contained many items on diseases of the brain, the nerves, and the heart.[60] Among them was *Traité des Nerfs* (1785), a work by the Swiss pioneer of occupational medicine, S. A. Tissot.[61] In another volume, *Treatise on the Diseases Incident to Literary and Sedentary Persons* (1772), he reports that 'Famous preachers and illuftrious profeffors have often been known to expire even in their defks'.[62] Such contributions comprise an emerging specialty whose modern flowering arrives with Charles Thackrah's *The Effects of the Principal Arts, Trades, and Professions* (1831)[63] and volume 1 of John Forbes's *The Cyclopædia of Practical Medicine* (1833), each of them published in the decade of *Middlemarch*'s setting.[64] This occupational approach establishes a cluster of symptoms around an unchanging model of working practice. To that extent, its weaknesses reflect the readiness of physicians to assume a necessary connection between scholarship and a sedentary life. The Romantic revival of 'peripatetic' philosophy does little to alter this perception.[65] Instead, the medical literature places authors in an occupational class whose disease profile is defined by prolonged immobility.[66] This process of classification holds surprises, nevertheless: not least in disregarding familiar social hierarchies. Forbes files the diseases of literary men under the general heading of the 'DISEASES OF ARTISANS', a disinterested grouping that precedes the reverse aspiration discussed here in later chapters.[67] Thackrah, similarly, compares 'The position of the student',[68] to other seated occupations, including stay-makers, milliners and tailors.[69] By way of remedy, Tissot recommends 'country diverfions', and a reversion to the 'natural' pursuits of 'an hufbandman and a gardener'.[70] Thackrah, for his part, calls for 'an hour's labour in the mill or warehouse, or digging in the garden.'[71]

This moderating return to the physical settles into orthodox opinion as the century proceeds. In *The Intellectual Life* (1873), Philip Hamerton links 'the physical activity of men eminent in literature' to the 'energy to their style'.[72] Samuel Smiles' chapter on 'The Literary Ailment', in *Life and Labour* (1887), notes a related tendency among 'brain-workers' to 'demand physical exercise'.[73] Woodwork becomes a particular focus for such redirection. Eliot had previously explored gentlemanly resorts to handiwork in her *Scenes of Clerical Life* (1857): Maynard, we are told, was 'much given [. . .] to carpentry, considered as a fine art, without any base view to utility'.[74] Casting a retrospective glance at this period, such pursuits become a satirical subject in Samuel Butler's *The Way of All Flesh* (1903), whose narrator reports that 'the exercise of sawing, plaining and hammering proved exactly what' the aunt of the novel's directionless hero 'had wanted to find – something that should exercise, but not too much'.[75] This controlled exposure reflects a common emphasis on fine-tuning – on the remediation of a 'sallow face'.[76] Just as *Middlemarch* reveals a new world of occupational disease, so it also rehearses this language of cures. Lydgate locates the source of Casaubon's illness in 'the common error of intellectual men – a too eager and monotonous application'. Though the diagnosis stresses a behavioural issue requiring individual reform, his 'error' is ascribed to a class of person, and becomes thereby collective and occupational.[77] Casaubon is urged to take up 'shuttlecock',[78] and Mr Brooke earnestly advises that he should 'make toys, table-legs, and that kind of thing'.[79] This move, from 'toys' to 'table-legs', surreptitiously queries forms of support that leave us merely playing at life. In this way, Eliot's novel offers a retrospective, and notably ironised, reception of medical answers to mental distress. Where authors themselves are concerned, it also hints that the strategy is double-edged, in as much as it taints mental exertion with a suggestion of disease. This manner of prescription remains pertinent, all the same, because it introduces artisanal labour to new social spaces, and thereby creates room for the authorial intelligence to migrate across a previously taboo mental-physical boundary.

Even more worrying than the imputation that literary composition makes you ill is the suggestion that literature is not work at all. What 'work' actually means was, and remains, an open question. Keith Thomas notes 'the absence of any single, universally acceptable definition.[80] Most theorists of the subject have imposed order by sharpening and codifying the available terminology. Arendt, for instance, distinguishes 'labor' from 'work':[81] 'Labor', for her, is a toilsome and brutally cyclical activity that tracks 'the biological process of the human body'; 'work', by contrast, is undertaken by the human fabricator (*homo faber*) in conditions that reconcile the *vita activa* and the *vita contemplativa*.[82] It 'corresponds to the unnaturalness of human existence' in denoting vocation, purpose, and fulfilment.[83] Richard Sennett suggests that Arendt failed to recognise the intelligence and personal fulfilment involved in practice of the crafts.[84] However this may be, the ordinary semantic overlap between 'work' and 'labour' makes for a confusing differentiation, and perhaps explains why William Morris, when memorialising a similar distinction, front-loaded and poeticised it as 'useful work *versus* useless toil'.[85] Among twentieth-century critics, Raymond Williams follows Arendt in distinguishing between 'work and labour', albeit attending more closely to the changing usage and social valence of these keywords.[86] In the age of the capitalist, he observes, 'labour' means 'that element of production which in combination with capital and materials produced commodities'; 'work', on the other hand, develops its primary, if not exclusive, modern denotation as 'regular paid employment'.[87]

The search for a watertight definition is understandable given the array of overlapping terms. Such efforts seem misguided, even so: not simply because terminological clarity has proven elusive, but because these persistent difficulties disclose an opportunity for analysis. Siskin calls this 'classification ambiguity', an attribute that accounts both for 'Literature's power as well as the sense that it is powerlessly detached from the real world'.[88] The fugitive meanings of 'work' are precisely what animate the present study. Indeed, it is a crucial feature of working life that explanations for what we do are positioned so precariously between the ideal and the necessitous, the fulfilling and the painful, the frivolous and the useful. Work's significance crystallises as such in the fear of a possible exclusion.

Understanding why this possibility troubled so many writers requires cognisance of the varied forces conspiring to present labour as the paramount value. The Gospel of Work's magnetism is the more notable for provoking a backlash almost upon its inception. Thomas Hood's 'The Song of the Shirt' (1843) garnered praise for exposing the inhumanity of calls to 'Work! work! work!' without respite.[89] More directly, Mill observed that 'There is nothing laudable in work for work's sake'.[90] Recent contributions by Chris Louttit and Rob Breton challenge the very existence of a unitary Gospel.[91] This is conceptually helpful: evidently, different factors determine what praise of work means in different cases. Only, a resort to plurality misses something at the rhetorical level: most notably, the coercive force of the slogan's very singularity. Instead of modifying an inherited phrase, the following discussion registers multiple threads by showing how distinct cultural and religious influences forged temporary alliance in favour of a unitary claim.[92]

One such influence dwells in the 'background noise' of religious Dissent. Ever since the publication of Max Weber's *The Protestant Ethic and the Spirit of Capitalism* (1904–5), modern economic attitudes have been read through the lens of Reformation theology.[93] A number of studies – from the 1990s onwards – return to Weber's counter-intuitive premise in denying the connection between 'absolute predestination' and 'passivity'.[94] John Hughes, for instance, charts 'an undeniable shift in thinking' that reverses the ancient subordination of the *vita activa* to the *vita contemplativa*.[95] In a Victorian context, these issues apply most directly to the influence of the Evangelical Revival, and the renewal of the Nonconformist conscience. A striking number of the figures discussed in this book reveal an additional connection to the Calvinism of Lowland Scotland.[96] In her work on this tradition, Susan Manning elaborates a relevant conviction that Calvinist '"conversion" is the beginning of a strenuous life of toil', not an opportunity to sit back on one's laurels.[97] Weber's absolute distinctions remain questionable all the same; and there have been attempts in recent years to cut a different path. Drawing on Werner Sombart's formative rebuttal, James Aho cites the prior existence of bookkeeping among the merchant guilds of medieval Venice, and the double-entry system devised in 1494 by Luca Pacioli.[98] Even the 'classic' texts of Victorian work speak with more than one voice. Weber quotes Carlyle's claim that the 'unexampled tyranny' of Puritanism 'was "the last of [all] our heroisms"', yet gives no account of the same writer's dalliance with monastic precepts.[99] *Past and Present* (1843), most obviously, champions not just Cromwellian piety, but Benedictine routine. Nor is Carlyle alone in displaying an ecumenical tendency: Ruskin likewise derives a Low Church medievalism from mixed cultural and religious roots.

Unsurprisingly, the more one moves from a conception of 'labour' in the abstract to specialised notions of craftsmanship, the more that neo-Catholic, or at least neo-monastic, theologies come into play. The last phase of this book reveals a related interchange between Calvinist investments in work as a founding value, and the extension of Catholic theologies of creation to human composition and human making. This arises most notably in the figure of the forge as portrayed by Gerard Manley Hopkins, and through the incarnational 'letter-craft' of Eric Gill. It becomes clear, moreover, that this new materialism relies for its emancipatory significance on a holistic sense of the spiritual in the physical. A theological strand likewise unites the book's written sources with a visual dimension, where the emphasis is less on working, than on appearing to work, and the ways in which artists make writing legible, and spiritually accountable, as physical labour.

The connection between work ethics and theology is longstanding, then; and so too is the complexity of their interrelation. This prompts the question whether the 'Gospel of Work' harbours anything new beyond the slogan – and, if it does, why that should arise in the 1830s rather than earlier. Even Smiles thought he was re-inculcating 'old-fashioned but wholesome lessons'.[100] Briggs, for his part, suggests that only 'The sense of gospel' is fresh here.[101] While that seems credible, the unusual force of the Victorian call to work invites further explanation. An answer lies in the way that it enables otherwise competing ideologies to find common cause. The mixed origins of Chartism present the most prominent example of this effect. Storing up capital, either on earth or in heaven, might seem a singularly bourgeois strategy; but among the Chartists an Augustinian tendency runs in parallel with that impulse. Work is seen as fallen, but also humanly unavoidable, and therefore dignified. As Anne Janowitz observes, the same recourse to Dissenting origins could serve to empower, even as it restrained in other ways: 'Chartist visionary communitarianism', she explains, 'often drew upon [. . .] visions of community that had been central to radicalism in the seventeenth century'.[102] This utopian perspective is no more apparent than in the way that 'Puritan' or renunciatory influence co-exists with a conception of labour that lays claim to personal and collective sovereignty.[103] In this case, the substantiation is not just customary or vernacular, but based in John Locke's assertion of a link between the business of 'subduing or cultivating the Earth, and having Dominion'.[104] Supplementing Locke's position, Smith's Labour Theory of Value emerges from this ground as a gauge by which to discover the real price of things. Modified by David Ricardo in the early nineteenth century,[105] it produces an unforeseen consequence in enabling a disenfranchised artisanal class to lodge proprietorial and political claims.[106]

This effect was not lost on the economist John Cazenove, who observed alarmedly in 1832 that the doctrine 'That labour is the sole source of wealth [. . .] unhappily affords a handle to those who would represent all property as belonging to the working classes'.[107] These theoretical and political developments witness the rise of what Hughes calls 'ontologies of labour', or 'theories which attempted to understand the very nature of labour'.[108] Expressed first as Romanticism, and then Marxism, such 'ontologies' ally working-class Puritanism to the proposition that labour confers sovereignty, and even happiness. The latter notion animates Marx's conception that 'the productive life is the life of the species'.[109] Though largely unfamiliar with Marx's untranslated works, the Chartists drew cognate principles from Owenism, and from the Romantic tradition of idyllic husbandry.[110] At the same time, their bid for political enfranchisement relied on the proposition that 'toil and trouble' – to employ Smith's reapplication of *Macbeth* – establishes inalienable rights.[111]

The example of Chartism illuminates, in this way, a characteristic feature of the early Victorian Gospel of Work: namely, its capacity to lay in abeyance competing and sometimes contradictory ideological premises, and to do so while exerting an apparently singular or monolithic form of cultural pressure. By harnessing the collective force of competing ideas, it guarantees the idea of 'work' peculiar potency. This potency finds favour not only with Benthamites, Evangelicals, and Chartists, but with groups less obviously susceptible, among them writers who worried about the social and ethical status of their vocation. As Valentine Cunningham notes, the new rich were exposed by their chapel-going to a dignified working mundanity, which fostered shared 'attitudes and theological assumptions'.[112] If not in chapel, then at the broader cultural level, the writers discussed here began to wonder whether authorship might lodge similar claims.

* * *

Although this book concentrates on manual and artisanal models, the experience in question – namely, removal from, and consequent longing for, physical forms of work – is almost by definition middle class. Without ignoring scope for overlap or interface, my discussion pertains to the problem of the already 'educated' writer who worried that writing was an evasion of honest work. This distinction is particularly helpful in the case of writers who adopted dual strategies. Anthony Trollope famously describes the 'allotted number of pages every day' completed alongside his duties at the Post Office. In that respect, he invites an analogy with bureaucratic process:[113] more pertinent, though, and less well known, is his accompanying comparison of book writing to the persistence of cobblers and 'any other workman'.[114] It is in testing this last, apparently improbable, allusion that these chapters find their subject. Naturally, the relationship between literature and labour also concerned working-class writers, and many existing studies address that conjunction.[115] As Salmon's discussion of Edward Paxton Hood reveals,[116] there were even working-class writers who wished 'to "widen and liberalise" the term "Labour" to include professional, middle-class occupations such as surgeons and authors'.[117] Hood's focus is nevertheless on working-class aspirants, many of whom found authorship attractive precisely because it lay beyond their ordinary cultural and working milieu.[118]

Apart from revealing gaps between experience and aspiration, the social mutuality of this move into new territory afforded opportunities. My examples reveal, for instance, a sustained discursive challenge to what E. P. Thompson calls 'The distinction between the artisan and the labourer'.[119] Ruskin pointedly conflates the two on describing his attempts to acquire the skills of road sweeper; and as discussed in Chapter 4, he also encouraged his Oxford undergraduates to acquire an aptitude for road-mending. Equally, the forms of prowess celebrated respectively by Gerard Manley Hopkins in 'Harry Ploughman' and 'Felix Randal' (see Chapter 5) channel a creative charge that is as amenable to agricultural toil as to deft hammerwork. If the distance of a middle-class gaze softens boundaries that would otherwise be keenly felt, it is often the case – at least in technical terms – that the dividing line between skilled and unskilled collapses on close inspection. The actor Richard Burton offers an instance of this effect on recollecting 'the lords of the coalface', among whom his father was renowned for an ability to dislodge from the seam twenty tons of coal by applying a No. 2 mandrel at the right spot, with the right force.[120] While the emphasis shifts across the date-span of this book towards a formally constituted craftsmanship, the discourse of skill is rarely absent from that of visible effort: a fact recognised and harnessed by Carlyle's application of the term 'author-craft' to his own 'sweated' version of literary labour (see Chapter 1).

Being middle-class in this period did not of course preclude a relation to the world of manual labour. Carlyle had been to Edinburgh University, but his morally austere father was of the labouring class. The self-educated daughter of a carpenter turned land agent, George Eliot was marked by the Evangelical tradition and its esteem for honest toil; so, too, was Barrett Browning, with the complicating factor that her family wealth came from sugar and slavery in the West Indies. William Gladstone, John Ruskin, and William Morris inherited personal wealth derived, respectively, from the slave plantations of British Guiana, from the Spanish wine trade, and from copper mines in Devon and Cornwall. *The Work of Words* shows how writers brought this silent inheritance – of labour origins and labours relations – into consciousness. In some cases, a connection is directly articulated, as where Ruskin symbolically replants on his Lake District estate the liquid wealth he has inherited from his father's sherry business; in other cases, it is more deeply encoded, most obviously in Gladstone's performances of an agricultural labour inflected by his inheritance of slave wealth. As Lesjak notes in relation to labour more generally, there is an element here of 'seeing the invisible' at the same time as denying or repressing it.[121] Where enslaved labour is concerned, that dialectic is especially telling; and while a full treatment of its role as an absent presence warrants a study in its own right, I explore several examples relevant to the forms of authorial self-fashioning under discussion.

From an initial focus on Carlylean labour doctrines, my attention shifts towards their ramifying legacy, both as transmitted directly, and as hybridised, through Ruskinian work ethics, proto-feminism, Victorian socialism, guild socialism, distributism, and early fascism. Carlylean influence is a helpful marker not only because its effects are traceable and explicit across this broad swathe of historical and cultural activity, but because it embodies and articulates several tendencies that might otherwise seem confusing, both in the nineteenth century, and as revisited today: notably, the convergence of Left and Right positions in labour politics; the persistent imbrication of theology with material and democratic relations; and a deep anxiety about the role of apparently non-instrumental, literary, or 'invisible' activities at a moment of crisis.[122]

Tracking such legacies carries risks as well opportunities. There is a danger, for instance, that the terms set by Carlyle's dominant contribution will limit the range of debate. His doctrines are masculinist in their orientation, and one might expect this to restrict the scope for exploring female experience. Chapters 3 and 6, on Barrett Browning and Olive

Schreiner respectively, show that this does not always follow: indeed, that Carlyle's labour theories contained within them unlikely opportunities. His influence is striking, as such, less for its orthodox transmission than for its fugitive after-effects. The aim here is not to affirm or endorse a canon of authors, but to account for the formation of a particular literary-artisanal inheritance. This includes registering the forms of limitation, malaise, and bias, to which it is prone. In this regard the historical situatedness of gender interacts crucially with class. While the nostalgia that middle-class male writers felt towards artisanal routine relied on feelings of loss, social guilt, and deracination, their female counterparts rarely reported the same experience. As numerous critics have discussed, most literary women were occupied with a more pressing struggle, one in which success depended on asserting the credentials of a middle-class intellectual.[123] The appeal of a working identity at odds with that withheld prize was likely to be limited.

An interchange between literature and domestic handicrafts, such as embroidery, was more common; but the middle-class coding of such activities resists the convergence in question between literary identities and working-class occupations. As Talia Schaffer observes, domestic handicraft was already the principal standard of comparison, so that 'Intellectually ambitious women, therefore, often regarded handicraft with strong hostility.'[124] Middle-class women nevertheless took part in debates about the division of labours. Dinah Craik, for instance, referred to the 'female handicrafts, in contradistinction to female professions'.[125] This helpfully registers the kinds of differentiation – of work as well as ambition – running through early debates on the Woman Question. Harriet Martineau, likewise, saw a role for 'cultivated women' in 'the improvement of our national character as tasteful manufacturers', specifying that this would be achievable if men would remove their jealous obstructions.[126] Later in the century, the Arts and Crafts movement enabled middle-class women to pursue such occupations more publicly without losing class status.

The foundation of the Guild of Women Artists became the focus, as such, for a new generation of female artist makers – among whom May Morris is only the most prominent.[127] For the purposes of this study, however, Barrett Browning and Schreiner stand out because they translate this physical turn into a specifically literary context. And they do so by reinventing the terms of their writerly labour: in effect defying Margaret Oliphant's notorious warning that women would be reduced to 'lesser men' by entering male domains.[128] Schreiner provides an especially resonant test case, in that her philosophical holism encourages a restless crossing between forms of intellectual labour, political labour, agricultural labour, maternal labour, and housework. All the while, she combines the material with the transcendental in ways that recall Barrett Browning's combination of vatic and artisanal premises. In this respect, both writers respond to attitudinal changes set in motion by a wider re-evaluation of manual labour.

* * *

Revealing the longevity and adaptability of an authorial strategy more usually linked to the 1840s and 1850s these chapters track its legacies deep into the period of modernism, bringing to light historical ironies and political valences that are otherwise easily missed. As such, the book establishes the origins of Arts and Crafts ideals in literary culture, and through the lionisation of the artisan tracks their continuing importance and operation well beyond the *fin de siècle*. In generic terms, too, this study extends beyond familiar ground: in addition to novels and poems, it addresses these debates through the distinctive qualities of letters, diaries and artworks. The testamentary process by which these forms seek to prove or synthesize work attracts particular attention. Encompassing this historiographic and formal range, the book's focus on Great Britain affords a sample of activity situated at a confluence between nationally inflected discourses of work: namely, the residual influences of Scottish Calvinism and English Puritanism, and more recent interactions between German Romanticism, English utilitarianism, American Transcendentalism, European Marxism, English guild socialism, and Italian fascism.

Non-British writers are included whose prolonged or formative residence in the United Kingdom catalysed an exchange of ideas. This makes particular sense in the case of a writer like Schreiner, whose movements between London and the Cape Colony reflect established networks of imperial exchange. At the European level, the Continental origin of Calvinism, and of Weber's underpinning 'Protestant ethic', offers a further basis for amplitude. Indeed, German philosophical idealism inflects Carlyle's materialism, and the related sensibility of Thoreau and Emerson. These intellectual genealogies warn against too strict a cultural focus, as does the obvious fact that writers rarely observe national boundaries in their own reading or correspondence. This is apparent even where the subject seems most vernacular: as discussed in Chapter 5, Dickens draws on the American poet, Henry Longfellow, when evoking the rural blacksmith's trade, while Walter Crane's socialist evocation of a bonneted William Morris shows him working at a double-horned Continental anvil rather than the more familiar London pattern.

A book of this kind nevertheless relies on limits, and an understanding that certain paths are well-worn or might better be handled in a dedicated study. There are, for instance, many volumes that address American cultures of work, so that I confine my attention to cases where the overlap with Britain is conspicuous.[129] Equally, I treat the Anglo-French assimilation of these debates elsewhere, in a co-edited volume on *The Labour of Literature in Britain and France, 1830–1910* (2018).[130] It shares the present concern with cultural production, but looks beyond the artisanal analogy to consider a broader spectrum of literary engagement with work. Just as it is not possible to cover every angle, it has been necessary to be selective about the writers chosen: rather than include an extended discussion of Edward Carpenter, for instance, I explore related ideas through Schreiner, the benefit being that her eugenicist ideas form a bridge between the holistic labour ethics of late Victorian socialism and the forms of prejudice arising from its encounter with New Imperialism, and then syndicalism. In the interests of focus, likewise, it is not possible to explore every aspect of the writers under discussion.

As previously intimated, a form of medievalist anti-capitalism attends the workshop and guild models handed down by Carlyle. While this influence escapes the standard categories of Left and Right, it may still be characterised. The book's last area of concern approaches this question through the ethical problems attending the craft tradition. Many writers deployed artisanal identity and cultures of apprenticeship as points of resistance to the fluidity of capital, or to routine effacements of labour in the object. Consciously or unconsciously, those working within this framework relied on forms of hierarchy inspired by the bonds connecting apprentice to master. Mercantile capitalism converges in some cases with feudal premises and with plantation slavery. While my concern is with skilled working process rather than associationalism *per se*, the two ideas interact as models of the writer-craftsman develop social and organisational ambition. Tracing this trajectory invites exploration of the authoritarian currents that flow through medievalist conceptions of labour, and their connection to a subsequent decline of artisanal approaches. The final part of the book charts a related move towards ideas of social hygiene, as exemplified by Ezra Pound's characterisations of usury as a threat to craftsmanship. The resulting analysis matters from the point of view of understanding the genealogy of more recent revivals of artisanal culture; it also delineates the uncertain scope for forging connections to literature, and for defining the value of intangible pursuits. It stands, too, as a suggestive case of intellectual inheritance, of the ways in which a conceptual lineage can be traced along lines of resemblance, even as changes in the genetic code, and multiplying ancestral lines, complicate and disperse determinative and causative origins.

PART I
ANXIOUS VOCATIONS

Without exactly coining the phrase, Carlyle's *Past and Present* stands as an irregular summation of the Gospel of Work. To '[k]now thy work and do it', he avers, is 'The latest Gospel in this world' (10:196). Work operates here as an absolute good – indeed, as 'Religion' (10:200) – and the dividing lines are correspondingly stark: on the one hand he invokes the 'unworking Dilettantism' of a partridge-trapping aristocracy (10:182); and, on the other, regiments of diligent but unemployed workers (10:197). Only, Carlyle begins at the edges to nibble away at this definitional absolutism. And it is here that he addresses the more specific concerns of this book. As Chapter 1 demonstrates, the implication of his conviction that 'a man perfects himself by working' (10:196) is that authors too must consider their status as workers. By 1843, Carlyle was still quoting Goethe, notably his injunction to 'Work, and despair not' (10:135). But the distinction advanced 'between work and sham-work, between speech and jargon' (25:196), imperils the place of poetry and fiction in his economy of values. Though admitting that 'The spoken Word, the written Poem, is said to be an epitome of the man', he is still drawn to ask, 'how much more the done Work' (10:158). Equally, his wry allusion to the pitiful 'day's-wages of John Milton's day's-work, named *Paradise Lost*' (10:19) betrays an anxiety not only about literary rewards, but about the equivalence of different 'day's work'. The aim here is not to repeat the well-known story of Carlyle's increasing and oddly self-defeating Philistinism, but to probe the uncertainties that shadow his categorical rhetoric, and the ways these condition his vocational placing.

Once Carlyle's difficulties in satisfying himself are understood, it is easier to appreciate the ironies of his legacy, and the forms of projection it invites. At the level of direct influence, several Carlylean preoccupations recur across the cases surveyed in later chapters. If, in *Past and Present*, work resolves down to the undifferentiated category of 'worker', there subsists a parallel emphasis on variable manual skill, the effect of which is to refine attention beyond the polar opposites of 'work and sham-work' (10:25). With this in view, Chapter 1 explores associated conceptions of craftsmanship and the 'maker'. Apart from encompassing practical mastery, the last role harbours a transcendental conception hospitable to ideas of poetic vision. And it unfolds a cosmic understanding of the labourer as the 'truest emblem there is of God the World-Worker, Demiurgus, and Eternal Maker' (10:229). As discussed in Chapters 5 and 6, this notion of the artisanal founder, who partakes in God's own handiwork, gathers renewed importance at the end of the century. More than anything, though, Carlyle's prominent position in this book depends not on his broad association with the Gospel of Work, but on his uneasy innovation in adapting it to an idea of the writer as physical worker: championing, in effect, a (labouring) 'hero as man of letters'.

This is not to suggest that he finalised an unalterable template. As Chapters 2 and 3 demonstrate, he was more often a subject of awkward and grudging, but ultimately creative, assimilation. Chapter 2 focuses on the artist and diarist, Ford Madox Brown. Though descended on his father's side from Scottish labourers, Brown's background was far removed from that of Carlyle: he spent his childhood in the footloose world of the Channel ports, from where he proceeded to study fine art at Antwerp.[1] The last circumstance makes a connection yet more unlikely, given Carlyle's 'scarcely suppressed contempt' for painters.[2] But while in the doldrums of his career, Brown sought comfort by 'steeping himself in Carlyle and gloom'.[3] The older man exercised an appeal in this way – an appointed outsider, scorned and neglected, yet heard. Brown worried equally about the primacy of doing over thinking, and like Carlyle responded through recourse to a purportedly honest labour. Most significantly, he answered anti-artistic scorn, and his own anxieties, by casting painting as a form of visual accountancy that brings work to the surface. While Brown famously portrays and celebrates visible musculature, he also converts mental labour into a recognised currency, apparently inspired by Carlyle's unflinching interrogation, 'where is thy work? [. . .] Swift, out with it; let us see thy work!' (10:156). This form of showing favours the bare measure of output, and the proof of living sinew; and one might expect a corresponding difficulty in reaching terms with the written word. Brown, nevertheless, is a painter who bridges the divide between image and word, in a process analogous to his physical depiction of invisible labour. This commitment crystallises in the form of a discursive exhibition catalogue, a diary, and the quotations attached to his picture frames.

Chapter 1

Carlyle's 'Author-Craft'

In his essay on 'The Negro Question' (1850), J. S. Mill refers dismissively to Carlyle's 'pet theory [. . .] about work'.[1] His attack proceeds on a familiar utilitarian basis: if authority is to be invoked in the matter of a social question, we need to know its source, its legitimacy and the limits of its jurisdiction. In colonial contexts, as discussed in Chapters 3, 4 and 6, the Gospel of Work was indeed an instrument of domination, which was all the more pernicious for its vagueness. It is in his overall account of Carlylean thought that Mill misleads, largely because he resorts to caricature. By presenting his antagonist as a practitioner of metaphysical moonshine, he neglects the complex influence of Carlyle's social placing, and the nuances of his philosophical position. This is most apparent when he lambasts Carlyle for suggesting an equivalence between 'such work [. . .] as is done by writers' and 'real labour', the latter being 'the exhausting, stiffening, stupefying toil of many kinds of agricultural and manufacturing labours'.[2]

An important ethical question is at stake: Mill rightly calls out Carlyle's audacity in preaching to people about their working conditions. And he legitimately questions the implication that authorship is equivalently punishing – not least since Carlyle was addressing harshly indentured plantation workers, including former slaves. What he misses, all the same, is the less hieratic position that motivates Carlyle's pronouncements: his concern to forge a connection between the transcendental function and the material world, so that 'ordinances' can flow in more than one direction.[3] And while the tendency remains to regard Carlyle as a secular prophet, pronouncing from on high, his social background casts that role in a different light. A university-educated man of letters, with decidedly aristocratic social connections, he was nevertheless the son of a poor man, who was first a jobbing stonemason, then a builder and finally a farmer.[4] By implication, Mill's jibe about 'stupefying toil' falls wide of the mark. From his youth, Carlyle had a better acquaintance with such labour than Mill credits. But apart from being a case of social misrecognition, the exchange reveals an enduring blind-spot about the varieties of labour admitted by Carlyle's Gospel. By definition, the underpinning experience was not direct: he was, after all, a writer. But if not direct, it could still be meaningfully indirect, and as such instrumental. The first two parts of this chapter consider an inherited encounter with a kind of labour that Mill does not register as part of the 'pet theory': namely, the artisanal construction work undertaken by Carlyle's father as a young man, and the ways in which he reconceives it in relation to his own work. This could happen rhetorically and metaphorically, but also through equivalence. The last part considers another referred context: that suggested by his approving review of Ebenezer Elliott's *Corn Law Rhymes* (1831) (28:136–66), a volume heralded as the production of a 'true' poet, with 'labouring' credentials capable of healing the rift between eloquence and 'real work'. Assigning the main event of poetry in this way, the review opens a revealing gap between Carlyle's sense of Elliott and the actual conditions of his poetic and labouring life. Taken as a whole, the chapter also hints at an attendant cost, revealed through a gradual retreat from metrical and technical definitions of poetry. This removes tools for distinguishing the poetic function from the prophetic, and means that Carlyle struggles to divide conscious versification from the accidents of a working rhythm. For the practising poets considered in later chapters, this makes him less a definitive example than a prompt to experimentation.

Books and Buildings

A crucial dividing line runs through Carlyle's philosophy of work. By the time of 'Occasional Discourse on the Negro Question' (1849), 'might' (20:46) was unquestionably in the ascendant. But while an attraction to force was a longstanding feature of his outlook, it dominates here at the cost of an earlier emphasis on the refinements of craftsmanship. It was through poetry, crucially, that Carlyle first approached these artisanal roots of his 'pet theory'. In his youth, he was a fervent champion of Robert Burns, Goethe and Friedrich Schiller; and while in the grip of an idealist phase habitually applied the term 'poet' to indicate philosophical distinction. The rule-breaking mechanisms of poetry were even considered useful, in as much as they peeled back the 'sham' of appearances to unveil the 'real'.[5] What makes Carlyle repudiate these early enthusiasms is hard to determine; but the death of his father marks a clear watershed. It left him troubled by the possibility of a broken inheritance, a fate understood in terms that combined matters metaphysical with criteria based in occupation and class. The following discussion charts Carlyle's attempts to heal that division. This represents a departure, in that James

Carlyle is often read as an inhibiting precedent: Ian Campbell identifies his strict Calvinism as the source of lifelong doubts about the value of poetic expression,[6] while David DeLaura sees his attitude as 'a revealing test-case of Carlyle's uneasiness with virtually all contemporary creative work'.[7] Chris R. Vanden Bossche acknowledges the importance of the paternal example, but characterises the relationship in Freudian terms as a tussle for authority.[8] But rather than being a source solely of constraint, or a prompt for rivalry, his father's rigidity also inspired poetic solutions. Redefining the scope of poetry to encompass the building of bridges and the raising of walls, the son seeks not to exclude his father's working legacy, but to transform and assimilate it. Thus Carlyle finds in the memory of his father the resources to close the gap between the literary life and the mason's trade. From there, he imagines what a refurbished poetry might be. The effect is to turn Mill's characterisation on its head. Instead of imposing intellectual conditions on agricultural work, Carlyle's literary vocation justifies itself before the imagined 'real work' of his father's physical exertion.

There are many textual contexts for this process, and consequently many possible constructions of it.[9] But perhaps the most revealing arises from the private obituary that Carlyle wrote to mark the passing of his father in 1832. Already coming to terms with his arrival in the literary world, and with the social 'anarchy' witnessed on recent visits to London, he was now being changed – or rather returned to his origins – by the act of recalling the paternal presence in words. Published posthumously as part of *Reminiscences* (1881), the recollections of James Carlyle are nevertheless carefully devised.[10] While frankly acknowledging the differences between father and son, the author seeks to convince himself – and perhaps also a ghostly auditor – that he can bridge the gulf that separates them. This task commences with an expression of gratitude: registering the role of his father in funding his education, he speculates, 'Nay, am not I also the humble James Carlyle's work?' (3). Whatever the father has made, by implication, cannot be wholly alien, so that we admit the possibility of a worker in flesh as well as a builder in stone.[11] Less easy to contain is the recollection that 'Poetry, Fiction in general, he had universally seen treated as not only idle, but *false* and *criminal*' (10). Carlyle admits that his father was unaffected by his own 'noisy and enthusiastic' attention to the poetry of Burns (9), but foregrounds compatible approaches to 'the Wisdom of Reality' (9). Harmony is restored through precarious re-description: 'The Poetry *he* liked (he did not call it Poetry) was Truth' (9). In a logical equivalent of bridge building, Carlyle spans the distance in this way between sanctioned and irregular premises.

The narrative perspective in this case is complex: even as Carlyle acknowledges his father's intransigence – notably, his 'most entire and open contempt for all idle tattle' (6) – we sense a subsequent narrowing between it and his own position. Indeed, he characterises himself increasingly along the same lines: as an opponent of eloquence, a kind of anti-Burns never distracted from 'virtuous industry' by 'rich men's banquets' (26:314–15). Where Carlyle gives Burns credit for his 'poetry', he does so at the cost of a guilty internalisation, a reproduction of his father's suspicion of undirected speech. Something similar happens when the older Carlyle dispenses advice to aspiring writers. To C. A. Ward, he contrasts 'the questionable enterprise'[12] of literature with '*work* in this world*', a stern benchmark implying that authors absent themselves from social reality by default.

And yet puritanical suspicion of rhetoric proves not merely a negative response, but the basis for a 'substantial' alternative. In place of empty words, Carlyle entertains the thought that 'a portion of this Planet bears beneficent traces of his strong Hand and strong Head' (3). His reformed version of 'speech' promises as such a material equivalent of literary fame.[13] Of course this process can evince its own form of strain. When Carlyle explains that 'good building will last longer than most Books' (23), he only seems to widen the gulf between poetry and paternal authority.[14] Equally, the material emphasis can feel wrongheaded, implying as he does that a book's value stands by the longevity of its physical edition rather than by its successive dissemination and reproduction as text. Ultimately, though, the idea of a material-intellectual succession wins out. '[S]mall differences' (4) in modes of construction loom large at this point, as between 'Palace-building and Kingdom-founding, or only of delving and ditching'. We also gather that the building of walls draws on faculties normally reserved to the artistic imagination. Thus Carlyle accords his mason-father the transcendental powers of a poet, '"uniting the Possible with the Necessary" to bring out the Real' (9). '[B]uilding (*walling*)', he claims, 'is an operation that beyond most other manual ones requires incessant consideration, ever-new invention' (24). In this way, a join completes between the practical and the creative imagination.

As Carlyle develops these recollections, and the distinctions they prompt, his method shifts from the comparative to the parabolic. This change is signalled by a primal scene, in which he imagines the father's mundane apotheosis on becoming 'William Brown's first Apprentice' (22). He relates how 'the two "slung their tools" (mallets and irons hung in two equipoised masses over the shoulders), and crossed the Hills into Nithsdale, to Auldgarth, where a Bridge was building' (22).

Personal transformation coincides with ritual admission to a 'noble craft', and significance attaches to all the accidental details: to the 'slung' but instrumental 'clothing', and the bodily experience of a balance that reconciles heft with skill. The same manner of doing arises from a summer scene in which the son pictures the father 'diligently, cheerfully labouring with trowel and hammer' (24). James Carlyle was merely a 'hewer' (22) at the bridge, but joins the company of those 'cunning hands' who piled it together. As an appreciative description, the allusion to 'cunning' evokes a form of 'knowing' purged of the rhetorical 'craft' that contaminates eloquence. It heals the division that sees '*kenning* and *can-ning*' – that is, cognition and ability (*OED*) – 'become two altogether different words' (28:142–3). The scene thus conjures an untroubled home for qualities that the mason shares with the writer. It promises refuge for a restless literary intelligence otherwise lacking a mandate. This scenario's resonance intensifies once one appreciates how the same trope replicates across subsequent works. The fictional Editor of *Sartor Resartus* (1836) describes his construal of German sources as like building 'a firm bridge for British travellers' (1:62), a 'stupendous Arch' by which to 'evolve printed Creation out of a German printed and written chaos' (1:63). Carlyle, this is to say, recruits the image of bridge-building not only to contact his father's memory, but also to heal the rupture between literary vocation and manual occupation. Meanwhile, the allusion to 'chaos' betrays a connection to Carlyle's latter-day project of imposing order, on the land as much as on the culture.

The spanning operation does encounter limits, however. Just as Carlyle celebrates the otherness of this 'substantial' occupation, so he also consigns it to the past, and confronts its present degradation. His father, he explains, 'wisely quitted the Mason trade' to become a farmer, 'when universal Poverty and Vanity made *show* and *cheapness* (here as everywhere) be preferred to Substance' (30). The connection between letters and artisanship is in this way restored, albeit not in a way that promises fulfilling partnership. Instead, they become unhappy and accidental partners in a debased situation. Carlyle writes despairingly in 1833 that 'Literature, one's sole craft and staff of life, lies broken in abeyance'.[15] In *Reminiscences*, he observes similarly that 'the age of Substance and Solidity is gone' (6), a remark that abandons all hope in plotting an adequate course between the literary and the tangible. Certainly, Carlyle was constitutionally prone to despair. But the next part of this chapter connects the more positive strategy he articulates here to a wider pattern, detectable in his early writings, that sees stylistic and scholarly values aligned self-consciously with the disciplines of a manual craft.

Carlyle's 'Craftmanship'

Absorbed in the self-aggrandising thesis of 'The Hero as Man of Letters' (1840) (5:194–5),[16] Carlyle observes privately that 'The only Sovereigns of the world in these days are the Literary men'.[17] This strand of thought understandably dominates critical accounts of his position, but he was also drawn to humbler affinities. In a letter to the House of Commons concerning the petition for a copyright law, Carlyle described himself as a 'Writer of books'.[18] This homely prepositional phrase suggests a calculated unwillingness to lodge claims based in learned authority. It also encapsulates and distils a call for legal recognition of authorship as an honest and 'useful' labour.[19] Opting for 'writer' over 'poet', he subtly disclaims the unremunerative 'privilege' of sacerdotal speech. The appended specification – 'of books' – insists meanwhile on the tangible outcome of authorial process. His phrasing, as such, expresses a more or less consistent view of literature as a made thing, and of poets as makers, in recollection of the Scots usage in *makar*.

The tenor of these examples owes its origin to an earlier, and more concerted phase, in which Carlyle sought to draw literature into the orbit of a workshop culture. In 1827, most notably, he praised the 'Singer-guilds' of Nuremberg, among whom poetry was 'taught and practised like any other handicraft' (26:32). In one sentence, he prefigures so many of the questions that recur across this book: the question, for instance, of literature's practical teachability, its level of equivalence with other trades, and the extent to which authors might learn from regions of Europe – notably, the metallurgical heart of Bavaria – that have preserved guild-based structures. Having travelled in this way, he commences a search for cases close at hand. One living example arrives in the form of Allan Cunningham, a poet and biographer who was apprenticed in his youth to a stonemason. As if registering their guest's overlapping identity, Jane Carlyle calls him 'a genuine Dumfriesshire mason still'.[20] This description improves on the condescending 'portrait' of Cunningham printed the following year in *Fraser's* 'Gallery of Literary Characters': 'Like Ben Jonson', the article states, 'he began with trowel and mallet, which he abandoned for divine poetry'. But the accompanying image is more Carlylean than the text [Figure 1.1]: it shows Cunningham seated next to a pile of books, and holding a mallet against one leg. Rough creases and an open-legged posture lend ambivalence to his 'genteel' attire, while the lines of a fashionable tie shade into the appearance of a workman's neckerchief.

Responding the same year to a letter from Mill, Carlyle quibbles with a term of intended praise: instead of appearing to be an 'Artist', he hopes

Figure 1.1 Anon., 'No. XXVIII Allan Cunningham, Esq.', 'Gallery of Literary Characters', *Fraser's Magazine* (August–December, 1832). World History Archive / Alamy Stock Photograph

that 'a few years' will see him 'stand forth in his true dimensions, an honest Artisan'.[21] Though self-deprecating, the request evinces pride, and a resolution not to be 'placed'. It offers, too, a commentary on Carlyle's stirring resolution, expressed in the reminiscences of his father, to '"write my Books as he built his Houses"' (8). In stylistic terms, Carlyle likewise reanimates this memory of a man who 'seldom or never spoke except actually to convey an idea' through an emphasis on 'craftmanship' [*sic*] in style.[22] Thus he advises Edward Strachey to 'Be *wisely brief*', 'not in phrase only, but still more in *thought*'. The writerly virtue of concision likewise enters artisanal territory through a sculptural exclusion of the '*un*essential', and a workmanlike resolution to 'hit the nail on the *head*'. Complimenting Elizabeth Gaskell on *Mary Barton* (1848) that same year, he recommends an effort to 'reject the *un*essential more and more'.[23] Jem Wilson, he imagines, would know 'very well that one should *hit the nail on the head* [. . .] *not* beating on the intermediate spaces, – if we *are* smiths.' Having taken the analogy some distance, he goes a step further in claiming shared occupation with those who hammer and nail.[24]

When discussing his own work, Carlyle imagines words as a physical substance or texture. As early as 1822, he explains to his brother that

'Grammar in writing is like fingers and arms in a manual trade'.[25] It operates, accordingly less as a tool deputed to fashion material than as the agent of manipulation. Addressing his father in 1823, he advances a related distinction, this time between forms of writing: 'I lay aside my author-craft,' he notes on penning this letter, 'and willingly betake me to another sort of writing'.[26] Not all allusions to 'craft' allude to manual standards of excellence: the OED rightly notes that it is 'sometimes applied to any business, calling, or profession by which a livelihood is earned'. But here the compound term 'author-craft' – resonant as it is of the German traditions already invoked – performs a more specialised function, suggestive of affinities between the calling of authorship so unfamiliar to James Carlyle, and the stonemasonry or farming that filled his working life.

The instruments of writing receive similar attention. In 'Early Kings of Norway', Carlyle explains that 'The Icelanders, in their long winter, had a great habit of writing; and were, and still are, excellent in penmanship' (30:201–310). Far from suggesting craft in the generic sense of the word, 'penmanship' here evokes the application of an instrument to paper. This is writing, but it is also manifestly physical.[27] Substantial words have to be cut to shape and *made* to fit. A related sense of blockage is strong in Carlyle's accounts of writing. While such complaints bear on his notorious digestive difficulties, explanations based in the action of writing are worth considering.[28] In *Past and Present*, he exclaims that 'the very Paper I now write on is made, it seems, partly of plaster-lime well smoothed, and obstructs my writing' (10:141). The letter to his brother, in which he defends the value of grammatical study, contains a passage that extends this vision of obstruction and resistance. Recommending 'perseverance', he cites 'The small worm on the coasts of the Mediterranean' who 'perforates a rock of flint by continued application'.[29] It is here that the correspondence between a reluctant raw material and the role of craftsman emerges most clearly.[30] No natural link arises between the substance and the final product; no built-in telos guarantees the emergence of a 'civilised' form. The parallel is entirely reliant on the agency of a skilled individual who keeps going in the manner of an apprentice motivated by a distant goal.[31]

As previously intimated, Carlyle's faith in craft as an alternative value system began to ebb in later life. Though already implicit in his father's resignation of the mason's trade, life in London after 1834 hastened the disillusionment. There, he complained of poor standards – epitomised by 'villainous [Cock]ney shoes' – and a 'second trade' of 'puffery' that subordinated the doing of work to the necessity that you 'convince the world that thou hast done it'.[32] Faced with this arena of inflated claims, his conception of 'doing' relies increasingly on an alternative standard, on demonstrations of force and sudden fulfilment.[33] Such values inform his distinction between those 'in the dilettante line' and 'the active poets', who 'are incessantly toiling to achieve, and more and more realise' (26:261). As a strategy of self-representation, it focuses less on a quiet internalisation of his father's example than on a visceral celebration of it through demonstrations of muscular strength. It also happens to be less credible as an approach to self-representation than an 'author-craft' based in perseverance, meticulousness, and tradition. This explains why Carlyle increasingly prefers a vicarious relationship with sweated realities – an example of which is discussed below – and why his confidence in literature pulls away from formal or crafted characteristics towards a spectacle of empowered insight.

The Pen and the Hammer

Six months after writing the reminiscences of his father, Carlyle published a review essay entitled 'Corn-Law Rhymes'.[34] Appearing in the *Edinburgh Review*, in July 1832, it describes the life and work of the 'Sheffield radical', Ebenezer Elliott, a man understood to be a poet and 'a middle-aged Mechanic, at least Poor Man, of Sheffield'.[35] The portrait follows of Elliott as a 'quite unmoneyed, russet-coated speaker; [. . .] a Sheffield worker in brass and iron' (28:138). Unburdened by education or social connections, Elliot represents 'nothing or little other' (28:138) than what is required. From these apparently simple materials, Carlyle achieves a firm weld between poetry and artisanal identity. Rather than look to his own ancestry, however, he now invests the desired qualities in a third party: a literal embodiment of the spirit he imagines will renovate the speaking function. In this respect, his method resembles Jane Carlyle's recollection of Allan Cunningham's visit, noted down in the same year. Only, here, Carlyle's mode of portraiture does not reflect personal contact with the subject. Indeed, he had never met Elliott. This circumstance confuses the level of embodiment in question, and leads to forms of misrecognition that illuminate the author's developed habits of projection.

Existing commentary on Carlyle's review tends to stress its announcement of a democratic muse. Karen Wolven, for instance, argues that it expresses an urge to demonstrate literary ability in the uneducated and the poor.[36] Though narrowing the gap between author and subject, Carlyle's respect for his 'peasant father' makes this emphasis credible. In a notice that neglects the distance implied by Elliott's quotation marks, the *Westminster Review* observes that the 'Author' of *The Village Patriarch* (1829) 'calls his book "A Poor Man's Poem"',[37] before commending it as a social 'thermometer'.[38] Carlyle does challenge the truism that 'poor men do not write', but is not overly concerned with matters of inclusion, or with the possibility of inspiring other 'working men' (28:138). Rather, he is motivated by Elliott's supposed capacity to revitalise the whole poetic project. Following his father's death, and also Goethe's, he looks for examples of literary endeavour capable of regenerating authorship. In Elliott, he finds a poet 'who can handle both pen and hammer' (28:139). His 'voice' allows no confusion with 'idle tattle', because it comes 'from the deep Cyclopean forges, where Labour, in real soot and sweat, beats with his thousand hammers "the red son of the furnace"' (28:138). Elliott, in short, represents a solution to the central conflict between quiet integrity and guilty speech that runs through *Reminiscences*. He is welcomed as a new hope, 'an intelligible voice from the hitherto Mute and Irrational' (28:138).

Though Elliott had received assistance from Robert Southey many years previously, it was Carlyle's review that proved the major turning-point in his career.[39] Apart from popularising Elliott, it influenced the views of subsequent writers, who likewise attributed poetic features to the labouring aspect of the man. Dickens observed in *Household Words* that 'His poetry is just such as, knowing his history, we might have expected'.[40] Elizabeth Gaskell includes epigraphs from Elliott's works in *Mary Barton* (1848), notably a passage from *The Splendid Village* (1833), which prefaces her description of learned weavers botanising and reading Newton's *Principia*.[41] Two biographies appeared in 1850, one by January Searle, the second by the poet's son-in-law, John Watkins.[42] And, in 1854, a shorter work was published by J. W. King.[43] Carlyle declared Searle's study 'worth very little'.[44] He seems, nevertheless, to have inspired its descriptive assumptions. In phrases that acknowledge strength without renouncing mythology and simile, Searle calls Elliott a 'Cyclop', 'a strong man; a sort of gigantic Titan'.[45] King likewise has Elliott singing with 'the strength of a Titan', and notes the 'unpoetic element' of surroundings where 'busts of Shakespeare, Achilles, Ajax, and Napoleon,' are kept 'in the midst of piles of iron and steel'.[46] In this way, Carlyle develops, and then inspires, a critical language able to encompass the virtues of the 'hard-working, practical man'.[47]

Up to a point, Elliott plays along with this image. In the preface to the edition noticed by Carlyle, he responds to reviews in the *New Monthly Magazine* and the *Athenæum*.[48] In so doing, he registers – and makes no attempt to confute – the 'supposition that they are the work of a mechanic'.[49] He alludes here to Edward Bulwer's reference to 'a common mechanic', but also his own apology in the preface to *The Village Patriarch*.[50] There he remarks that 'If my composition smell of the workshop, and the mechanic, I cannot help it'.[51] One should not 'wonder', he proceeds, 'if mechanics write well in these days'.[52] This is all well and good, but Elliott's justification for assuming that identity is actually rather scant.[53] A letter addressed to Watkins, and later published in his biography, illustrates the complexity of his subject's social position: having thanked Watkins for the dedication of lay sermons, Elliott pleads in postscript, 'Do not address me Esquire' (originally, a shield bearer or gentle aspirant to knighthood). 'I have been a hard-working man all my life,' he explains, 'and am now a humble tradesman with a very large family to maintain, and so they call me a big man, because we cannot get into a very small house.'[54] Having disclaimed noble associations, he unfolds additional confusion. Seeking to explain a discrepancy of outward impression – a 'humble tradesman' in a big house – he inadvertently draws attention to it. As an assertion of identity, Elliott's words backfire; but along the way they highlight a problem of 'placing' that warrants further investigation.

If Elliott's involvement in Radical politics justifies his reputation as 'the poor man's friend' (he was a founder of the Sheffield Mechanics' Anti-Bread-Tax Society), it did not make him a poor man himself. He is better described as a 'jobbing merchant'.[55] Though claiming descent from Border cattle thieves, he must equally account for his father, who received a 'first-class commercial education' in Newcastle-upon-Tyne.[56] Alluding to his mother, whose 'ancestors had lived on their fifty or sixty acres of freehold time out of mind', Elliott acknowledges that 'I have made out my descent, if not from very fine folks, certainly from respectables'.[57] As the 'nominal proprietor' of the Rotherham foundry of Clay and Co., his father made no great fortune; but it was enough to send his son to school. What eventually caused Elliot to work in the family foundry was not a collapse of fortunes, but 'a punishment' for truancy.[58] This experience lasted until he was twenty-three. It seems to be Elliott's sole qualification for considering himself 'a working-man', though on this subject he also protests that 'I am not aware that I ever did so call myself'.[59] A comparison with Dickens's spell in Warren's Blacking Factory misses the mark: rather than mourning the end of his education, Elliott welcomes his escape from a situation that breeds feelings of inferiority. This being so, his career never did resemble 'that of a common working-man', as Watkins observes.[60] His role would rather be that 'of a master – of one whose head sets to work the hands of others.'[61]

Direct exposure to the trade cycle brought ruin and prosperity to Elliott in equal measure. In a letter to Macvey Napier, written after his review was finished, Carlyle acknowledges fresh information: his subject, he reports, is 'now, rather improved in circumstances' and 'keeps some little hardware shop'.[62] Even then, he wrongly calls him 'Reuben Elliott' (28:144); and his prefatory description of one 'bred an actual hammer-man or something of the sort' reinstates the image of a poet who 'by his skill in metallurgy, can beat out a toilsome but a manful living'.[63] In fact, Elliott gave up being a 'hammerman' in any exclusive sense long before, on assuming the management of his father's foundry.[64] He was declared bankrupt in 1816, at which point he moved from Rotherham to nearby Sheffield, where he set up as an iron dealer.[65] No longer directly involved in manufacturing, he entered a lucrative trade in which 'he made 20*l*. a day, sitting in his chair, without seeing the goods'.[66] According to Watkins, he lost one third of his savings in the crash of 1837, leaving him with £6,000.[67] This implies that Elliott was worth in savings alone the sum of £9,000 at the time of Carlyle's review. Tokens of respectability followed, including frequent listing under various resolutions and petitions published in the local press.[68] In the late 1820s, Elliott sent one of his sons to Peterhouse, Cambridge, after Southey pulled strings.[69] These facts do not contradict Elliott's claims about his origins, and there is no reason why intermittent wealth should transform his class position. But they inevitably complicate Carlyle's attribution of poetic qualities to a union in one person of the pen and the hammer, and his insistence on a 'personal battle with Necessity' (28:138).

That Carlyle never actually met Elliott explains how his testimony could diverge so radically from the reality of the poet's life. But it is not just Elliott's social background that eludes his descriptive categories: the poetry, too, resists the sinuous materialisation attributed to it. This is not so surprising, given the belated nature of the discovery: far from being a quintessentially Victorian poet, Elliott's style and aesthetic identity were formed in the first two decades of the century.[70] His poetic 'conversion' was owing not to life in the foundry, but to the chance revelation of James Sowerby's *English Botany* (1790), a work that led him out into Sheffield's near countryside in search of flowers to paint.[71] A largely decorative and derivative poetry is the result, heavily influenced by Romantic conceptions of communion with Nature. In *The Vernal Walk* (1802), 'serpentine rills rejoice' and 'Mountain torrents shine', while an opening address to the sun as the 'unbounded sea of light', evokes the seasonal poetry of James Thomson.[72] Unsurprisingly, given the accompanying pastoral lament for 'POOR DAMON, hapless lover!', the poet appears not as a 'smith', but as a 'bard of nature', who 'Warbles his rustic song'.[73] As Elliott moves through the phases of his career – from praise of Nature, to literary satire, and then socio-political satire – the mood darkens.[74] Priorities change, and at that point he leaves the Romantic legacy to one side, preferring to warn that 'Rivelin's side is desolate' ('The Tree of Rivelin').[75] Even when consumed by social purpose, though, he cannot resist alluding incidentally to the landscape, to ornamental flourishes of 'rock and rill'.

A scene of walks not just for Elliott but for many workers engaged in the metal trades, the Rivelin Valley exemplifies the co-existence in Sheffield of pastoral environments and water-powered grindstones.[76] In title and setting, 'The Tree of Rivelin' unsettles the binary distinction between 'natural sensitivity' and the identity of 'northern, industrial poet'.[77] Watkins's account is unusually perceptive in noting the discrepancy between this cultural work and the Cyclopean myth. He dispels the 'burly ironmonger' image, reporting that Elliott was 'of nervous temperament, weak in body', with 'sympathies' that were 'continually vibrating with torture, like the strings of the Æolian harp in a rough wind'.[78] Even Searle contradicts some of his earlier testimony in admitting surprise on first meeting Elliott, and finding him 'a man of short stature, instead of the bulky Titan I had pictured him in imagination'.[79] In this way, authorial fashioning that stresses 'natural vigour' (28:139) – in Carlyle's phrase – runs up against reality in the form of the poet's actual body.

Elliott himself responds to his late reputation as a 'mechanic', and here, too, a discrepancy arises: 'Is it strange', he asks, 'that my language is fervent with a welding heat, when my thoughts are *passions*, that rush burning from my mind, like white-hot bolts of steel?'[80] An apparently metallurgical 'welding heat' is reconfigured in Romantic and affective terms to become '*passions*'. The strongest evidence Carlyle can adduce for a 'Vulcanic dialect' comes not from the poetry, but from the earlier part of the same long sentence in the Preface: 'He says [. . .] his feelings have been *hammered* till they are *cold-short*; so they will no longer bend; "they snap, and fly off," – in the face of the hammerer' (28:148). Taken as a whole, Elliott's original sentence begins and ends in the 'heart', and is not about wielding the hammer, but about being hammered.[81] Carlyle's mixture of paraphrase and quotation obscures the effect of this treatment, which is that the poet's feelings 'snap – and fly off in sarcasm', as material figure is converted suddenly into mordant polemic.[82] It follows that Elliott's trajectory is more 'conventional' and more affective than his admirers wanted to believe. He realises, rather than resists, Raymond Williams's analysis of the early nineteenth century as a period when the '*Artist*' and '*artisan*' were parted along lines of 'sensibility' and 'skill'.[83]

No single phase of Elliott's career perfectly exhibits the synthesis of labouring subject and muscular style that Carlyle's description encourages. Even amid his 'political phase', the references to labour are Shelleyan: less glorifications of manual prowess than opportunities to extend a theme of tyrannical oppression. This is most apparent in the fourth of six poems entitled 'Song', which intones the message that 'freedom's foes mock'd labour's groan'.[84] Elliott's opposition to the Corn Laws and the 'tax-bribed plough' lead him, equally, to satirise pastoral convention. While this fits the image of an urban poet, it sets him against the agrarian tradition of labour poetry that aligns working rhythm with poetic rhythm.[85] The anti-reaper poem, *'Rogues* v. *Reason'*, exclaims 'Your cause is thresh'd – 'tis time! forgive | The husk that casts ye out; | And with your horrid bread-tax live, | Or try to live without.'[86] The 'time' of political reform runs counter, here, to the timing of the scythe. Elliott's perspective is that of the master of an enterprise: he resents the privileges accorded to rural landowners, leading him to the simple equation of his poem 'Reform', that 'They murder'd hope, they fetter'd trade'.[87]

Elliott introduces himself as an instinctual free-trader, and this no doubt reflects his father's economic positioning; only, it is the failure of his business that clinches the political direction of travel, and it is in this respect that Carlyle misjudges Elliott most seriously.[88] He never countenances Elliott's Radicalism, but misreads its orientation, its appeal to competition (rather than co-operation), and its roots less in 'sweat' than in the politics of a trade position.[89] Though genuinely interested in securing the poor man's bread, Elliott makes no attempt to distinguish that cause from the business-owner's unbridled capacity to compete with Continental enterprises. Indeed, he breaks with Chartism as soon as it abandons its opposition to Protection.[90] Carlyle projects his hostility to 'Competition' and *'Laissez-faire'* onto Elliott, unaware that these are idols to his 'Corn Law Rhymer'.[91] Given the close alignment in this period of working-class politics with free-trade arguments, the confusion is understandable.[92] The effect, nevertheless, is to aggravate the discrepancy between Elliott's poetic impetus, and the Carlylean view of it as intrinsically related to the life of the forge.

Elliott, as we have seen, is not what Carlyle imagines him to be. He can afford to rent a handsome stone villa, and is more iron-dealer than hammer-handler. These facts are relevant not so much in themselves than for what they reveal about Carlyle's emotional and intellectual priorities. They reveal in particular his need to believe that somewhere – elsewhere – literature and work might be reconciled. They also disclose his method, in deputing the task to an inspired 'mechanic' not obstructed by the 'dead letter' of education.[93] A similarly vicarious solution would later be employed by Ruskin, when identifying Sheffield as an arena in which 'workers in iron' could re-form the possibilities of artistic expression.[94] In both cases, the pressing concerns of an educated patron are vested in the artisan, a figure whose fixed social position becomes the basis for a new era of untrammelled creative expression.

A persistent irony haunts this discussion of Elliott's social position: namely, that his labouring class credentials were no more impeccable than those of his reviewer, himself the son of a stone mason. Carlyle, in this respect, is misled. But he also recognises in Elliott an opportunity. By clothing him in the garb of a workingman, he reserves the possibility of a manually-inflected art, one unpolluted by 'idle tattle'. As such, the misrecognition is best understood as a species of wishful thinking: Carlyle witnesses, through his review, the stature of an 'active poet', one who realises a lettered repetition of his father's work on the bridge at Auldgarth. In a final twist, this process of identification eventually unsettles Carlyle's willingness to indulge Elliott as an exception: in the closing remarks of his review, he cannot help asking, 'Whether Rhyme is the only dialect he can write in; whether Rhyme is, after all, the natural or fittest dialect for him?'[95]

* * *

Carlyle employs several coping strategies after embarking on his career as a man of letters. The first, articulated in *Sartor Resartus* and in *On Heroes* (1841), foregrounds artistic insight to the extent that he equates the poet with the prophet and the philosopher. By contrast, his private letters and reminiscences venture an internalisation of his father's status as a craftsman in a strategy closely linked to his early appreciation of poetry. Both affinities undergo pressure after his arrival in London. He earnestly hoped to write his books 'as he built his houses', but the same resolution employs the figurative sleight of hand that his father disdained. In its place, a toiling – rather than crafted – model of literary work begins to gain traction. By insisting on the strenuous labour, sweat, tears, and even pain, induced by composition, he could at least adduce the physical symptoms associated with visible labours, and with the occupational diseases previously discussed. Meanwhile, Carlyle gravitates towards forms of work that lie fully outside himself, often focused on superhuman levels of strength and resolution. As such, the review of Elliott's poetry is significant even at a generic level. A review, after all, is a referred form: one that projects and explains more than it participates. All the while, Carlyle sustains compositional theories of the vatic, the artisanal and the toiling, in changing relative concentration. If this creates problems and restrictions for those operating in his wake, the next two chapters demonstrate that the same legacies could also be generative.

Chapter 2

Ford Madox Brown Among the Brain-Workers

As the cases of Cunningham and Elliott demonstrate, there is a strong tendency towards verbal portraiture in the method by which Carlyle isolates artisanal characteristics. This chapter turns from the case of a writer who redescribes his vocation in visual terms to that of an artist who portrays Carlyle himself, and who likewise indemnifies intellectual labour by making it visible. Ford Madox Brown is best known for his large-scale canvas, *Work* (1852–65) [Figure 2.1], a painting much studied by art critics, and routinely seen as visualising a central Victorian value. Yet the

Figure 2.1 Ford Madox Brown, *Work*, 1852–65, oil on canvas. © Manchester Art Gallery / Bridgeman Images

circumstances of its composition contain a commentary not only on the fraught connection between the labour of mind and the hand of the artist, but also on the difficulties encountered by a discourse of authenticity that relies on processes of representation, staging and demonstration.

In its final form, *Work* depicts a group of navvies mending a road who are watched from one side by likenesses of Carlyle and F. D. Maurice. It is an arrangement that differs markedly from the design that first inspired the commission of its patron, Thomas Plint [Figure 2.2].

Apparently unhappy with the painter figure who originally stood at the sidelines, Plint asked Brown 'to introduce *both* Carlyle and *Kingsley*' in substitution.[1] He duly contacted Carlyle to arrange a sitting, and quietly discarded the suggestion of Kingsley in favour of Maurice. The legal complications arising from Plint's death in 1861 ensured that it was not until 1865 that the painting could appear in public.[2] In that year it was shown as the centrepiece of a one-man retrospective, 'The Exhibition of *Work*, and other Paintings' ('The Gallery', Piccadilly, 1865), an event whose billing simultaneously describes a specific painting and testifies to all the artistic effort it involved. The self-authored catalogue that Brown published to mark the event discloses a related double logic, resembling as it does interpretative art criticism as much as exhibition or sales description.[3]

Figure 2.2 Ford Madox Brown, 'Study for the Oil Painting *Work*', 1852–56, watercolour and pencil on paper. Image courtesy of Manchester Art Gallery

Among the commentaries that Brown includes, the long entry on *Work* stands out. Amid the action and colour of the street scene, he identifies 'the British excavator or navvy' as the 'outward and visible type of work'.[4] Meanwhile, Plint's concern with personality recedes in favour of delineating 'types and not individuals'.[5] Carlyle and Maurice are recognisable to the right, but are described anonymously as 'brain-workers who, seeming to be idle, work, and are the cause of well-ordained work and happiness in others'.[6] This conception of a 'seeming' idleness, and the idea of 'seeming' more generally, offer one focus for this chapter. The word allows a dual acknowledgement that what appears to be the case may count for a lot, and yet be at variance with reality. Apparent idleness emanates from the brain-workers' genteel attire, as also from their reflective pose and removal from physical labours. But that impression equally reflects a history of attitudes. Danahay rightly observes that Brown's claim in the catalogue 'does not negate the fact that they look idle', or lessen the influence of the Protestant work ethic in producing 'contradictions in both Brown's prose and his painting'.[7] Distinguishing his treatment from Colin Trodd's 'transition from "vision" to "authority"', he registers the complications of visual and verbal witness.[8] It is worth dwelling, all the same, on the importance of being seen – in this painting, and in Victorian culture more generally. D'Israeli remarks, pertinently, that the lack of reward garnered by 'intellectual pursuits' results from their 'objects' being 'so invisible', and so rarely 'palpable to observers'.[9] As the theologian Horace Bushnell noted in 1848, 'the writer himself is hidden, and cannot even suggest his existence'.[10] Several questions arise from this observation. Does the same representational quandary apply to the artist: that is, to the figure purportedly in command of the visual field? Is Brown attempting to translate Carlyle's Gospel of (authorial) Work onto a painted canvas, in an effort to redeem his own related labours? And, equally, might *Work* offer a remedy for literary invisibility, by conferring the kind of presence that attracts respect to other occupations?

In a detailed and authoritative account of Brown's *Work*, Barringer identifies the painting as an exercise in achieving 'incontrovertible verisimilitude'.[11] My own reading builds on his findings, but differs in exploring Brown's paradoxical attempt to make visible less what is seen and understood as 'reality' than a labour of mind that is not normally detectable. The first part discusses the depiction of the writer's face, and asks whether the sight of a writer can be a metonym for invisible professional processes. The second part moves away from the painting as a finished object, to consider its genealogy. In so doing, it addresses the handiwork of representation itself. A painting may take work as its subject, but can our appreciation of that subject ever extend to the medium in which it is rendered? Such questions invite a clearer delineation of the relationship between painters and 'brain-workers'. The last part turns from Brown's painting to his writing: specifically, the personal and professional diary that he kept during this crucial phase of his career.

Seeming Idleness

Work now hangs in Manchester Art Gallery, not far from the town hall where murals also by Brown depict the origins of the city and its industry. The painting has been described variously as 'a comprehensive depiction of Victorian reality',[12] an 'allegory of Victorian labour',[13] and a study that 'endorses Carlyle's Gospel of Work'.[14] Many take it to symbolise the industriousness of an entire epoch. The canvas's scale, its obsessively rendered detail, and its appeal to a 'universal' subject, invite these forms of attention. But something is missed if we neglect the associated difficulties that the painting – indeed, any painting – encounters when depicting the labour of mind. Alluding to George Hicks' *The Sinews of Old England* (1857), Barringer illuminates a wider turn of painterly attention towards the muscular and morally upright labourer.[15] Brown's leadership in this area was achieved by persisting unfashionably with the conventions of history painting, which he absorbed while studying at the Antwerp Academy under Gustaf Wappers. An emphasis on working from life establishes the innovation of this approach. Rather than honouring cold universals, he freezes instances of vital being.[16] A sonnet published with the catalogue announces this programme: by means of a 'weird art', it pledges to 'transmute poor men's evils,' so that 'Their bed seems down, their one dish ever fresh.'[17] Such representational work acts on the body to arrest change. By illusion or alchemy, it enlivens and preserves the staple satisfactions of 'bed' and 'dish'.

But what of 'work' that strains the mind more than the 'flesh', and whose 'art' is all the more strange for not being seen? The catalogue is often taken to evince intellectual confidence – triumphalism, even – in stating the existence of 'brain-workers', and the reach of their ideas as the 'cause' of 'well-ordained work'.[18] Yet the stylistic awkwardness of its gloss complicates the visual proof. The parenthetical clause and suspended verb, in 'who, seeming to be idle, work', run defensiveness and assertiveness in parallel.[19] Acknowledging how things might look, Brown pre-empts the popular imputation, and the inner fear, that thinkers are 'idle'. Having done so, the case is pressed that work need not be available for inspection. Trodd writes, accordingly, that *Work* gives primacy and sovereignty to the 'eye of the intellectual'.[20] But if the catalogue questions mere appearances, it derives little obvious support from the canvas. The viewer's gaze settles only slowly on the drab pair occupying the right-hand position. Their visual survey is less assured, and less in command of the scene, than one might expect. Even as we notice them, our attention is referred sideways by Maurice's focus on the central group, or thrown back on itself by Carlyle's partial return of stare. The effect resembles a drama of frustrated certainty. Such impressions do not amount to a council of despair, though. The relegation of 'brain-workers' to a peripheral position is in fact part of the point. We are witnessing the beginnings of an urge to emulate, or at least learn from, the desirable element in physical labour, and of a concern to turn invisible work to more obvious advantage.

Brown's allusion to 'brain-workers' participates in this revisionism. Its provenance is hard to determine, but the first *OED* citation comes from 1844, a review published in *The Christian Teacher* (1844) that weakly counters reports of 'apoplexy, epilepsy, inflammation of the brain, and dyspepsia' by citing examples of the 'longevity of brain-workers'.[21] Although the phrase itself does not appear in the title under review – William Sweetser's *Mental Hygiene* (1843) – the commentary seems indebted to those works by Tissot and Thackrah on occupational disease that I have previously discussed.[22]

In Brown's hands, the phrase functions more positively: imbued with refurbished literalness, it dwells less on the over-worked cerebrum than on a mental power to conceive good works. Ten years after the exhibition of *Work*, the American political economist Calvin Colton hinted at this possibility, on writing that 'laborers [. . .] are not confined to those who engage in manual toil'.[23] Infused with fashionable interest in the physiology of mental disturbance, Brown's preference for the embodied 'brain' suggests a new avenue.[24] Even the abstraction of 'mind' begins to enter the physical arena, as Henry Maudsley's *The Physiology and Pathology of Mind* (1865; 1867) would corroborate.[25] Both usages admit scope for muscular effort, conflating an imperceptible idea of mind with the visible presence of a bodily organ. As a man whose business was making things visible, Brown occupies a revealing position in these debates. The portrayal of work, and especially 'brain-work', represents a crucial test, as such, of artistic scope. Discussing the question of representation more broadly, Elaine Scarry includes painting among 'Forms of art that have no temporal element', and which therefore 'convey the "activity" of work with more ease than does literary narrative'.[26] This takes us some distance, but the examples given here – Jean-François Millet's *The Sower* and the *Seated Girl in Auvergne Spinning* – are all manual and demonstrable. For Brown, the question is not solely how to represent action in a static painting, but how to impart an industrious appearance to otherwise invisible processes of writing and thinking.

In the first major study of Brown's life and achievement, Ford Madox Ford (né Hueffer) draws attention to the 'literary ideas' lying behind his grandfather's works.[27] His point concerns the dynamic relation between literature and visual art, but also pertains to the translation of unperceived experience onto the visual plane. Among the younger Pre-Raphaelite artists, likewise, literary affinities encourage an absorption of Catholic symbolism and iconography. And it is apparent that the impulse of religious art to depict spiritual phenomena provides an additional basis for converting abstract ideas into glowing physical reality. Discussing the riddle into which one navvy shovels dirt, John Walker mentions that Carlyle uses it 'as a metaphor of the sifting process, which is necessary to obtain worthy leaders'.[28] As such it materialises a process of judgement, standing for the broader idea that physical forms may point to mental conceptions. Equally, Brown's placing of the contemporary sage in the 'market square' puts a 'higher' form of teaching back within earshot and eyeshot.

The body, in this respect, stands for more than immanent physicality; it, too, is a kind of symbol. Brown regards faces, in particular, as a reliable window into the obscurity of active thought. His art repeatedly implies that literary achievement can be shown through the authorial visage. In this respect, he combines Continental history painting with a more intimate mode of portraiture, geared towards intimations of the internal life. One of his most ambitious paintings, *Chaucer at the Court of Edward III* (1847–51), installs the father of English poetry at the heart of civil power.[29] A related work, *The Seeds and Fruits of English Poetry* (1845–53), borrows the niches usually occupied by saints and fills them with writers, ranging between Shakespeare, Milton, Thomson and Burns.[30] The logic of sight and 'showing' is apparent, too, in Brown's *Wilhelmus Conquistador (The Body of Harold)* (1844–61), a composition in which political events are evoked by the physical witness of a dead king.[31] The features used to model Geoffrey Chaucer are actually those of a contemporary poet, Dante Gabriel Rossetti. The painted face performs a double service, as such, evincing poetic intelligence at the level both of signifier and signified.

The Biblical mottos engraved on the frame of *Work* initiate this emphasis on the meaningful façade, even as they enact the ways in which writing verifies looking. The central inscription, 'In the sweat of thy face shalt thou eat bread' (Genesis 3. 19), finds its realisation in the navvies' facial perspiration. A further Biblical quotation adorns the right-hand side of the frame: 'Seest thou a man diligent in his business? He shall stand before kings' (Proverbs 22. 29).[32] As a rhetorical question, it aptly evokes the priority of inquisition and inspection. The 'face' here is not just a mark of what lies within, but a more permanent substitute for the inner world, the last word in an evidential process that recognises 'diligence' by process of sight and survey. Brown's emphasis on painting from 'life', and in the open air, contributes to this logic of visual scrutiny: as an artistic procedure, it sheds light on hidden details, just as Carlyle, in submitting to the artificial eye of a photograph, had to be lured into the open from his study.

Difficulties nevertheless complicate Brown's answer to the problem of intellectual invisibility. As Gregory Dart observes, he 'possessed a marked preference for Carlyle's early books'.[33] The painting itself is not so clearly aimed. It combines elements of the social concern of *Chartism* (1840) with the privileging of 'action' propounded in *Latter-Day Pamphlets* (1850). Bobus – the Houndsditch sausage-maker shown electioneering in the background – comes from *Past and Present*, a volume published twenty-two years before *Work* was exhibited, and nine years before Brown began painting it. Far from being trivial, these matters problematise the idea that an author's visage may stand for a specific literary content. Brown, perhaps, senses this on entering the unconvincing disclaimer that, despite taking 'personages of note' as models, he intends them to 'delineate types'.[34] Barringer, for his part, notices the image of Carlyle as a 'sneering, gap-toothed, prophet', who has failed 'to live up to the criteria of masculinity, physical activity, and assertiveness that identify the workers'.[35] There is nothing in the catalogue to suggest that brain-workers should measure up physically, but the painting's visual language certainly diagnoses the intellectual vocation in terms of relative incapacity. The problem is partly conceptual, and partly a matter of the strain involved in representing what is invisible. In as much as the term 'brain-workers' suggests physicality, Brown probes the limits of Mill's distinction between bodily and mental labour. But he has not found, nor even sought, a way of evidencing this intellectual pressure on the picture plane.[36]

The same limitation arises from Brown's correspondence with Carlyle. Replying to an initial invitation to sit, Carlyle explains that he is in a poor condition to help, because 'l[ost] deep in the belly of an ugly Enterprise'.[37] It is as if Brown's plans to depict authorship, by painting a famous brain-worker, are exposed to incidental refutation. For Carlyle, the work in which he is engaged – his laborious effort to complete *Frederick the Great* (1858–66) – feels neither active nor passive, but irrevocably internal, and therefore outside the painterly field of view. A further difficulty concerns the polarisation of intellectual labour and manual labour enshrined in the catalogue. Brown, like Mill, imagines an eternal principle that separates different types of person. At least initially, this prevents him seeing that reasoning and problem-solving are an essential component of most practical tasks. These complications dawn on Brown only later, when musing that the tract-distributing lady might 'be benefited by receiving tracts containing navvies' ideas!'[38] '[E]xcavators', he concludes, 'are skilled workmen, shrewd thinkers chiefly'. Certainly, Brown makes a case for the existence and persistence of invisible things, but he does so by extending a principle of showing that excludes such processes. Equally, the challenge of visualising what cannot be seen sees him falling back on the writer's face or likeness. The risk is that he merely confirms the primacy of visibility as a test of work, that he reinstates, rather than queries, a more conventional method of visual survey. Brain-work proves incapable of standing for itself, with the result that it is converted into something it is not.

A more convinced understanding of Brown's method arises from the Pre-Raphaelite division of labour between word and image. In an otherwise laudatory review of 'Mr Madox Brown's Exhibition', William Michael Rossetti worries that the 'descriptive-catalogue scheme' might 'tempt some painters to be less careful and emphatic in telling their story upon the canvas, knowing that they can fall back upon the explanation which the catalogue supplies'.[39] A recent critic goes further in calling the catalogue a 'dangerous supplement'.[40] Brown's commentaries might put his pictorial imagery in a semantic straight jacket, but the process of revealing this verbal limit happens to be conceptually generative, heuristic even. By relying on the catalogue to alert the viewer to the existence of 'brain-work' Brown acknowledges a problem: namely, that painting, taken alone, possesses inadequate means for testifying to labour of mind. What cannot be inspected cannot be counted. Thus, Brown's pictorial experiment activates conflicts already latent within the broader Calvinistic tradition: suspicious of iconography and what 'seems', it responds by treating knowledge of election as a kind of invisible credit, evinced by works that mimic the thing itself. A similar conflict, between suspect appearance and necessary proof, haunts the bourgeois attitude to the visual arts, as revealed by wealthy merchants who dismiss art but make an exception for portraits commemorating patrons, founders, and civic worthies.[41] By partially representing (or even distorting) invisible labours, Brown's *Work* becomes a provocative witness, mimetic of an enduring problem.

Apart from advancing a Pre-Raphaelite conception of the 'sister arts', the text of the catalogue exploits a cultural glitch in pitching bourgeois principles of demonstration against Protestant conceptions of the self-speaking 'word'. The latter assumes a power to see through appearances into the invisible processes of thought. To employ a phrase popularised by W. J. T. Mitchell, the result is a truly 'composite art', albeit one that comes dangerously close to a division of labour, where the word deals in essences, and the vision in accidents.[42] Biblical quotations play their part; but the supplement on which Brown relies most heavily is not a painted banner, nor is it the graven surround that augments Rossetti's paintings. In this regard, the catalogue functions as a watch or ward, a witness to the variable testamentary power of images and texts operating at different levels of remove. Far from threatening the canvas's ability to signify, it participates in a larger conception of 'the work', even while registering its generic and physical distance from the painted original.

Idle Observers

As previously noted, Brown originally cast the figure of painter in the right-hand position of *Work* [see Figure 2.2]. Rather than gazing at the navvies from the margin, his eyes are cast down. Resigning the task of observation in this way, he suggests a person who idles even within the bounds of a purportedly idle profession. The frivolous action of his cane, meanwhile, signals an absence of serious business. Brown models similar body language in *The Hayfield* (1855–56),[43] a work that depicts a painter reclining against a haystack, with one arm held aloft, as if renouncing the work of the brush. In this way it realises – even provokes – Carlyle's hostility towards artists, his warning that 'This is no world where a man should stand trimming his whiskers, looking on at work'.[44] What then does it mean for the brain-workers to step into the artist's shoes? While links between them rest on shared professional commitment to observation, the alignment cuts both ways. Carlyle and Maurice are acting just as painters must do: observing a scene with purposes obscure to the onlooker, so that they appear idle. The differences between these figures are worth exploring, however; and in so doing, we must read against the grain of continuities instantiated by the painting's history. While the artist is drawn into the orbit of the intellectual worker, and while Brown convincingly evokes a shared experience of occupational stigma, that conflation turns out to be neither inevitable nor unproblematic. '[L]ooking on', very evidently, is a function that Brown confronts and complicates, but also reclaims.

   The state of his profession was an ongoing preoccupation for Brown, and indeed an evolving artistic subject. On a bad day, he reports how 'A loathing of my vocation seized me' [. . .] Work, work, work for ever muddles a man's brain'.[45] Brown was not alone in this respect. Painters of his generation suffered a special kind of status anxiety. Paula Gillett attributes this to an almost universal experience of 'basic uncertainty' about 'the legitimate functions served by the painter's work'.[46] Walker further elaborates the complex bind of these 'gentlemen of the brush', in claiming that artists are 'unusual among intellectuals because, besides thinking, they make things with their hands'.[47] This singularity makes Brown's interchange between word and image especially relevant when considering the competing allure of handiwork. At the same time, he was not above worrying over social impressions. According to Ford, his father objected to his 'obvious trend towards the ungentlemanly life of an artist'.[48] The mother of his second wife disapproved of the match due to 'the disreputability of his profession'.[49] These perspectives query the notion that he replaced the artist figure with two intellectuals because their equal status was a settled matter. On the contrary, the painting's headline distinction between brain and hand would be even harder to sustain had Brown retained the artist from the preliminary study.

Unlike their literary peers, Victorian artists also lacked legal acceptance of their power to create intangible wealth.[50] It was not until 1862, when the Fine Art Copyright Act passed into law, that they benefited from the Romantic conceptions of property previously accorded to authors. (The right to license and profit from engravings was previously vested in the new owners of the physical painting.) These broken forms of recognition explain why visible – and therefore manual – forms of labour assume so much importance for Brown. If the work's intellectual content cannot be owned by the artist after sale, the next best thing is to lodge that claim at the point of presentation, through a visual – and therefore, enduring – realisation of 'brain-work'. Brown's vehemence in berating Plint for comments on the 'dilatoriness of artists' and 'the shortcomings of artists as compared with dealers' suggests the urgency of this need to refute through demonstration.[51] A tension arises, all the same, between a desire to live up to this social pressure – and perhaps, also, the law's insistence that what actually accrues value is the intellectual labour invested – and the social hazard posed by too close an alignment with the labour of the hands. Brown's answer, as intimated, is to bind the artist to the brain-worker.

Several of his contemporaries would conduct similar experiments. Samuel Smiles, for instance, includes a chapter on 'Workers in Art' in *Self-Help* (1859).[52] Three years later, P. G. Hamerton published *Thoughts About Art* (1862), a work that decries the worldly prejudice suffered by the 'noble' arts.[53] These Victorian accounts of artistic endeavour were anticipated – as Smiles acknowledges – by Joshua Reynolds.[54] Reynolds describes artists as 'workers' involved in an 'exertion of mind'.[55] He prefers pains of accomplishment to 'the effect of enchantment', and rejects 'inspirations of genius' not tied to 'well-directed labour'.[56] A conscious investment of labour guarantees aesthetic value, as well as professional status: 'The value and rank of every art', he avers, 'is in proportion to the mental labour employed in it, or the mental pleasure produced by it.'[57] Though believing in artistic 'labour' as a form of exertion, Reynolds insists that the accompanying 'mental pleasure' distinguishes painting from a 'mechanical trade'.

Was the painting of *Work* an exercise in proving artistic labour? Barringer understands its 'elaboration of detail and the hard-won verisimilitude' as the mechanism by which Brown could 'assert his mastery over the whole social scene', 'a manual worker and a brainworker'.[58] Contemporary reviewers certainly recognised a testament to personal work in the painting – if not necessarily manual work – whether in praise or disdain.[59] Single artist shows were rare in the 1860s, but Brown's retrospective successfully publicises his achievement, while spurring the completion of unfinished work.[60] After a year of unprecedented productiveness, he could show 'upwards of a hundred works'.[61] '[S]ome three thousand people' attended, exhausting 'about two-thirds of that number of catalogues'.[62] Even Gladstone paid a private visit.[63] 'The result', Brown proudly observes, 'is that people begin to say I must have been a very hard-working man all my life, a thing they have hardly given me credit for as yet'.[64] If *The Exhibition of Work* lives up to its name in both these senses, it also makes an exhibition of painting itself. In a letter to Lowes Dickinson, Brown reports having 'painted in Heath Street here (it being 6 ½ feet long) on a truck fitted up by myself for the occasion, to the astonishment of all well-regulated people'.[65] Painting *en plein air*, in this way, Brown takes his work out of the studio, and into the street. The effect is to witness his use of oils in public, and thereby include his vocation among the typology of London professions.

But just as the painted faces of brain-workers disguise interior processes, so the surface effects of artistic labour have a habit of frustrating Brown's search for inner truth. In particular, the union between intellectual labour and what Barringer calls the painting's 'transcript of the physical word' begins to pull apart.[66] The scale of the canvas, for instance, necessitates a degree of scenic reconstruction, which conveniently draws on Brown's early training as a history painter. Despite foregrounding his 'realism', Ford stumbles across this issue on noting the quality of *'tableau theatrique'* in Brown's work.[67] Verisimilitude, it seems, is inescapably linked to staging. But it is at the level of the body and the pose – whether of brain-workers or navvies – that the artist's eye is drawn closest to the lived reality of work, and at the same time removed from it entirely into the alternative arena of 'seeming'.

This is most apparent in Brown's use of a studio photograph as the basis for his portrait of Carlyle. Commenting on an early study,[68] Holman Hunt warns his friend that 'such fitful contortions in a human face seem to me very painful when for hours, years, and ages they remain the same – as in a picture'.[69] The advice is striking for the fact that Carlyle's mouth is actually closed in the photograph by Charles Thompson.[70] Artistic liberties of this kind are commonplace, but they complicate Ford's claim that 'The picture was not to be, and should not be regarded as a work of generalisation or allegory, but as an actual moment, caught and recorded'.[71] At issue is the capacity of the brain-worker to stand for a larger idea, including the identity of the preliminary study's suppressed artist. The painting vouches for reality and disregards it at the same time. It honours an observational faculty whose value as 'honest' work is challenged by its own observational diligence, where that diligence entails routine practices of artifice and modelling.

In related ways, Brown's sourcing of models contorts and fragments the canvas's naturalistic snapshot. Working over such a long period, he cannot capture an entire scene in the present. Individual studies, composed many years apart, must be compiled into a whole. This leaves him working within a composite, and therefore highly artificial, time-frame. In his diary, Brown mentions going to Gray's Inn Lane 'to look for Irish people', noting that 'I painted at the head of the man mixing mortar'.[72] In January the following year, he 'painted in the young working man, the hero of the picture, all but his legs', and finally he 'painted at the legs of the hero in the large picture'.[73] Isolating fragments for painterly attention might be an inevitable part of the process, but fitting together deracinated body parts recalls the queasy articulations of Dickens's taxidermist and bone curator, Mr Venus.[74] *Work* remains a testament to the observational power of its artist, and of art more generally. But it performs this role less as an expression of coherent results derived from continuous effort than as the function of a composite and theatrical process.

The genealogy of the painting harbours one further check on the subtle conflation of the artist and brain-worker. Death, in particular, haunts the canvas's parade of visibility. After beginning to paint the baby of 'a poor woman' found in Holborn, Brown learns that the child has been taken ill and died.[75] He is obliged 'to rub out' what he has done. Disjunctions between life and representation arise even as Brown captures the vitality of the navvies. The catalogue text registers 'the melancholy fact, that one of the very men who sat [. . .] lost his life by a scaffold accident, before I had yet quite done with him'.[76] More than a sad epilogue, this information throws into doubt the association between visibility and living presence carefully cultivated by the 'real time' descriptions of the catalogue. As Brown's 'life drawing' faces the expiry of its subject, the sinews of the workmen assume a ghostly shape. A memorial function steals upon the painting and we are reminded that 'captured' flesh is still fugitive, and that the artist has relied on a conception or idea of life, rather than on life itself.

Brown's *Work* highlights the observational labour performed by artist and brain-worker alike. Its silent, unacknowledged aspects, in particular, are externalised through a depiction of the brain-workers' gaze. By making the work of perception a subject of art, Brown delineates a new social claim. The dividends reaped by Carlyle and Maurice are less obvious, not least because their social position at once invites and resists a direct comparison. In their apparent idleness – defined, as it is, by contrast with the exertions of heroic navvies – they inherit the reputational problems of their artistic predecessor. Even for the artist, the benefits of *seeing* work are strictly limited. A prevailing logic of visual survey ensures that multifarious thought processes become purely observational: a branch, in effect, of (noticeable) painterly diligence. Equally, *Work*'s compositional history discloses Brown's serial reversion to metaphysics, as efforts to capture and observe reality return him to the spectral world of absent presences. Becoming a brain-worker crystallises an opportunity for the painter: it isolates and redeems the invisible aspects of a profession that lives by visibility. Yet by separating observation from the act of guiding a brush, Brown also misses the intelligence or 'craft' underlying manual process, and obscures the shifting reality of the painted subject.

Disciplines of a Diarist

Brown, as we have seen, extends a visual depiction of the writer into a proof or demonstration of brain-work. The literary import of his anxiety about intangible labour applies equally to his own writing, and in particular to the private notes he made about his professional life. As a verbal testament to his progress as a painter, Brown's diary stands as a predecessor to the catalogue's commentary on brain-work. 'Should every one keep a record of his daily acts & sentiments,' he proposes, 'the history of the world would be made out in a way that no historian could distort however illiberal or enthusiastic in his nature'.[77] This confidence in the accuracy of self-witness converts diary keeping into a ward against distortion, an indelible testament whose checks on the public record promise a reform of historical method itself. His method of 'fixing' work on the page betrays, as such, a settled confidence in the imperishable power of words. In this respect, his example differs from the others discussed in this book. Far from anxiously performing literary work, his writing captures the daily record of an artistic labour more nervously conceived. The diary is of central interest, all the same, for the ways in which it supplements Brown's revisionary account of 'seeming', not least his displaced yearning for an unstigmatised hand. It commands interest, too, for modelling a form of writing more centrally enrolled than literary fiction in the value systems of commercial life. In this respect, Brown's daily account doubles as a mercantile account book, albeit one that privileges the aims of art over the financial ends of stock taking.

Despite alluding to the history of the world, the diary's animating spirit is more theological than historiographic. The first book opens with a 'short retrospectary [*sic*] glance at the events which have led to my undertaking' the Chaucer painting.[78] As this more representative entry suggests, Brown's thoughts are geared to self-investigation and self-reform. The Calvinist inheritance passed down from his father supports this view of the diary as a spiritual record. In this tradition, as Manning observes, 'The burden of the proof of election falls on the self-investigating conscience'.[79] The role of this 'internal observer'[80] in self-transformation recalls the form of St Augustine's *Confessions* (397–98).[81] It also follows paths less travelled by Protestant minds. Challenging the Weberian orthodoxy that excludes Catholic traditions, Aho traces modern accountancy to the 'sacrament of absolution [. . .] implanted in the fertile soil of the [medieval] Italian trading centers'.[82] Brown's own version of confessionalism first emerges in entries describing *Chaucer at the Court of Edward III*, a work begun in Rome, and specifically endorsed by his deceased wife, Elizabeth ('Lizzy').[83] According to Brown, she 'prophecied that it would ensure me ultimate success, [. . .] and *ordered* me to complete it after her death'.[84] '[I]n fulfilling her behest', he intimates, 'I am breaking one of her strongest recommendations, I have parted from Lucy', Lucy being Brown's motherless daughter, who was lodging with a maternal aunt.[85] Following this admission, he enters a prayer and a complaint: 'O! God! ought not that thought to make me strive & struggle agains [*sic*] indolence.'[86]

Though directed at God, his confessions lack the form of an intercessory prayer. Rather, the whole cycle of confession, witness and judgement plays out on a private page. With no priest to impart absolution, the conscience loses its outlet: in Weber's words, it is 'doomed by an inexorable

fate, admitting of no mitigation'.[87] As Brown's succeeding cry suggests –
'O! the hell of poverty!!!' – this lack of 'mitigation' introduces a distinctly
unconfessional breaking-point. From an address to God, he slips into a
wail of self-pity. Such modes are closer, in fact, to self-justification than
confession, suggesting a blended form, akin to James Hogg's *The Private
Memoirs and Confessions of a Justified Sinner* (1824), where the privacy
of memoir fuses with the form of the unanswered entreaty.[88] The story of
Elizabeth's dying wish is not an opportunity to admit fault at all: rather,
it sketches a supposedly unavoidable conflict of laws, where adhering to
an initial 'order' explains the breaking of a 'recommendation', an effect
at once technically consistent and morally spurious.

The repressed confessional element returns to the surface of the diary
at moments of gratuitous admission and self-castigation. Not long after
his first entry, Brown records several instances of lapsed effort connected
to oversleeping. On 5 September 1847, he writes that he 'Got up late, got
to work late, did little'.[89] On 25 September, he reports feeling weary at
close of day, and falls to the familiar self-attack: 'am a very swine – shall
never get the painting done in time – am a beast & a sleepy brute'.[90] On
7 October, he chastises himself, using the same words in reverse order:
'I am a brute & a sleepy beast'.[91] Such terms of reproach are mortifying,
but they also presume a divided self, one capable of hosting a senseless
and destructive force. Dramatising in this way a Calvinist moral quar-
antine, Brown's self-chastisement integrates an 'evil double' who recalls
Robert Louis Stevenson's bestial Mr Hyde.[92] This way of thinking seems
to have circulated among his artistic acquaintance in similar terms: the
young William Morris would compare himself to 'a lazy, aimless, useless
dreaming body'.[93] Both men associated dreaming with a failure of will,
a descent into lumpen physicality.

Though gratuitous, such self-castigation forms part of Brown's mission
to account for the way he spends his time. A related urge towards confession co-operates with the discipline of quantification, and in particular the
form of the ledger that haunts the diary. In her discussion of *Robinson
Crusoe*, Q. D. Leavis argues that Defoe's fictional 'day-dreams' were ones
in 'which the solid unromantic bourgeois interests ruled', with their 'tire-
some balancing of pros and cons in every possible situation'.[94] An early
theorist of bookkeeping, Defoe represents a particularly fruitful precedent
for thinking through Brown's own 'mental stocktaking'. 'A tradesman's
books', he contends, 'are his repeating clock, which upon all occasions are
to tell him how he goes on, and how things stand with him in the world'.[95]
The strict function of such books is to financialise time, but Defoe also
understands their upkeep as a virtue in itself. Bookkeeping – like diary
keeping – expresses a discipline of self-inspection, a willingness to face up

to the whole picture and see the damage. Defoe casts this process as a double action: 'As every thing done must be set down in the Books, so it should
be done at the very time of it'.[96] The repeated 'done' in this case turns
an outlay into an act, and finally a record of diligence. Meanwhile, the
discipline of bookkeeping stands in for the larger project of self-scrutiny,
enabling the idea of 'credit' to shift from the financial field into the moral
arena. As Weber notes dismissively, 'the old mediæval idea (even ancient)
idea of God's bookkeeping is carried by Bunyan to the characteristically
tasteless extreme of comparing the relation of a sinner to his God with that
of a customer and shopkeeper'.[97] For Defoe, the books are not a bridge or
analogy, but a reliable tool of navigation in both spheres: 'A Tradesman's
books', he insists, are 'like a Christian's conscience'.[98]

Brown's diary is not itself focused on the financial account; his version
of credit dwells instead on daily gains (and losses) of time, measured as a
function of work achieved. In this respect, his moment of rising acquires
an over-determined significance. On an unusually good day – 10 November 1847 – he 'Got up at 7 got to work by 9, painted at the study of the
green gown with the yellow hood till ½ past 3, went out for a walk till
¼ to 5 – set to work again at 7 & worked till 12 at a drawing of Burns
(10 hours work).'[99] Even more vigorous work occurs on 18 April 1848,
involving repainting, glazing, mosaic work and visitors.[100] Following a
string of frenzied entries documenting between ten and seventeen hours'
work, his closing report of '(18 hours)' arrives here as the climax of a
strong run. The satisfaction produced by routine notation is palpable, and
the diary's gearing towards credit and proof acquires a life of its own. In
the resumed diary of 1865–66, the entries are abbreviated to single lines,
concluding almost always in a bracketed declaration of hours worked, the
expressive prose of the first entries now tried, tested and boiled down to
the essential information.

Brown's practice as a diarist does not adhere to bookkeeping principles in all respects. Failing to observe proper accounting neutrality, he
understands 'negative' entries as enduring setbacks. When the results are
favourable, he salves his conscience by counting hours spent at the easel;
when they were not so favourable, his self-directed procedure leaves him,
simultaneously, in the position of worker and foreman. The entry for
2 November 1847 indicates when Brown wakes up, and at what time
'work' commences: 'Got up at 7 & to work by 9, painted the study of the
ermine cloake of ye ladië with ye sideless gown'.[101] In this way, he declares
a 'wasted' interval of two hours. An even more horrified testimony appears
two weeks later: 'Got up at 10! drank beer the night before & eat Bread
and cheese!' (14 November 1847):[102] Sometimes, Brown's self-disgust
leads to a breakdown in the notational system, staging in effect a failure

of diligence: the entry for 27 November 1847 begins unconventionally, 'Got up I know not at what hour'.[103]

This insistence on absolute loss represents Brown's most obvious departure from the measured tally of an account book, where the debits for each day will be set against the progress of an entire financial year. In his mind, by contrast, negative entries are never made up. And while he condemns backsliding, he also unintentionally produces it. This occurs through the perpetuation of category errors and perverse disincentives to preparatory effort. Exertion not easily classified as 'work' – at least, according to Brown's narrow definition – is automatically annulled. Thus his complaints of incurable 'indolence' reflect not personal failure, but a refusal to enter all things 'done' in the 'books'. On one occasion, he ponders the events of the previous few days: 'Yesterday I turned a servant out of doors and we walked far enquiring for another'.[104] As to 'The day before,' he admits, 'I forget, I only know I did not work'. The day's texture is obliterated as the declaration 'did not work' evacuates the need for further distinguishing detail. An earlier entry, for 7 November 1847, offers a particularly gloomy record of a day gone awry, as he attempts working at 11am, only to feel 'so miserable and dejected' that he gives up.[105] Brown's dejection follows reports of sleeplessness in a previous entry.[106] Having eluded its effects by getting to work 'before 9' and working '6 hours', it eventually catches up with him. Though evidently restored by the walk and company mentioned on 7 November, the diarist cannot resist the self-castigation of '(000 work)', a triple nullity that cancels all preceding matter.

The problem with such insistent and doleful accountancy is that it counts some things and ignores others. Here, 'work' is not 'vision' or observation – as practised by seemingly idle brain-workers – but the bare measure of hours spent at the easel. Routine tasks are excluded, for fear that the symbolic gains reserved for painting will be diluted. On 6 September 1847, Brown complains 'Have not worked to day [*sic*]'.[107] Then he mentions 'having been out all the morning to the costume shop', and among other things, 'bought 10 yards of flannel for draperies', 'engaged a model for tomorrow', and 'ordered a movouble [*sic*] seat for my painting steps'. This does not sound like a morning spent in vain: all the more striking, then, that such tasks are not entered in the ledger as work. As Manning aptly remarks, the 'findings' of 'the self-investigating conscience' can be 'radically untrustworthy'.[108]

Brown's notion that diary entries stand against distortion becomes increasingly hard to credit, not least because he ignores Defoe's advice to enter all things 'done' against a neutrally determined account. Perhaps this is not so difficult to understand: even when properly undertaken, bookkeeping deals in fictions. While commercial accounts take the financial position as an indicator of the way things stand 'in the world', there are occasions when broader measures of achievement provide a better indication of prospects.[109] Brown's accounting currency is hours worked, not money, but with comparable effect, in that he applies a uniform measure to messy incommensurables. According to Aaron Brown, it is precisely this emphasis on 'consistency' that 'entails accounting fictions'.[110] Such fictions, in common with legal fictions, take a functional end in being fanciful; their purpose is to make things work in pursuit of a larger goal.[111] In legal contexts, that goal is justice; in accounting, it means balancing the books, an imperative that can mean 'numbers with no basis in reality have to be plugged in, side-by-side with objective, measurable values'.[112]

Accountancy also encounters problems with the past, in that the picture granted is of 'a past that never actually existed, in the sense that by the time all information became available, it was out of date'.[113] As an informal record, rather than a balance sheet, Brown's diary is only partially susceptible to this critique; still, the forms of 'knowing' distortion it practises are analogous. Brown consciously sacrifices truth to a broader conception of balance, which he links in turn to a larger professional aim: namely, his development as an artist. As a sequential accumulation of evidence, the diary encourages stocktaking, and emphasises what has been gained or lost. But, as noted, he regards these as absolute quantities, and neglects what might be recouped tomorrow. The future in this scheme is an inadmissible sort of account. In this respect, Brown knows the danger of punishing himself for unavoidable chores but persists because of the disciplinary gains involved. He broaches these forms of awareness on acknowledging that 'I am in reality employed at *business* all my time, from the moment I get up till I go to bed'.[114] The phrase 'in reality' briefly upsets Brown's selective accounting model. Most revealingly, he alludes to 'time lost in preparations', a formulation that contains a world of self-imposed strain. Indeed, it discloses the true nature of Brown's narrow tally: rather than an oversight, or simple meanness, it shows itself plainly as an accounting decision. The diary, it follows, is less confessional than it is self-regulating, an instrument designed to incentivise hours spent directly at the canvas. 'Preparations' are of course prerequisites for this kind of work – Brown admits to being 'employed at *business* all my time' – but his supposedly 'dreamy', unpurposeful, manner requires their curtailment.

Accounting fictions may drive production, but production is in turn endangered by false lows, and equivalently false highs. A fixation on daily results crowds out the planning required to sustain performance over time. The entry for 2 January 1855 indicates that Brown 'worked at the navvies', and found 'the pot boy a triumph', and 'the mortar-man perfection'.[115] His entry for the 3 January suggests an altered form of productive consciousness: 'I feel in the most ethereal & extatic [*sic*] state possible'.[116] The following April he reports spending 'all day at the designe of "Work"', so that the effort 'is now to me a species of intoxi-cation'.[117] The 'sleepy beast' of impaired consciousness seems finally to have reached terms with the fastidious diarist who keeps the daily account. Such feverish absorption resembles what Geoffrey Hill calls 'the kind of exhaustion that is involved with prolonged and intensive labour on the work in hand': the kind that can 'release quite unexpected graces of inspiration', and yet be a 'falsely mystical ecstasy'.[118] Such inward resources are not always easy to summon; because exhaustion entails an abdication of creative agency, there can be a long wait for the right mood. In Brown's case, this 'extatic' feeling gives way quickly, and revealingly, just two days later, to concerns about being 'Very perplexed & low in spirits'.[119] Productive elation depends, moreover, on an overvaluation of the point at which a work exhibits 'perfection', or comes together, to the neglect of those more frustrating or 'distracted' labours leading up to it.

Brown tolerates distortions arising from his irregular accountancy for their effect in stimulating renewed effort, rather as Trollope speaks of blank days in his working diary 'staring me in the face, and demand-ing of me increased labour'.[120] His methods also prove operationally damaging, as can be seen when such fictions overwhelm the rhythms of artistic practice in favour of a narrow measure. Equally, the conceit that hours manually employed at the easel equal 'work' proves more power-ful than the essential facts of preparation and planning. No longer func-tioning as an instrumental fiction, the tally of hours becomes a flagrant illusion, a licensed mendacity that conflicts with his otherwise frank investigation of the self. Though in itself an exact method, its effect – ironically – is to obstruct the broader principle of diary keeping. In this regard it recalls the Calvinist double bind of a state of election whose result is not 'works', but the appearance of work going well. This more fundamental fiction overrides the principle of accounting itself, prompt-ing Brown's reliance on transcendental certainty and justification, and flouting the priority he otherwise accords to showing over seeming.

* * *

Brown's written commentary on *Work* makes a case for the invisible labour of mind. As a visual artist, though, he represents things seen on a visual plane. This sense of an art that inhabits the surfaces rather than the depths is precisely what animates Carlyle's suspicion of painters. Brown answers this challenge by bringing brain-work into the visual field, and making the visage of the writer emblematic of invisible work. The unfortunate effect is to reinforce, rather than challenge, the prevailing logic that rewards only demonstrable processes. As substitutes for the earlier figure of an artist, the painted brain-workers propose a dialogue between the brush and the pen, at least where the genealogy of the painting is concerned; and the composition invites a similar exchange between these discrete instruments and those held in public by the navvies. Several critics ascribe a conscious demonstration of work through the painterly exercise of observational power, an attribute shared by artist and brain-worker alike. While this seems credible, a union of painting with testimonial functions ultimately eludes Brown. The visual account strains to confirm a working equivalence between the faces of the brain-workers and the navvies' active sinew. Rather than presenting a transcript, physical fragments, and substituted tools, are assembled into a staged whole. The diary, too, mistakes appearances for progress, effacing 'preparations' in privileging the brush's more definite testament.

The convenient fictions of personal accountancy acquire in this way a troubled life. By resorting to the emblematic face of the writer, or adducing a synthetic detail that matches the immediacy of navvy labour, Brown takes the logic of a painted tally as far as it can go. And perhaps it is revealing that he is alone among the cases discussed across this book in favouring observational functions – whether painterly or writerly – over a more processual account of art as craftsmanship. He is left, consequently, with an effort to prove and improve intellectual labour, an effort that must fail for as long as the bare record of things seen is accepted as the sole token of production. Such 'failure', nevertheless, has an unintentionally productive result: through its manifest shortcomings, *Work* tests in a traceable way the distortions necessitated by an exclusively visual standard of proof. Internal contradictions are disclosed not just as a representational *impasse*, but as an irregular subject matter. Although not immediately realised, this fosters the possibility of a shift away from Brown's solution – of an encoded authorial visage – towards the principle of a thinking and self-speaking hand.

PART II
WRITERS AT WORK

Carlyle and Brown typically address labour in a form that is physically manifest, while sending attention away from the body of the observing writer in favour of a diverting spectacle. The next two chapters cover situationally diverse examples that mark a distinct change. Instead of referring 'real' physical work elsewhere, they hold on to it, and in the process keep the body of the writer centre-stage. Chapter 3 explores a crucial, but paradoxical case. During her years as an invalid, Elizabeth Barrett Browning felt imprisoned by her bodily circumstances. She was correspondingly keen to develop a transcendental theory of poetry. Undaunted by the apparent conflict, she nevertheless embraced Carlyle's Gospel of Work as applied to writers, drawing equally on its artisanal and toiling strands. Much of the ensuing discussion concerns the forms of associated – and conflicted – embodiment practised by her poetry and her letters. In this regard, it would be a mistake to interpret the sick body as a compliant element. As historians of Victorian invalidism have shown, there is a quality of resistance about the passivity of the sick-room.[1] In Barrett Browning's case, the same applies to the poetic work that happens there, sharpened and animated though it is by pain and palpitation. Rather than conceding ground, her physical withdrawal licenses and intensifies a philosophy of determined literary action.

Chapter 4 addresses personifications of a more literal 'literary labour', beginning with Gladstone, who combines Homeric scholarship with woodcraft, and then Ruskin, who mixes lecturing with road-mending, harbour-building and axe-work. These cases restore the theatrical emphasis and sense of demonstration discussed in Part I, but with the difference that the writer's body becomes the interface between contemporary working practice and the ideal of a physical-cerebral self. The chapter closes with a discussion of William Morris's integrated theories of human making and literary composition. His self-conception as a writer acquires particular significance in charting moves towards the writerly craft ethics of the late nineteenth century. As is well known, he also engaged in practical design activity through the work of Morris

& Co. His lectures, meanwhile, assert an equivalence between the fine arts, and the crafts of 'house-building, painting, joinery and carpentry, smiths' work, pottery and glass-making, weaving, and many others'.[2] As if further guaranteeing the standing of these 'lesser arts', Morris insists that all 'real art is the expression by man of his pleasure in labour' (22:42). He thereby extends Ruskin's labour theory of art value, and his exclusion of painful or fallen experience, while audaciously revising the Benthamite calculus. Labour, in this respect, is fully instrumentalised: no longer an external imposition, it becomes a reliable tool, directly applicable to self-betterment and human flourishing.

Chapter 3

Barrett Browning's Poetic Vocation

Though not alone among political liberals in celebrating Carlyle, Elizabeth Barrett Browning seems an unlikely admirer of his labour theory. He assumes a masculine identity, after all, and a performance based in strength and able-bodiedness. By contrast, her most productive period coincided with the years she spent in confinement as 'a confirmed invalid'.[1] Undeterred, Barrett Browning confesses herself 'an adorer of Carlyle',[2] even keeping an image of him in her bedchamber.[3] Writing to Robert Browning early in their courtship, she calls him 'the great teacher of the age'.[4] Perhaps she sensed an opportunity to please by praising his friend; but the affectionate bias runs first and foremost in the other direction. As Rosemary Ashton observes, it was not her lover's esteem, but Carlyle's modest praise of Browning's poetry that 'predisposed her to like and admire him'.[5] Indeed she had already committed herself in critical prose, having anonymously co-written a laudatory essay on 'Thomas Carlyle' for R. H. Horne's compendium *A New Spirit of the Age* (1844).[6]

Carlyle's insistent allusion to the 'man' of letters understandably distracts critics from his influence on a poet better known for lamenting a dearth of literary 'grandmothers'.[7] But the clues are not entirely hidden. Barbara Dennis observes that 'Elizabeth admired the "strong man" in politics',[8] while Angela Leighton notes her related attraction to father figures.[9] Several recent studies have begun to explore and clarify the connection with Carlyle more directly. Beverly Taylor assesses Barrett Browning's engagement with 'the hero as poet',[10] while Marjorie Stone sees the figure of Romney in *Aurora Leigh* (1856) as a kind of distillation of the Carlylean emphasis on 'labour and action',[11] a reading that assigns Aurora the utopian side of his prophetic creed, and posits a 'subversion' of his 'authoritative stance'.[12] This chapter extends recent treatment of Carlylean legacies, but does so less in relation to models of heroism than in addressing the material and workaday aspects of Barrett Browning's proposition that poets should be 'workers'. Equally, it broadens attention beyond the field of *Aurora Leigh* – where Carlylean influence interacts complexly with other, not always consistent, strands such as Romney's Fourieurist socialism – to include an earlier generic field. This reveals Carlyle's literary Gospel of Work as an effect negotiated in the messy 'real time' of daily epistolary labour. Though far from uncritical, the resistance this mounts takes the form less of 'subversion' than of militant orthodoxy.

The first part of the chapter argues, accordingly, that Barrett Browning's admiration presents a case of doctrinal purism and revisionism strangely combined. She upholds the principle of the poet-worker, even in the face of Carlyle's recantations. But when criticising him she speaks as 'his disciple'.[13] The second part examines the relationship between Carlylean work ethics and the terms of the 'Woman Question' as posed in the 1840s and 1850s. The concern here is with the role of female identity in thinking through the bodily expressions of labour that Carlyle increasingly favoured. The last part explores Barrett Browning's status and identity as an invalid, and its influence on her method of making writing 'work'. Though in some respects a source of incapacity, her bed-ridden condition engenders a productive routine of correspondence, a variety of literary expression well adapted to the conditions of her secluded life. As such, Barrett Browning's work ethic is not a commitment at variance with her invalidism or her position as a middle-class woman. On the contrary, such circumstances contain the defining feature of her approach: a creative adaptation of Carlylean precepts that simultaneously fulfils the letter and refines the spirit.

'Song is work': Barrett Browning's Poetic Labour

Barrett Browning's annotations to Shelley's *Essays, Letters from Abroad, Translations and Fragments* (1840) reveal a pronounced sympathy for the vatic theory of poetry:[14] the 'Poetic art', she would later claim, is 'a divine guess'.[15] This emphasis on the transcendental seems at odds with the very idea of a poetic *labour*. Certainly, her appraisals of literature favour divine, or organic, process over evidence of human toil: of Tennyson's *Maud* she complains that 'there is an appearance of labour in the early part', and that 'the language is rather encrusted by skill than spontaneously blossoming'.[16] But while such remarks weigh in the balance, they do not support an intractable division between Apolline poetry and literary craftsmanship.[17] On the contrary, Barrett Browning seeks a coherent alternative to such oppositions. And it is to Carlyle's 'active' conception of the 'Vates poet' (5:84) that she looks in developing a synthesis.

This influence applies most intensely in the period of her famous epistolary exchange with Robert Browning (1845–46). As love letters, their primary purpose is to build intimacy, venturing large steps forward and small steps back. The long interval between receiving Browning's first letter, and meeting him in person, encourages a form of projection that causes the image of the absent lover to assume the lineaments of a personal fantasy. The common ground of poetry benefits from a similar effect, conferring a quality of speculation and experiment that recalls formal poetic manifestos. In this reserved space, Barrett Browning characterises her physical-poetic ideal as a Spartan regimen: 'if a work is worthy, honour must follow it'.[18] Such statements often appeal to the etymology of 'poet', in ποιητής or 'maker'. But, equally, they insist on equivalence with other vocations, whether more practical or less so: 'I have *worked* at poetry', she tells a friend: 'As the physician and lawyer work at their several professions, so have I, and so do I, apply to mine'.[19] Writing in January 1845, Browning acknowledges a conflict between enjoyment of her poetry, and his 'duty' as 'a loyal fellow-craftsman' who 'should, try and find fault'.[20] Barrett Browning, in turn, offers a grounding and a justification for the 'kind of obscurity' that brought criticism to Browning's poetry.[21] She does so by translating it into the language of communal craft practice, whereby his 'graver cuts deep sharp lines, always', achieving 'an extra-distinctness' of image and thought.[22]

This conception of literature as a practical exercise applies equally in evaluating the work of other writers. A novel sent by 'Mr Chorley' attracts the qualifying observation that he is 'A feeler .. an observer .. a thinker even [. . .] – but a maker .. no'.[23] An important instance of this encounter – between languages of craft and languages of labour – arises from Barrett Browning's report of an exchange with the proto-feminist author, Anna Jameson. In answer to Jameson's suggestion that 'carpet work [. . .] led the workers into "fatal habits of reverie"',[24] Barrett Browning 'defended the carpet work as if I were striving *pros aris et focis*, [. . .] & said not a word for the poor reveries which have frayed away so much of silken time for me'.[25] While these efforts conduce to the communal good, her retort suggests a conflict between actual carpet work, and the literary labour for which it is an analogy. At the same time, Barrett Browning acknowledges a double significance. Applied to her own existence, she discovers both a crucial productive faculty (it is 'silken', even if 'poor'), and a fraying effect damaging not only to literature conceived more practically, but also to life itself. In this latter sense, the monotony of textile work is transferred to literature, pervaded here by a whiff of Tennyson's 'The Lady of Shalott', and that artisanal malaise which drives the weaving women of *The Bacchae* to leave 'loom and shuttle' (1235) in search of feast and frenzy.[26]

Answering a further reply – to the effect that 'you may do carpet work with impunity' while 'writing poems all the while."!'[27] – Barrett Browning denies the supposed synergy: 'Think of people making poems and rugs at once', she exclaims, 'There's complex machinery for you!'.[28] Poetry, she resolves, should be reconciled with labour, not seen as a secondary enterprise. Making rugs, or 'netting a purse', and making poems are both serious forms of work, and will never be frivolously combined without dropping stitches: 'Art, you know, is a jealous god & demands the whole man .. or woman'. [29] In her Preface to *Poems* (1844), she puts the same position another way: 'I never mistook pleasure for the final cause of poetry; nor leisure, for the hour of the poet'.[30] A further significance attracts to this exchange with Jameson as revived in a letter to Browning of 20 to 23 August 1845. In it she alludes to the system of secrecy necessitated by her father's 'patriarchal ideas of governing grown up children', and the sense of living in a 'harness': 'a side-world', in effect, 'to hide one's thoughts in, & "carpet-work" to be immoral on in spite of Mrs Jameson'.[31] In this regard, she registers how literature has granted her 'liberty' in the family. This spares her 'the disingenuousness – the cowardice – the 'vices of slaves'!' which she attributes to her brothers, who are 'constrained *bodily* into submission .. apparent submission at least .. by [. . .] being dependent in money-matters on the inflexible will'. Though leading to a defence of her 'father's heart', these words propound a comparison of his household – run as if by 'divine right' – with the conditions of a slave estate.

This point carries a double significance, of course, in that her family's wealth on both sides was derived from slavery and related Jamaican investments.[32] More personally, Barrett Browning benefited from the patronage of John Kenyon, and a legacy from her uncle, each of whom received compensation payments for slaves under the 1833 Slavery Abolition Act. Barrett Browning alludes to this inheritance in December of 1845, on sharing her ambiguous yearning to 'own some purer lineage than that of the blood of the slave!' – since 'Cursed we are from generation to generation!'[33] Two, not necessarily incompatible, possibilities flow from suggesting a lineage from slaves – one has been questioned by genealogical research, while the other implies a retributive burden incurred by the forebears who spilt their blood.[34] For present purposes, the related ambiguity of 'carpet-work' is crucial. At one level, as we have seen, it aligns literature with paid industrial labour; but in this letter it is simultaneously aligned with enslaved labour and with its evasion as a cover. It is a double one, at that, as the phrase increasingly stands for literature without naming it.

In 'The Runaway Slave at Pilgrim's Point' (1848) – a work submitted two years prior to publication in the abolitionist annual *The Liberty Bell* – poetry is likewise associated with flight. Here, the letter's generational curse transmutes into the curses of a protagonist who avenges poetically by disdaining given rules of articulation.[35] Perhaps revealingly, these letters precede the fallout from Carlyle's 'Occasional Discourse on the Negro Question' (1849). That text disclaims any wish to see plantation workers 'slaves again' only to realign that term more approvingly to 'mean essentially "servant hired for life"' (40:672–6). All the while, it engages in racial slurs, attacks on abolitionist 'Exeter Hall philanthropy', and relativisations of new-found personal liberty. Four years earlier, Barrett Browning saw the dividing lines less clearly, and certainly less than she did on publishing 'Curse for a Nation' in the *Liberty Bell* of 1855.[36] That poem's strain of Carlylean prophecy is pointedly qualified by its rage against bondage and feudalism.[37] And its famous malediction, as Stone observes, is at once dictated and self-writing.[38] In these letters, by contrast, Barret Browning imputes an overlap between divergent forms and situations, moving as she does uncomfortably between an idea of poetry as evasive domestic liberator, poetry as a variety of industrial labour, and herself as enslaved in Carlylean fashion to an unremitting literary vocation.

In as much as she defies Carlyle at this time, the tactics are loyal and affectionate, and recall the approach taken to her father. Only here literature offers no 'side-world', it being the very subject under discussion. Once again evaluation of another's work forms the crux: writing to Browning in February 1845, she asks 'And does Mr. Carlyle tell you that he has forbidden all "singing" to this perverse and froward generation, which should work & not sing?'[39] As a rebuttal of the Gospel of Work in its philistine aspects, her words refuse the implied opposition of art and effort, and yet go further: 'And have you told Mr Carlyle that song is work, and also the condition of work?'[40] Pre-figuring Brown's description of 'the brain-workers' as 'the cause of well-ordained work and happiness in others', she combines Carlylean concern with the root of things, and a similarly derivative linguistic register – this, even as she pushes into the more radical territory evacuated by her idol. The rebuttal nevertheless draws its force from her concurrent insistence on uncritical devotion: 'I am', she admits, 'a devout sitter at his feet – and it is an effort to me to think him wrong in anything'.[41] Devotion in this account entails an unsettling of faith, combined with an uneasy or 'ruffled' feeling, induced by the thought of Carlyle 'putting away, even for a season, the poetry of the world'.[42] Crucially, he is found to be in the 'wrong' not because his creed promotes an intrinsic disregard for poetry, or indeed because she intends a 'subversion' of sage discourse, but because he has not adhered consistently to the letter of his own doctrines.[43]

Referring to an early exchange of letters, Barrett Browning fears that 'his opinion was I had mistaken my calling'.[44] She later discovers that Browning received the same 'prodigious advice', 'to write your next work in prose!!'.[45] There are grounds, as discussed in Chapter 1, for doubting the force of Carlyle's anti-poetic position, but increasingly he understands poetry as a philosophical abstraction rather than a specific metrical practice. Barrett Browning does not address these sources of ambivalence, preferring to privilege bardic status over the evidence of words and actions: Carlyle, she avers, is 'a poet unaware of himself'.[46] Later that February, she replies to Browning's reassurances with a restatement of her view that he 'fills the office of a poet – does he not? . . . and he discharges it fully'.[47] She betrays no inkling of what Daniel Karlin calls Carlyle's discovery that 'he could worship "song" [. . .] while advising every actual poet of his acquaintance to turn to prose'.[48]

Despite the element of blind faith, Barrett Browning develops several points of objection aimed at her mentor. In each case, she deploys a distinctly Carlylean vocabulary while extending the logic of his propositions beyond his area of comfort. A more than usually vociferous rebuttal reports 'reading Carlyle upon Cromwell',[49] and lamenting his 'praise for dumb heroic action as opposed to speech and singing'.[50] She goes on to clinch the basic principle that words constitute deeds: 'As if Shakespeare's actions were not greater than Cromwell's!'[51] Meeting Carlyle's philistinism with the remonstrance that he should be more Carlylean, she insists equally that thought and 'song' should always be 'working'. The Carlyle who emerges from Barrett Browning's letters is, in this regard, a perfected version of the man, derived not from aberrant sayings, but construed selectively from his writings. At its most radical, this idealised version underwrites positions that are not particularly Carlylean, as where she states that 'one may be laborious as a writer, without copying twelve times over.'[52] Equally, she proclaims freshly that 'one may work one's verses in one's head quite as laboriously as on paper'.[53] Such statements add up to an unannounced departure from Carlyle, in privileging confidence and self-forgiveness over self-punishment.[54] Thus, on confessing that 'I have been idle lately I confess', she refuses the temptation to condemn herself for inhabiting 'the castle of Indolence'.[55] Instead, she sees things in the round: 'Do I mean to be idle always? no! – and am I not an industrious worker on the average of days? Indeed yes!'[56]

If there is an element of class privilege at work in this self-forgiveness, the generosity radiates outwards as well. Her claim to be a 'laborious'

writer holds in the best sense. Instead of abandoning 'doing', she liber-
ates it from the field of demonstration, so that the site of labour inhabits
a sphere of mental process rather than bare demonstration. She registers
the same point in a humorous aside on claiming that her lapdog, Flush, is
'not [. . .] a physical-force dog'.[57] Rather, he is 'a hero after the fashion of
Mr Carlyle' where 'the intellectual is preponderant'.[58] In the process, she
approaches a rounded, or perfected, conception of Carlylean principle
that exceeds the example of the man himself. Repudiating the cruder
Calvinist concern with appearances, her words dispense with analogy in
favour of the bolder claim that writing inseparably *is* labour, and that the
unseen may be embodied in the manner of the physical. As the next part
of this chapter shows, this move from analogy to identity is broadly conceived, and as such presents challenges linked to the Carlylean distinction
between metaphorical clothes and essential being.

'The writer bodily': Women and Work

Barrett Browning's defence of the precept that 'song' is 'work' would
offer a straightforward understanding of her professional identity
were it not for the gendered valence of 'work' in the Carlylean lexicon.
Carlyle admits in *Two Notebooks* that 'there are "female geniuses"
too'; only, he adds that they are 'minds that admire and receive, but
can hardly create'.[59] The question arises whether those not addressed
by the Carlylean mantra, or indeed actively ignored by it, could sal-
vage something from its claims. Several woman writers of the 1840s and
1850s recognised that Carlyle's emphasis on physical graft harboured
opportunities: notably, in converting a universal duty to work into the
beginnings of an aberrant right to do so. Indeed, as Taylor observes,
'the influence of *Heroes* on mid-Victorian feminist activists deserves
fuller scrutiny'.[60] The following discussion answers this challenge by
setting Barrett Browning's Carlylism in the broader context of the contemporary 'Woman Question'. It notes, in particular, the appeal of his
emphasis on writerly being. Though initially coded and clothed as male,
this approach eventually lodges in the body as a purported site of truth
and authenticity. We witness as such a response to Carlyle's calls that is
simultaneously consistent and uninvited.

The Gospel of Work in this manifestation offers an ethically-charged
basis for resisting anti-feminist precepts, not least the stereotype that
middle-class women were consumers of luxuries rather than produc-
ers. In an early example, Caroline Norton highlights the immoral uses
to which husbands could devote the literary earnings of their wives.[61]

Attention later turns from earnings to the right to work itself, and it is at this point that the Society for Promoting the Employment of Women (1859) identifies new openings for women in clerical work. Perhaps the foremost writer and campaigner on these issues was Anna Jameson, and it is no accident she was among Kenyon's dinner guests on the evening in July 1851 when Barrett Browning first met Carlyle. Jameson was on the brink of publishing her two most influential works: *Sisters of Charity Catholic and Protestant, Abroad and at Home* (1855) and *The Communion of Labour: A Second Lecture on the Social Employments of Women* (1856).[62] Like her friend and correspondent, Jameson makes no secret of admiring Carlyle: indeed, she exchanged letters with him on several occasions in the 1830s and 1840s. Faced with Carlyle's conflation of work with male personhood, she refuses to accept the necessity of resignation or exclusion: rather, she understands shared humanity as a given, and reverses the terms of the debate, insisting that women had been unjustly deprived of their participant birthright. The world, she declaims, 'is a place in which work is to be done, – work which *must* be done'.[63] This work, she insists, is '*good* to do', 'at once the condition of existence and the condition of happiness'.[64]

As Linda Peterson notes, Jameson believed that 'the domestic realm should be extended into the world at large'.[65] In this regard, her position resembles that articulated by Ruskin in *Sesame and Lilies* (1865). Certainly, the author treads a fine line between approving differing roles – the man who 'governs, sustains' as distinct from the woman who 'cherishes, regulates' – and elaborating an alternative.[66] Ultimately, though, she queries the notion that women should be 'always under tutelage, always within the precincts of a home'.[67] This she does by proposing a shared domestic enterprise – a 'communion of labour' – whose principles can expand within those limits. Jameson evokes not just a thirst for work, but a solemn need of it. 'The woman cries out', she avows, '[. . .] to perform worthily her share'.[68] This idea that depriving people of work constitutes an injustice, even a violence, recalls Carlyle's arguments in *Chartism* (1840) (29:135). So, too, does Jameson's call for worker armies, formed from the unjustly unemployed.[69] In *Sisters of Charity*, she combines a Protestant sense of mission with the disciplined medievalism of Carlyle's *Past and Present*. She is 'no friend of nunneries',[70] but observes that 'the Calvinistic reaction against the dominant Church' was 'not favourable to women'.[71] Soon after, Barbara Leigh Smith [Bodichon] made a related case in *Women and Work* (1857).[72] Like Jameson, she spots an advantage for women in the Carlylean conviction that 'No human being has a right to be idle'.[73] If work is a duty, it follows that it should be available to all. These writers might equally have built on women's literature of the previous century, but the precedents offered no clear direction of travel:[74] as Jennie Batchelor shows, Charlotte Smith had insisted that writing is 'as physically demanding as that of "the Daniads or of Sisyphus"', whereas Mary Wollstonecraft's new intellectual order assumed 'the differentiation of mental and manual labour.'[75] In this context, Barrett Browning's exposure to Jameson opens new horizons. Her mediated version of Carlylean work ethics warrants attention, this is to say, alongside its more direct influence. At the very least, Barrett Browning shares Jameson's disposition to find out what, in Carlyle's teachings, would serve the purpose of ambitious women.

There are moments when Barrett Browning's absorption in Carlylean terms becomes self-defeating. In one letter, she vows 'manfully to wade thro the waves of learning [. . .] unmindful of either the rocks of disappointment or the waves of labour'.[76] If the bald imperative to proceed 'manfully' has a whiff of false-consciousness, it nevertheless harbours a crucial distinction. As Leighton notes, Barrett Browning had a descriptive preference for the 'manly, not masculine'.[77] This catches a broader Victorian tendency – apparent in writers such as Tennyson and Morris – to apply the word 'manly' in denotation of 'honest' or 'upright' behaviour, with a gender inflexion less conscious than might now seem credible.[78] Barrett Browning likewise admires the 'strength' that makes 'honesty' possible, and while Victorian contemporaries commonly mix up such attributes with manliness, the focus of her admiration falls on the attribute rather than its origin. Of Harriet Martineau, for instance, she writes that 'she calls herself the strongest of women, & talks of "walking fifteen miles one day & writing fifteen pp. another day without fatigue [. . .]"'.[79] Apart from admiring the physical feat, these words celebrate Martineau's use of the heroic boast. Barrett Browning, as such, goes beyond the imitation of narrowly 'male' virtues witnessed in her early letters. A more subversive trade in attributes emerges, signalled less by apparel or role playing than by new ways of being.

If, as Mary Sanders Pollock argues, these 'cross dressed' epithets subside by the time of *Aurora Leigh*, they are quickly replaced by an enlarged conception of female artistic capacity and identity.[80] An increasing interest in Carlyle's philosophical essentialism – a doctrine suspicious of fluidity, whether in trappings or deeper truths – provides one credible explanation for this turn. Matthew Campbell reads the same development through an injunction in 'The Hero as King', which requires 'every man [. . .] to speak out; to act out, what Nature has laid in him.'[81] While this model of 'speaking out' retains an idea of performance, it simultaneously posits a 'natural' expression of selfhood. Here, then, the artistic function channels actions. These, in turn, determine and reproduce being. This is more than a role or mask, as Barrett Browning would make clear when answering reviewers who lament '"if I would but change my style"!'[82] 'But that', she counters, 'is an objection (isn't it?) to the writer bodily?' 'Buffon', she adds, 'says [. . .] that "Le style c'est l'homme"'. Rather than see style as a selective interpretation of the self – in the manner of her critics – she regards it as the unalterable expression of being. Only, Barrett Browning recasts this category as 'the writer bodily'.[83] That the body stands in for this essence is revealing of her departure from Buffon's looser understanding of *l'homme* as denoting character, or personality. By shifting the emphasis from a generically male identity to a recognition of physical facts, and therefore difference, she signals the matter of her womanhood as the deep, unavoidable and unjust cause of critical objection.[84]

Barrett Browning returns to this question the following year, on correcting Kenyon's suggestion that 'I had said there was nothing in him [Carlyle] but manner'.[85] Buffon figures again, but in defending her position she argues that 'what is called Carlyle's mannerism, is not his dress, but his physiognomy – or more than that even'.[86] Having read 'Carlyle upon Cromwell', she follows suit in commending his being 'very much himself, it seems to me, everywhere'.[87] All writers, she implies, have a licence, and a duty, to be themselves. Discussing a related sense of 'Of blood and brain swept outward upon words', Campbell draws attention to the way that 'Aurora authenticates her utterance through a sounding of the rhythms of her own body'.[88] And yet this recourse to physical being does not go untroubled. Most notably, it crystallises the problem of reception at issue in this chapter: that is, how Barrett Browning navigates the influence of a thinker who simultaneously assumes a male subject and emphasises the primacy of being over performance. This problem is anticipated in the letters, but it is in *Aurora Leigh* – as many critics note – that it interacts with the wider question of poetic vocation.

Aurora – like her author – is assailed by two, intermingled prejudices. First, she must endure the lectures of Romney Leigh, who addresses his cousin and her sex simultaneously: 'Women as you are, [. . .] We get no Christ from you – and verily I We shall not get a poet' (II. 220).[89] It might seem that Aurora's task is to demonstrate that women can be poets; but the situation is more complex, in that Romney also disregards poetry: 'But men, and still less, women,' he adds, '[. . .] Scarce need be poets' (II. 41).[90] Aurora thus steers a difficult course: insisting both that women can be poets, and that poetry is not just valuable, but in keeping with a concern to improve life. Amidst this double insistence, poetry is defended as an aid to practical functions – 'your Fouriers failed, I Because not poets enough' (483–5)[91] – while Romney must learn that the 'singers' stand among God's number as 'workers for his world' (1233–4).[92] Barrett Browning thus sustains the intellectual and transcendental functions attracting her to poetry in the first place, while cultivating a newly physical, rhythmic, and labouring identity. The result is a concern with bodily intelligence that anticipates Olive Schreiner's *Woman and Labour* (1911), a work discussed in Chapter 6 that thinks through 'field work' and 'brain work' in relation to the equally conscious *labour* of pregnancy.[93] Equally, it seems no accident that the bodily aspect of Barrett Browning's own poetry should develop as a marked tendency after she gives birth in 1849.

An integrative agenda proves elusive, all the same, because the interaction between social expectation, social amelioration, and self-realisation, is so complicated. Once Barrett Browning has established the value of poetry as a professional and social aim, she needs to show that women can be poets, a requirement preceded by a need to show that women should work, and that they should work in that particular way. In these circumstances, clear demands delivered from a stable subject position are not easily lodged. These conflicting forms of awareness are concisely evoked by an item of post, arriving from America in 1845. Bemused, and amused, she observes that it was 'addressed to .. just my name .. poetess, London!'.[94] Struck by its having made its way at all, she remarks on 'the simplicity of those wild Americans in "calculating" that "people in general" here in England, knew what a poetess is!'[95] The envelope's casual allusion to a poetic profession discloses a remote – and perhaps comforting – confidence in the force of an artistic category. Barrett Browning finds herself thus recognised by the postal system, but not by the literary world. While the irony of this staggered acknowledgement diagnoses a problem, it also reveals how things might be different.

Letters, Invalidism and Poetic Labour

The previous example conjures an idea of epistolary 'address' that shows Barrett Browning's identity as a poet crystallising as a matter of occupational identity.[96] The remainder of this chapter considers the generic and circumstantial crux of this problem. Even as Barrett Browning moves towards a consciously somatic writing position, much of her communication with the outside world manifests itself not through the bodily presence of voice, but through the surrogate offices of correspondence. Having the quality of an intellectual calendar, a report on reading and poetic experience, her letters to Browning coincide – as previously noted – with her longest period of confinement. With this circumstance in view, it is striking that she characterises them less as a substitute for physical presence than as a primary action. Being a repository of the idle faculties that she excludes from the poetic, they acquire a sacrificial function, as writing literally thrown away, or given up to social intercourse. Yet they also exploit this secondary status: more than disposable jottings, they become a testing ground for unconventional work ethics and marginalised modes of production. This effect dwells in her position as an invalid, but also highlights the ways in which all writers rely to some extent on delegated address.

Barrett Browning worries, all the same, that her correspondence might be tainted by its close association with incapacity. As if in recollection of Harriet Martineau's *Life in the Sick-Room* (1844),[97] she admits that 'talking by the post' brings to mind 'people shut up in dungeons [. . .] scrawling mottos on the walls'.[98] Such visions reflect a conviction that poets shut out from 'the outward aspects of life' are at 'a lamentable disadvantage'.[99] The manuscript of this letter reveals a striking interpolation of the word 'outward',[100] which pointedly amplifies her concern about the inward and secluded life she had been living since the death of brother in July 1840.[101] Barbara Dennis ascribes her ill health to 'a form of tuberculosis', a verdict that leans heavily on George Pickering's medical assessment that she 'suffered from a chronic lung affliction'.[102] Retrospective diagnosis misleads, however, in de-emphasising the vagueness of the malaise, a self-reinforcing attribute that ensures the capacity of invalidism to signify at the level of perception and identity. The vagueness, in this respect, is less diagnostic than symptomatic. As Maria Frawley notes, an avoidance of medical details among invalids reflected a scripted 'sick role'.[103] Dennis broaches the same question when discussing Barrett Browning's discouragement of visitors 'to the point of refusing their advances with lies'.[104] Elizabeth Berridge takes such suppositions the furthest, in that she interprets illness as a 'cover': 'a common enough loophole for frustrated and intelligent Victorian women'.[105]

In dealing with her suitor, Barrett Browning alternates between downplaying her condition as a temporary impediment – conceiving illness, even, as a malleable state – and presenting it as a non-negotiable fact. The latter tendency informs her habit of self-mythologisation, according to which she speaks of 'leading a life of such seclusion',[106] like Mariana in the moated grange, or a hibernating dormouse.[107] Less playfully, she reflects on the time-decaying action of a life lived in 'Books & dreams', and the distant prospect of 'the outward world'.[108] This last vision aligns not only with the end of winter, but with all that lies beyond 'the threshold of one room'.[109] Beyond these complaints – and in the spirit of Martineau's chapter on 'Some Gains and Sweets of Invalidism' – she nevertheless admits the advantages, indeed, the seductions, of an identity formed within the compass of a bedchamber.[110] This, to some extent, runs against accepted critical wisdom. Discussing a group illustration of women authors in *Frazer's Magazine*, Peterson stresses the connections between authorial status, social involvement and physical visibility.[111] Barrett Browning eludes these connections simply by being bed-ridden. Unlike Brown's 'brain-workers', she remains resolutely out of view. But rather than consigning her to obscurity, her predicament suggests an alternative basis for personal repute.[112] The commentary in Horne's *A New Spirit of the Age* has her 'Confined entirely to her own apartment, and almost hermetically sealed', indeed 'scarcely seen'.[113] This supposed lack of visibility extends to the pointed omission of an author-portrait, and playful speculation as to 'the very existence of the lady'.[114] Such allusions tally with Barrett Browning's self-description as a 'disembodied spirit'.[115] They are additionally complicated by the irony that she contributes her own essay to Horne's volume, a circumstance that lends a sense of discourteous erasure to the editor's jocular speculations.

This emphasis on withdrawal – even resignation – might collude with perceptions of unphysical, and therefore unlaboured, composition. But just as Barrett Browning's invisibility does not rule out status or repute, so the discourses of retirement and labour are able to co-exist. Evangelicalism, as Frawley notes, 'ratified affliction as God-Given', so that the concept of 'work as worship' mingles strangely with a form of worship based on self-seclusion.[116] Convalescence, as such, presents as a peculiarly conflicted predicament.[117] The essay on Barrett Browning in *A New Spirit of the Age* reconciles these tendencies through an emphasis on her bedridden labours. Dwelling on an 'indefatigable "work" by thought, by book, by the pen', it opens the possibility that an invalid might yet be thought a 'worker'.[118] While this conception of mental effort certainly pertains, it could also generate frustration. In an early letter to her mother, Barrett Browning declares a willingness to employ 'any mental exertion' that might be required to 'shake off bodily torture'.[119] 'I HAVE exerted all my energy', she complains, including 'all the muscular power of MIND', but found bodily anguish 'repressed' instead of 'overcome'. This anxious report represents an early example of bodily metaphor applied to mental process: her 'exertion' requires 'locomotive' and 'muscular' power. Evaluative and linguistic deference to the action of the limbs wards off the charge of malingering, but potentially concedes too much ground, leaving her vulnerable to a definition of work that excludes anything not physical. Indeed, she proves susceptible to the culture's privileging of action: '[I]f I could "rake & hoe"', she laments, '.. or even pick up weeds along the walk'.[120] When reporting 'much head-work of my own',[121] she guiltily confesses that 'bodily exercise is different', that the effort of projection entailed by correspondence has made her 'inclined to be idle'.[122] While the letter to her mother indicates prior sources for this tendency, her self-description as a 'devout sitter at his [Carlyle's] feet' ironically frames this problem as one of intellectual 'influence' encountering stubbornly physical limits.[123]

Barrett Browning's complaint that she feels poetically disabled by confinement reflects Carlyle's rhetoric of mobilisation, and its relation to work; but it builds, too, on the peripatetic or excursive element in Romantic literature and philosophy.[124] The same applies to Martineau's chapter on 'Nature to the Invalid', where a window view ensures that the 'mind has had an airing'.[125] Barrett Browning's dependence on morphine suggests a further connection to Romantic precedents, though in that respect she conceives motion as a problem, and the drug as its solution. Complaints of 'palpitation' effectively rule out exercise as a remedy, despite Browning counselling her to walk outside.[126] In this respect, morphine serves less as a dissipated alternative to healthy movement than a release from agonised trembling. Associations with imagination and contemplation, as figured by Thomas De Quincey, are avoided: no sublime journeys through hallucinated spectacle take place, and few connections are made to poetry. Only at the close of her explanation does she suggest to Browning, in a hand so slanting that it might fall off the page, that 'the lotus-eaters are blessed beyond the opium-eaters; & the best of lotuses are such thoughts as I know'.[127] Insisting in this way on a difference between the Homeric flower, and her own 'amreeta draught', she implies no quarrel with Odyssean adventure.[128] The movement she hopes to still is rather the trembling induced by drug withdrawal.

Notwithstanding the possible advantages of physical retreat, Barrett Browning speaks of the sick chamber as an evasive action, the recourse of 'one who could have forgotten the plague, listening to Boccaccio's stories'.[129] Indeed, she wishes to avoid the 'unbecoming' spectacle of 'infirmity', and thereby ward off any association between sickness and her poetry.[130] This places her letters in the awkward position of a buffer. They become the guardian of many qualities determinedly excluded from the poetic, and a crucial arena in which she negotiates the conflict between her acceptance of Carlyle's injunction that all should 'work' and the daily reality of physical confinement. Letters can be written in bed, and as such function as the symptomatic context for a stationary predicament, while providing the means by which it is structured and perpetuated. Apparently relishing the idea of a disembodied reach, Barrett Browning explains that 'I write in fact almost as you pay visits, . . .

& one has to "make conversation" in turn, of course'.[131] The emphasis here is on a social action, notwithstanding the cloistered predicament of the author. She would have letters governed by the same expectations, and the same scope for reply and debate, as polite intercourse. Even as her 'almost' signals awareness of the conceit, these remarks afford a glimpse of a more intimate, reciprocal, and remote epistolary form.

Letters represent an escape from the pedestrian life on the literal level that they entail words being conveyed by paid emissary. In the hopeful early days of their correspondence, the written word seems less a substitute than a full-blown alternative, its declaratory power overcoming all effects of labour and distance. As Browning playfully boasts, the disproportion between effort and outcome can be absurd, and in its way alchemical: 'Three scratches with a pen, even with this pen, – and you have the green little Syrenusæ where I have sate and heard the quails sing'.[132] The exoticism of far-off location magically resolves into the writer's singularly fixed station. In the manner of Emerson's provocation that 'the wise man stays at home',[133] Browning concludes that 'all you gain by travel is the discovery that you have gained nothing, and have done rightly in trusting to your innate ideas'.[134] These reassurances later conflict with the argument he adopts as a suitor wishing to remove her from the parental home. At that juncture, travel becomes less an effort 'to prove limitation' – as Arthur Hugh Clough would write in *Amours de Voyage* (1849) – than a bid to overcome it.[135] Browning's flattering consolations give way, accordingly, to thoughts of an Italian journey that will realise his lover's yearnings for 'another atmosphere'.[136]

Written communication occurs at an attractively safe distance for Barrett Browning, its ebbs and flows not only predictable with the post, but susceptible to regulation and control. Love 'on the page' can be purified of the physical, and its development carefully regulated, at least until she finds herself writing that 'it is certainly not my turn to write, though I am writing.'[137] Epistolary decorum, and longing for a more reciprocal outlet, pull in this way against the form's unilateralism and univocalism. Signalled by the present participle in 'I am writing', these qualities allow a written voice to exceed the present without losing its identity in time. Something of this power informs the so-called 'posting rule' in English contract law, a principle introduced by *Adams* v. *Lindsell* (1818).[138] In a fictional meeting of minds, the rule gives the offeree power to form a contract at the point of dispatch. By disregarding the labour and practical agency of the postal service – which might in reality lose or misdirect a letter – it invests the offeree with an enhanced power to overcome gulfs of distance and lags of time. The analogy is inexact, but the informal conventions of courtship correspondence achieve something similar. Barrett

Browning's replies bind the offeror, Browning, by virtue of being committed to the post. In this way, contract formation models a less codified emotional meeting place. If Browning, instead, is the offeree, then the comfort comes from knowing that a meeting of minds may already have occurred, and that no additional note will cross disastrously.

The necessary gap between utterance and reciprocation admits a similar analysis. With letters, there is always room for a reply, or a delay akin to Barrett Browning's quibbles about the right season for meeting.[139] This, too, is a source of comfort, though one that consoles with a measure of self-delusion when a fruitless wait is overtaken by a second, forgiving, suspicion that the note has been misdirected or intercepted. Whereas *Adams* v. *Lindsell* enforces a resolution through the mechanism of a legal fiction, lovers more readily take refuge in the practical gaps between expression and delivery. Among several works disclosing a contemporary preoccupation with letters, Herman Melville's 'Bartleby, the Scrivener' (1853) alludes to the United States 'dead letter office', a facility in which undeliverable offers and acceptances are kept 'alive' in perpetuity.[140] Most contracts are rendered void by the death of one party; but this repository conjures the idea that some undead vitality might be preserved by the post's capacity to carry a surrogate will, cut loose from physical presence. Browning likewise wonders whether letters might have a life of their own. He refers to 'the distance so palpably between the most audacious step there, and the next .. which is no where, seeing it is not in the letter'.[141] Letter-writing as such resembles a kind of 'going' in itself, albeit confined to the motion of a single irrevocable 'step'.

This sense of miraculous travelling arises, too, in Carlyle's *Past and Present*. Musing on the historical window afforded by *The Chronicle of Jocelin* (c. 1173–1202), the narrator reports that 'The most extinct fossil species of Men or Monks can do, and does, this miracle, – thanks to the Letters of the Alphabet' (10:44). But what if the 'fossil species' in question is a living poet? In that case, the startling animation of such missives heightens an unfortunate contrast with their embalmed originator. Dante Gabriel Rossetti's report of a meeting with the Brownings carries something of this impression: of 'Mrs B', he remarks that 'She looks quite worn out with illness, & speaks in the tone of an invalid'.[142] By 'tone' he implies not only the speech characteristics of a stock character, but the more unstable notion that her animation and presence of speech are tinctured by their deathly opposite. Carlyle, for his part, gasps in awe at the power of the dead 'voice' to communicate through lettered remnants. But he also formulates a political theory of speech, one that predicts a new class of public orator, or 'Speaking Man' (10:243), capable of replacing the dissipated governing class 'with a living voice, nay in a living shape, and as a concrete practical exemplar'.

The 'tone' that Rossetti detects in 'Mrs B's' voice questions this connection between speech and 'living'. Barrett Browning informs Mary Russell Mitford that Carlyle *'writes thoughts'*,[143] and in that respect she herself resists Carlyle's emphasis on physical presence, on thinking and being. The audible suggestiveness of 'song' in its conventional denotation as written poetry helps her with a related argument: poetry, for her, is not inferior to speech, but possessed of cognate powers. Refusing to see writing as a surly upstart railing against supplemental status, she insists on the possibility of life less in the writer, or speaker, than on the page. Letters, as such, challenge the monopolies claimed by human speech. She perceives no deficiency in them, nor even much sense of 'printed' limitation.[144] Not merely a substitute for audible presence, they propose an available and genuinely voiced alternative. And because she believes her letters can 'converse', they do not betoken an absence of 'ourselves'.[145] Responding to Browning's missed opportunity of 'really seeing' her,[146] she claims to have 'learnt to know your voice' as a correspondent.[147] Words function here as Coleridgean 'living Things', able to transmit presence as subjects in the world.[148] Looking back on their early exchanges, Barrett Browning assures her lover that his are 'vital letters'.[149] They are trustworthy carriers of identity, but more than that: 'I felt your letters to be you from the very first'.[150]

By May 1845, Browning complains that 'it is high time you saw me, for I have clearly written myself out!'[151] Instead of fulfilling a surrogate presence, the epistolary routine strikes him as little more than a necessary evil. The following year, Barrett Browning is still defending the social primacy of the form: 'It is a way of meeting, .. this meeting in letters'.[152] Elsewhere she acknowledges the desiccated oddity of the 'talking', and even its subversive possibilities:[153] 'You are to be made out by the comparative anatomy system', she writes, 'You have thrown out fragments of os [bone] .. sublime .. indicative of soul-mammothism – and you live to develop your nature, .. if you live.'[154] 'Soul-mammothism' is Carlylean phraseology: the narrator of *Past and Present* invites the reader to 'peep' into the past, as if 'a deep-buried Mastodon [. . .] were to *speak* from amid its rock-swathings' (10:43). But her humour in this passage endows written words with a denatured vitality that marginalises, or renders unnecessary, the 'speaking voice' Carlyle himself privileges. And where that voice does break through into the discourse of the letters, its life energy is disembodied or supernatural: '[T]hese are the days of Mesmerism & clairvoyance', she teases, on claiming an impossible knowledge of Browning's 'skulls & spiders'.[155]

Just as Barrett Browning imputes qualities of voice and vitality to the (un)dead letter, so she associates the epistolary form with
unconventional modes of production. While this recalls Henry David
Thoreau – who wonders 'If I cannot chop wood in the yard, can I not
chop wood in my journal? – the 'work' performed by her letters takes
its origin in an awareness of incapacity, and the same invalidism which
precludes physical submission to the Gospel of Work.[156] Barrett Browning's resistance to the idea of bedridden work, and the likelihood of
Carlyle's disapproval, even precipitates a kind of perversity. This signals
the awkwardness of her condition, but also its powers, and its capacity to enact labour. Letters document activities – in a manner similar
to a diary – and the narratives they contain impose a form on passing
time. They also become material artefacts, proofs of effort in a manual
script. This testimonial function applies not only individually, but to the
accumulated weight of correspondence, and the possibility of posthu-
mous publication. Barrett Browning acknowledges this on suggesting
that Mitford's correspondence might one day appear in 'folio shape'.[157]
In the same letter, she speaks of signing and sealing her 'contract' as
Browning's 'articled' correspondent.[158] But contrary to the finalities of
Adams v. *Lindsell*, their agreement always stresses the unfinished nature
of epistolary work. The result, in fact, is a flirtatious compact, one that
entails 'taking no thought for your sentences, (nor for mine) – nor for
your blots, (nor for mine) nor for your blunt speaking (nor for mine),
nor for your badd speling (nor for mine)'.[159] We are reminded of all the
ways in which letters stop short of presentable work: if they count as
'production', their raw or unrefined artfulness still disclaims the effort
reserved for published literature.

Hovering between work and distraction, distance and presence, these
courtship letters share many of the qualities that trouble poetry, to the
extent that they readily stand in for it. The association promises certain benefits: letters possess a straightforward social utility – and a stable
addressee – that poetry lacks. In defending her experience of having 'lived
all my chief joys, [. . .] in poetry & in poetry alone', Barrett Browning
approaches a conception of the sufficiency, and even the advantages, of a
vicarious form.[160] While the genius of poetry enlivens her correspondence,
the social purpose of the letters rubs off on the poetry. And when the letters report on the work of poetry, they become in themselves a form of
production, as literary criticism. In this role, they declare and fulfil ends
that go beyond the immediate object of communication. Finally, the connections between literary writing and this mode of loving by letter upset
any sense of the letters as an arena – as Leighton puts it – in which Barrett
Browning appears merely 'as the heroine of a love story'.[161] Unconven-

tional modes of production arise even in those letters concerned with illness. When Browning complains of a headache, and his correspondent returns sympathy, a kind of currency is exchanged.[162] Supposedly fixed ailments prove linguistically malleable, at least amid the communicative aims of courtship. Just as Carlyle's dyspepsia coincides with an increasing valuation of action, so Barrett Browning's high estimation of active pleasures deals in the 'signal disadvantages' that rule them out.[163] Her idealisation of untrammelled physical prowess makes most sense, this is to suggest, in the context of a dialectic between incapacity and action. In these conditions, ablebodiedness operates less as a condition than as an enticing metaphor.

Once viewed in the light of these connections, between invalidism and physical work, letters and exertion, Barrett Browning's 'Carlyle-ship' seems less at odds with her personal circumstances.[164] Her manner of living through correspondence, meanwhile, articulates and partially resolves her predicament as an invalid worker. This means reconceiving what possibilities of 'life' and 'voice' are available in writing, and indeed what unconventional forms of productivity it evokes. Letters emerge as records of daily effort, collectable eventually in a volume or corpus. They are also external markers of literary production, reporting the progress of particular poems or essays. Criticism combines, as such, with a labour of love – with flirtation, in short. That, of course, should never be 'laboured' in the sense of earnest or dogged. As love letters, they perform their own specialised form of work; and they stand in for other written works, even as they disclaim the status of work for themselves. In this capacity, they provide a comforting, and sometimes experimental, proxy for poetic and literary production, benefitting from a confidence of witness and audience not usually enjoyed by 'invisible' cultural labour. In this respect, their function is to point the way.

* * *

Cycling between a vatic theory of poetry and an ecstatic materiality – whereby the poet appears as worker, maker, and seer, all at once – Barrett Browning follows Carlyle in combining artistic vision with social responsibility. As a practising poet, however, she resists her mentor's effort to redefine poetry as an insight or wisdom not concerned with metrical realisation. Instead of rejecting him, she holds him to the standard of his previous sayings, perpetuating a more amenable version of Carlyle than he himself justifies. She knew his thoughts on 'female geniuses', but like Jameson, Norton, and Smith spots an opportunity in his dogmatism. She turns Carlylean essentialism against itself. Dropping the ventriloquism of her earlier writings, she ultimately appeals to a version of Carlylean sincerity. This, by the same token, enables her to channel, and ultimately celebrate, the 'writer bodily', necessitating and justifying an appeal to her position as a woman. At the same time, Barrett Browning holds keenly to the Romantic legacy; and defends the poetic against complete assimilation by the social. Instead of renouncing the intellectual life, in the manner of Carlyle's more philistine outbursts, she casts herself (and him) as its guardian.

Of all Barrett Browning's circumstantial departures from the Carlylean blueprint, her invalidism is the hardest to reconcile with a philosophy of action; but here, too, she spots an opportunity. By shifting the site of physical presence away from the body, to the medium of correspondence, she broadens the sphere of literary agency. Letters cease, in turn, to be distractions, and become modes of social and literary production. Importantly, a rebellious instinct is not what leads Barrett Browning to depart from these Carlylean tenets, but rather her imagined orthodoxy. Unlike Brown – who inherits a restless need to *show* the world that he is working, even as he disagrees with Carlyle, and whose agonised self-chastisement excludes both artistic preparations and the diary itself from the sphere of production – she dispenses with the daily quota. If this reflects the received confidence of an upper middle-class woman, it also evinces a reasoned understanding that the poetic mind needs only to be industrious 'on the average of days', that the workshop of a skilled 'maker' is the model not the power loom. According to her philosophy of immanence, letters are not merely proofs of imperceptible work, or a simple testament to being, but an action in themselves, a way of carrying on life and labour in defiance of physical or temporal limit.

Chapter 4

Participant Observers: Gladstone, Ruskin, Morris

In the first and second parts of this chapter, on William Gladstone and John Ruskin, the emphasis shifts to a more gestural or performative approach. The question of demonstrating work arises again, but rather than representing physical tasks in their association with the labouring classes, they are here displaced and refracted through the body of the middle-class writer, a figure who selectively performs that work in a personal capacity. As Siskin pertinently observes, georgic literary forms offered a 'means by which the work of writing itself came to be seen as a potentially heroic activity'.[1] This development underpins the turn towards 'husbandry' apparent in my examples, and in the case of Gladstone, there are links between Virgilian precedent and 'the promotion of landowners' virtues' or 'nation building'.[2] Only, there is less emphasis in this case on an interaction between 'the heroic and the professional'; and little on deploying the georgic as 'a tool in the making of modern professionalism'.[3] The georgic operates here not so much to symbolise and empower 'professional' labours than to displace disembodied work. In that way, it re-fashions literature in its own image.

In this respect, georgic tropes interact with a cluster of mid nineteenth-century movements, beginning with revived interest in the Greek gymnasium.[4] As if avoiding Charles Kingsley's 'Isle of Tomtoddies' – a place of 'all heads and no bodies' – the followers of Muscular Christianity extended these principles of physical wellbeing into a broader field of human experience.[5] Glimpses of a more integrated human life are equally prevalent in American literature, owing largely to the legacies of Carlylean idealism and the New England culture of unified sensibility. So writes Thoreau: 'Can there be any greater reproach than an idle learning? 'Learn to split wood, at least.'[6] Far from defending the literary life by re-describing it as 'work', he accepts the customary slur of an idle distraction, proposing instead that writers atone for their defective calling by doing something else with compensating vigour. This spectacle of the author as labourer endures on both sides of the Atlantic well beyond the century's close. By contrast with the fashion for depicting authors at their desks, it is an outdoor tradition. In this respect, the writer is seen demonstrably 'at work', but in an unaccustomed arena.[7] Recent criticism has presented this literary turn towards physical life as a manifestation of masculine anxiety.[8] Or it has stressed a theological migration away from contemplative withdrawal in favour of action in the world.[9] In what follows, my emphasis falls rather on a performed continuum between displays of manual work and the nature of writing itself. As such all three cases witness an unusually immersive form of literary 'field work'.

Gladstone's Odyssean Toolshop

Gladstone's modern reputation has been shaped primarily by his actions as a statesman. In that capacity, he created the Liberal Party, led the great reforming government of 1868 to 1874, and sought (unsuccessfully) to enact an Irish Home Rule bill. The following discussion considers the less familiar subject of his career as a man of letters.[10] It began while he was still a schoolboy at Eton, where he wrote verses on classical, and reverential subjects.[11] These activities were preparatory, of course; but as one gleans from The Glynne-Gladstone Papers (Gladstone's Library, Hawarden), they established a lifelong habit of literary composition. Its forms of expression range from the epic *Palmyra* – an early poem in rhyming couplets written at Eton – to the light verse of 'There was an old woman of Cambridge' (GG/1453), a limerick written towards the end of his life. To these compositional interests must be added his prolific career as a scholar, which ranges from translations of Horace to detailed studies of Dante and Homer.

Of course, Gladstone was not alone among Victorian statesmen in nurturing literary interests. As a politician-writer, he warrants notice for refusing the temptation to render literature a merely displaced setting for the working out of political ideas.[12] But even there, he is not completely alone. What really sets him apart is his willingness to test and reinvent the boundaries between literature on the one hand, and on the other a 'practical' life that simultaneously encompasses and exceeds the sphere of party political debate. John Morley remarks pertinently that Gladstone 'had none of that detachment, often found among superior minds', and that his 'instruments' were 'the sword and the trowel of political action'.[13] Exploring a more invigorating, and more probing, connection to agricultural pursuits, Morley's subject does just that. But he also reaches beyond the glancing comparisons of rhetoric: Gladstone grasps not just 'the trowel of political action', but also the trowel itself. While this activates matters of prudence and policy that concern his prime ministerial experience, it also involves active participation in the physical work of his estate. These two outcomes are different in kind, yet firmly linked as reflections of Gladstone's Homeric enthusiasms: his understanding, for instance, of Odyssean statesmanship as a matter of unified sensibility and multifarious intelligence. They also speak to the legacy of his father's position as a slave-owner: in effect, linking literary labour to a third category of 'practical' experience, that of bonded labour.

Gladstone's personal engagement with manual work began with an early interest in woodturning.[14] A diary entry from 1858, which mentions 'my first lesson' in tree-felling (31 July 1858), signals a new trajectory, and a pastime that would endure for many decades among the trees of his estate at Hawarden, North Wales.[15] In the first sustained study of this part of Gladstone's life, Peter Sewter indicates that Gladstone spent a portion of 1,071 days on wood-cutting.[16] Such activities were unusual in landed gentlemen, yet became a basis for his public reputation. Among the thirty axes that remain on display in Gladstone's study at Hawarden Castle, one – a silver-headed specimen – was presented by the men who built the Forth Bridge.[17] He reciprocated with volumes of 'improving' reading, in an exchange that simultaneously enshrines divided roles and the possibility of shared talents. Unsurprisingly, his hobby also attracted the attention of enemies. In a famous parliamentary speech, Lord Randolph Churchill imputed a destructive and self-appeasing motivation, in claiming 'The forest laments in order that Mr Gladstone may perspire'.[18] For Roy Jenkins, similarly, this 'obsessive form of recreation' led to his estate being 'considerably denuded' through 'arboreal slaughter'.[19] Churchill correctly senses the possibility of ulterior purposes, but misleads through his picture of deforestation. While the danger and the exertion of tree-felling attracted Gladstone, it was neither wantonly destructive nor purposeless. Woodland management required (and does still) the thinning out of weaker or misshapen trees to create light and space for the saplings coming through.[20] Sewter provides valuable context in noting the 'air of neglect about the estate at Hawarden' when Gladstone married into it.[21] Focusing exclusively on felling operations also obscures his commitment to planting trees, as well as his concern to cultivate, to fructify, and to steward. The many books on forestry, agriculture and small holding added to his library track a deepening of these holistic approaches.[22] A similar picture emerges from the tree measurements and related notes that survive among Gladstone's papers.[23]

More private meanings of woodman's work are mediated through the pages of Gladstone's diary. Aimed at justifying his use of time, this document transforms the ancient precedent of Augustine's *Confessions* into a distinctly bourgeois project.[24] As Peter Jagger remarks, it served as 'a kind of "account book"'.[25] Gladstone – like Brown – came from Scots Calvinist stock. His father, John, co-founded a kirk and Caledonian School early in his time as a Liverpool merchant. With the rise of his fortunes he converted to Anglicanism, a change that helped his second wife, Anne MacKenzie Robertson, become active in the city's Evangelical networks.[26] The diary inherits this ecumenical tendency, in reconciling traditions of confession with Protestant modes of self-scrutiny. Through the systematic notation of daily reading, alongside political and manual tasks, we derive a total survey of Gladstone's life and times. Rather than documenting outward productivity, however, he understands all kinds of personal industry in relation to spiritual progress. With each passing birthday, he takes stock: turning 17, for instance, he finds little reason 'to congratulate myself'.[27] The following year, he offers a similar 'retrospect of time misapplied or lost' through 'idleness';[28] in 1832, he promises to bind himself 'down to work', suppressing 'natural sluggishness' through a 'painful and chastening exertion'.[29] In these remarks, a felt responsibility to work coincides with an inner conviction of moral turpitude, focusing on 'indulgence of bodily intemperance'.[30] A catalogue of infractions dated 26 October 1845 lists 'idleness' as a prominent shortcoming.[31]

In a further hybridisation of Calvinist, Anglican and Catholic practices, Gladstone would scourge himself, and then register that event by entering a lambda in his diary. Marks on the page become a key, in this way, to marks on the body. Literary works with erotic content were an especial prompt for self-flagellation, among them medieval fabliaux, and 'a book marked "Rochester's poems"'.[32] Other such prompts included his notorious 'rescue work', pursued in the company of prostitutes – a diversion with charitable aims, but occasionally titillating effects. Such acts belong to a programme of Tractarian piety that encompasses several less sensational activities: among them, fasting and monitoring the number of hours spent in bed each night. An annotated copy of Anthony Horneck's *The Happy Ascetick* (1724 edn) in Gladstone's Library confirms an interest in '1. VOWING, 2. FASTING, 3. WATCHING and 4. SELF-REVENGE'.[33] He has marked a passage indicating that 'Fasting hath got fo ill a Reputation among us, becaufe the Roman Church hath miserably perverted the ufe of it'.[34] In the same work, we find related underlinings: 'working the Mind into very low, and humble thoughts of ourfelves, and of our worth.'[35] Later in life, Gladstone would mark passages on 'The Discipline of the Body' in George S. Barrett's *Religion in Daily Life* (1893).[36] A preoccupation with fasting extends to Gladstone's general reading: in his copy of *Early Letters of Thomas Carlyle* he enters a 'v' against the words, 'being this day upon the fasting list (not from religious but medicinal motives)'.[37]

Gladstone's recourse to woodcraft might seem connected to this longing for pain and punishment. Woodchopping, after all, exhausts the body, and in that way exhausts physical urges: among those to which Gladstone was liable, Peter Stansky lists 'masturbation', 'pornography' and 'his attempts to save prostitutes'.[38] Indeed, the lambda disappears from his diaries in the summer of 1859, a timing that coincides roughly with the first wood chopping entries. We might conclude – as Gladstone's biographers often do – that whip and axe fulfil similar purposes, standing in for each other as agents of a pain that shades into pleasure. Ian Gibson makes the pertinent observation that Gladstone lived at Eton under the superintendence of Dr Keate, a 'most notorious flogger'.[39] The shared Eton background of Charles Algernon Swinburne – another champion of the whip – corroborates this sense of a habit founded in early classroom experience.[40] For further expression of this topical nexus between erotic and working impulses, one might look to W. H. Hudson's *A Crystal Age* (1887), an eerie utopian fiction whose love-crazed protagonist resorts to tree-felling 'with the frantic energy of a Gladstone out of office'.[41] In this scenario, the hero takes on 'some unusually violent task, such as would exhaust the body and give, perhaps a rest to the mind'.[42] Gladstone himself observes this much on noting that 'in chopping down a tree you have not time to think of anything except where your next stroke will fall'.[43] As I mean to show, however, wood chopping serves purposes that extend beyond the economy of erotic life. Most notably, it sits on a continuum with the intellectual life, to the extent that Gladstone consciously theorises it as the basis for an enlarged creative consciousness.

The keyword linking ascetic versions of woodchopping to therapeutic or purgative versions is 'exercise'. The 'best exercise' recommended by *The Happy Ascetick* is spiritual in kind, a formalised mode of discipline or self-control. A less certain role for 'exercise' informs a celebratory portrait showing Gladstone surrounded by roundels listing aspects of character or experience, among which 'EXERCISE' appears alongside an axe.[44] A revealingly imprecise emblem, the axe hesitates between social utility and a purer expenditure of energy. Similar tension emerges from an anecdote in which Herbert Gladstone recalls his father being 'quite irritated when in a *Punch* cartoon he was drawn as cutting trees a foot or two from the ground', since sound economy required cutting at ground level.[45] Only Herbert adds that it 'did not matter', 'as we were out for exercise'. It is equally clear that neither end prevails unchecked, and that Gladstonian purposelessness revises rather than abolishes its objects. Insensibility to this balancing act recurs across the newspaper coverage of life at Hawarden. A *Times* editorial sketch from 1877 relates how, on a visit to the estate, a delegation from the Bolton Liberal Party found their leader chopping wood.[46] In the midst of his official 'retirement' from politics, this manner of 'exercise' easily resembles a folly. The reporter surmises that his 'Bolton audience must have looked forward [. . .] to the moment at which the axe was to be dropped, and the woodcutter to give place to the statesman'. Gladstone, it is true, was 'much more than a feller of trees'. But the more probing implication is that he saw tree-felling as an integral, rather than ancillary, concern. In a manuscript text from August 1858, he commends the 'relaxation & refreshment' to be found in 'alteration of different employments', yet enters the caveat that 'all should have an end'.[47]

Ascetic or therapeutic explanations for manual activity recede yet further once Gladstone's contacts with reporters are viewed as performances, adapted to communicating political or philosophical messages. As previously noted, Danahay attributes the turn towards strenuous labour in the period to an emasculation of the male writer within the 'female' domain of the home.[48] This model fits Gladstone less well: as a man of wealth and position, his intellectual work was never all-encompassing. And he did not experience his home – his estate – as a confined or confining environment. In *The Sinews of the Spirit*, Norman Vance dwells on the category of 'manliness', but applies a model more pertinent to Gladstone.[49] Instead of presenting performed masculinity as a defensive measure, he locates its sources in an approach to churchmanship that promotes action in the world. In two respects, Gladstone's woodcraft evades a precise fit even with this model. The advocates of muscular Christianity prioritise sports and battle in their accounts of worldly action, with an emphasis on '*agon*, race' or 'contest'.[50] Gladstone welcomes these classical echoes, along with the revived language of gymnastic exercise. But for him the axe signifies something more than sport, as does his challenge to the common prejudice that manual work is degrading. And he rejects the opposition between action and religious seclusion set out, for instance, in Thomas Hughes's *The Manliness of Christ* (1879).[51] Drawn to incarnational thinking from the time of his exposure to the Oxford Movement, Gladstone's spiritual sinews tell a different story.[52] When he looks to monastic traditions, he recognises a model of purposeful work rather than a sphere of renunciation. A book from his library entitled *The Benedictine Lay Brother*[53] contains marked passages on the 'menial work of the monastery' and on work conceived as a mode of 'action' or 'prayer'.[54] Notice lines also appear against 'Do not make the mistake of devoting yourself to prayer instead of working'.[55] *The Rule of Our Most Holy Father Saint Benedict* also appears among his books.[56] A key source for modern conceptions of manual labour as spiritual labour, it also substantiates a sense of denominational amplitude.

As for many of his contemporaries, Gladstone's reception of 'dangerous' Catholic sources relies on a broader, popular mediation (and containment) of monasticism. Indeed, his practice and rationalisation of manual labour draws heavily on Carlyle's *Past and Present*, a work he reports reading in July 1843.[57] Its portrait of a well-ordered life, orchestrated by the firm and directive Abbot Samson, tallies with Gladstone's early sense of how authority should be exercised. And though its initial appeal reflects the virulently authoritarian Toryism of his youth, it equally informs his moderation towards Anglo-Catholicism.[58] Carlyle, after all, offers a resolutely Protestant view of medieval monastic life, one geared towards the relatively uncontroversial proposition that 'Work is Worship' (10:233). Gladstone later claims that the Sage of Chelsea's powerful individuality contains 'fragments both of justice and wisdom', despite 'selfish' and 'intolerant' ways.[59] He also sympathises with Carlyle's attention to artisanal virtue: his edition of *Ebenezer Elliott*, for instance, contains a pencilled index with entries for '141. Grinders' and '246. Carlyle'.[60] Woodmanship, too, finds its sanction in Carlyle. A passage marked for attention in Gladstone's copy of *On Heroes* reads 'I suppose the right good fighter was oftenest also the right good forest-feller, – the right good improver, discerner, doer and worker in every kind'.[61] For Gladstone, as for Carlyle, the worker's remit extends beyond the felling of trees to encompass broader programmes of improvement and discernment. Equally, Gladstone's 'passion for order' – as H. C. G. Matthew calls it – allows a convergence between estate husbandry and the Carlylean view of labour as an action that simultaneously forms environments and selves.[62]

Gladstone hopes to be considered 'a labouring man myself', to be 'acknowledged as "a comrade" of the workers'.[63] A related aspiration emerges from his copy of Carlyle's *Reminiscences*, in which he marks the resonant phrase, previously discussed, 'Let me write my books as he built his houses'.[64] David Bebbington interprets 'Gladstone's tree-felling', and his reputation as 'the People's William', as aspects of an effort to restore a 'fraternal spirit between the classes'.[65] His visit to workers constructing the Forth Bridge belongs to this tendency, as does his sympathy for 'Cottage industry, or small culture (*petite culture*)'.[66] Running in parallel with this fraternal impulse is a belief that intellectual labour should re-engage with manual labour. A pact of mutual benefit likewise underpins Gladstone's foundation, in 1891, of the Hawarden Young Man's Society, established 'for the purpose of physical training and recreation'.[67] Opened by his son, Herbert, the Society stood next to the previously established Mechanic's [*sic*] Institute and Literary Improvement Society (1854). Nearly all mentions of tree-felling in Gladstone's diary enshrine this commitment to varied occupation. One entry cycles between an ecclesiastical matter ('Convv. With Bp of Oxford'), an interval of 'Tree-cutting while the party went to Mold for S. P. G.', and readings from five authors (De Gassicourt, Rousseau, Hume, Lessing, Taylor).[68] A similar entry lists educational instruction ('Latin with Stephen'), letter writing, more books, and 'Music in evg' alongside the 'Felling of the three Beeches'.[69] At this point, any impression of normal energies is suspended: Gladstone emerges as a man not only indefatigable, but reluctant to divorce scholarship from physical feats.

His readings in Carlyle provide a further clue to this unusually unified understanding of divided time. The following passages in his copy of *On Heroes* ('The Hero as Poet') are marked: 'A vein of Poetry exists in the hearts of all men' and 'no man is made altogether of Poetry'.[70] From this idea of dual natures, Gladstone recovers a conviction that mutual reliance governs the relation of the parts. Tree-felling likewise has an invigorating effect on the compositional process. When he hits a problem in his writing, a bout of exercise shifts the blockage. On 21 August 1878, for instance, he recalls having 'Worked on England's Mission', a subject that is 'difficult', and 'has required some rewriting.'[71] The same difficulty quickly gives way to 'Woodman's work'. These entries from the late 1860s and early 1870s illustrate the frequency with which scholarly activity ends in recuperative 'axe-work':

> Worked on Homer. Woodcutting.[72]
> Worked on Homer. Felling trees.[73]
> Worked on Homer. Felled a lime at the Rectory with H. G. Dined at the Rectory. Read Scott's Swift–Stanley's Westmr. Abbey.[74]
> Worked on Homer. Read Nabathaean Agriculture (Renan on) [. . .] We felled a good elm. Round game in evg.[75]

While these shifts from scholarship to manual labour lend an impression of relief and sustenance, Gladstone also works in the opposite direction. His 'first lesson' in tree felling gives way to reading 'Herring's Letters & Appx. – Hume's Life & Corrsp. – Cicero's Epist. Ad Famil[iares].'[76] On 28 December 1867, he undertakes 'Woodcutting in aft', in between 'papers and private affairs', Homeric studies, and reading 'Baker's Abyssinia'.[77] The previous week, he lists items of political correspondence alongside the note, 'Returned to my woodcutting'.[78] The rest of the entry mentions 'Corrected proofs & revised my Article on Phoenicia' and 'Homeric conversation with Stephen'.[79] Yet this is called 'A day of settling down'.[80] Another marked passage in Carlyle's 'The Hero as Poet' shifts the emphasis away from differentiated intellectual and spiritual attributes towards an underlying unity: 'For body and soul, word and idea, go strangely together, here as everywhere.'[81] The diaries, more generally, enshrine this alliance of 'body' and 'word'. In April 1876, Gladstone reports that he 'Worked on Athenè' and 'Also worked with my sons on the great Beech Tree'.[82] This broad application of 'worked' to literary and manual tasks confers a confident symmetry on apparently diverse functions. Forestry, moreover, aligns with book-making as a productive process. In 'Woodcraft with Herbert. Worked on Preface to Mycenean Volume', the constructive qualities of woodman's work bleed into the kindred labour of building a preface.[83]

Gladstone further extends his 'woodmanship' into his intellectual life through his study of Homer,[84] a preoccupation expressed through *Studies on Homer and the Homeric Age* (1858), *Juventus Mundi* (1869), *Homeric Synchronism* (1876), the primer on *Homer* (1878), and *Landmarks of Homeric Study* (1890).[85] Several critics trace through these works a connection between liberalism and Greek heroism.[86] Homer's portrait of Odysseus as a king warrants particular attention in this respect. Though remote from modern forms of monarchy, heroic conceptions of kingship appeal to Gladstone's notion of statesmanship as legitimised by the cultivation of diverse faculties. '[I]n heroic Greece', he observes, 'the king [. . .] was not the fountainhead of the common life, but only its exponent' and 'The source lay in the community'.[87] Straying in this way from his Tory roots, he proposes a model of kingship conferred by an ideal of behaviour. Indeed, he approves the expectation that 'The Homeric king [. . .] should be emphatically a gentleman'.[88] This title hardly applies comfortably to the wily Odysseus, but Gladstone includes him among those rulers who cultivate an 'intense corporate or public life'.[89] In *Studies on Homer*, he gives the additional example of Paris, who took 'the chief share in the erection of his own palace'.[90] An ensuing portrait of Odysseus – as one who 'proves himself a wood-cutter and ship builder in the island of Calypso', while remaining 'no stranger to the plough and the scythe'[91] – evidently recalls Gladstone's own devotion to the attainment of a 'comprehensive' self. He goes on to cite Odysseus's challenge to Eurymachus, 'to try which of them would soonest clear the meadow of its grass, which drive the straightest furrow down the four-acre field'.[92] This is not yet a wholehearted espousal of democratic notions: the tasks of agriculture are converted almost too readily into aristocratic tests of prowess. But such passages show Gladstone moving towards a conception of general capacities, one that he would develop further in later works.

Juventus Mundi (1869) appears at the height of the enthusiasm for wood chopping, and it is here that a change commences. Though alluding similarly to 'the kingly character in Homer' as 'all-comprehensive' – one that 'embraces even the manual employments of honourable industry'[93] – this study departs from the tone of haughty proof. The sense of sporting challenges recedes, and we are invited to recognise actions as productive of identities: 'Odysseus' is 'a wood-cutter and ship-builder'; he is 'the carpenter and artisan of his own bed, so elaborately wrought'.[94] A portrait emerges of the Greek chieftain as author of his own material reality, an 'all-comprehensive figure' whose woodcutting and agricultural employments are praised as instances of an 'honourable industry' that exists outside the 'higher faculties' of 'Judge, General, and Priest'.[95] Odysseus's own 'skill' makes him, as such, a 'king' adapted to an increasingly meritocratic age. From among the 'inferior professions of partially skilled hand-laborers', ' the woodman' and 'the pilot' acquire special prominence, as roles in which 'skill avails far more than force'.[96] As this would imply, Gladstone's analysis extends beyond the pages and readership of his Homeric scholarship to encompass his own life. His portrait of a statesman-king indirectly addresses his own dual status as head of a household and sometime leader of an island nation. A whiff of the self-fashioned hero emerges, likewise, from his diary, where he reports splinter injuries sustained while woodcutting.[97] In other ways, his diary evidences a link between political and domestic policy: one entry reports 'Much rumination: on imperial concerns – & on Homer', as if one thought would lead to the other.[98] More publicly, a political cartoon on 'Cabinet-Making' (1880) registers an otherwise unlikely convergence between statecraft and joinery [Figure 4.1]. The incongruous instrument of a woodman's axe, and the stooped figure of the Prime Minister as workingman, acknowledge and resist the utopian comprehensiveness of the statesmanship in question.

What, then, are the implications of this analysis for Gladstone's self-conception? In the ancient world, he argues, 'both the useful arts and the fine arts had a social dignity',[99] a dignity signified by their 'common designation δημιόεργοι'.[100] This status informs his sociology of the period: among a list of Homeric 'professions' – encompassing '1. Seers', '2. Surgeons', '3. Artificers', and '5. Heralds' – Gladstone includes '4. Bards'.[101] A later work, on 'Contact Between the Assyrian Tablets and the Homeric Text' (1890), refers likewise to 'the qualities and the methods, of the Maker or Poet', and to the 'institution, dignity and influence of the Bards'.[102] And while Gladstone observes perplexedly that the 'song' belonging to Achilles is 'almost the only gift which is not ascribed to the

Figure 4.1 Joseph Swain, 'Cabinet-Making', *Punch*, 8 May 1880. By permission of the Master and Fellows of Magdalene College, Cambridge

all-accomplished Odysseus',[103] he declares that 'The two protagonists are evidently the two greatest orators of the Poems'.[104] He realigns manual skill in this way with the poetical and political aspects of character, all under the broad category of δημιόεργοι.

The neatness of this identification is troubled all the same. As Bebbington notes, Gladstone admired Aristotle's 'understanding of the good life'.[105] But he also embraced forms of labour that Aristotle considered inconsistent with citizenship.[106] A related complication concerns Gladstone's understanding of slavery. In the third volume of *On Homer and the Homeric Age*, he writes that Achilles in the inferno 'does not choose the slave, but the labourer for hire (θητευεμεν is his expression), as the type of a depressed condition upon earth'.[107] From here, he reaches the dubious conclusion that the position of the slaves was 'analogous to that of domestic servants among ourselves, who practically forfeit the active exercise of political privileges, but are in many respects better off than the mass of those who depend on bodily labour'.[108] Insisting that 'cruelty or oppression' were not necessary conditions,[109] Gladstone defends the Homeric world against association with modern-day slavery. In the process, he posits a category of 'benevolent' slave-holder, one not irrelevant to the claims of his own father, John.

John Gladstone's position as a merchant slave-owner has long been acknowledged by biographers.[110] Having graduated from corn dealing to the Imperial trade with India, he was drawn into land ownership through the foreclosure of mortgages held by indebted sugar planters. Further acquisitions followed, to the extent that he was, by the 1830s, a major owner of human capital in Central America and Jamaica. The magnitude of this operation emerges from S. G. Checkland's calculation that John Gladstone received payments of £93,526 for 2,039 slaves under the Slavery Compensation Act 1837,[111] an outcome owing largely to the offices of his son in Parliament who, with other MPs sympathetic to the West Indian interest, converted the proposals for a transitional loan into a grant. Surviving deeds and inventories pertaining to the Gladstone family properties conjure the grim reality of their Demerara plantations: one lists '7 ranges of Negro Houses 100 feet long each of 24 wide', as well as slaves carrying names such as 'Glasgow', 'Fowler', 'Ned', 'February', 'John Brown', 'Goliah', 'Nelson', 'Coffee', 'Jupiter', and 'Cicero'.[112] A 'Table of Compensation rates for slaves in British Guiana, c. 1833' clinches the prevailing logic of the human being as chattel. The sums listed range between '1. Head People . . . 87.8.0 ¾', '2. Tradesmen . . . 68.8.0 ½' and '5. Inferior Field Labourers . . . 36.0.5'.[113]

Not merely a prominent plantation owner, John Gladstone was a leading apologist for slavery under reformed conditions. In 1830, he published *A Statement of Facts . . .*,[114] a pamphlet that defended the plantation owners' 'right to property'.[115] As if foreshadowing his son's pastimes, he mentions that some American slaves freed as a consequence of 'the last war' were unsuccessfully taken to Trinidad, where they were vainly offered 'every inducement to influence them to work, either on plantations, as wood-cutters or otherwise'.[116] Not long after the abolition of slave-holding, a letter in the *Sheffield Independent* declared that 'The name of Gladstone deserves to be forever infamous, as one of the most greedy and remorseless of West Indian slave owners, whose estate in Demerara was made notorious over all others by the number of negroes worked to death', a 'man, the very walls of whose house are cemented with human blood, whose whips, and manacles, and treadmills have scarcely yet perished from the earth'.[117] The issue had been reignited by new government measures against the importation of sugar from American slave plantations. John Gladstone was in a particular position to benefit, having successfully imported a workforce of so-called 'Coolies' from India. In this he was inspired by the apprenticeship system to which former slaves were transferred by the Slavery Abolition Act 1833, a measure that exchanged feudal bonds for capitalistic bonds of contract and debt.[118]

Notwithstanding Checkland's detailed study of the family business, it is only in recent years that historians have explored its attitudinal and political legacy.[119] In Parliament, Gladstone exerted his influence to ensure that British trade policy never conflicted with his father's reconfigured interests as an employer of indentured labour. As Roland Quinault shows, he defended the apprenticeship system, and even opposed the disclosure of compensation payments.[120] In later life, he pursued a protectionist policy that benefited the interest of colonial sugar growers. When his father died, he inherited £120,000, and briefly became an owner of Demerara estates. It is darkly ironic that a man who benefitted so bounteously from the bonded labour of enslaved Africans should spend his free time performing agricultural tasks. It is striking, too, that Gladstone employs the figure of the lash to betoken self-flagellation, the whip being a notorious symbol of the slaving party.[121] One reading of these facts suggests a man tormented by guilt. In this account, he uses the purgative of an associated labour to re-perform, and thereby absolve, the punishments doled out by his father's overseers. Checkland edges in this direction: as the son of a planter, he notes, 'William had found himself in a very difficult position'.[122] Gladstone's attitude to slavery evolved over time, but there is little to suggest that he suffered pangs in this direction. Though it was his brother Robertson's lot to take over the business, his father deputed the intellectual and moral justification of slave owning interests to William.[123] An associated sense of slavery as a conditional, rather than absolute, evil runs through Gladstone's statements on the subject. In his address to the Newark electors he draws on his father's 1830 pamphlet, insisting that government should 'let emancipation go hand in hand with fitness to enjoy freedom'.[124] He even declares – in a manner that recalls both his father and late Carlyle – that 'I would not free the slave without assurance of his disposition to industry'.[125] Not for the first time, work figures as a defining attribute and qualification.

The striking characteristic of these positions is that they combine a publicly moral or humanitarian agenda with the unspoken reality of family advantage. However intellectually contorted the message, Gladstone seems unaware of the strain. He addresses a coincident benefit, not an inconsistency. Speaking in Liverpool, in 1886, he includes the abolition of slavery among ten subjects upon which 'the masses have been right and the classes have been wrong'.[126] In the 1890s, he observes that 'the advance of social opinion generally on that dreadful subject has been immense'.[127] Towards the end of his life, he acknowledges 'the sad defects, the real illiberalism of my opinions on that subject'.[128] It is even possible that Gladstone's actions against absentee landlords in

Ireland unconsciously offered recompense for his father's even more distant possessions. And yet the conditionality of his position never entirely recedes. Gladstone adds of his past opinions that 'they were not illiberal as compared with the ideas of the times'.[129] While one might expect a degree of cognitive dissonance – informed by the impossibility of accepting that his father was an unrepentant sinner – the issue prompts no obvious personal crisis.

His participation in agricultural tasks seems not, then, a function of ancestral guilt; nor was it a gesture of sympathy in favour of the slaves and 'apprentices' held by his family. Instead of freeing the slave, he ennobles 'servile' tasks in such a way as to defend or redeem the process. Gladstone, this is to say, models an exemplary performance of servile labour, one that conveniently narrows and expands the meaning of emancipation. He neither denies, nor shirks, the labour associated with enslaved roles. He joins it, rather, to moral and intellectual qualities, and even to qualities of rule and oversight. Ultimately, the necessity of compulsion falls away. The more certain effect, however, is to release the slave owner from guilt. In this way, ideological compensation follows financial compensation, and slavery takes its place in a history of institutions charged with preparing the stuff of humanity for new roles. The endurance of 'servile' labour beyond the endurance of slavery becomes, then, an implicit defence of that system, a defence that relies on a rehabilitation of the labour itself. The unfree premise of that labour recedes in this scheme, because attention is redirected towards the variable moral progress and conditions of its subjects.

The possibility that a king, a statesman, or a man of letters, might share in such labour becomes the ultimate vindication of its necessity – the necessity, that is, of its voluntary execution where willed, and of its coercion where unwilled. This reading of Gladstone's woodcraft – as an unconscious apology for slave labour (if not for slavery itself) – relies upon an extrapolation. But it offers one way of tracing continuity through the otherwise baffling terrain of the Glynn-Gladstone archives, a terrain that extends from the deeds of slave estates to Gladstone's late correspondence with voluntary associations devoted to beekeeping, rabbit-farming, livestock rearing, and other forms of cottage economy.[130] These apparently miscellaneous contexts witness the slow evolution of a Gladstonian pastoral: a bloody pastoral, but one complacently untroubled for so long as the dignity of labour – whether enslaved or transfigured into Odyssean heroism – remains the founding value.

A related problem concerns Gladstone's characterisation of Odysseus. His reading of Homer insists on an open and honest connection between manual labour and statecraft. When Gladstone's Odysseus ploughs a field, his action implies no subterfuge: the exemplifying labour resists conversion into magic, deceit or unwarranted privilege. These conditions reflect an 'absence of priests and merchants', a class of person whose business 'too much resembled that of the kidnapper or swindler'.[131] And yet, Gladstone adds, it is 'the reproach of seeming to belong to this class that smartly stings Odysseus'. On writing these words, the profession of his own father cannot have been far from consciousness: a merchant whose trade resolves likewise into absentee ownership of land and human capital.[132] In Odysseus's case, the sting lodges deeply not because he works in commerce – though his wanderings are fugitive in their own way – but because the comparison aptly characterises his turn of mind. Adorno and Horkheimer identify Odysseus in just these terms. Comparing 'the solo manufacturer Crusoe' to the trading instincts of the cunning Odysseus, they recognise a kind of proto-merchant, for whom 'Deception is a mode of exchange'.[133] In this distillation of the trafficking impulse, the method becomes the commodity and the commodity the method. By contrast, Gladstone – like Ruskin – reserves a place for the honest merchant, for a mercantile impulse not wedded to mendacity. This insistence is in itself revealing. '[C]unning' stings so smartly because of its wider currency in the lexicon of moral encounter. It arises, most notably, in John Henry Newman's famous retort that 'I scorn and detest lying [. . .] and slyness, and cunning [. . .] quite as any Protestants hate them'.[134] Rather than suppress lying, most eminent Victorians imply its containment through recognition. Carlyle, for one, evokes the possibility of a nobility blended with wily tendencies: in *Sartor Resartus*, he traces 'Title' and 'King' to '*König* (king)', where 'anciently *Könning*, means Ken-ning (Cunning) or which is the same thing, Can-ning' (I:198). This passage of etymological play accommodates – indeed, celebrates – 'cunning' by resolving it into the Scots form 'kenning', itself evoking an innocuous 'wisdom', 'knowing', or 'teaching'. Dubious connotations are acknowledged, then; but within a sifting process that confirms a source for true authority. More mischievously, Oscar Wilde exploits Odyssean 'lying with a moral purpose' as a pressure point in his campaign to outrage his peers and predecessors.[135]

What sets Gladstone apart, in this respect, is his concerted effort to separate out such attributes, to admit no necessary convergence between heroic impulses and fugitive ones. Apart from deterring association with the 'shorthand' methods of the trickster, he extracts Odysseus's reputation from such latter-day corruptions as Virgil's 'maltreatment of the Homeric characters'.[136] The 'Ulysses of Virgil', he contends, 'simply represents the naked ideas of hardness, cunning, and cruelty'. He is '*durus, dirus, sævus, pellax, fandi fictor, artifex, inventor scelerum,*

and *scelerum hortator*'.[137] But while Gladstone insistently diverts attention away from Odysseus's faults – here, by dwelling on Trojan and
Roman perfidy – he cannot entirely ignore the familiar conception of
Odysseus as a master of cunning. Choosing an appropriately hesitant
phrase, he admits in *Homer* (1878) that 'His prudence so commended
by Athenè, leads towards craft'.[138] In 1890, he observes a 'universality
of accomplishment' culminating in a 'design leaning towards craft'.[139]
If an idea of deception arises in the first case, the 'leaning' in question
delivers not a commitment to cunning, but something at the trickier end
of an innocuous 'prudence'. In the second case, Gladstone absorbs such
'craft' into the remit of government. In place of a prince of darkness, he
installs 'the prince of policy', or 'design'.

Gladstone draws closest to the flaws of his hero on admitting a 'tenderness (to say the least) for fraud under certain conditions'.[140] Along
with 'Athenè', this for Odysseus is more than a matter of 'stratagem';
on the contrary, they jointly find in it 'a satisfaction'.[141] But he pointedly
resists any suggestion that this is a defining feature. Though it 'became in
after ages the keynote of the character',[142] he refuses to see that outcome
as inevitable: rather, 'it is in Homer only one of several features highly
distinctive'.[143] Odysseus, he implies, has a multi-faceted character, and
the prominence of 'cunning' in his modern reputation commits a distortion. Homer, we are told 'has awarded to him a many-sidedness, such as
is possessed by no other hero'.[144] He is 'a master not only in war, but in
government and in every industrial pursuit'.[145]

The related epithet, applied to Odysseus at the beginning of *The
Odyssey*, is πολύτροπον, meaning 'of many turns'.[146] Gladstone copes
with this word by reassigning it: its usual senses of 'wily', 'flexible',
and 'cunning', recede in favour of Odysseus's versatility as a statesman and a craftsman. He may even have imagined the more innocent
'turns' of the lathe, whose hobbyistic employment led to his admission
to the Worshipful Order of Turners in 1876.[147] However this may be,
Gladstone understands πολύτροπον as referring not to a single aspect
of Odysseus's character, but to a wholesome capacity for interchange
between skills. The editions of *The Odyssey* in Gladstone's Library
– most of which he received as gifts from their translators – suggest
an influence in this direction. G. A. Schomberg renders πολύτροπον as
'versatile',[148] while S. H. Butcher avoids 'shifty' with 'of many shift'.[149]
Rev. Lovelace Bigg-Wither's professedly 'literal' translation follows
Gladstone with 'the many-sided man',[150] and Sir Charles Du Cane
opts for the more innocuous, 'versatile'.[151] At the level of the language
itself, these Victorian instances of 'Englishing' struggle to combine
praise with realism.

In his modern reading of *The Odyssey*, Pietro Pucci contends that Homer achieves the 'feat' of making 'the trickster and the sufferer one person'.[152] Gladstone, by contrast, hopes to take the trickster out of the craftsman, before making one multifaceted figure out of the craftsman, statesman, and king. In this respect, he favours not the 'knowing' of a sly strategist, but that concerned with humble occupations, with ploughing the field, or with fashioning the timbers of the marriage bed. Gladstone's differentiating formulation prioritises 'craft' in this artisanal sense, according to which 'The chamber of Achilles is rich as a museum; that of Odysseus as a toolshop'.[153] The less savoury tricks of the wily hero he downplays, leaving in relief a profusion of skills (or 'turns') represented by the full inventory of tools on display. Instead of 'civilising' Odysseus in the manner of earlier translators, Gladstone emphasises 'primitive' virtues. As E. J. Feuchtwanger observes, this philosophy casts a virtuous circle around his political convictions, according to which 'the moral sense of the masses' is perceived as 'sounder than that of their social superiors'.[154] Just as the body of the man of letters requires the salutary check of physical exertion, so the body politic needs those employed in the 'toolshop' of the country to be healthy.[155] Belief in this convergence of morality and skill profoundly affects the location of heroism in Gladstone's account. In a typically unconventional reading, he claims that *The Odyssey* sets forth 'the domestic character of Odusseus [*sic*] in his profound attachment to wife, child, and home'.[156] He is a 'model of the domestic affections', a man 'yearning for the day of escape from the arms of a goddess'.[157] The same family-type informs the spirit of a photograph from 1898, which shows the Gladstones – axe-wielding *pater familias* accompanied by sons and wife –[158] arranged around an enormous felled tree [Figure 4.2]. Diary entries, likewise, dwell on 'Treecutting with my sons'.[159] All of this contrasts with Tennyson's Ulysses, for whom home and family are a condition of stasis rather than achieved action ('How dull it is to pause' (22)).[160]

But we should not rule out a Gladstonian variety of self-deception, and even cunning. The 'yearning' to escape mentioned in relation to Circe recalls the mixed motives of his 'rescue work' with prostitutes: '[T]hese talkings of mine', he writes in his diary, 'are not within the rules of worldly prudence'.[161] The word 'prudence' deserves attention here and elsewhere in Gladstone's works. As used in *Homer*, it acknowledges the possibility of a policy that 'leans towards craft' yet avoids outright 'cunning'.[162] And it occurs in his aphorism, 'Liberalism is trust of the people, tempered by prudence; Conservativism is distrust of the people, tempered by fear'.[163] More than a polite substitution, 'Prudence' ventures a middle way. Gladstone's usage steers us towards

Figure 4.2 Photograph of 'Mr Gladstone and Family Felling Trees at Hawarden'. North East Wales Archive

the less subversive elements within the etymology and semantic field of 'cunning'. 'Prudence' also activates the latter aspect of Aristotle's distinction between poesis and praxis (or action): it tells us how to act and how to make decisions.[164] And though it is a politician's virtue, it enters an Odyssean relation with poesis and eloquence. Gladstone welcomes this association, but must accept that the same versatility exposes him and his hero to a broader array of human experience. In this enlarged context, the meaning of 'craft' as a practical value seems more than ever open to question. Either Gladstone must redefine adventure so that it is more narrowly consistent with 'Christian prudence';[165] or some version of prudence must be tolerated that can 'lean towards' without actually succumbing.[166]

The cunning in craft infiltrates the 'canning' of craftsmanship most obviously when wood-chopping becomes an exercise in public relations. Gladstone invites this question on observing that the Homeric monarchs used 'publicity and persuasion' to exercise government.[167] Recalling Abraham Lincoln's propagandist pose as 'rail splitter',[168] Gladstone's woodmanship occupies a related form of political theatre.[169] Wood-chopping, as Matthew notes, was 'a skill well respected in the countryside';[170] and as Peaple and Vincent show, 'to *vox populi*, wood cutting eminently brought out the heroic aspect of their hero.'[171] In these contexts, Gladstone is not so careful to define his terms; and he entertains modes of showing otherwise troubling to the Puritan conscience. These proclivities reflect his own habit of theatre-going – which counts, for Jagger, as an example 'of how he was not beyond compromise.'[172] Joseph S. Meisel also registers this pastime, but goes further in stressing Gladstone's employment of taught theatrical method. He was, he proposes, influenced by eighteenth-century rhetoricians who systematised theatrical gesture.[173] This language of the dispatch box may not translate directly to the woods of Hawarden, but it corroborates a sense that bodily movement – and manual labour – might in its way persuade.

Morley's famous account of the statesman being roused from wood-chopping by a royal telegram bears out these forms of dramatic attunement. Having declared his 'mission to pacify Ireland',[174] Gladstone's words are subsumed back into the mute eloquence of the task: he 'never said another word till the tree was down'.[175] In painting this scene, Morley leans heavily on newspaper reports. *The Times*, most notably, observes that 'The chips that flew beneath the vigorous strokes of Mr Gladstone's axe will long serve as proofs that the retired statesman is still strong enough for other work.'[176] An editorial sketch in the same edition quotes Gladstone's son saying that the display proves his father 'not yet past work'.[177] But 'work', here, is less the object of signification than an idea of 'retirement' recast as activity. While many of the axes that Gladstone received as gifts were cherished as objects of usage, their iconographic function persists in this context: in images of the statesman at work, the length of the blade turns toward the viewing eye, as if appealing to ideas of reform and strong leadership. The axe's nature, in this respect, is rhetorical as well as instrumental, a political function that dawns readily on journalists attending his sylvan shows. *The Times* article even speaks of Gladstone's 'appearance in character' being 'a little overacted', and his silence on political questions a little too complete to be genuine'.[178] Rather than dwelling on primitive virtue and honest labour, the reporter imputes an 'artistic effort', one that 'would have been perfect if we could only bring ourselves to believe in it'.[179] Believability is here compromised by questionable dramatic power, but also by the structural question of whether it is actually appropriate to suspend disbelief.

Despite his best efforts to confine 'craft' to 'prudence' or 'policy', Gladstone's identification with an artisanal hero admits a drift from 'skill' or 'wisdom' towards cunning. His citation of ancient equivalents for his family's involvement in slave-holding likewise commits an evasion: a mode of mercantile cunning that gives the worst work to somebody else. Gladstone's own performance of manual labour, I have argued, seeks no atonement for that family legacy, whether obviously or in veiled ways. Rather, it extends the paternalistic politics of his youth, according to which 'servile' labour paradoxically delivers self-mastery.

Reversals of this kind are relevant, but Gladstone does not reproduce Hegel's master-slave dialectic, within which the roles of 'Lordship and Bondage' are exchanged and synthesised.[180] Instead he relies on a combination of inherited Toryism, Christian submission, and family advantage. The problem, as he sees it, is not that the labouring function – or even the institution of slavery – is intrinsically degrading. As if throwing a moral lifeline to his father, he argues instead that the blame lies with other masters, with cruel masters. His conception of labour, in this respect, is surprisingly feudal: he worries less about freedom and unfreedom than about working conditions and the operation of *noblesse oblige*. In the party-political sphere, Gladstone's woodcraft acquires a distinct valence, which more closely reflects his reputation as a reformer. The spectacle of a senior politician labouring in the woods was not without emancipatory meaning for the millions living by the work of their hands. And there is ample evidence that tree felling retained a private meaning in Gladstone's life: as primal husbandry, as meditative practice, as a method of estate management. This message is inescapably modified all the same once these scenes are mediated, and the actor becomes conscious of an audience. The private meanings of woodcraft give way, in this context, to the partisan theatre of a controlled 'retirement', to a spectacle that closely resembles not just the craftsmanship of Odyssean statesmanship, but its politic embrace of 'publicity and persuasion'.

John Ruskin, Professor of Digging

If, as argued, Gladstone's obvious differences from Carlyle obscure deeper affinities, the position with Ruskin seems quite otherwise. Consciously styling himself Carlyle's literary and political heir, Ruskin claimed that he and his 'Master' were at one in all things, as if in a 'minority of two' (28:15). In fact, the alliance was more complicated than these attestations suggest. Whereas Gladstone's commitment to gymnastic renovation retains an emphasis on Carlylean toil, pain and self-denial, Ruskin associates labour more actively with pleasure. His Scottish affinities are Highland rather than Lowland, and though schooled in Evangelical piety, he emerges free of self-doubt, or any impulse toward self-inspection. Relatedly, he favours social objectives over personal or spiritual trial. In his hands, the labour ethic develops into an exemplary practice, even a mode of teaching, closely tied to a conviction that the work of the hands can be, and should be, a source of fulfilment. God, he claims, 'intends every man to be happy in his work' (12:341). This conception of wellbeing – what Morris would call 'man's pleasure in successful labour'

(22:23) – represents a shift in the development of Victorian work ethics, and a crucial staging post in the cultural legacies addressed by this book. While it places a check on the absolutism of Carlylean labour theory, it also offers a new basis on which physical work can interact with art and 'intellect' more generally. As detailed in what follows, Ruskin probes the limits of this cerebral-physical emphasis in the course of two interrelated labour experiments, the first among his undergraduates at Oxford, and the second at Brantwood, his estate on Coniston Water in the Lake District. The literary significance of each emerges through a dynamic translation of text into agricultural experience, and then of the latter back into the former.

Writing to a family friend, Ruskin confesses a compensatory motive for such thinking. Though admitting that his mother was right in suggesting that his 'weak constitution' made 'athletic exercise dangerous', he laments that she 'lost sight' of 'a very certain truth – that an important part of a man's education is to make him Manly'.[181] As previously discussed, it is not clear that Ruskin means 'masculine' when he attributes this 'manly' aim; he refers, rather, to the danger of cossetting that impedes a child's development of responsibility and resilience. Despite the deficiencies of his upbringing – or, perhaps because of them – he sets great store by self-administered lessons. In *Praeterita* (1886), he recalls his 'original instinct of liking to dig a hole, whenever I got leave' (35:426), a reversion to 'instinct' that effectively by-passes faults of education. Exercising this 'excavatory fancy or skill' produces pleasure; but Ruskin simultaneously insists on its end-use, on its resulting in a 'useful furrow' (35:426). His 'happiest bit of manual work' comes at the behest his mother 'in the old inn at Sixt' (35:428), when, on taking 'the strongest broom I could find', he 'cleaned every step into its corners'. These activities extend deep into adult life, always with a sense that such work is in the nature of play: fun, experimental and operating within safe limits.[182] His main strategy relies on the primacy of personal experience, acquiring tacit knowledge of what others might cultivate in his wake. Before giving advice, he observes, 'it would be well if we sometimes tried it practically ourselves, and spent a year or so at some hard manual labour, not of an entertaining kind – ploughing or digging, for instance' (16:399). A more therapeutic emphasis emerges from the tale told by Ruskin's Venetian friend, Count Zorzi, who finds him one morning 'with a hatchet in his hand', 'splitting certain logs for firewood' (29:19). 'When he had set me a sufficiently good example', Zorzi continues, '[. . .] he advised me to take exercise in the same way from time to time, assuring me that wood-cutting was a kind of gymnastics very beneficial to health' (29:19). The 'play', here, derives from an impression that Ruskin is discovered or embarrassed in the performance of an eccentricity. This gives way, in turn, to a characteristically pedagogic recovery of poise as he goes about setting an example to his friend.

These convictions are not confined to anecdotal recollection, but make their way into Ruskin's more serious aesthetic and economic treatises. As early as *Modern Painters*, he promises gains in 'bodily health' and 'happiness' to the upper classes if – 'however clumsily' – they would make 'serviceable' the physical exertion of their amusements (7:429). A great positive effect will follow, he adds, if 'men undeniably of the class of "gentlemen" [. . .] would [. . .] enter into some of our commonest trades' (7:429). *Munera Pulveris* (1872) spells out a more immediate implication in stating that 'merely rough (not mechanical) manual labour [. . .] *should be done by the upper classes*', since '*bodily health, and sufficient contrast and repose for the mental functions*' are '*unattainable without it*' (17:234–35). In an apparent borrowing from the teachings of Xenophon, and perhaps also Thomas More's *Utopia* (1516), he then resorts to a harsher realism, in stating that 'All criminals should at once be set to the most dangerous and painful forms of it' (17:234). Such work is not suited to those possessing 'lordly' qualities, glossed as 'tending towards rule, construction, and harmony' (17:236). While these class-inflected terms run against the spirit of his other pronouncements, the dividing line depends, crucially, on a reformulated class system that perfectly grades character. An alternative version of the political order emerges, in which Ruskin naturalises social positions according to individual moral capacity.

Less retrograde labour relations inform Ruskin's proposition that 'All professions should be liberal'; and, famously, that 'the workman ought often to be thinking, and the thinker often to be working' (10:210). In this way, he refers the word 'liberal' to its French and Latin roots, implying that freedom and generosity might redeem manual as well as intellectual labours. As such, he upsets a whole tradition of disdain for the work of the hands, running from aristocratic stigmatisation of manual labour in modern Europe, back through Cicero's assertion that 'no workshop can have anything liberal about it', to Aristotle's exclusion of farm hands from the franchise.[183] At issue is the mistaken notion that 'one man's thoughts can be, or ought to be, executed by another man's hands' (10:200). Whereas the alienation of thought is but one instance for Marx of a broader division of roles, Ruskin understands it as the fundamental lapse from which all else follows. Rejecting the supposition that 'manual labour is a degradation, when it is governed by intellect' (10:200), he advances a conception of alienation that stresses the evil in frustrated imaginative capacities. This 'union of brain and handwork' (17:59) – as Cook and Wedderburn call it – runs not just from hand to brain, but also from brain to hand: a denial, in effect, of 'The Platonic separation of knowing and doing' (Arendt), but also a personal enactment of that denial.[184] This – as previously seen – takes the form of a moderating return to the physical, and thereby an avoidance of that 'degenerate state' wherein the scholar 'tends to become a mere thinker' (Emerson).[185] Ruskin likewise argues that '[I]t is only by labour that thought can be made healthy' (10:201); indeed that 'manual work' is 'often in measure refreshing'. Only, this is more than mere refreshment: he proposes no less than a wholesale modification of physical relations to the intellect. Seen in this light, manual labour reveals mental challenges of its own. In *Praeterita*, Ruskin speaks of having 'worked with a carpenter' (35:427) as if recalling the tutelage of the drawing masters employed by his father. Celebrating the levels of skill and mental acuity involved, he applies the language of medieval labour in terming this tradesman a 'master'. Tales of road sweeping work similarly: recalling how he 'swept bits of St Giles's foot-pavements', Ruskin transmutes brooms and trowels into honoured implements requiring nice handling. And he deepens the sense of integrating labour with thought by imagining 'studentships' in the use of these tools.[186] 'The painter should grind his own colours', he explains, and 'the architect work in the mason's yard with his men' (10:201). According to this philosophy, the work of composition becomes intimate with its materials, an insight only available to those schooled in apparently basic and tedious tasks.

When Mahatma Gandhi translated Ruskin's *Unto this Last*, he included a note to the effect that 'the life of the tiller of the soil and the handicraftsman is the life worth living'.[187] This 'life', as Ruskin sees it, is an agrarian affair. In philosophical, as well as technical terms, it is also pre-modern. Having reimagined the feudal order, he engrafts the flexible virtues of Odysseus, evoking a world in which one should 'Teach the plough exercise as carefully as you do the sword exercise' (18:419). Rather than acting externally, the self-culture in this case operates *'inside'* the 'breast' (27:399); and it acts on the symbolic organs of 'lungs' and 'heart' (27:399). The model, here, is 'the broad chest of Theseus [. . .] a hero's heart, duly trained in every pulse' (27:399). Evidently, this recalls Gladstonian heroic culture and martial-agricultural training; but a difference resides in the insistent return to a quality of mind, to 'thoughtful labour' (27:296). These links between field cultivation and education are ultimately enshrined through the work of the Guild of St George – the utopian landholding enterprise that Ruskin founds in 1871 – and its associated Monte Rosa Company. Recent studies by Sara Atwood and Mark Frost offer a detailed account of this subject.[188] My own discussion focuses on the link between agricultural labour and Ruskin's identity as a writer. I am particularly concerned with a mode of intellection that develops 'limbs of mind' (16:366) through the formation of whole landscapes. This interface, between cultivating mental and physical capacity, and shaping space, is no more apparent than at Ferry Hinksey (now, North Hinksey), where Ruskin applied undergraduate labour to the repair of a village road on the edge of Oxford. Traversing this derelict pathway *en route* from Abingdon to Corpus Christi College, he witnessed an opportunity 'to show my Oxford drawing class my notion of what a country road should be' (20:41).

Having mentioned the idea of road-mending in a lecture, Ruskin soon after persuaded two undergraduate friends, James Reddie Anderson and Alexander MacEwen, to recruit participants. They, in turn, would persuade Ruskin to persist when he feared the academic world would think 'he had turned to this experiment of engineering because he could not do the work of his chair'.[189] The 'first list of Oxford workmen' – comprising students gathered at Balliol College on 16 March 1874 – includes 'Anderson, Forbes, Mallock, Wilson, Stuart Wortley, Fitzroy, Hoare, Toynbee, Wedderburn, Montefiore, Vaughan'.[190] (Andrew Lang, Hardwick Rawnsley, and – reputedly – Oscar Wilde, would join them the following year.) On 30 March, Ruskin left for Italy, having directed his gardener, David Downs, to help the undergraduates with practicalities. By 2 May, Ruskin was apologising to Arnold Toynbee for not having kept adequately in contact. Reporters from the national press had visited the site, and letters were exchanged in *The Times* and the *Daily News*.[191] Returning to England on 22 October, Ruskin resumed the 'councils' or breakfasts held in his rooms, and spent a day at the 'Diggings [. . .] with my "merry men"'.[192] The following summer, Ruskin gleefully reported 'gaining influence with the men', and a prospect of the road's completion.[193] The landowner's surveyor inspected the finished works on 20 June, finding that 'The young men have done no mischief to speak of'.[194]

Most existing commentaries on the dig measure its success as a practical venture without fully addressing its character as a labour experiment. A common, and understandable difficulty arises from the confusing array of reasons Ruskin gave for the work. Three distinct objectives appear in a letter sent to Henry Acland: drainage of stagnant water, the restoration of cottages, and simple beautification (20:42). In Ruskin's mind, at least, the practical end of the dig was less crucial than the message of its working process: 'Make what recruits you can', he urged Anderson, 'to the theory that one's chief exercise ought to be in useful work, not in cricket or rowing merely' (37:735). Readers of *Fors Clavigera: Letters to the Workmen and Labourers of Great Britain* (1871–84) (hereafter, *Fors*) were likewise encouraged to 'learn common forge work, and to plane and sew' (29:249). In parallel fashion, Ruskin redirects under-graduate brain-work away from the library towards an arena of social, physical, and intellectual improvement. A recent experience of breaking stones with a 'workingman' in Iffley only sharpened his sense of the accompanying mental difficulty.[195] 'Diggings', he informs Joan Severn, 'involve many questions, and are in fact a business I should like to take up wholly, with no lectures' (23:54). Enlarging the same principle, he tells Anderson that 'the best national forms of education and scholar-ship must begin in agriculture' (37:85), while digging should be viewed as 'an art' (20:43). Some observers obligingly characterised Ruskin as a philosopher of manual labour: Rawnsley, for instance, recalls him 'sit-ting cheerily by the roadside we were improving, breaking stones not only with a will, but with knowledge'.[196] Ruskin, meanwhile, bestows on Downs the title of 'Professor of Digging' (20:44). Apart from suggest-ing what a 'foreman' to undergraduates might be, this sobriquet aptly describes Ruskin himself. In the window of an Oxford shop consecrated to cartoons, 'INO' depicts him with pick and shovel in hand, wearing the incongruous garb of a working man, over the caption, 'President of the Amateur Landscape Gardening Society' [Figure 4.3].[197]

Figure 4.3 Caricature Portrait by INO, 'No. XVI, Great Guns of Oxford, President of the Amateur Landscape Gardening Society', 1874, Ruskin College, Oxford

The caption to Douglas Bliss's cartoon, 'John Ruskin and the Hinksey Diggers' (1863), offers a more pointed view on 'The Gospel of Labour at the Home of Lost Causes: Professor Ruskin Takes a Class Out to Make Roads'.[198] But Ruskin was not really taking his class 'out'. Rather, he was extending the medium of university instruction to encompass a broader field, as if converting the methods of a lecturer – who illustrates points by practical example – into another medium. '[W]hat he said in his lectures,' observe Cook and Wedderburn, 'he always went on to *show*' (20:31). Instruction in this way converges with doing, and labour with illustration. By encouraging his students to 'discover what the work of a day-labourer really was' (20:31), he 'lectures'; or, at least, re-imagines what a lecture might be. This process reaches its culmination and fulfilment at Brantwood, where several of the dig's participants would extend their effort to reunite the word with the world. Initially exemplifying the verbal discourse of academic lectures in the 'practical' environment of a construction site, the point of address soon shifts to a parallel gap between the printed page and a working Lakeland estate. Just as Ruskin would speak of 'reading a building as we would read Milton and Dante' (10:206), so he begins to reclaim and make legible whole landscapes. Brantwood itself was not short of literary associations. It was the former home of the radical printer, W. J. Linton; and Ruskin knew that its lands had been a possession of the Cistercian Order in the Middle Ages. In one lecture, he offers related praise to St Benedict the 'Captain of the Host' of 'the working saints', alongside St Bernard of Cîteaux (33:236). If St Bernard's rule provides a context for the social mission of Ruskin's scholar navvies, and the apportioning of the day, it also sheds light on the connection between estate management and Ruskin's work as a writer.

As previously observed, the literary side of this dual commitment attracts notice as part of the 'writers in their studies' pictorial genre,[199] a journalistic mode that also chronicles Gladstone at Hawarden.[200] An article by Wedderburn, which describes walls 'rightly covered with bookcases and cabinets',[201] witnesses a hub of production whose products are captured as if 'on the bench'.[202] W. G. Collingwood's painting, 'John Ruskin in his Study at Brantwood' (1882) elaborates this sense of a literary workshop.[203] Sitting with quill in hand, Ruskin appears in the centre of a scene of open drawers and discarded sheets. The composition recalls Dürer's 'St Jerome in his Study': here, too, light streams through a window to illuminate the work, while Ruskin's cat appears in place of Jerome's lion. This sense of the study as scriptorium supplements Ruskin's particular method of seizing the day, in a monkish shift-pattern of alternating labour. 'Mr Ruskin rises early', Wedderburn explains, '[. . .] and writes for three hours before his guests are down'.[204] Collingwood, similarly, writes that 'Like Montaigne, he does not pass the night in his study, but takes "to-day" by the forelock'.[205] The other labours of the day emerge through his description of the hall, whose marble table reveals an indicative still-life of 'soft hat, and thick gloves, and chopper', all hinting that 'he has come in from his afternoon's woodcutting'.[206]

Just as at Oxford, Ruskin imagines himself leading a band of amateur navvies. A paper silhouette from the period shows him at the head of a 'working party', climbing uphill with staff and billhook ('chopper') in hand. Rather as Collingwood depicts Ruskin holding a pen in the morning, this instrument reveals the labour of the hour. In the manner of Gladstone's axes, it also gathers a symbolic function. Writing to Susie Beever, Ruskin reports that he 'was all that afternoon seeing the blacksmith make a chopper!'[207] Now housed in the Coniston Museum (19:20), it denotes a preoccupation with the cutting edge – on his estate but also across the history of civilisation, as evidenced by 'axe-hewn church altars' (18:136), and even the 'hatchet edge' (6:228) of mountains. In his most sustained account of sharp-edged tools as gauges of culture, Ruskin explains that 'the characteristic weapon of Hephæstus [. . .] is not, as you would have expected, the hammer, but the clearing-axe, – the doubled-edged πέλεκυς', used by Ulysses to cut down trees (20:247). He repeats this conception in *Fors*, on observing that Richard the Lion-heart's 'main tool' was 'an old Greek one, and the working God Vulcan's – the clearing axe' (27:57). In this way, once again, he reactivates the *culture* in agriculture.[208]

Ruskin's journal entries from the period likewise allude to 'cutting woods', '[c]hopping wood', and 'pleasantest wood work'. Rather than addressing something outside the manuscript medium, they restore the project of hillside clearance to artistry and language. On 8 February 1878, his fifty-ninth birthday, he records being 'down at 7 [. . .] ready either for writing or woodchopping'.[209] The two prospects seem continuous, as if following from the same initial letter along a common path. Clichés recover their material origins only to flow back into metaphor. Ruskin likewise refers to 'the chapter on cleavage for *Deucalion*, and a good deal of practical cleavage in cutting out the lawn-tennis ground'.[210] Equally, an interchange between material and immaterial dimensions animates a letter to Beever: having identified 'Stalk' as 'a Saxon word', he reports that 'I'm finding out a great deal about the thing though not the word, for next "Deucalion," in chopping wood.'[211] Another incursion of woodcraft into letter craft occurs when Ruskin addresses his cousin, Joan Severn, in their accustomed baby-talk, to report 'Mees got such a booty chopper!'.[212] Next to the word chopper, Ruskin pens a likeness of his billhook [Figure 4.4], a tool suggesting the full array of agricultural, intellectual and biological interaction.

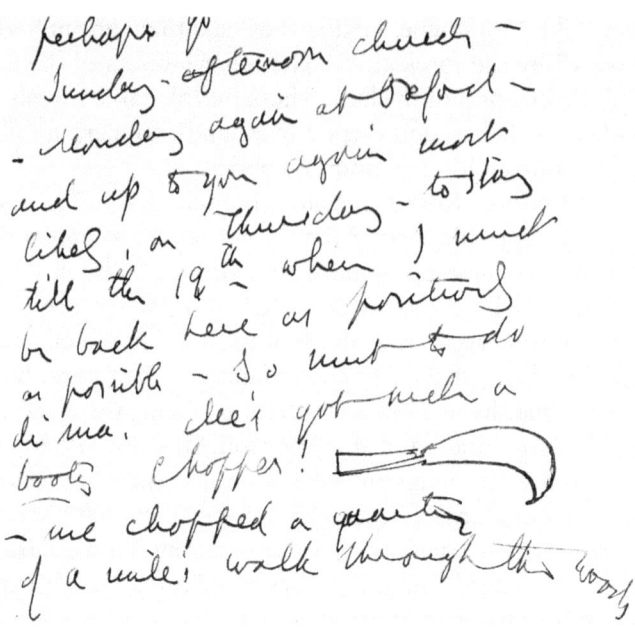

Figure 4.4 John Ruskin, sketch of billhook, pen and ink, detail from 'To Joan Severn' ('Darling Pusiky') (April[?] 1873), The Ruskin: Library, Museum and Research Centre, Lancaster University

Its tang is left anatomically visible deep in the handle, while the pronounced curve of blade recalls the beak, or eponymous 'bill', of the feathered creatures celebrated in *Love's Meinie* (25:1–186). Ruskin writes that the bill represents the whole of a bird's 'economical and practical life', 'at once its sword, its carpenter's tool-box, and its dressing-case' (25:30–31). In *Proserpina*, the link between bird and blade is made more explicit still: there, beaks act 'with two edges vertically, like a knife on a plate or an axe or chopper on a block, the name "bill" being originally given to the weapon from its resemblance to the bills of birds of prey' (15:183). As so often in his writings, an etymological rationale underwrites and naturalises an apparently chance resemblance.

Ruskin also re-prints authors whose works bear on the integration of practical and literary life. Letter 61 (January 1876) of *Fors* announces this agenda, notably the inclusion of 'the two first Georgics' (28:500) among his *Bibliotheca Pastorum*. These literary-agricultural plans come to fruition in a new translation of Xenophon's *Economist* (or, *Oeconomicus*) (31:1–102), chosen as he explains to J. S. Blackie, because 'my own political economy is literally only the expansion and explanation of Xenophon's – and Xenophon's, simply Homer's in lowly and daily practice' (37:550).[213] Ruskin may have quibbled with Gladstone's emphasis on Homer as the root of the Greek divine system, but he shares an urge to celebrate the heroic and domestic economy of the early classical world, most particularly 'the two ideals of Kingly passion and patience, in the stories of Achilles and Ulysses' (36:16, 13). In keeping with the notion that 'the economy of the field is the first science' (36:7), the translation would serve as the first of a series aimed at 'British peasants' (36:9). As such it sheds light on Ruskin's bibliographic efforts to address the work of the estate.[214] Indeed, several key ideas flow from the *Economist* into the projects he carries on at Brantwood. Foremost among these is the principle of benevolent oversight, derived from Xenophon's portrait of rulers who value agriculture as much as the planting of garrisons (31:48). Understanding the productivity of the land as a measure of national virtue, Cyrus works the fields himself, never sitting 'down to dinner without having first earned it in the sweat of my brow' (31:49). And he has planted the very trees of the garden that Lysander admires. Xenophon's dialogue offers guidance not only on farming, but widens its scope in presenting agriculture as a form of 'physical training' that 'makes the overseer more manly' (31:50). Agriculture, so conceived, 'teaches us to help one another' (31:51), and in that respect differs from the competitive world of undergraduate sport or learning. Finally – and in a manner suitably geared to Ruskin's own position – Socrates concludes that 'husbandry is not so irksome to learn' (31:78), and for that reason engenders no jealousy as to trade secrets. In a manner redolent of Gladstone's agricultural displays, 'planting and sowing' are reconfigured as an invitation to demonstrate prowess. Indeed, they are commended to those who 'find especial pleasure in being watched at work' (31:78).

The act of literary translation emerges as a particular locus for combining literary cultivation with soil cultivation. Prescribed by Ruskin as a challenge at one of his breakfasts for Oxford 'diggers' (31:3), the Englishing of Xenophon begins as a challenge to the willing. Answered initially by Wedderburn and Leonard Montefiore, W. G. Collingwood subsequently took the latter's place, and the two men travelled to the Lakes for the summer vacation of 1875. Over subsequent weeks, they fell in with Ruskin's routines at Brantwood (31:18), 'reading it out to him, and he following our translation with the Greek'. If this was the 'morning's work', the afternoon saw them acquiring a more practical training in Xenophon's economics, as they helped Ruskin fulfil a two-year-old plan[215] to build a 'new harbour' (31:18) at the lake edge.[216] This 'Robinson Crusoe' work belongs to a wider literary horizon and symbology.[217] His accompanying sketches exploit a resemblance between the angle of wall against the lake and the curve of a bird's bill (or, billhook). Elsewhere, Ruskin notes that 'The ancients likened the form of this harbour to a sickle, and on the coins of the town we find a curved object, within the area of which is a dolphin' (9:464). Having previously resorted to employing a local farmer's son, the arrival of Wedderburn and Collingwood provided an opportunity to reassert the amateur principle, as well as to resolve any 'interference' (27:505) between literary and practical functions. As Ruskin explains in *Val D'Arno* (1874), 'Intelligent laying of stones is always delightful; but the fancy must not be limited to its contemplation' (23:86–87). Collingwood's playful report that 'the old game of the Hinksey digging was played over again' contains a revealing emphasis on recurrence, a conscious linkage of apparently different contexts.[218] The erection of a scholarly monument – in the form of a translation – closes the circle opened the previous year at Oxford. To this extent, the message of Oxford – where Ruskin calls undergraduates away from lectures – cannot be appreciated without contemplating its conclusion at Brantwood, where the 'laying of stones' reunites with the handling of words.

A broader remit for 'translation' also comes into view, one that reaches beyond Xenophon to include turning students into stonemasons, and back again. Taken together, these metamorphoses belong to a larger effort, by which Ruskin brings literary productions into alignment with his physical and human environment. From the world of the waterside, up through clearing operations on the hills, to the very top of his estate, Ruskin gradually moves, enrolling his household in the channelling of water, in the creation of a moorland garden, and finally in a scheme to grow hardy varieties of wheat. Managed for centuries as coppice land – first by the monks, and then by local charcoal burners and colliers – the overgrown woodland becomes a focus for these efforts.[219] And a related fantasy develops, of 'transmuting ground which never yet, since the mountains were made, has been of the smallest use to man or beast' (30:51). In this respect, too, a connection forms between agriculture and lecturing. When communicating with large audiences, Ruskin would use bespoke models, diagrams and large-scale drawings. In similar manner – as Fiona Loynes has it – Ruskin turns his estate into a laboratory, or 'experimental playground'.[220] In effect, this opens a new chapter on his 'boy-gardening' (35:427).[221] It serves, too, as a kind of surrogate business. Brantwood, after all, was the enterprise into which Ruskin invested funds inherited from his father's sherry concern. By these means, he returns to the soil the capital of a mercantile enterprise. As for Gladstone, then, a memory of commercial 'estate management' haunts the second generation in which the family agriculture assumes a more settled and domestic form. Such haunting precludes the complacent assertion of ancestral or aristocratic logic, rendering each intervention in the landscape an act – necessarily – of self-fashioning. And this self-fashioning bleeds increasingly into landscape design. Ruskin leaves off coppicing, for instance, so that tall, slender stems can grow out in a fashion reminiscent of Botticelli landscapes,[222] and he imagines the terraced garden as 'a paradise of terraces like the top of the purgatorial mount in Dante'.[223] Ruskin also conducts field trials: cultivation without heather burning, for instance, or testing an 'old theory of saving water' using reservoirs.[224] The impulse, as Collingwood astutely observes, is that of a 'civil engineer'.[225] Francis O'Gorman's claim that Collingwood wanted to re-masculinise Ruskin sheds a different light on this comparison.[226] But Ruskin engages in engineering without needing to be an engineer; and the work in question is closer to a kind of model making. Even while forming landscapes, he alters them in controlled conditions, and always in dynamic interplay with a master text or master allusion that binds the conceptual play of intellect into the intelligent laying of stones.[227]

From the apparently various operations of a road dig, of woodcutting, of harbour building, and hillside gardening, there coalesces a consistency and a coherence, underpinned by personal and textual allusion. In the manner of an Oxford 'illustrated' lecture, this combination of translation and construction suggests the artful unity of a cultural product. Like all such creations, it exhibits contradictions and internal tensions. These are evident, not least, in the reliance on professional help, as where Ruskin made Downs available as a 'thoroughly good foreman [. . .] for work too disagreeable for your own hands' (38:89), a fixer able to graft or buy the students out of trouble. And, notoriously, the resurfacing work would quickly disintegrate.[228] Weathering, flooding, and use by heavy farm vehicles hastened a destructive process set in train by the diggers' use of a weak Oxford oolite.[229] In their memoirs, the diggers cited their feeble bodies,[230] an untrained clumsiness,[231] and a failure to master the 'difficult work of stone-breaking' (20:43). Wedderburn reports, relatedly, that 'scoffers (Dons included) used to come and stand on the top of the banks while we dug' (20:43).[232] This sense of being mocked provided a defensive rationale for internalising negative commentary. Wilde strikes the most subversive note. It was not just a technical failure, but a failure of scholarship: 'like a bad lecture it ended abruptly – in the middle of the swamp'.[233] In this way, he invokes only unachieved continuities between working and writing.

But there are reasons to look beyond the dominant view of the venture as a dead-end. Understood as a labour experiment, the skill on show becomes less important than the nature of the encounter. As

Loynes observes, 'the fact that his [Ruskin's] schemes were not always economically successful did not detract from their value as instruments of learning'.[234] Even the difficulties faced by the undergraduates – whether physical or mental – bear out Ruskin's division of the earth's inhabitants into 'the peasant paymasters – spade in hand [. . .]; and, waiting on them all round, a crowd of polite persons' (27:184–85). The dig questions this unfair transaction. The mockery endured by the diggers acquires, in this respect, a sacrificial utility. The new road may have been of limited use, but the processual logic of its construction yields a rich and compensatory meaning. Attending to this heuristic logic – rather than to the technical results – also reveals a more interesting basis for critique. For instance, the theatrical nature of Ruskin's experimental method threatens the distinction he upholds between utility and mere play. Even if the inexact fit is part of the point, the instructive side of 'showing' too easily sheers away from the purported purpose of the 'doing'. The undergraduates' encounter with manual labour entails a mode of 'passing' that reflects, and generates, physical and social awkwardness. The sketch by 'INO' belittles the concept of a playful amateur in similar fashion: ill-fitting clothes suggest Ruskin's unsuitability for the new role, while his ambivalent expression – part visionary gaze, part workaday resignation – punctures the pretension of an ennobling labour [see Figure 4.3]. His superimposed appearance implies a superimposed remit. These effects are matters of perception rather than a witness to Ruskin's intentions; but they disclose the dig's deeper logic, its awkward casting of social and professional roles. In photographs of the working party, contorted postures and expressions express a vaguer sense of contortion, signalled here – but not necessarily resolved – by the diggers' offer of their bodies to the task.[235]

J. Nash's intelligent portrayal of the dig ('Amateur Navvies at Oxford') underscores this sense of spectacle [Figure 4.5]. As Barringer demonstrates, the image comically inverts the scene of Brown's *Work*, and may even be a 'deliberate pastiche'.[236] Both compositions feature a raised bank upon which people are variously idling and spectating. Both make labour – that most unobtrusive and 'natural' of daily activities – an object of public interest, and as such an event. And both feature a group of 'navvies' occupying the centre ground. In Brown's painting, however, the bank falls away to the right, whereas Nash raises it to a commanding position above the action: here, the 'brain-workers' graft, and the labourers watch or lounge. The pattern of inversion is not complete, however. As in the surviving photographs, Nash decks out the undergraduates in white flannels and straw boaters. This observance of social origin subtly invokes Ruskin's original call, for men

Figure 4.5 J. Nash, 'Amateur Navvies at Oxford – Undergraduates Making a Road as Suggested by Mr Ruskin', *The Graphic*, 27 June 1874. © Marcus Waithe

'undeniably in the class of "gentlemen"' (12:343). A more perfect mimicry would efface the meaning of this gesture, so the undergraduates work without resigning their primary identity. In *The Pickwick Papers* (1836), by contrast, Dickens has all the players at the village cricket 'dressed [. . .] in straw hats, flannel jackets, and white trousers – a costume in which they looked very much like amateur stone-masons'.[237] Whether 'amateur navvies' or 'amateur stone-masons' the primacy of resemblance over being is essential to the spectacle. This accords with Ruskin's less flexible observation that 'There is rough work to be done, and rough men must do it' (18:417), in as much as the undergraduates are manifestly not 'rough men', but another fashion of man involved in unaccustomed work. The danger is that casual onlookers miss this meaningful hesitation, and infer a disqualifying premise, a failure to follow through.

These revised, or process-based, outcomes are further complicated by the question of audience. In as much as he predicts or models this in advance, Ruskin envisages a university crowd comprising the students and college fellows attending his lectures. Nash's image includes donnish spectators, but also represents a collection of labourers on the raised bank. Unlike Brown's *Work* – where the brain-workers' attention validates manual work and self-validates intellectual work – this working-class gaze unsettles. Two irregular interpretations arise. Either the undergraduates have been 'found out' in an inauthentic guise: their labour converted into recreation, rather as the ferryman in Morris's *News from Nowhere* (1890) is compared to a 'refined young gentleman playing waterman for a spree' (16:8). Or, a darker comparison forms, not with freely volunteered labour, but with labour commandeered or coerced without pay. In this parallel vision, Downs becomes the overseer of a tied labour gang, working for Ruskin in his capacity as absentee 'master'. This unofficial reading casts the audience of working men as freemen, looking down quizzically on a party of would-be slaves or convicts dressed in fatigues.

Ruskin follows Carlyle in thinking benevolent overlordship preferable to a life under tyrannous contract. In this regard, a Christian belief in the virtue of submission combines with an inherited vein of Scottish Toryism, which detects cant in the liberal preference for impersonal relations over feudal guardianship. Though Ruskin enthusiastically condemns systems in which 'The workman was [. . .] a slave' (10:189), and pities the life of the Helot Greek, he shares with Gladstone a reluctance to condemn slavery in absolute terms. This reflects a deep attachment to principles of household loyalty and obedience – to a non-monetary economy, in short. Though he defends slavery only when its discussion impinges on this feudal principle, there were occasions – as Frost shows – when his negligence, absenteeism and high-handedness caused hardship to his working-class subordinates.[238] Ruskin's visit to Hawarden in 1878 throws these convergences into sharp relief. The episode is pertinent because of a report that 'A third member of the party' was 'welcomed with special warmth as one of the band of Hinksey "diggers"' (36:80), and in the same connection, because of what Ruskin said to his host when he was there. Responding to talk of the 'good work' performed by the Quakers, he remarked provocatively 'I don't think that prisons ought to be reformed, I don't think slavery ought to have been abolished, and I don't think war ought to be denounced'.[239] As Hilton suggests, Ruskin wilfully exaggerates, and indeed contradicts previous statements.[240] Only, exaggeration is also a feature of Ruskin's rhetorical method: one that he uses instrumentally elsewhere to isolate truths and realities. Here, however, he misses the mark, because he misreads the contours of Gladstone's politics. The two men stood closer in these respects than he seems to guess. Ruskin's voluntary economy hesitates, likewise, between a socially integrated labour model and one that recovers virtuous submission from the awkward contingencies of human misery.

At Oxford, and at Brantwood, Ruskin aims to integrate his writings with his deeds. The result is a kind of translation loop, within which he converts the learning of the lecture hall into material that can be laid on road or harbour wall. These activities, in turn, underpin the translation of Xenophon's *Economist*, a work whose content dwells on related forms of social translation. Ruskin likewise re-models landscapes as self-reinforcing texts. In this regard, he achieves a remarkable unity between practical works and the life of the mind, even at the level of the sharp-edged implements applied to clearing his woodland. On the other hand, Xenophon's recommendation of agriculture over mechanical or artisanal tasks interferes with Ruskin's broader support for craftsmanship. Equally, he feels that his writings are not 'working', at least not beyond the experimental zones of his professorship and his estate. The timing of the dig coincided with a period of distress engendered by Rose La Touche's rejection of his marriage proposal. This established a pattern of mental strain, which led after her death to his most serious breakdown, in 1878. Those attending him at that time cite habits of over-work: a labour of mind, in effect, that renders him out of his mind.[241] Ruskin himself queries the diagnosis of 'over-work', insisting that 'I had not been then working more than usual' (19:386). He points, instead, to an alarming impression that 'nobody believed a word' of his books (19:386). His mode of showing by illustration is susceptible, likewise, to semantic interference. 'Work' presents as 'play' when ostentatiously displaced, and 'doing' can become 'acting', or a distasteful 'passing'. Equally, the emphasis on manual intelligence becomes dystopian, or just not credible, when combined with an emphasis on submission or servitude. I have argued, even so, that Ruskin successfully renounces ends in favour of meaningful process; and that he does so while drawing an idea of utility into the ken of intellectual procedures more usually deemed intransitive. In this regard, the problems attending his labour experiments are not easily separated from their achievements.

Morris's Song-Craft

Where William Morris is concerned, the primacy of literary effort is not so certain, and the theatrical nature of the manual component less clear-cut. Nevertheless, a quality of 'passing' is likewise detectable. Addressing the Trades' Guild of Learning in 1879, Morris issued the tentative request, 'Will you, [. . .] look upon me as a craftsman who shares certain impulses with many others [. . .]?' (22:81). Being the Oxford-educated heir to a mining fortune, he knew that his artisanal credentials were peculiar, forced even, and that his wearing a craftsman's smock would always resemble a gesture. Indeed, he sensed the awkward irony of his role in stewarding a tradition created not by middle-class artists, but by the working people of the past. As a writer he stands out, even so, because far from merely performing craftsmanship, he earned his living by practising the applied arts. While Gladstone and Ruskin stressed an invigorating interchange between distinct activities, Morris posited a common fabric, pinned in his case to a closely theorised conception of the poet as all-round maker. Including the poet in this way granted Morris a place to stand, a position of strength from which to survey the wider workshop of his applied activities. Halliday Sparling's claim that 'Morris was master of many [crafts], practising them all at the same time and together' speaks directly to this self-image.[242] In a book notable for such apologetics, Sparling repurposes the phrase 'Master-Craftsman' to signify not an eminent position in the trade, but rather the scope of a consummate all-rounder. In the process, he registers an aspect of Arts and Crafts philosophy that defies not only the industrial division of labour, but also a more traditional emphasis on specialisation. While this breadth complicates relations with the artisanal past, it pays dividends in other areas. In particular, it grants the Morrisian poet leverage to test the technical, ethical and social limits of 'craft', understood here less as a guild secret than as a facet of human creativity.

Morris's attitude to vaticism, most notably, offers an insight into his understanding of artistic creation, and the versions of poetic labour that he wished to disclaim. While Sparling's quotations from Morris's private conversation were recalled at a distance of several decades and without aid of notes, his memories in this area seem accurate in spirit.[243] 'Inspiration be damned for a yarn!', his 'Morris' exclaims, 'It belongs to the mystery-man's bag of tricks'.[244] In as much as 'inspiration' applies at all, it is here converted into a matter of manual intelligence. This account tallies with J. W. Mackail's memory of Morris assailing 'Romantic' theories of creation through the transcribed outburst, 'That talk of inspiration is sheer nonsense [. . .], there is no such thing: it is a mere matter of craftsmanship'.[245] Mackail recalls, in addition, that Morris 'never spoke, or apparently thought, of poetry as involving more than the craftsman's qualities'.[246] A 'trained aptitude of hand' conveys the idea that poetry is a manual endeavour, in which skill meets the resistance of substance. References to 'honest work', and 'sheer honesty and serious workmanship', accord with this notion that physical effort is frank, and so ethically privileged.[247] There is something of this in Morris's bluff tone: his scorn for unwarranted sophistication, or self-evident 'nonsense'. The 'inspiration' model also transfers the source and labour of literary composition away from the poet, and as such mistakes the nature of poetry itself. Poems require individual effort, individual attention, because they are conceived as made things, subjects of human fashioning. Paradoxically, this 'thinginess' implies a path towards textual independence, so that while their inception as works represents an act of will, they gather further value, sophistication and mystery once the 'tools' are put down.

A further pronouncement from Morris's table talk bears on compositional rhythms and the apportioning of the day. Once again, he registers an impatience, a sense that these questions in their essence are simple: 'If a chap can't compose an epic poem while he's weaving tapestry,' he ventures, 'he had better shut up, he'll never do any good at all.'[248] The question shifts in this way from the ultimate source of art – itself a relatively abstract and long disputed matter – to address the versatility of the maker. May Morris alludes to the same question when she examines the 'Bellerophon drafts' meant for *The Earthly Paradise*. Noting the 'places where Morris breaks off at times in the very midst of a passage',[249] she insists that 'holders of traditional views about poetic inspiration [. . .] must modify the imagined picture of their poet in his frenzy of inspiration letting nothing earthly enter into the sacred place at such a moment'.[250] She even dedicates a section of 'Workshop Notes' to manuscript versions of his poems, showing 'his progress as a craftsman'.[251] Hoping to refute her father's reputation for 'easy and unlaboured' work, she sees him 'teaching himself to throw off the hesitations of apprentice-work'.[252] And she stresses 'how early' the poet 'learnt the necessity of matter-of-fact labour in the process of moulding and finishing', conjuring in the process a 'picture of the craftsman, sitting at his task'.[253] Alluding to the illustrations for a planned edition of *The Earthly Paradise*, George Wardle recalls how 'Mr Morris became possessed by the idea of cutting the blocks himself: and he took them all in hand and carried them through'.[254] A mixture of self-determination and chaos informs the prosecution of such tasks, as Edward Burne-Jones makes clear in a sketch of Morris at his carving bench [Figure 4.6].

Staring into the detail of the block, he removes parts of its surface in rough and warm-hearted fashion, as if in anticipation of Walter Pater's claim that all art consists 'in the removal of surplusage'.[255] Discarded burins lie scattered around, displaced by fits of anger or simple distraction. Morris's crossed feet add the sense of a self-comforting physicality harnessed to the mental concentration of production.

This rough-and-ready attitude results from Morris's casual movement between media (10:190). Remarking on his 'breaking off in the sheer middle of the impassioned Sthenoboea's apostrophe to Love',[256] May Morris notes that her father was unusual among 'great poets', in that he 'was liable to be called away to attend to firm-business at many moments of the day.'[257] This does not preclude excellent results, however: he has a

Figure 4.6 Edward Burne-Jones, *William Morris Making a Wood Block for 'The Earthly Paradise'*, n.d., pencil caricature. British Museum

capacity, she insists, 'to take up the thread again without effort or loss of time'.[258] There may be nothing in the nature of poetry that rules out this way of working: registering points in the manuscripts that show Morris breaking off in the middle of things, she restores a workaday context to the apparently seamless published text. In this way, father and daughter dismiss the ruling authority of inspiration, while the metaphor of taking up 'the thread' lends the sense of a flexible and dynamic process not vulnerable to spoiling. Once picked up, the weft takes the same undeviating route through the warp.

This willingness to flout principles of specialisation reflects the Pre-Raphaelite tendency towards playfulness and amateurism. 'The division of labour', Morris declares '[. . .] has pressed specially hard on that part of the field of human culture in which I was born to labour' (22:82).[259] The same condition prevents him 'getting help from others' – prevents him, in short, from serving an apprenticeship, or drawing on the skilled labour of established figures – and compels him 'to learn many crafts' (22:82). A related combination of audacity and heroic revivalism inspires Morris's personal motto, 'Si je puis' [If I can].[260] From Pre-Raphaelitism, he inherits the idea of the mixed media artwork, which re-establishes links – dormant in England since the Reformation – between the written word and the visual arts. But he also understands this free movement between media as a function of the intrinsic challenges presented by the projects in hand. Thus planning an illustrated poem draws his attention to the materiality of books as finished objects, dependent on harnessing different media and different trades; from there, he addresses the other, free-standing objects upon which books depend – the wood blocks, for instance. A book, Morris believes, 'has a tendency to be a beautiful object'; but the common production of 'ugly books' obliges him to abandon the accustomed arena of literary composition, to consider illustrated page setting; and in his last decade, to publish complete volumes through the Kelmscott Press.[261]

Having championed integrated objects, Morris's attention turns to the patterns of integration that might govern a society. In a lecture on ancient Iceland, he alludes to 'the feudal or hierarchical period when manual labour was far from being considered a disgrace'.[262] This historical precedent buttresses an already instinctual preference for a broad distribution of faculties, freeing him to promote a world in which 'the greatest men lent a hand in ordinary field and house work, pretty much as they do in the Homeric poems'.[263] In a manner recalling Gladstone's commentaries on Homer, Morris's translation of *The Odyssey* emphasises an association between versatile leaders and a well-made world. Only here the emphasis is not so much on the democratic credentials of the carpenter statesmen, as on a versatile prowess working above the bedrock of unalienated skill. His Odysseus lives in a 'house well-built' (13:92), its walls consisting of 'ashlar stones close-fitting' (13:340). This vision offers no protection against the sundering forces of epic; and it does not entail democratic principles.[264] It promotes, rather, a unity of domestic and public dignity, an effect that lifts the reader out of the unheroic present into a new economy of value.

Morris's rapid movement between media reflects a belief in the common basis of all crafts, including poetic composition and bookmaking. The portrayal of Bow-may, a female archer in Morris's *The Roots of the Mountains* (1889), tests this principle in a fictional context. 'Even as she was speaking,' we read, 'she had notched and loosed another shaft, speaking as folk do who turn from busy work at loom and bench' (15:334). Eloquence leaves martial prowess undiminished, and in that respect verbal salvos enter ready comparison with the discharge of arrows. This affinity is referred in turn to the world of the spinning shed and workshop, in a further illustration of Morris's interoperable poetics. Several of the anecdotes about Morris's working habits cultivate the same image. In describing Morris's poetry as a 'sub-trade' of manufacturing, Henry James errs by imputing a hierarchy of value; but he rightly registers Morris's radically integrated view of cultural and material production, as well as the question of relations between his poetry and his business activities.[265] As if imagining Morris's likely answer to James, Walter Bagehot remarks that 'the great man himself, William Morris, is composing the drawing-room, as he would do an ode'.[266] Far from seeing his 'trade' as a threat to his genteel status as poet, Bagehot conceives it as a natural accompaniment. If one could 'compose' a drawing-room, perhaps one might also 'weave', 'build', or 'hammer out', a poem. According to Sparling, he would stand 'at an easel or sitting with a sketchbook in front of him, charcoal, brush or pencil in hand, and all the while be grumbling Homer's Greek under his breath'.[267] The alternating stylus, the parallel language – of literature as well as Greek – and the 'unhesitating' productiveness, evoke an ideal of flexible aptitude, one that proposes and vindicates an expansive conception of craft.

The same material-rhetorical affinity underpins connections between composing epic poetry and weaving a tapestry. Aptitude in one craft breeds aptitude in others, leading to cross-fertilisation and a cumulative stock of expertise applicable across different fields (22:82). A sense of how this might work emerges from a letter sent to A. J. Wyatt, a Cambridge don whom Morris charges with supplying a plain prose translation of *Beowulf*: 'I have rhymed up the lines of Beowulf which you sent me', he reports, and '[. . .] should be very much obliged if you could send me some more *as soon as possible*'.[268] '[If] you will supply me with matter', he adds, 'I will undertake to be through in 2 months.' The letter shows Morris procuring literary materials in the same way as he acquires pigments for Morris & Co. In a scene that recalls D. G. Rossetti's satirically incongruous sketch *The Bard and Petty Tradesman*,[269] Morris briskly announces a compositional timetable determined by a need to get the 'product' to market. Wyatt, meanwhile, emerges as a supplier of raw material. In a process far removed from conventional notions of poetic composition, Morris has 'rhymed up the lines of Beowulf'. Embellishments are applied: a process difficult in itself, but routine for a practised craftsman. If not exactly mechanical or thoughtless, the process of conversion evokes the relatively mundane tasks undertaken by Morris's employees, whose work on block-printed wallpaper Peter Floud describes as 'repetitive handwork'.[270] *Rhyming up*, likewise, is a matter of 'mere craftsmanship'.

As previously noted, Morris's emphasis on flexibility and versatility flouts not only modern divisions of labour, but also the lines of specialisation instituted by guilds and livery companies. Indeed, the matter-of-fact practicality of Morris's pronouncements can sometimes feel closer to the tone of a man of affairs than an artisan. Or, rather than channelling the craftsman's accustomed restraint, it evinces a writer's freedom in moving between genres. We might look, instead, to Ruskin's 'confession of imperfection' (10:190) as a measure of his craft affiliations, though not coincidentally it also expresses the vision of a middle-class amateur. The serialised version of *News from Nowhere* contains inconsistencies that might recall the trial and error of handicraft.[271] Only, such errors were common, and did not rely on an ethos of craftsmanship, being more in keeping here with the divided attention of a newspaper editor who was also an author, businessman and political campaigner. There is a fine line, evidently, between errors that reflect the priority of process over premeditation, and those that reflect haste or over-committed energies.

As a claimant to the title of craftsman, Morris knew that his breadth of activity was unusual, unhistorical even. Admittedly, the artisans of the past pursued ancillary trades to support their income – rather as Shakespeare's father would supplement his trade as a glover by dealing in wool.[272] Morris finds some related comfort in the thought that 'The Plays acted on solemn occasions at York and Wakefield were done by the very men who produced the arts of the period, the workmen of the crafts of those places'.[273] But the context here is devotional and seasonal – and so unlike his routine movement between poetry and weaving. By contrast with the specialised organisation of historical work, Morris celebrates artists as 'representatives of craftsmanship which has become extinct in the production of market wares' (22:373–74). Precisely because their historical masters are 'extinct' – and, less avowedly, socially ill-matched – loyalty is owed less to a trade than to a method, or spirit, of work. This privilege entails a responsibility, to 'do our very best to become as good craftsmen as possible' (22:373–74), and to uphold craft values that could not survive under the more concerted pressures of trade. But the source of this mandate – to represent values not directly inherited – is never specified. Indeed, the breadth of the claim, and the cause, reflect a position of self-appointed oversight. In this respect, the 'confession of imperfection' resembles less a description of medieval methods than a convenient warrant for the artist-craftsman's enlarged jurisdiction.

How does this expanded remit translate into the field of literary experience? The poet – unlike the historical craftsman – shares the mercurial attention and range of Morris's modern 'representatives of craftsmanship', but at the same time possesses an antiquity and authority unavailable to the latter. The poet, in this respect, provides a way through. Imbued with the ideal afterglow of an integrated vision, it is a role that confers lineage without the need for apprenticeship. In its Norse version, especially, it encompasses learning and social status.

From this position, the modern artist-craftsman glimpses a more comfortable basis for unified sensibility. In his lecture on 'Early England', Morris states that the Norsemen 'were not ashamed to work with their own hands'.[274] They were warriors, he admits, but also 'shipwrights, housebuilders and armourers', and 'almost every one could settle a copy of verses on occasion'.[275] The expansive root of the word *craft*, in the Germanic *kraft* ('power'), informs his confidence in making this case.[276] As Ian Felce claims, it seems likely that Morris's understanding of craft as a matter of 'agency and efficacy'[277] derives from 'his acquaintance with the Old Norse word *kraptr* or *kraftr*'.[278] This attribute consequently secures a connection between poetry and a broader creative potency, while offering a bridge between Morris's status as a powerful man – able to move between different contexts – and the artisanal spirit he hopes to harness. Felce's quotations from G. Vigfússon's Old Icelandic-English dictionary are pertinent: they include the compound nouns '*krapta-skáld* (literally a "power-scald" i.e. a "poet whose song has a magical power") and *krapta-maðr* (a "strong" or "powerful" man)'.[279] In these ways, a conception of the poet as *skáld* [bard] binds intermingled forms of 'skill', 'power', and 'magic'. This vision acquires a central place in Morris's cultural theory, signifying an imaginative freedom that might, eventually, be shared among all craftspeople.

But how should we understand the undiminished power of this figure in the modern age? Both before and after his conversion to socialism, Morris conceives handicraft as an exemplary practice pending fulfilment, a holding position, necessary until a larger reformation of conditions can take effect. The poet in this account works beyond that scheme, as if an ensign for the future integration of artistic, social and political power. Morris nevertheless confers a capacity to stand apart, drawn from a conviction that words belong to craft, and that craft is unalienated when practised outside the commercial system by artists in touch with the old unities. Although Morris leaves no comprehensive statement of this compositional theory, a reasonably coherent picture emerges from his table talk, and from the reports of people who knew him. As noted, he rejects 'inspiration' in favour of a poet's necessary 'craftsmanship'. But this seems less a poetic 'Gospel of Work' – whereby poetry is recruited to work's position as a personal and social value – than a statement of poetry's source in human fabrication. As such, its interface with cognate activities extends beyond the 'sister arts' of Pre-Raphaelitism to include the sister crafts. All the while, Morris rejects analogy in favour of identity: poetry is not just 'like' weaving, but consists in the same substance as other crafts, and in the same labour process. Even if the materials are different, a deeper structure binds. It is tempting to read a poetics of interruption into Morris's pattern of work. Only, the movement away from poetry towards some other craft is not experienced as a decided break. Applying a slightly different model, Stephen Arata has characterised this tendency as a matter of 'diffused attention', understood as a virtue arising from Ruskinian work-pleasure, and perhaps inspired by 'the practice of many traditional craftsmen [. . .] of propping up books beside them to read while they worked'.[280] While this speaks suggestively to Morris's flexible powers of concentration, Arata's emphasis on cognitive operations and the 'acting up' of weavers' self-education does less to catch the implied equivalence between operations: the invented, rather than 'traditional', sense that lessons learned in one medium are routinely applicable in others, so that the trades comprise not a series of 'other things', but a single field of attention.[281]

Walter Crane once claimed that Morris 'had a textile imagination', in that 'his poems and romances seem to be woven in the loom of the mind'.[282] The craft of weaving certainly exemplifies this sense of an intrinsic affinity between poetry and the 'lesser arts'. And the 'loom of the mind' is a helpful and arresting figure: it captures Morris's determination to manipulate otherwise abstract qualities of imagination. Weaving, after all, offers a seductive counterpart to the poet's craft: etymologically, the word 'text' derives from the 'tissue of a literary work (Quintilian)', or 'that which is woven, web, texture, f. *text*-, ppl. stem of *tex-ere* to weave' (*OED*). On giving a weaving demonstration at the Arts and Crafts Exhibition of November 1888, Morris announces himself 'the author of *The Earthly Paradise*', and in so doing performs a basis for these connections.[283] The Burne-Jones sketch of this escapade emphasises not only the theatricality of working in front of an audience, and the frame's curious hesitation between classical pediment and scaffold, but also the less calculated display of Morris's nailed undersoles, his workman's boots [Figure 4.7].

Unlike Brown's 'brain-workers', this presentation has Morris unselfconsciously meeting the challenge of the work, rather than the eye of the onlooker. He was not, of course, the first to explore affinities between weaving and poetry: the example of Dante – a poet featured among the Pre-Raphaelite canon of worthies – demonstrates a longer history, as well a source of influence. Building on Robin Kirkpatrick's discussion of Dantean composition,[284] Michael Hurley characterises the *terza rima* of the *Commedia* in ways that speak to Morris's idea of a poetry consisting of woven stuff.[285] If Dante's preference for craft over mercantile transaction offers a precedent for seeing poetry and textiles as involved in a functional relationship, it also illuminates the civilisational import of an otherwise commonplace comparison between texts and textiles.

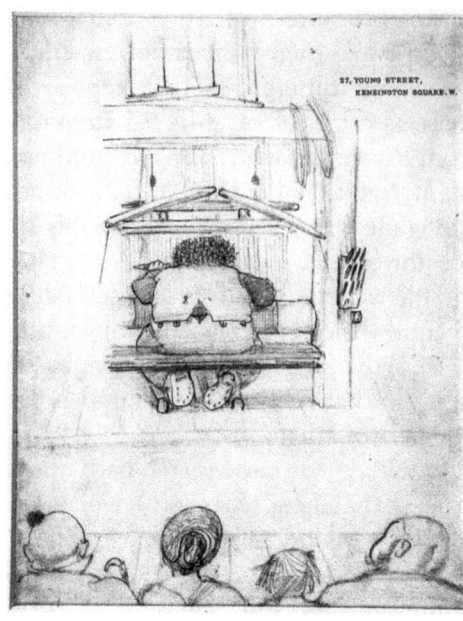

Figure 4.7 Edward Burne-Jones, *Caricature of Morris giving a Weaving Demonstration*, n.d. William Morris Gallery, London Borough of Waltham Forest

For Ruskin, likewise, 'the disuse of the spinning-wheel' (30:328) is a sign of national decline. 'Athena holds the weaver's shuttle,' he explains, 'not merely as an instrument of *texture*, but as an instrument of *picture*', where 'picture' stands for the interest of art-loving societies in 'household pictures, from the web of Penelope to the tapestry of Queen Matilda' (20:269). Morris ranks tapestry as the 'the oldest way of ornamenting a cloth', to the extent that 'The figured webs of the Homeric poems were probably of this kind of work' (22:272). The last allusion evokes a kind of *mise en abyme*, where a textile-resembling literary text contains within itself a textile committed to representational art. In the process, Morris imputes a substantial and historic quality, moving as he subsequently does to the British Museum's 'scrap of cloth of the ancient Central American civilisation so woven' (22:272). The 'figured web' expresses in this way an embedded and enmeshed artistic philosophy.

This sharing of characteristics between poet and craftsman acquires particular importance in the matter of analogies between artistic and divine creation. The capacity of warp and weft to simulate not just pictures, but to gather worlds from two dimensions, becomes a way of conceiving poetry's own conjuration of the complete vision. As discussed, Morris advances this agenda not by resorting to a supernatural theory of composition, but by removing the distinction between craft and magic, between divine creation and human creation. *Sigurd the Volsung* (1876) – a free adaptation of *Volsunga Saga* – contains the most probing expression of this notion. It opens with a description of the Volsung ancestral dwelling:

> There was a dwelling of Kings ere the world was waxen old;
> Dukes were the door-wards there, & the roofs were thatched with gold;
> Earls were the wrights that wrought it, and silver nailed its doors;
> Earls' wives were the weaving-women, queens' daughters strewed its floors,
> And the masters of its song-craft were the mightiest men that cast
> The sails of the storm of battle adown the bickering blast (12:1).

The poem apportions roles among the Volsungs in unfamiliar ways: dukes are also 'door-wards', earls' wives double as 'weaving-women'. Far from contracting dishonour, this association of craft and government enhances individual social dignity. The reader, meanwhile, could be forgiven for confusing this 'dwelling of Kings' with the poem's entire epic universe. Morris's description fills out all available space, accounting for each and every detail in a conventional but necessarily expansive way. Just as the production of a carpet infused with fancy and intellect is a potentially world-transforming event, so this description traces the Volsung world back to a series of human craft acts. The magical or divine business of creation combines in this way with artificial forms of human production. Importantly, it is an effort communally expressed. It differs as such from the condescension or whim discerned by Browning's Caliban, who complains that 'it pleaseth Setebos to work, | Use all His hands, and exercise much craft' (185–86).[286] In Morris's vision, by contrast, the craft-as-creation model operates from the ground up.

Morris's *Iceland Journals* include descriptions of landscape that compare geological features to the constructed forms of human houses (8:76).[287] While this conceit domesticates an awful magnitude, it also construes mountains as architectural forms. The Volsung world is likewise the work of craftsmen, a made thing that spurns the potent mystery of Setebos's agency. As these lines from *Sigurd the Volsung* demonstrate, Morris goes beyond even the quaintly generative acts of the King James Bible, according to which 'God made the firmament, and divided the waters' (John 1. 7):

> Day-long they fared through the mountains, and that highway's fashioner
> Forsooth was a fearful craftsman, and his hands the waters were,
> And the heaped-up ice was his mattock, and the fire-blast was his man
>   (12:103–04).

'[T]hat highway's fashioner' implies a single world-maker, but also allows the possibility that different 'highways' are the work of different craftsmen, an implication that closes the gap between a house wrought by 'weaving-women' and the world itself. A sense of the metaphorical nevertheless preserves the alterity, or magic, of this handicraft. Its author is 'fearful', and its instruments in 'hands' and 'mattock' sound more like figures than literal implements.

As 'song-craft', the poetry that animates this world enjoys an equivalence with the work of those house 'wrights' who are also earls. The 'lesser' and 'greater' arts converge, in this way, so that the poet contributes to the fashioning of all things: not just 'songcraft', but 'Tales of the framing of all things and the entering in of time' (12:4). While the bards who service these yarns are powerful ('the mightiest men') and brave ('that cast | The sails of the storm of battle') (12:1), a consolidation of 'song' and craft extends and dignifies the role of poetry. The physical world assumes associated qualities in the telling. Thus, for instance, in 'The sails of the storm of battle adown the bickering blast', 'bickering blast' confers a rhetorical quality on the tempestuous wind. And the physical space of a 'garth' acquires an association with 'rhyme', complicated in turn by an organic capacity for 'blossoming'. In these ways, Morris imagines a 'songcraft' that punctuates, rather than simply recalls, the 'entering in of time'.

The forms of potency associated with *kraptr* embrace both the idea of consummate skill, and the possibility of magic. In this regard, Morris sails closer to the wind than does Gladstone. Indeed, he actually admires the shifty side of Odysseus's character. In his own translation of Homer, the relevant epithets are largely positive in tone. His hero is 'the wise-heart, crafty of lore' (13:325), 'the Shifty, the man who wandered afar' (13:1). He likewise embraces connections between intellectual wiliness and skill in handicraft. In the course of shaping a bed-post, Morris's Odysseus 'lopped away the boughs of a long-leafed olive-tree, [. . .] shearing the bole from the root up full well and cunningly' (13:340). The connection, here – between prowess in handiwork and a kind of opportunistic acuity – is unmistakable. As noted above, the same sympathies condition Morris's fondness for the 'fascinating drolleries of Brer Rabbit and Brer Fox' (12:17–18), and the antics of Tom Sawyer, notably his ruse in 'deputing his labour, so that his neighbours ended by struggling for the privilege of working for him' (12:20). In 'moments of naughty exaggeration', May Morris recalls, her father declared this a '"little lesson in economics" [. . .] worthy of Odysseus' (12:20). Writing on the same literary type, Carl Jung argues that '[a]nyone who belongs to a sphere of culture that seeks the perfect state somewhere in the past must feel very queerly indeed when confronted by the figure of the trick-ster'.[288] This yields a striking definition: if Morris's medievalism avoids simple-minded nostalgia, he nevertheless admires perfect states, as well as aspects of the feudal past. Far from just feeling 'queerly', though – or seeking to exclude this influence – Morris deliberately admits the trickster.[289] A 'little lesson' suggests a course of instruction, perhaps on the folkloric origins of capitalistic behaviour. It also recalls the title of Morris's 'A King's Lesson' (1888), a parabolic short story whose more orthodox resolution, to 'make an end of the craft of kings and of lords and of usurers' (16:297), prompts the notion that 'there should be but one craft in the world, to wit, to work merrily for ourselves'. While this allusion to kinds of 'craft' forges a distinction, it also acknowledges the word's amplitude. Moreover, the Tom Sawyer school of trickery persists beyond the folkloric phase into the formalised and respectable era of bourgeois life: it is 'like an old river-bed', as Jung observes, 'in which the water still flows'.[290] Equally, there is something more to the antics of Tom Sawyer than a warning, something that exceeds an instrumen-tal purpose: Morris also seems to be entertained. Merriment, in this respect, characterises not only the craftsman, but also the modern sole trader in cunning.

This occasional tolerance of the 'naughty' leads to a more straight-forward admiration of audacity in literary heroes. Wilde notices it on observing that 'Athena laughs when Odysseus tells her "his words of sly devising," as Mr William Morris phrases it'.[291] Arguing that great liter-ary works are more properly considered the product of whole societies than individuals, Carlyle likewise offers the example of the 'craftsman', or 'the smith', whose 'cunning methods' consist – quite legitimately – in passing off the communal effort as his own: 'how little of all he does is properly *his* work!' (5:98). By way of illustration, he remarks of the *Divina Commedia* that 'only the finishing of it is Dante's' (5:98). Carlyle's point is that we admire such works no less for that knowledge. Even where matters of production are concerned, a frisson of primitive naughtiness attracts respect. As the case of Tom Sawyer suggests, this recognition leads to a cathartic acknowledgement of capitalism's dan-gerous appeal. The 'little lesson' in question refers, then, to self-knowl-edge. Morris delivers just such a lesson in *News from Nowhere*, in the form of an 'old grumbler', who resembles the author, while mourning the loss of the 'spirit of adventure' (16:149) that animates literature in the old days of 'good sound unlimited competition'.

In *Sigurd the Volsung*, Regin most clearly embodies the compellingly dark side of human ingenuity. A failure to combine craft with martial prowess throws his character out of balance, compromising the 'integrity' of his aims and his craftwork. As such he stands apart from the more love-able Odysseus. Excellence of fashioning, it follows, may not always work in the service of truth. Even here, though, Morris evinces a kind of respect. Employing a Chaucerian blazon to introduce Regin's character, he reveals an uncomfortably close alignment of policy, rhetoric, craft and poetry:

> [T]he lore of all men he knew,
> And was deft in every cunning, save the dealings of the sword:
> So sweet was his tongue-speech fashioned, that men trowed his every
>   word;
> His hand with the harp-strings blended was the mingler of delight
> With the latter days of sorrow; all tales he told aright;
> The Master of the Masters in the smithying craft was he;
> And he dealt with the wind and the weather and the stilling of the sea
>   (12:62).

Morris does not forget what draws us to Regin. The phrase 'tongue-speech' verges on tautology, but with its union of the tool (tongue) and the product (speech) it discovers something admirable in the execution, drawing attention to the 'made' quality of Regin's beautiful lies. While 'competition' informs the less wholesome side of a positive category, such as 'adventure', cunning emerges equally as one aspect of a larger category, in craft. The key, perhaps, is not to isolate virtues from vices, or to tolerate a social order in which cunning operates free of craft's productive energies. Odyssean cunning seems less 'modern' than that of Regin. But in both cases we recognise a troubling convergence between 'competition' and 'cunning', each of them mutually attractive.

Equally, Morris's interest in the relationship between textiles and the 'stuff' of the imagination encourages him to confront literature's trickier associations (20:274).[292] His ambiguous characterisation of Circe, who first enchants and then aids Odysseus's men, is indicative. In Morris's translation, the advance party of sailors finds a 'goddess or a woman' (13:142), 'where a great web' she 'was weaving and singing shrilly-clear'. The dimensions of this web overwhelm the sailors' hold on reality, and we are put in mind of a spider's web. Circe, it follows, is a sorceress who passes her time in composing a deadly fantasy in thread. The initial uncertainty about whether she is a mortal keeps alive a connection with specifically human treachery. In the story of Penelope, Morris exploits a further opportunity to combine ideas of false construction with steadfast loyalty. Famously, she delays the suitors in setting 'to gear a great loom' (13:280). Morris has her 'Stay the urging on of my wedding till this web to an end I have sped' (13:280). The effect is to re-domesticate the hall, to reinstall her own work in favour of male urging, while the growing shroud for Laertes sets up a rival narrative – an act productive, albeit mournful – in place of the suitors' wasting designs. Penelope's craftwork may represent a wholesome rejoinder to the bullying of the suitors, but as the lines run on Morris refuses to disguise its connection with secrecy and deceit: 'And through the day my weaving in the mighty loom I plied, | And undid my web in the night when the torches were set by my side' (13:280). Undoing diurnal labour in this way, Penelope stages a kind of anti-production through nocturnal unpicking. Her defence lies in securing Odysseus's interests while he is abroad. He, in turn, spares her the wrath of his homecoming. The difficulty remains that she has 'beguiled them': in effect, she has combined the domestic with the deceitful. This characterisation evidently places her among the beguiling witches who preoccupy the Pre-Raphaelite imagination. As Nina Auerbach shows, such treachery – closely entwined as it is with 'women's work' – draws on a mythic anti-feminism that also discloses a 'dangerous mobility', an 'otherworldly power'.[293]

While such dynamics are often active in Morris's work, the case in relation to textiles presents complications. He was, after all, a weaver himself. And his interest in the convergence of craft and cunning extended – like his own activities – beyond woven contexts. Writing about the Norsemen, for instance, he raises the matter of irregular offensive methods. He begins by excusing their using 'these weapons of deceit', on the basis that 'when they do it is an act of war'.[294] Penelope's domestic craft likewise harbours just and warlike intention. As if to clinch his point, he introduces a Homeric parallel:

> [C]ompare the curious passage in the XIII book of the Odyssey where Athene, a Goddess, is delighted with Odysseus for telling her an intricate series of lies; which indeed he is always doing, and cannot even resist the temptation of one last lie at the expense of his poor old father, which from my modern point of view I really think was too bad: again in book XIX Autolycus, Odysseus' mother's father, is spoken of as outdoing all men "in thievery and skill in swearing," clearly with approval.

Odysseus fibs in pursuit of strategy; but he is also an inveterate liar, one who tells lies for the sake of lying. Morris recognises as much when drawing a contrast with 'the Northman' who 'would not lie to his friend and still less to himself'.[295] The Greek hero, he goes on, 'cannot even resist the temptation of one last lie at the expense of his poor old father'.[296] Hence the exasperation in 'I really think was too bad', a clause that evinces the kind of disappointment caused by an unruly friend. So, while Penelope's actions are compatible with the code of 'the Northman', her own husband practises a more gratuitous form of deceit. He gets away with it, though, and the double-standard goes unexplored. A fairer study might cast an audacious heroine of the Becky Sharp type – whom Thackeray likewise associates with the devious textile arts, in 'little Circe's toils'.[297] Morris's omission discloses a further double-standard, or at least a kind of differential tolerance, operating at the heart of his fictional and political economy. Morris recalls and condemns 'the modern method and the parent of all falseness', what he terms the legitimised swindling of modern capitalism. Even so, he remains susceptible to the trickster-hero's appeal, to a figure who cannot help himself, who 'cannot even resist the temptation of one last lie'. As his reference to Tom Sawyer confirms, he understands and senses the conflict; indeed, his airing of it in the safe environment of the family group might be taken as acceptance of the bargain.

Further complications arise when Morris examines the particularities of weaving as a technique and a medium. Even in its primitive state, the work of the loom resembles a mechanical product. This means that it resists the kinds of personal finish applied by the human hand. As Morris explains, weaving is 'not so much of an art as pottery and glass-making, because so much of it must be mechanical' (22:249). And yet, he adds, 'it produces beautiful things, which an artist cannot disregard' (22:250). Aside from the compensation of beauty, the problem of machine-monotony is overcome as Morris appreciates 'the web growing day by day almost magically' (22:250). Such magical growth provides an intriguing commentary on the exclusion of divine acts from the Volsung world, where manual effort becomes independently generative. Later in this passage from 'The Lesser Arts of Life' (1882), Morris invokes other sources of romance, among them the pleasure of working 'in a pleasant place' with 'a book or two to be got at' (22:250). Mechanically-generated magic evidently makes weaving a special case. As such, it unsettles the assumption that craft always depends on the human hand.

Conscious of the danger in this drift from human agency to the magic of automation, Morris reinstates an idea of 'integrity' more redolent of Gladstonian thinking. '[T]he real way to deal successfully with designing for paper-hangings', he contends, 'is to accept their mechanical nature frankly' (22:260). Thus a return to Pugin's insistence on the declaration of structure – on rendering 'the *useful* a vehicle for the beautiful' – mitigates the moral and aesthetic harm threatened by a necessary evil.[298] He also attempts to backtrack. Seeing no reason to 'doubt that mechanical pattern-weaving was practised by the Greeks in their earlier and palmy days' (22:273), he guesses that this would have been restricted to 'the simpler kinds of patterns in piece goods, diapers, and so forth.' This leaves room for more personal agency in the creation of sophisticated pieces.

Eventually we reach a pared down and specialised version of the craft, distilled to its human essence,[299] at which point, Morris concludes, 'we no longer need the help of anything that can fairly be called a machine' (22:251). The only equipment required is 'a frame which will support heavy beams on which we may strain our warp' (22:251). In these conditions, he assures us, 'our work is purely handwork' (22:251). Such distinctions are evidently unstable, as John Henry Dearle – Morris's textile designer – would acknowledge on reporting how 'At the site of ancient Carthage (55 BC) has been discovered the remains of a loom which had been capable of utilising power and which seems to have anticipated many of the mechanical contrivances which have been applied to looms of the 19th century'.[300] Moreover, there is special pleading in Morris's 'anything that can fairly be called a machine', in that 'fairly' simultaneously registers and dismisses the possibility that 'a frame' put to this use could be called a mechanised aid. When discussing 'tapestry-weaving' (20:194), he likewise argues that art 'has thrown aside all mechanical aid [. . .], its loom being a tool rather than a machine' (20:194). He relies, as such, on an unspecified philosophical difference between 'tool' and 'machine'. A 'tool', we infer, lacks the deceptive qualities reserved to machines. It also lacks the machine's demonic capacity, its imagined self-will. A tool, moreover, transfers human intent, and a human imprint, on to the workpiece so as to insure against magic or misdirection. However this may be, a primitive loom is not wielded in the manner of a conventional tool, as it does not require continuous contact. By definition, it stands apart. Even if originally guided by hand, the shuttle's subsequent lift into flight, with the industrial age, evokes a potential for independence. This troubles, or at least tests, the distinction that Morris hopes to maintain. All the while, he admires the 'magical' growth of the web, so that one can connect even these thorny matters to the larger question of trickery and the trickster in literature, and indeed to the author's dependence on the same qualities.

Morris's admiration for poetic audacity may seem at odds with the working model of literature discussed in previous chapters. Celebrating craft values in literature does not, for him, mean suppressing an unruly element. On the contrary, he recognises a vaunting quality in characters as well as in writers, so that while literature may be 'a mere matter of craftsmanship', it is not by extension 'laboured'. The connection between cunning and deceit proves less easy to police. In the case of Penelope, the tricky expedient of undoing work in a good cause finds itself enmeshed in the textures and textiles of a legendary female deceit. In the case of the Norsemen, Morris identifies similarly irregular methods, which are likewise reserved exclusively for war or the defence of family. The problem, for Morris, is that Odysseus – as the chief representative of the craft-cunning nexus – rarely respects this idea of a last resort. More than the means to an end, lying for him stands closer to a compulsion, even an art form. Morris hardly approves of this behaviour; nor, indeed, does he regard lying as a synonym for art itself, in the manner of Wilde's satirical dialogues.[301] Rather, he recognises an irregular tendency, a glitch that works alongside the virtues of handicraft, carrying the potential to generate either magic or runaway automation. Just as Morris allows 'Odyssean lies' into *News from Nowhere*, so he knows that art cannot be kept pure or unsullied without losing its essence. Equally, he appreciates that the 'resistance' of a raw material cannot be eliminated without fashioning something bland and lifeless. This generates, in effect, a work ethic accommodating of craftsmanship and audacity, vitality and risk.

* * *

The three parts of this chapter draw together a broad professional and social range, as well as diverse artistic and generic preferences. Each case details an attempt, all the same, to reconcile poetic, governmental, and intellectual practices with the 'honest' qualities of physical labour. Manual work figures notably as a personal action and a public spectacle, susceptible less to 'proof' in the manner of Brown's legible sinews than to a living embodiment of dual faculties: an exemplary performance, in effect. Gladstone's Homeric ideal of the warrior-worker king inspires his conception of an integrated personality, and he profits from Benedictine principles of alternating occupation. Only, a selective relationship with these models, and a determined exclusion of cunning from statecraft, embroil him in ethical complications, and irregular forms of inheritance. Even when 'retired' from politics, amidst the rhythms of the Hawarden day, his occupations are shadowed by the legacy of his father's mercantile guile, and his enslaved workforce. These circumstances impart a dark edge to the voluntarism underpinning his ideal of the complete statesman. Gladstone cannot be accused of cynicism or flagrant manipulation, but the positions and poses he adopts – as dutiful son, as politician, and as woodman – never diverge from his personal and political interests.

Ruskin's relationship with voluntarism is similarly troubled and troubling: he prefers unpaid service to wage labour;[302] and through a curious mixture of feudalism, chivalry, and primitive communism, imagines freedom as the fruit, rather than the bane, of a bonded position. His concern to shape landscapes in the image of texts – and people in the image of ideals – ensures controlled conditions for his experiments. A sense of control arises, likewise, from the fantastical premise that a new edition of Xenophon would be read by British peasants. When the laboratory conditions lapse, though, the results are revealing, as when his road-making undergraduates find themselves observed by agricultural labourers. It is not that Ruskin avoids such encounters: the pages of *Fors* encourage just this meeting of minds. But the presence of a working-class gaze in Nash's composition prompts an irregular thought: that 'amateur navvies' are not constructive imposters, at all, but class enemies employed in unfair competition or some form of strike breaking.[303] In all three cases, an effort to spread faculties widely, to combine brain with brawn, while replacing payment with service, throws up problems of placing and performance: a nervousness about fugitive identity issuing from others, but also a preoccupation with authority and control embedded in the primary vision. Apart from revealing a persistent rigidity, affecting the mid-Victorian philosophy of integrated faculties, this last aspect bears on my final chapter and its discussion of similar concerns among poets and artists of the early twentieth century.

Whereas Gladstone understands woodchopping as a revitalising break from literary researches, Morris posits a fundamental similarity between these activities. The irony, as demonstrated, is that this capacity to move between different crafts and different media is fundamentally a modern development: that is, a symptom of Morris's historical moment and social position, rather than anything sanctioned or predicted by the guild system. Morris's defiance of specialisation is at once a condition of his unapprenticed status, and a mark of his class position. To the figure of the poet, like the gentleman artist, he accords an unusual level of immunity: exemption from divisions of labour, from commercial pressures, from boredom even. Nor, in his mind, are poets justified in fretting over their working status. Even if besieged by hostile forms, the modern bard remains for Morris a proud survivor, a figure capable of exercising general competence across different media, a figure who possesses and preserves powers destined to be shared by all. He never flinches, even so, from the possibility that craftsmanship might shift into a realm of unsettling artifice and cunning, and this, too, reflects his insistence on a labour of mind. Such magic is sometimes figured as the opposite of manual craft, as an anticipation of automation, and by extension of machine-minding. But craft itself has dealings with sorcery: a fact revealed by the slippery distinctions between artifice and cunning, machine and tool. Morris does not entirely break the presumption that manual labour is healthy, and literary activity suspect; but he accepts that both entail moral risk, and that this risk dwells in an attribute too valuable to be excluded.

PART III
CRAFT CONSCIOUSNESS

Even where the emphasis of previous chapters has been on sheer toil or invigorating labour, my examples have been closely tracked by discourses of manual skill and apprenticeship. Part III considers a more fully realised version of this craft-consciousness, where the emphasis falls on the associated malleability of words. Chapter 5 explores the most popular of these literary-artisanal tropes: namely, the implied connection between the writer and the blacksmith. Running from late Dickens, through late Ruskin, to Hopkins, it demonstrates a common attraction to the idea of the literary artificer, albeit one that is troubled by the forge's Promethean glow. While Salmon demonstrates the foundational role of 'Carlyle's invocation of literary 'guilds' and 'apprenticeships' in *Sartor Resartus*',[1] the following discussion reveals how these models became instrumental at the level of their linguistic tooling. This effect is also derived from Carlyle, but rather than feeding into the novelistic tradition of self-development, it fosters here a resurgent trope of linguistic making, which gradually intersects with the Arts and Crafts movement in the last decades of the century. The chapter charts an early encounter between these approaches through the pages of Dickens's *Great Expectations* (1861), a novel highly sensitised to languages of labour, but also – as we shall see – to distinctions between licensed and unlicensed tooling.

The stakes involved in this turn towards literary handicraft are worth considering. Reflecting on a fashionable turn towards artisanal versions of literature, David Masson observes in 1873 that the 'poems and songs' of the Anglo-Saxons 'were *made* – were actually fabricated for them out of their language by word-smiths'.[2] Masson's last term appears in the *OED* as the first instance of its use. As such it evokes the period's revived interest in Old English, a language whose compound methods of word formation inspire both the morphology of this coinage, and an associated challenge to reified distinctions between culture and craft. Such thinking inspires, in turn, a new generation of 'word-smiths', each of whom presses archaic linguistic resources into the service of analogies between literary composition and metalwork.[3] Addressing the 1850s – specifically the battles to establish authorial property – Pettitt notes that 'authors risked unmasking Romantic ideas of autonomy and spontaneous creation, and exposing the more homely craft of the writer beneath'.[4] In subsequent decades, as my examples suggest, a new generation adopts a less embarrassed attitude towards 'homely craft'. Far from taking strategic refuge in Romantic ideas, they attack them. In broad terms, though, Pettitt's point holds true: any departure from a mixed model is a risky strategy. This part of the book attends to the gains and the losses involved in lodging occupational value in one place, as well as the ways in which craft 'magic' smuggles in through the back door some of the potency associated with earlier discourses of 'spontaneous creation'.

Chapter 6 explores the continuing influence of these ideas in the early twentieth century, not only through the legacies of the Arts and Crafts movement, but as redefined by Guild Socialism, Distributism, and Syndicalism. The three figures discussed – Olive Schreiner, Eric Gill and Ezra Pound – may appear disparately positioned. But each shares a transitional role set between nineteenth-century labour ethics and the disciplines of a new political aesthetic. Moreover, each draws on and adapts the strategies explored in previous chapters. Schreiner engages actively with Carlyle, Ruskin and holistic philosophy; Gill and Pound, for their part, reformulate notions of apprenticeship and the material letter. In all three cases, a form of social hygiene emerges that troubles attempts to establish literary work ethics on an institutional or collective basis. The reception and reinvention of this legacy has consequences for our conception not only of modernism, but for an understanding of more recent attempts to redefine literary effort.

Chapter 5

Songs of the Forge

Building on connections previously discussed between poetry and weaving, this chapter addresses an equally searching comparison of writing to forge labour, one that prioritises matters of process over what Jean Baudrillard calls 'productive finality', but which also registers forms of visibility.[1] Amidst the symbology of craftsmanship, the figure of the blacksmith stands out because of an enhanced power to signify and represent. Ruskin's note on the twenty-first capital of the Doge's Palace in Venice conveys something of this. He describes its eighth side as showing a figure who '[. . .] beats with a large hammer on a solid anvil' under the caption 'FABER SUM' [I am a maker] (10:420). The Latin 'faber' serves a broad purpose in this respect, in that it elides the difference between 'smith' and the wider category, 'maker'. This ability to speak of labour in general also influences political representations. Walt Whitman, for one, splices metallurgic figures with democratic politics, utopian communalism, Eastern mysticism, and erotic life, in visions of '[b]lacksmiths with grimed and hairy chests'.[2] Re-domesticating this American trajectory, the radical English poet and campaigner, Edward Carpenter, sets his *Towards Democracy* (1883) to the 'solid beat of steam and tilt-hammers',[3] while praising '[l]overs of all handicrafts and of labor in the open air',[4] chief among them '[t]he blacksmith'.[5] For Carpenter, as for Morris, the image of the blacksmith becomes a symbol of socialism, a rallying cry for a newly conceived aristocracy of labour.[6] As previously noted, Walter Crane puts his depiction of a smith fashioning a sword to a revolutionary use as the emblem on the front of a Socialist League membership card [Figure 5.1].

While the blacksmith's ability to signify at the general and political level guarantees a prominence and potency, the questions entailed by the medium of metal are not superficial either, whether understood technically, theoretically or representationally. This applies equally to the forge's role as an interface between manual and literary intelligence. Widely read on both sides of the Atlantic, Henry Wadsworth Longfellow's 'The Village Blacksmith' (1841) epitomises the revived image of

Figure 5.1 Walter Crane, Socialist League Membership Card, Hammersmith Branch, 1885. William Morris Society

the forge as a place of dignified, but also intelligent, labour.[7] In a manner that pre-empts the spectacle of Ford Madox Brown's *Work*, the poem issues a powerfully visual invitation to admire 'a mighty man';[8] and by means of the last stanza's Wordsworthian turn, activates a middle-class conscience stirred to admiration, even envy, by a vision of working-class labour. *The Blacksmith's Forge*, a terracotta relief by Ruskin's protégé, Benjamin Creswick, contributes an additional idea, at once localising and widening the emphasis on spectacle [Figure 5.2]. The composition includes several children, who 'Look in at the open door' of the 'flaming forge'. Their embedded infant eyes cast the blacksmith as a mighty provider, whose capacity for force is tempered by care.

But Longfellow's blacksmith also 'looks the whole world in the face', and in that way reverses the direction of 'brain-worker' scrutiny.[9] In a move that anticipates Dickens's attention to this subject, the poem also presents a striking transformation of a working scene into art and music: not only as a dynamic image, but at the level of sound patterns, so that we 'hear' the blacksmith 'swing his heavy sledge | With measured beat and slow'. Longfellow's coda ventures a further manipulation of intellectual materials, in combining a metallurgical version of the fates' work of spinning – 'Our fortunes must be wrought' – with the more active resolution to shape 'Each burning deed and thought!' This convergence

Figure 5.2 Benjamin Creswick, *The Blacksmith's Forge*, terracotta relief, 1886.
© Collection of the Guild of St George, Sheffield Museums Trust

of rhythm and thought lends the poem a special significance, not least in thinking through the kinds of knowledge and virtue that manual labour might instil. This approach inspires in turn the 'The Forge' chapter of *Moby Dick* (1851), in which a 'sea blacksmith'[10] uses 'gathered nail-stubbs' to produce a harpoon.[11] As Ahab hammers, the union – or weld – of the mental and the manual completes: a novelistic microcosm of what happens when a schoolmaster goes to sea as 'a simple sailor', and a smith becomes uprooted from his homeplace.[12] Creswick, too, honours this connection: most notably, as part of his scheme for the decoration of the Bloomsbury Library in Birmingham (Jethro Cossins and Barry Peacock, 1890). Amidst terracotta relief panels representing rural labours, sports, domestic comfort, and leisure, he includes a composition devoted to industry that features a scene of forge labour, flanked this time not by children at play but by two figures reading.[13]

The blacksmith, finally, is more than a throwback: his services were retained in the nineteenth century as the best recourse for rural communities requiring fast repair of agricultural and household equipment; and he survived the twentieth century by moving into vehicle maintenance, specialist farrier work, and architectural restoration.[14] This occupational history evinces an independent, uncollectivised condition, and as such bears a resemblance to the position of the writer. While many 'cottage' industries fall by the wayside, both figures wonder whether they are still supposed to exist, and yet continue to do so. The different parts of this chapter engage, accordingly, with the degree to which writers recognise something of themselves in the image of forge labour. The first part – on *Great Expectations* – discusses the portrayal of Joe, and his apprentice, Pip.[15] Apart from testing the relation between forge production and literary production, Dickens's novel offers a response – simultaneously sceptical, knowing and idealised – to the Victorian romance of the metalworker. From this consideration of how craftsmanship operates in the arena of fiction, the second part explores Ruskin's real-life dealings with the metalworkers of Sheffield and Worcestershire, and the ways in which such interactions play out at the level of Ruskinian literary theory. The last part addresses Gerard Manley Hopkins's equally strong attraction to metallurgical premises, and as such widens the theological ambit beyond Protestant models. Dickens and Ruskin sensed liberation in the idea that words and ideas might become the material components of an honest labour; Hopkins likewise admired Carlyle's doctrine of work, but he takes the putative affinity between literature and metalwork in new directions, viewing it rather as a perilous site of union between divine creation and a deputed power to represent.

The variousness of these cases – ranging between a popular novelist, a Victorian sage, and a Catholic priest – demonstrates the deep and broad penetration of the literary-artisanal analogy under discussion, while throwing into relief certain common preoccupations. In different ways, as we shall see, Dickens, Ruskin and Hopkins, honour the forge as a discrete and singular zone. Equally, each invites a convergence between metalwork and literature, arising from a sense of the Promethean power, and force, of blacksmith and writer alike. Within this scope we witness, too, a concern with malleability, and music; and an associated form of anxiety or guilt, focused on the manipulation of materials and on the repurposing of things given, received or stolen. This idea of force prompts, in turn, an emphasis on violence, whether in the fashioning of objects, the coining of lives, or the casting of characters. This implies that the metallurgic analogy is not simply a strategy, or a quaint affinity, but a stringent basis for testing the relationship between literature and the material world. Less tolerant of risk than Morris, these cases also prepare the ground for the Carlylean legacies discussed in Chapter 6. As such, they announce a resumption of anxiety, based here in the relationship between processes of language and acts of creation.

Harmonious Blacksmiths

The earliest of the works discussed in this chapter, *Great Expectations*, is more often treated as a study of benefaction, or an adaptation of the *bildungsroman*, than as an account of the relations between writer and craftsman. But the novel's wider concern with authentic being is crucially invested in the metallurgic turn discussed above. The same goes for its attention to the correct placing of things – whether of tools in the workshop, or of life in relation to its developmental stages. In making a case for this alignment, the following discussion draws on studies by William Cohen, Steven Connor and Tom Paulin that explore connections between the novel's linguistic fabric and its metallurgic 'heart' in Joe's forge, a scene of production as well as a zone of feeling. Each, in addition, highlights the moral complexity of the fabrication process, and its dependence on ideas of force. My own contribution draws these sceptical accounts of metallurgic coining into dialogue with what might be termed the 'romance of the forge', a sentiment that preserves Longfellow's manual ideal. Responses that focus on plot often struggle to account for this function, because Pip's experiences tend so remorselessly towards *illusions perdues*. To appreciate its enduring power, we must instead focus on elements of writerly texture, on moments when Dickens's labour as an author breaks through the surface of Pip's mediated and fallen relation to the forge. Far from suggesting a mere connection, these moments betoken a reflexive attention to the matter of authorial labour itself, to rhythms of composition that correspond to the novel's complex music, consisting as it does of hammer strokes, thuds, cardiac beats and other percussive movements. While such affinities partake in a romance of kindred labour, they also make an open study of its costs.

Dickens commonly romanticises his working-class characters – Peggotty, for instance, in *David Copperfield* (1850). But he rarely extends this sentiment to the labouring life itself.[16] Childhood memories of the blacking factory precluded any personal yearning towards 'honest' labour. Physical work remained for him an unregenerate affair, a matter of fallen necessity, not far removed from the dismal mutterings of convict speech overheard by Pip: 'Mudbank, mist, swamp, and work; work, swamp, mist, and mudbank' (230). But while his Guild of Literature and Art established letters on the footing of a middle-class profession, Dickens himself struggled to keep his writing – or, at least, his mental conception of its strains – at the desired, or even a desirable, remove. Just as Carlyle resorts to the lurid fantasy of being 'chained to my galley-seat and oar [. . .] nearly dead of toil and despair', so Dickens mobilises the language of slavery to conjure the feeling of lost agency and abjection inspired by his writing schedule.[17] As Chris Louttit notes, he called *Dombey and Son* 'my approaching bondage', and complained of being 'kept in actual bondage for weeks together' by the demands of *Great Expectations*.[18] Such labour is shorn of Ruskinian satisfaction: the writer is declaredly spent of all resource yet simultaneously committed to the persistent fiction that this condition is 'actual' rather than comparative or simulated.

Exploring this cross-contamination of physical and mental states by a different route, Cohen understands the novel's 'manual conduct' primarily in terms of the sexual shame associated with masturbation.[19] While the textual evidence for autoeroticism is limited, this argument stands in suggestive relation to Siskin's commentary on the contrast between philosophy and 'the actual world' as characterised by Marx and Engels: namely their occupying 'the same relation to one another as onanism and sexual love'.[20] Onanism, in this account, is deemed a crime against 'productivity'. Equally, Cohen links instances of 'manual shame' to the novel's lack of any 'explicit scene of writing'.[21] This he attributes to the writer being 'ashamed of his hand' as the novel's productive source.[22] Dickens's broader representation of work and 'handicraft' evidently differs from the celebratory positions explored in previous chapters. But he also speaks with more than one voice. In this connection, we must account for the radiant glamour of forge work as dramatised in *Great Expectations*, and for its associated allure as extended to writing.

In fact, Dickens's efforts to align the smith's work with writing go well beyond the romance of Joe's labour: they eventually encompass the novel's broader concern with manufacture (of people as well as things), and include injuries sustained by the same assimilation (among them, abuse, violence and theft). This process commences in a view of literary composition as continuous with metalworking: sentences are forged, and discrete components are fire-welded. There is an element of timing and discernment here: one must strike (and write) while the iron is hot, but equally remove the workpiece from the fire before it overheats and drops off. When this continuum is allowed, it dwells in the struck rhythm of the forge and the pulse of the sentence. As the hammer forms the iron in the fire, a parallel conception emerges of language as a malleable element made soft by fancy and fixed hard by sudden quenching. Joe's forge obligingly resembles that portrayed in 'The Village Blacksmith', and it likewise courts the admiration of educated readers. The connection is not accidental: Dickens and Longfellow had been friends since first meeting in Boston in 1842.[23] At a revealingly extra-diegetic point, Pip experiences a physical memory of Joe's bodily frame: 'O dear good faithful tender Joe,' he exclaims, 'I feel the loving tremble of your hand upon my arm' (140). This strength of arm recalls Longfellow's archetype, but with an additional tenderness. Pip performs the corresponding role of Creswick's child who peeps in while the work is happening. In this environment, the blacksmith is the total person. He pits his strength against a stubborn material but stays in touch with the softer texture of things and feelings, including the sensibilities of a readership that also 'peeks' into this scene of labour.

If the connection between blacksmiths and wordsmiths draws on elements of stock labour-romance, it depends equally on Dickens's willingness to mix that ideal into the novel's murkier currents. He originally cast Joe as a 'good-natured foolish man', but the novel focalises much of the naive adulation and compensatory fantasy directed at him through Pip's illusions.[24] Our view of the forge is consequently second hand, as if replicating the novel's own generic distance from manual operations. Equally, the forge reveals a darker side when Joe's role as custodian is bypassed. Working alone, and under duress, Pip removes a file as if in aboriginal appropriation of the forge's power, an act whose meaning hesitates between an infernal and a Promethean defiance of law. The mythic aftermath of this deed dawns when Magwitch's agent comes to the village, and surreptitiously attracts Pip's attention to his peculiar manner of stirring his glass '*with a file*' (78). The episode supplies a further instance of misuse, the reassignment of an object whose original magic depends on its association with Joe. The file in this new aspect commands an uncanny significance, at once familiar and out of place: 'I was haunted by the file too', Pip confesses, 'A dread possessed me that when I least expected it, the file would reappear' (79), its instrumentality replaced by a frightening autonomy.

A hammer strike moves metal in a process that relies on physical presence, strength and skill; a file, by contrast, permanently removes material, taking it beyond the field of useful manipulation. And it does so not through practised force, but by means of the unvarying differential between hard teeth and soft metal. In *Great Expectations*, the file's power to break the band of a ring, or a shackle, even of an apprenticeship, comes cheap: it is 'portable property' (201), and becomes vulnerable as such to misuse. The kinds of trouble bred by this secondary usage proliferate uncontrollably. Pip recognises this on seeing that the weapon used against Mrs Joe is 'the iron I had seen and heard him [Magwitch] filing at', here put by Orlick to 'its latest use' (120). The disturbing thought arises that 'I had provided the murder weapon, however undesignedly' (121). He keeps quiet, fearing it is 'now more likely than ever to alienate Joe from me if he believed it' (121). Ironically, it is not the original misdeed that introduces a distance between them, but this sense of a lie by omission.

A further assault on the romance of the blacksmith arrives through an unnerving wordplay on the term 'forge'. Mrs Joe warns Pip that '[p]eople are put in the Hulks because they murder, and because they rob, and forge, and do all sorts of bad' (15). She feels herself victim to a counterfeit life in having taken a blacksmith as her husband. Pip, likewise, is described in a local newspaper as 'our young Telemachus', a phrase suggestive of shifty Odyssean paternity (231). Discussing the novel's interest in 'passing off', Connor observes 'the determining effect of authentic labour, as against the flimsy, light-fingered similitudes of the forger'.[25] '*Great Expectations*', he adds, 'tries to maintain its and its readers' confidence in its own metallurgic currency'.[26] The implication of such 'trying' is that the novel does not seal the association. The same newspaper describes Pip as 'a young artificer in iron', an allusion to the connection between falsehoods and the power to create. Even honest Joe is implicated: he independently forges the power of the state when making shackles, but sees this power instantly co-opted by a passing band of soldiers (31). Pip likewise finds the term 'artificer' maddening because it connects the virtues and the dangers of the forge to his new life, suggesting continuity between its power of unlicensed making and his project of self-creation in London.

Pip's relationship with the forge bypasses Joe in several other ways. Orlick, he reports, 'gave me to understand that the Devil lived in a black corner of the forge, and that he knew the fiend very well' (112). Orlick is 'kept' by Joe as 'a journeyman at weekly wages'; he is not, then, a master, and in that respect does not determine the forge's meaning (111). A grotesque pastiche of the novel's hero, Orlick, presages Pip's forms of footloose self-fabrication. It is Pip, accordingly, who performs the most far-reaching appropriation of the forge's power. Less through a single act than a series of imaginative practices, he conjures a realm of lost childhood innocence. These regrets for an existence in which he was 'content to be partners with Joe in the honest old forge' are themselves suspect (271). The recurring notion that 'there was no fire like the forge fire and the kitchen fire at home' proves a sentimental snare, a consolation that evades responsibility. Such thoughts do not console his sister – who finds herself 'Mrs Joe Gargery, who married the blacksmith' (3) – and will not serve Pip. Joe's local monopoly as *the* blacksmith insists on a settled and co-defined condition for his dependents, a rootedness that troubles characters whose fires are kindled instead by social ambition. On the day that Pip signs his indentures he feels he is going to the scaffold (105). A thick curtain falls on all the 'interest and romance' of his life (107). At the level of feeling, the institution at the heart of craftsmanship – the apprenticeship of skill, and placement – is in this way denied. Joe, correspondingly, can live up to Longfellow's archetype as 'a well-knit characteristic-looking blacksmith', but is hopelessly out of place 'in his holiday clothes' (23). And he is rendered mute by the adult Pip's habit of casting him in dumbshow 'at one of the wooden windows of the forge' (8).

Pip's self-torturing fantasies contain just enough truth to preserve the sympathy of his reader. But quite apart from that process, Dickens leaves room for us to imagine the forge as a site of alternative values. This bright prospect endures because, while Pip is telling his own story, his author reimagines the frustrated fixity of apprenticeship as a basis for verbal malleability and creation. The first clue to this process is situational. The forge, evidently, is not a domestic space in the manner of a middle-class writer's study. Yet Pip indicates that 'Joe's forge adjoined our house' (8), and that '[t]here was a door in the kitchen, communicating with the forge' (16). In different ways, blacksmith and writer recall the conditions of a pre-modern workplace. Such proximity between the professional and the domestic is double-edged, however: 'Home', Pip admits, 'had never been a very pleasant place [. . .] because of my sister's temper' (106), though Joe nonetheless had 'sanctified it'. When Jaggers arrives and offers Joe 'compensation' (140) for breaking Pip's bond of apprenticeship, a clash of cultures ensues. As a lawyer and agent, he assumes that roles are flexible, and value transferable.[27] Work for him is not personal, or domestic; contributions can be quantified, and expressed financially, rather as legal representation eliminates the necessity of acting in a case for yourself. Joe's position is complicated by his employment of Orlick for week's wages, an inconsistency that strikes at the heart of the fluid boundary between forge and kitchen. But the larger point is that the forge does not operate according to the depersonalised protocol of the commercial world. Joe senses this to the extent that he twice repeats the rationale for his indignation at Jaggers' having 'come into my place bull-baiting and badgering me' (141).

Although Dickens's letters evince a business-like manner, a hint of the Joe/Jaggers stand-off runs through his early clashes with publishers who hold him to contracts sealed prior to the enormous growth in his earning power. In this respect, Dickens shares Joe's view of work as inalienable. 'Cottage industries' – such as writing and smithing – assume a personal interest in work, which initially warrants Pip's otherwise evasive longing for the forge's 'honest old' heart (272). On abandoning his apprenticeship, Pip exchanges a principle of independence for one of indebtedness. Having 'believed in the forge as the glowing road to manhood and independence' (106), he refuses the apparent servitude of indentures. This may seem an occupationally specific dilemma, but there are connections here to Dickens's self-conception as a novelist. Troubled at time of writing over the 'placing' of his vocationally indecisive children, he unfolds resemblances between his work and that of the stoutly independent blacksmith. Both resist the wiles of agents, and both expect the imprint of labour to endure in their creations. Even more so than most writers, Dickens could boast of independence and self-sufficiency. Indeed, he was well placed to understand the risks and the benefits embraced by sole traders, having taken control of his work through self-publication.

Rejecting Joe's call to fashion useful objects, Pip erects new fronts of language and manners to ward off the lurking sense of himself as a finished product. One route to Pip's inner self remains accessible, however, and it is supplied by recurring images of the human heart. As a metonym for feeling, the heart mitigates the effects of social climbing because it naturalises a role for rhythmic art, and aligns Pip – albeit briefly – with the creative figures of author and blacksmith. If we apply Caroline Levine's detection of a rigidly spatial or painterly strain in modern conceptions of the novel, we may likewise find an influence running in the other direction, whereby the natural pulse of the blacksmith returns the form to its time-bound origins.[28] As Levine acknowledges, though, this move does not always harbour liberation. The distinction between time standardised, and a more anticipatory timing, which could be 'cyclical, polyrhythmic, and dialogic', is not always clear.[29] Quoting Martin Munro, she notes that '"repression had its own rhythms"', in that 'slave masters figured out that slaves would work better if they were singing'.[30] In *Great Expectations*, rhythms naturalise and console, but are also often fugitive. Whether or not the subject is a convict, this version of the Emersonian 'pulse-beat' seems less a reclamation of metre, than a body on the run. Out on the marshes, Pip reports that 'With my heart thumping like a blacksmith at Joe's broad shoulder, I looked all about for any sign of the convicts' (35).[31] The heart's beat – now, a metallurgical 'thump' – finds a visceral communicative object in Joe's adjacent body: a searching, alert and communicative 'hammering', that rejects the desensitised model of mindless percussion. Within a few lines, though, this intimate yet socially resonant sound meets its nemesis in the uncanny noise of 'the file still going' (35–36). The continuous, spectral motion of this instrument lacks the reassurance of a distinct cardiac 'beat', producing instead a constant slur. Having escaped the confines and regulatory structures of the forge, the noise becomes environmental.

This sense of a spectral visiting resumes when Magwitch calls on the adult Pip and sets his 'heart beating like a heavy hammer of disordered action' (319). Pip insists that he feels 'abhorrence', but the heart tells a different story. Pointing forward to Magwitch's declaration, 'I'm your second father. You're my son, – more to me nor any son' (320), it alludes darkly to the convention by which a master craftsman stands *in loco parentis* to his apprentice.[32] Here, though, the invited comparison is not with the sinister file, but with the disordered and disarranged hammer of surrogate fatherhood. The primacy of the beat rings out once again when Pip visits the forge towards the end of the narrative. On 'listening for the clink of Joe's hammer', he hears nothing: 'Long after I ought to have heard it, and long after I had fancied I heard it and found it but a fancy, all was still' (473). In its fullest confirmation of the heart's work, the forge's elemental beat ceases altogether on Joe and Biddy's wedding day. The scene's dramatic significance dwells in the initial fright; but it also gathers meaning from Pip's circular description of the aural landscape. Listening for the hammer strike, he has in some sense already heard it – in his mind's ear – while the actual sound conforms to a deeper pulse, intimate with powers of 'fancy' and imagination.

The connection between metalwork, culture and this somatically 'honest' heartbeat, sounds most clearly through the novel's attention to music and song. Visceral affinities between cardiac rhythm and dance suggest this link, but as a conscious theorisation its origins stretch back to Ancient Greece. Pythagoras is said to have discovered the harmonic correlation between the weight ratios and sonic intervals of different blacksmith's hammers.[33] In the light of this story, the forge as scene of music is less a conceit than a return to origins. Joe's anvil first strikes this note when the soldiers arrive. As Pip recalls, one 'opened its wooden windows, another lighted the fire, another turned to at the bellows,' and 'the rest stood round the blaze, which was soon roaring' (33). At last the tension breaks, as 'Joe began to hammer and clink, hammer and clink, and we all looked on'. The delicate balance between these sentences – the first piling up preparatives, and the second relieving expectation – turns retrospective description into a scene still present to eye and ear. As the repeating 'hammer and clink' signals this transformation, the onomatopoeia of the double tapped 'hammer' (knocking a rhythm at the anvil before the iron is struck) announces a long-delayed union of word and thing. Equally, the passage's lyricism places the ancillary function of words in abeyance, as if returning language to its roots in sonic drama.

The novel's most concentrated rendering of forge work hesitates between recollection, spectacle, and immediacy in even more complicated ways. Pip summons the memory of a 'song' that 'Joe used to hum fragments of at the forge, of which the burden was Old Clem' (95), St Clement being the patron saint of smiths. Though vividly dramatised, he narrates the scene from the perspective of his experiences at Satis House, where he is surprised 'into crooning this ditty' (96) to order. The episode starkly illustrates the nature of an abuse that encourages Pip to be untrue to his origins, to be complicit in his own ruin. But it also offers a study in the forge's power of artistic creation, and the dubious homage paid to it by the privileged and 'idle'. Amidst these complications, Pip's narrative brings to the fore a residual admiration:

> It was a song that imitated the measure of beating upon iron, and was a mere lyrical excuse for the introduction of Old Clem's respected name. Thus, you were to hammer boys round – Old Clem! With a thump and a sound – Old Clem! Beat it out, beat it out – Old Clem! With a clink for the stout – Old Clem! Blow the fire, blow the fire – Old Clem! Roaring dryer, soaring higher – Old Clem! (95–96)

The eloquence of this rendition imparts a purpose and dramatic intensity all of its own. Pip is recovering from language a new capacity to accompany this cardiac-metallurgic 'thump'. The question of an 'excuse' – in the technical as well as the layman's sense – prompts the question, what comes first? The beat out rhythms of work or the song? The ethics of work or reverence for the saint? The affinity between artist and smith, or the envy of one for the other?

As in the 'hammer and clink' passage, the words of the song exist in a grammatically and functionally worked-up state. Loosened by the heat, and by the push of a hammer head, the atoms of meaning shift. 'Thus, you were to hammer boys round' is uttered in a strange voice, not obviously Pip's, a voice that takes comfort in the forge and receives from it help and community by combining this peculiar 'were to' with the imperative address, 'hammer boys round' (95). Meanwhile, the succession of clean monosyllables, and the punctuating 'Old Clem', set a song 'on the anvil' (95–96). This is not so remote from Dickens's practice of embarking on a novel in serial form before finishing the whole, or even planning it fully.[34] The successive blows of this forging process, the variations called for by rhythmic or 'serial' necessity, reward periodical instalments as a high-wire act. A feat of this kind deserves an audience – one more immediate than any drawn by the considered totality of a book. As Pip recalls how he and the soldiers 'all looked on' (33), one easily imagines a scene animated by the admiration and envy of the writer himself.

Forge songs haunt Pip, too, in his later phase living as a 'gentleman', and under a new sobriquet. Complaining that 'Philip [. . .] sounds like a moral boy out of the spelling book' (177), Herbert Pocket proposes 'Handel for a familiar name', on the grounds of 'harmonious' friendship, of Pip's having 'been a blacksmith', and the 'charming piece of music by Handel called the Harmonious Blacksmith'. This episode takes its place in that broader project of Dickensian re-naming epitomised by the John Harmon/John Rokesmith/Julius Handford transformations in *Our Mutual Friend* (1864–65).[35] Handford – like Handel – suggests a 'handle', or nickname, and so stands here as a nickname for a nickname. A handle is also the fixing place for the blade of a hand-tool, recalling the process by which Pip, in Anny Sadrin's words, 'lets himself be "handled" by others'.[36] In its sinister aspect, such re-naming simultaneously re-makes Pip and obliges him to carry his origins around in freakish fashion. Re-naming also recalls the conditions of slavery. The famously entrepreneurial Handel appeared among 'The Names of the Adventurers of the Royal African Company of England', whose business involved the transportation of slaves in dire reversal of their human expectations.[37] Even the choice of composer is condescending, associated as Handel then was with provincial and amateur music making, as prompted by his recent centenary.[38] By re-naming the novel's protagonist, Dickens signals an ongoing hesitation between the roles of creature and creator: Herbert does not call Pip by the title of a musical work, but by the name of its composer.

Pip's new name, and the piece of music associated with it, recall the drawing room automata of the eighteenth century: a mechanical novelty more than a lived reality. At the level of the novel's thematic architecture, however, Dickens's interest in forge music is no picturesque contrivance. Fascinated by Handel, and drawn to 'The Harmonious Blacksmith', he explores the connection it formalises between his own creative mastery and the metallic songs of labour. Pip's first-person narrative leaves a space for these unrealised possibilities, for paths distinct from the emotional abuse he suffers, as also from his wayward expectations. A power of rising above the contingencies of plot reflects the depth of Dickens's interest in the piece. In *Dombey and Son* (1846–48), Mr Morfin expresses his 'frame of mind' on his violoncello, playing 'the Harmonious Blacksmith [. . .] over and over again, until his ruddy and serene face gleamed like true metal on the anvil of a veritable blacksmith'.[39] Such music-making exceeds the analogical, in approaching the 'true' and the 'veritable'. Morfin's 'latent harmony of a whole foundry full of harmonious blacksmiths' supplies a precedent, too, for the communal vision evoked by Pip's more optimistic conjurations of forge life.[40]

As editor of *All the Year Round*, Dickens marks the year of the Handel Festival by publishing 'Our Eye-Witness with Handel' (1859), an account by Charles Collins of how 'The Harmonious Blacksmith' came to be composed.[41] Collins's version of events differs from the more familiar story told by Richard Clark in *Reminiscences of Handel* (1836), itself reproduced from a *Times* article of 17 April 1835.[42] Clark has 'The great composer' overtaken by a shower when walking near Edgware,[43] a chance occurrence that recalls Pythagoras's similar apprehension on having 'Providentially [. . .] walked passed a smithy, and heard the hammers beating out the iron on the anvil'.[44] The composer takes shelter 'under a blacksmith's shop',[45] finding within this space a man 'singing at his work', as 'The varying sounds of the falling hammer on the metal mingled with the rude tones of the man's voice, and entered into the very soul of the attentive listener'.[46] Identifying the blacksmith as William Powell of Edgware, Clark claims possession of the very same anvil. An accompanying illustration carries the substantiating caption, 'THE HARMONIOUS BLACKSMITH'S ANVIL AND HAMMER'. Re-purposed first as an 'instrument' – which, when struck, 'gives the two Notes which Handel has made use of as the Key Notes – viz. B and E' – it now appeared as a holy relic.[47]

While Collins shares this emphasis on the thing itself – the very same anvil, he claims, 'was appropriately brought to the Crystal Palace for the Handel Festival' –[48] he departs from Clark by placing Handel at the organ in 'a country church' on a summer evening. Organ notes drift outside on the air, where another sound 'seems to bind the rest together, and measure out the time to them – a sound that, though it tells of labour, gives yet an added measure', a sound that 'comes from the blacksmith's hammer ringing on the anvil'. Because the composer does not leave 'his place', the affinity between art and labour arrives unbidden, as a gift. Both accounts emphasise a change of use, from instrumental tool to musical instrument, suggesting in turn a social ascent.

Great Expectations likewise distinguishes the forge as perceived by Pip from the forge as a zone of possibility, or liberty. In this last guise, the smithy promotes a vital and percussive model of literary production. Words become malleable objects whose ties are loosened and turned to the hammer's work. Similarly conceiving 'The Work of writing' as 'palpable work',[49] Paulin discusses the scene in which Joe chooses his stylus 'from the pen-tray as if it were a chest of large tools' (460), and tucks up his sleeves 'as if he were going to wield a crowbar or sledge-hammer'. This, he claims, heralds 'a utopian image', according to which 'writing and publication can resemble innocent labour, or a labourer can write and that seem natural'.[50] Although 'Utopian' is a helpful descriptor for the exemption that Dickens accords scenes of forge work, the novel is concerned less with something impossible or unrealistic than with a dialectic, staged between writing on the one hand, and on the other, ideas of licensed and unlicensed usage. Wemmick unconsciously registers this process when he employs a literary-metallurgical metaphor to describe Jaggers's reputation as 'Britannia metal, every spoon' (205). The passage measures Jaggers's invulnerability against an assayed inventory of household gear. In this it witnesses a further – albeit less anarchic – spreading of metallurgical premises beyond their 'native place' in the forge (469). A similar effect informs Pip's recollection of his first 'memorable day' at Miss Havisham's, as the 'first link' in a 'long chain of iron or gold' (73). Likewise, 'the sound' of Mrs Joe's 'iron shoes' is said to be 'quite musical' (51). Figurative seepage of this kind enacts the novel's preoccupation with re-use, and ultimately abuse. In an article that sheds tangential light on the linguistic implications of stealing a file, Kathryn Murphy discusses Thomas Hobbes's 'hygienic distinction between the proper use of language, and its four "Abuses", among which he includes "metaphor"'.[51] '"Abuse" or "abusion"', she observes, 'is the standard English rendering of the rhetorical trope of catachresis, in Latin *abusio*: the improper use of words, or the application of a term to something it does not properly denote.'[52] A similar problem occurs to Dickens, for whom social life and novelistic rhetoric are unavoidably implicated in a catachresis that deranges primary application and original meaning.

Using files and metallurgical figures outside the forge may appear straightforwardly unlicensed. But the novel is forever unsettling hygienic distinctions, testing the difference between fair and improper use. It is not always clear, for instance, that trouble always comes from the outside. The forge may be sanctified, but Dickens does not disguise its link to sporadic eruptions of violence. Colonel Quagg, the ogre blacksmith in George Sala's story from *Household Words*, differs in many respects from the gentle Joe; but that tale's elaboration of a connection between rhetorical and physical abuse is relevant.[53] Quagg, we are told, is 'not a harmonious blacksmith, or a learned blacksmith', but a man whose violence towards members of a local sect is galvanised by the language of his profession: 'I'll knock you into horseshoes and then into horsenails', he threatens.[54] Quagg is then beaten within an inch of his life by a passing preacher who defends his principles with his fists in a way not attempted by his co-religionists. As an instrument of conversion, his use of violence recalls Zeno's *argumentum ad baculum*, or 'the argument of the stick'. It applies, as Murphy observes, when 'an argument is only carried through the threat or exercise of force'.[55] Joe makes this connection himself, on recalling how he and his mother ran away from his father: his father could not bear to be without them, he explains, and having caught up with them, 'took us home and hammered us' (47). Joe distributes his energies differently from his father, whose domestic abuse is 'equalled by the wigour with which he didn't hammer at his anwil' (47). But this does not mean that blows are never implied. As Nicholas Shrimpton observes, 'Hand-to-hand combat is a conspicuous feature of the text'.[56] Jaggers seems conscious of a physical threat when bargaining with the blacksmith over Pip's future. In other, more obvious, ways the forge fails to keep a lid on violence, it being the source of several unlicensed types of 'hammering' (8), whether of Pip by Mrs Joe ('brought up by hand'), or of Mrs Joe by Orlick, who once struck dumb could only 'signify him by his hammer' (122). Just as the servant in Zeno's example must alter his beliefs under compulsion, so Dickens portrays characters caught in a cycle of abuse within which narratives of ineluctable destiny and self-blame co-exist.[57]

Paulin links physical abuse to the birth of language in the forge, and the alphabet's 'death signs'.[58] He enters a crucial caveat, though, in stating that 'Dickens knows and believes that his imagination isn't simply murderous, direct, powerful – it is also innocent and capable of a redeeming love.'[59] These two emphases are not necessarily on parallel tracks. In *Tristes Tropiques* (1955), Claude Lévi-Strauss enters a similar account of writing as death-dealing; and, in *The Savage Mind* (1962), expounds the equally relevant notion of 'bricolage', according to which (handy) objects are taken up by 'primitive' peoples and applied to purposes not originally intended or licensed.[60] Pip's mysterious visitor practises something similar on stirring his rum with a file, thereby re-making this tool as a spoon, and ultimately this 'spoon' as a covert signalling device. Orlick follows suit when he converts a discarded leg-iron into a truncheon. These appropriations point to interlinked advantages and dangers, to promises and threats, each of which resides in the forge's 'savage' difference from Jaggers's world of contract and exchange.

The language of *Great Expectations* recalls in this way the 'welding words' (II.575) of Browning's *Sordello*: at once instrumental, and prone to unexpected figuration, it simultaneously evokes purpose and impropriety.[61] On one level the dramatised affinity between words and metalwork redeems the forge as a site of honourable labour; on another, it is an affinity redeployed in the service of music, and beyond that, the writer who stands behind the blacksmith. In this way, the name, or 'handle', always recalls the 'Handel'. This effect is concisely evoked by a slippage between the two senses of abuse – its etymological sense of a re-use, and its familiar meaning, as a violence, an assault, that leads finally to the self-assaults of the traumatised victim. At stake in this borrowing is the inescapable connection between forge and kitchen, between words and hammer blows, between labour and violence. Such links are evoked most starkly by Pip's sister, who mutely registers her assault by tracing 'a character that looked like a curious T', and thus a hammer (122). Equally, Pip's independence and integrity are violated almost as soon as the novel begins. In this novelistic world, 'abuse' in its several senses underpins the operation of art, as well as the 'primitive imagination'. Pip longs for the fixity of the forge, and he regrets the 'decisions' of his life; and as readers, equally, we are invited to endorse this yearning. But the awkward fact remains that Dickens *requires* Pip's re-alignment: the exigencies of the plot insist on Pip's abuse, even his torture. He has changed shape too many times to recover his old form.

By contrast, the author of Pip's destiny is an empowered artificer or craftsman, able to fashion not just his subject, but the linguistic tools by which that subject is beaten and pushed. In this respect, the removal of the boy from the forge, and all the upheaval that entails, is disturbingly intimate with the renovation of the literary intelligence. Far from representing an ethical flaw, Dickens makes a virtue of this sad realisation by dwelling on it, by making it part of the novel's conscious fabric. The novel's power as art depends, then, on a recognition that the forge's violence cannot be separated from the same violence of metaphor that puts the tools of the forge within reach of the writer. The writer, in turn, enjoys a freedom to apply and misapply those instruments at will. Rather than wield it silently or gratuitously, Dickens makes an open study of this stolen power. A new subject eventually forms: rather than understanding the novel in its familiar guise, as a tale of the blacksmith-turned-gentleman, we witness an alternative vision, a necessarily guilty fable of the writer's stint as an irregular blacksmith. These conclusions widen our sense of the artisanal turn in late nineteenth-century writing: as a novel, *Great Expectations* embraces the idea of language made malleable, but it also reveals the terms of this linguistic malleability, and most particularly, the ethical malleability that licenses the work of a 'wordsmith' in the first place.

Nail-bearers: Ruskin's *Fors Clavigera*

As discussed in Chapter 4, Ruskin followed a routine of manual labour at Brantwood, where he sponsored a series of labour experiments that brought excavatory and agricultural exertion into heuristic encounter with literary experience. My attention turns, here, to his interest in the qualities of words, and the ways in which words themselves perform metallurgical work. *Fors Clavigera* (1871–84) forms the focal point: a series of open 'Letters to the Workman and Labourers of Great Britain' whose verbal substance engages less with public landscaping than with the combinations of skill and manipulative force associated with forge work. In one of the few sustained readings of *Fors* as literature, Linda M. Austin argues that Ruskin assumes a fixed relationship between language and things,[62] derived from an ever exceeding literary labour that defies Malthusian principles of scarcity.[63] The result, she claims, is a debased, or inflationary language, one that accedes unwillingly to 'nature's law of diminishing returns'.[64] Austin's analogy between currency and writing is helpful and suggestive; but Ruskin does not subscribe to a gold standard where language is concerned. On the contrary, he had long feared that the intrinsic value of things would not, and could not, underwrite the value of words.

The allusive title given to these letters offers a starting point. Ruskin's favoured translation is 'Fortune the nail bearer' (27:375). In addition, 'fors' encompasses several contradictory meanings: it could imply a willing submission to fate, or a will to power that employs a force inspired by 'the strength of Hercules' (27:28). Similar uncertainty applies to 'clavigera', which 'may mean [. . .] either Club-bearer, Key-bearer, or Nail-bearer' (27:28). Ruskin's periodic reference to the letters as 'playful', or involved in 'a kind of bitter play' (29:197), introduces further possibilities. This last reading casts language as a free element, exempt from laws of scarcity operating elsewhere. Describing writing as 'play', he also acknowledges – in ways analogous to Dickens's portraits of forge work – the consciously imperfect correspondence between work and words. By contrast with Miss Havisham's 'sick fancy [. . .] to see some play' (60), it suggests a mode of re-tasking that benefits 'worker' and 'writer' alike. Literary play is turned, accordingly, into literary labour. Ruskin, it follows, is keenly aware of words as instruments, and indeed of *Fors* in its entirety as a kind of tool, formed for the shaping of lives. As in *Great Expectations*, however, violence is a part of this process. And an additional concern arises: that this inflationary state is not circumstantial, as Austin would have it, but intrinsic to literary language, and in that capacity at odds with the craftsmanship to which it is drawn.

Fors's official purpose, as the printed organ of Ruskin's Guild of St George, may seem remote from this meta-linguistic thread. Inspired by Plato's *Republic* (c. 370–80 BC), and More's *Utopia* (1516), the Guild's focus was agrarian and technologically limited: machines were not prohibited wholesale, but steam-driven mechanisms were banned because they degraded the environment and created idle hands. Intrinsic value was favoured in coinage, as in other matters, to the extent that 'unearned' income – in particular, usurious income – was regarded with suspicion. As the Guild developed, it acquired an educational arm, through the foundation of St George's Museum. Located in Sheffield, and drawing on the city's traditions of metalwork, it was dedicated to 'the liberal education of the artizan' (30:39). The implications of this charter for sound workmanship bear most obviously on the audience of artisans that the museum courted. If *Great Expectations* addresses and remakes Longfellow's subject of the proud and independent black-smith, *Fors* addresses actual metalworkers.[65] Ruskin's open letters deserve attention, too, for their implicit commentary on the labour of writers, including the methods of their own author.

Parallels with *Great Expectations* extend beyond the metallurgical into the musicological. In Letter 76 (April 1877), Ruskin describes the 'real poetry' of Wordsworth as 'disciplined singing' (29:85). He com-pares this union of the 'natural' and the consciously ordered to 'Shef-field ironwork', a product 'Natural to Sheffield – joyful to Sheffield, otherwise an entirely impossible form of poetry there' (29:85). 'You don't, perhaps, feel distinctly', he ventures, 'how people can be joyful in ironwork, or why I call it "poetry"?' (29:85). Having posed this sug-gestive question, Ruskin omits any gloss. He answers eccentrically that 'the only piece of good part-singing I heard in Italy, for a whole summer, was over a blacksmith's forge' (29:85–86), the implication of such 'call-ing' being less an identity than that forge work fosters lyricism. 'But', he adds, 'I speak of better harmonies to be got out of your work than Handel's, when you come at it with a true heart, fervently, as I hope this company of you are like to do'. Where Dickens dramatises momen-tary convergences between direction and doing, between composer and worker, Ruskin reunites 'disciplined music' with a folk premise. As if activating the echo of 'clavier' in 'clavigera', the vision is of Italian forge labour transforming into art, an idea developed by the succeeding refer-ence to a music hall rendition by G. W. Moore, who was leader of the 'Original Christy Minstrels'. By employing an adjective derived from I Peter 1.22 (KJV) – 'fervently' – and embracing the advantage of 'a true heart' (29:85), Ruskin effectively summons an uncompromised version of Pip, one who proudly carries the name of the work, rather than the composer. Far from sponsoring a departure from the forge – in the man-ner of Magwitch's benefaction – Ruskin's patronage announces an effort to build a 'company' around it (29:85).

In *Fors*, as in *Great Expectations*, these converging literary and craft ideals dwell in a renewed sense of working rhythm. A recollec-tion of Swiss farm workers, 'threshing corn with a steady shower of timed blows' (28:132), epitomises this possibility. They were, Ruskin avers, 'as skilful in their – cadence, shall we, literally, say? – as the most exquisitely performed music, and as rapid as its swiftest notes' (28:132). The pattern of simile ('as skilful . . . as its swiftest notes') encounters a check in the form of the parenthesis: the labour process is rethought, and its cadence re-literalised as a material practice, 'an action or mode of falling' (*OED*) appropriate to the accompanying 'shower' of blows. The product, meanwhile, is less threshed corn than the 'music' of a combined feat. A similar labour voyeurism emerges from Letter 80 of *Fors*. It describes a visit to land near Bewdley, Worcestershire, given to the Guild by George Baker, then Mayor of Birmingham. Mindful of the area's reputation for small forged products, Ruskin's host asks 'if I would like to see "nailing"' (29:173). Later in the letter, Ruskin laments the punishing 'darg' allotted to 'the English Matron and Maid' whose work he witnesses.[66] In the first instance, though, the magic of the forge holds sway, an effect signalled by the way working rhythms steal into the letter's descriptive pattern:

> So he took me into a little cottage where were two women at work, [. . .] each with hammer in right hand, pincers in left [. . .] At a word, they laboured, with ancient Vulcanian skill. Foot and hand in perfect time: no dance of Muses on Parnassian mead in truer measure; – no sea fairies upon yellow sands more featly footed. Four strokes with the hammer in the hand: one ponderous and momentary blow ordered of the balanced mass by the touch of the foot; and the forged nail fell aside, finished, on its proper heap; – level-headed, wedge-pointed, a thousand lives soon to depend daily on its driven grip of the iron way (29:173–4).

Whether by direct command, or in the manner of 'Open sesame', Ruskin conjures the mythical action of the scene '[a]t a word'. Equally, he conveys an affinity between verbal balance and the true 'measure' of the forge. The choreography of hands draws us in: 'hammer in right hand, pincers in left', with 'Foot and hand in perfect time'. From here, an evenly balanced prose poem emerges, the natural measure of which invites a kind of lineation, with phantom endings at 'hand', 'blow', 'mass', 'foot', 'aside', 'heap', 'wedge-pointed', 'daily', and 'way'. A craft-intelligence inheres in the polysyllabic, yet definitive, 'One ponderous and momentary [. . .]'. Eventually the backed-up syllables explode, in the terminal stress on 'blow', itself a curious anticipation of the 'sudden blow' in W. B. Yeats's 'Leda and the Swan' (1924).[67] Here, too, something is engendered: a nail, used 'for fastening the railroad metals to the sleepers', that construes 'iron way' as 'railway' (29:174). Meanwhile, the broadly iambic progress of 'its driven grip' enunciates a philosophy of material consciousness, one that resolves the trochees, or spondees, of 'Four strokes' into the 'balanced mass' of an Old English caesura – 'Level-headed, wedge-pointed' – and concludes in the iambic, or end-weighted resolve of 'And the forged nail fell aside, finished, on its proper heap'.

Where does this 'iron way' lead? *Great Expectations* addresses the shape or 'career' of life, and the extent to which one forges or forsakes futures. Ruskin, too, incorporates these conflicting forces, though his conception of fortune-making differs radically from Pip's. In Letter 43

(July 1874) he notes that 'the current and continual purpose of *Fors Clavigera* is to explain the powers of Chance, or Fortune (*Fors*), as she offers to men the conditions of prosperity; and as these conditions are accepted or refused, nails down and fastens their fate for ever, being thus "Clavigera," – "nail-bearing"' (28:106). This qualified agency draws on principles of freedom that depend, paradoxically, on the necessity of offering correct answers to mortal questions of faith.[68] At the same time, an idea of hazard informs the more 'driven' characterisation of fortune-making. Ruskin explains that the 'book' presents 'the laws of Fortune or Destiny, "Clavigera," Nail bearing; or, in the full idea, nail-and-hammer bearing; driving the nail home with hammer-stroke, so that nothing shall be moved; and fastening each of us at least to the Cross we have chosen to carry' (27:230–31). The present continuous in 'driving the iron home' combines a sense of active process with finality – whether through appointed fate, or a fault in workmanship. Mistakes, as it happens, are intrinsic to 'unregulated' methods of handiwork: a condition the craft theorist David Pye calls 'the workmanship of risk'.[69] Something of this idea is conveyed by Ruskin's expanded title, '"How you may make your fortune, or mar it"' (28:107). Elsewhere he praises medieval craftsmanship for confessing its human imperfection (10:190). Far from being faulty, honest-hearted imperfection becomes a token of the beautiful. Here, though, Ruskin approaches a fatal fixing of the nail. In common with Pip, the line between immovable destiny and incriminating error is rarely clear, and while the coincidence of nail and flesh hints at Christ's Passion, Ruskin (like Dickens) contemplates the awful finality of such 'marring'.

This brings us to the harmful side of the hammer's productivity. Just as tools stolen from Joe's workshop equip Orlick's violence, so the 'force' in the Ruskinian 'fors' approaches the Carlylean philosophy of rule by force, and indeed the state's effective monopoly on it. In the matter of violence, and especially war, Ruskin is easily discovered in self-contradiction, attracted as he is at different points by a sublime power to impose will and by a hatred of wasted life. In *Fors*, though, we rarely encounter one without a tinge of the other. The eccentric folly of Wemmick's 'stinger' (206) colours Ruskin's direful allusion to 'the 35-ton gun called the "Woolwich infant"' (27:43). He succumbs, relatedly, to the despondent thought that, far 'from beating sword into ploughshare, [. . .] the sword is set to undo the plough's work' (27:298): another metallurgical transformation aborted by re-purposing. Such concerns invade not only the 'beating' rhythms of craftsmanship; they even inform Ruskin's complaint about the 'dreadful hammers' of the geologists, whose irreverent 'clink' sounds 'at the end of every cadence of the Biblical verses' (26:15). In this reversed version of the 'cadence' set by the corn threshers of Thun, Ruskin finds the music of scripture unnervingly materialised as the quarry of a hacking operation aimed at all settled truth.

In *Great Expectations*, a new fictional contract is required to assimilate the power of the forge. Its consequences are apparent in the movement between the lively action of Pip's heartbeat, and the horror of a disembodied thud. Ruskin likewise conjures an awareness of the connection between unwarranted force, and 'fors', through the sense of 'Clubbearer' in his title. Cardinal Manning summed up this discomforting resonance on comparing the experience (and interest) of reading *Fors* to 'the beating of one's heart in a nightmare'.[70] Austin, equally, notes Ruskin's approving account of Florence's military history: the city's governing class, she observes, extended 'the privileges of their own new artisan government', to include 'pillage, inheritance, and hoarding'.[71] Other letters relate facts rather than personal preferences; but they are marked by an unwillingness to suppress the roots of artisanal culture in exploitative power, in what Austin calls 'the power of the body'. Ruskin alludes, for instance, to Venice's plundering of Constantinople (9:24–5): an act that simultaneously defines the city's ambiguous relationship with Christendom and establishes its role as a treasury of fine things. Like Dickens, Ruskin perceives, and dramatises, this connection between giving, creating, and taking away.

Both writers express a similarly double-edged respect for working-class vocations. Ruskin concedes in Letter 28 (April 1873) that Dickens speaks like a hack about 'Independence, and Self-dependence' (27:518). He concludes, however, that the novelist's portraits of 'menials' are never disrespectful. When Biddy chides Pip for his condescension in offering to 'remove Joe into a Higher sphere' (135), she hints darkly at the fate of those who play at being authors in their own lives. There is no going back for Pip, of course; but, like Ruskin, Dickens locates freedom in conscious submission, and wisdom in a range of talents.[72] This position recalls Plato's 'myth of the metals', a lesson that applies despite the ways in which both writers worry over social mobility.[73] Yet Ruskin's attempt to find a place for the writer proposes a more developed theory of craftsmanship than anything Dickens entertains. His account of Christ's being 'brought up to a carpenter's craft' (27:218) differs profoundly from Dickens's contemptuous commentary on Millais's 'Christ in the House of his Parents'. Far from excluding this sphere of experience, he draws a parallel with God's 'handiwork' (29:55), 'the real Master of every trade being always a God' (27:403). Left to explain how works by Tintoretto and Titian 'could be done "wholly without religion"!' (29:88), he privileges human deeds – and by extension, practical acts of creation – over the delaying mechanisms of faith or divine action.

The primacy of craftsmanship is not then a matter of simple causation, but a question of ethical primacy: 'resolving to do our work well,' Ruskin avers, 'is the only sound foundation of any religion whatever' (29:88). Far from challenging or imitating Christian precepts, exemplary deeds become their instructional source. No longer aiming to divide human creations by theological end, he rewards the spirit of the process, redefining ideas of 'value' and 'production' along the way. Thus Ruskin concludes that there are 'two absolutely opposite kinds of labour'. If the first is 'labour supported by Capital, producing nothing', the second is 'labour unsupported by Capital, producing all things' (27:38). Mercantile consciousness and usury are thus figured as enemies of production. As the son of a wine merchant, Ruskin evidently feels a need to explain: his father, he hastens to add, owned the vineyards from which his wine was produced, so that he 'grew his wine, before he sold it' (29:408). It is a doubled-edged defence: if a merchant can be a farmer, then a farmer may be a merchant, and the distinctiveness of the agrarian value system looks less secure. Under improved conditions, however, Ruskin believes the values of the grower will prevail over those of the dealer. He wants his audience to become 'primarily, Gravers, Makers, Artificers, Inventors, of things good and precious' (29:408), hoping thereby to reverse the historical trend of the City of London, 'where chapmen have become the only dignitaries', and where 'we have [. . .] the Ironmongers' Company, but not the Blacksmith's' (29:408). As land becomes liquid, and commerce consumes confraternity, the impulse in these several cases is to reaffirm distinctions that have become blurred.

Relatedly, Ruskin insists on mutual adherence to ethical standards, formulated to ensure that the 'intrinsic value' (27:217) of craftsmanship is not debased or defrauded. '[T]he first law of St George's Company', is, then, 'to do good work' (28:140). While Carlyle confuses the distinction between 'maker' and 'monger' in his account of Ebenezer Elliott, Ruskin focuses instead on the nature and conditions of production. In this vision, even trading operations adhere to the values of craftsmanship, a principle succinctly expressed by his father's epitaph, 'an entirely honest merchant' (27:169). This broad ethical standard takes its source from words carved on Venice's first church, St James of the Rialto: 'Around this temple, let the merchant's law be just – his weights true, and his agreements guileless' (29:99). Sending a photograph of the inscription to St George's Museum, Ruskin notes its setting on 'marble so good that the fine edges of the letters might have been cut yesterday' (29:99). Even the discursive medium resolves into a conspicuously 'made' thing.

Ruskin thereby reiterates the ethical supremacy of making over trading, and in the process admits that merchants might learn as much from things made as from things written.

These regulatory principles are realised in a form of writing equally inspired by 'affectionate, honest, and earnest work' (29:87), by a resistance to usurious practice, and by a manual attention to 'the fine edges of letters'. The pages of *Fors* contain several articulations of this idea as it bears on the life of the mind. In Letter 9 (September 1871), Ruskin asks his audience to imagine 'a true and refined scholarship, of which the essential foundation is to be skill in some useful labour' (27:147). Letter 11 (November 1871) proposes that 'a true artist is only a beautiful development of tailor or carpenter' (27:186–87), and that 'in the house-producing-and-painting function, [. . .] the artist is still typically and essentially a carpenter or mason'. The essence of this affinity suffuses an account of Botticelli as 'the greatest Florentine workman' (27:372). Keen to demonstrate the value of a workshop system in which supremacy of skill trumps privilege of birth, he claims that all the early Italian masters 'began by being goldsmiths' apprentices;' (27:372) and were '[. . .] formed by the master-craftsman who mainly disciplined their fingers'. Such seamless modelling of the apprentice in the master's image differs markedly from the experience of the malformed Pip, whose given names and origins hail from outside the workshop. Ruskin further elaborates this contrast with *Great Expectations* through an insistence that 'Lippi and his pupil were happy in each other' (27:374). He goes on to add, however, that 'the boy soon became a smiter of colour, or colour-smith' (27:374). In that way, he re-activates Dickens's attention to the affinity between metalwork and violence, hammering and thumping.

The mythic source for this union of craft and intelligence also proves illuminating, arising as it does from a discussion in Letter 23 of the carved labyrinth in the southern porch at the Cathedral of Lucca, and an accompanying inscription, which reads: 'This is the labyrinth which the Cretan Dedalus built' (27:401–05; 27:510). In assessing that figure's significance as an artificer, Ruskin discovers a history of immaterial labour, one that transposes the image of tools in ways redolent of writerly process. Having invoked a homely equivalent for the inscription in the popular legend that '[t]his is the house that Jack built', he proposes that 'the name of Jack, the builder, stands excellently for Dædalus, retaining the idea of him down to the phrase, "Jack-of-all-Trades"' (27:403). '[T]he real labyrinth', Ruskin concludes, 'set the pattern for nothing; while Jack's ghostly labyrinth has set the pattern of almost everything linear and complex since' (27:407). This conception of the artificer's work – in setting 'the pattern' – yields a form of intellectual property that transcends any single material expression. Whereas Ruskin elsewhere focuses on a continuum between the craftsman and the fine artist, the literary applications in this case are more obvious, the field of concern being ghostly rather than visible, or manifest. On the other hand, the labyrinth itself – with all the confining complexity it implies – is not a particularly auspicious precedent for this aspect of *Fors*'s programme.

Dinah Birch observes that Ruskin understood the '"workmen and labourers"' of his title 'in the broadest sense', and that 'He was a workman and labourer himself'.[74] 'His work', she adds, 'lay in writing, and he considered *Fors* its culmination'.[75] Ruskin evidently did believe that literary artistry could take part in a wider reunion of craft and intelligence. However, his statements on this subject are not nearly as emphatic as those committed to the visual arts. Indeed, he resorts to special measures in convincing his readers, and himself, that it all makes sense. '[T]he constant object of these letters of mine,' he explains, '[. . .] has been to urge you to do vigorously and dextrously what was useful; and nothing but that' (27:449). He wonders all the same whether his own literary work qualifies as 'vigorous' and 'dextrous'. This thought plants an anxiety that never quite subsides. In Letter 16 (April 1872), he imagines an entirely insubstantial writing process: not so much unproductive as anti-productive, something closer to a confidence trick. Far from being an isolated lapse, it quickly applies to the whole field of written discourse. As in the previous chapter, we approach a version of the trickster's creed, expressed here as the ruling principle of modern economic life:

> "Here," the practical Englishman says to himself, "I produce, being capable of nothing better, an entirely worthless piece of parchment, with one thousand two hundred entirely foolish words upon it, written in an entirely abominable hand; and by this production of mind, I conjure out of the vacant air, the substance of ten pounds, or the like. What an infinitely profitable transaction to me and to the world! Creation, out of a chaos of words, and a dead beast's hide, of this beautiful and omnipotent ten pounds. Do I not see with my own eyes that this is very good?" (27:282).

Complaints about making 'money out of *nothing*' would later arise in the form of Ezra Pound's attacks on central banks.[76] The more local point rests on a concern that writing has become a form of conjuration, a perversion of divine, as well as artisanal, acts. A writer himself, Ruskin struggles to answer such charges to his own satisfaction. Letter 25 (January 1873) more or less acknowledges this state of confusion, in mentioning his having 'once or twice ventured to call myself your fellow-workman' (27:513). Three years later, he proposes that 'some forms of intellectual or artistic labour, inconsistent (as a musician's) with other manual labour, are accepted by the Society as useful' (28:645). Thus he grants himself, and others like him, a grudging allowance, so long as 'the intellectual labourer ask no more pay than any other work-man' (28:645). This last provision, revealingly, follows an admission that he can ply no trade, having never been taught, or brought up to one (28:644).

Exceptions of this kind reflect persistent worries over practical/literary non-equivalence, and a resulting sense of personal inadequacy. Even when Ruskin figures 'intellectual labour' as a possible contribution to the Guild, musicians and artists seem more on his mind than writers. And he often doubts the scope for mutual recognition: for instance, he painfully recalls having 'once or twice ventured to call myself your fellow-workman' (27:513). 'I have oftener', he adds, 'spoken as belonging to [. . .] those who are not labourers, but either live in various ways by their wits – as lawyers, authors, reviewers, clergymen, parliamentary orators, and the like – or absolutely in idleness on the labour of others' (27:513). Ruskin henceforth characterises himself as 'a makeshift Master' (28:644). There is a sense, here, not only of self-contempt, and a concomitant idealisation of others, but of role-play. This sense informs the contradictory assertion that literary work is 'always play, when it is good' (37:513). It echoes in turn his earlier allusion to authorship as 'bitter play' (37:513). '[P]lay', however – or at least enjoyment in work – is not fundamentally at odds with Ruskin's broader understanding of what work could and should be. It is confusing, in this respect, to find him applying the word 'play' as a slight on the seriousness of his own labours. The alternative possibility, that literature might elicit work-pleasure, is hardly credited.

Elsewhere, Ruskin defends his vocation: 'if readers of *Fors* think my letters too desultory,' he thunders, 'let them consider what this chief work [. . .] involves' (33:408). Challenging the perception that 'I write "easily"' (29:170), he complains that 'No one has the least notion of the quantity of manual labour I have to go through, to discharge my duty as a teacher of Art' (28:383–401). These outbursts are coherent in themselves, but present a mixed message when taken alongside passages of self-chastisement and despondency. Ruskin appears in the grip of some cognitive dissonance, caused by the strain of identifying himself as a workman while simultaneously upholding his authority as Master. Another source of strain concerns professional standards. Amid so many duties and commitments, he is painfully aware that he cannot maintain the exacting standards of workmanship he demands of others. This much he admits on compiling and publishing the mistakes in previous issues, and even discussing 'harmful misprints' (28:511). The fortune in 'fors' thus undergoes an irregular interpretation. To avoid submitting to 'such chances of error', he weakly explains, 'would involve a complete final reading of the whole' (28:511). And this, he acknowledges, is asking too much: it would mean having 'one's eye and mind on the look-out for letters and stops all along, for which I rarely allow myself the time' (28:511). In this respect, at least, his schedule favours hazard and chance over the principle of doing the best work.

For all these reservations about the place of writing among the crafts, enmeshed as they are in the author's shifting self-identity, it is worth considering Ruskin's project at the level of *Fors* as a whole. Different conclusions come into view when this approach is taken. Apart from *addressing* nail-bearers, he wants to put a tool in the hands of his audience: as Cook and Wedderburn put it, 'the book itself was to be a nail-bearer' (27:xii). Seen in this light, his variable agency as a literary worker recedes, to be replaced by the literary work itself, an entity that 'fastens' and 'nails down' our fate (28:106). Ruskin refers to *Fors* as something outside himself, and therefore beyond full control: as much raw material as author. This sense of the letter (and ultimately the book) as a tool ensures an instrumental purpose apart from uncertain authorial status. Readers are encouraged to place their trust in chance, but the results would not depend on interest. By contrast with his foregoing parable of the borrowed plane (27:381), the tool in question is wielded without paying rent to a capitalist (27:11–26). *Fors*, as such, powers no 'ghostly self-going planes' (27:90) of capitalist production. And its making has no recourse to Pip's phantom file. A self-publishing venture – aided by Ruskin's former student at the Working Men's College, George Allen – it unites the printing with the distribution, and circulates a limited stock in the manner of an artisanal product. At this material level, if in nothing else, Ruskin designates himself 'the first producer' (27:100). Answerable for the quality of the 'paper, binding, eloquence, and all' (27:100), he claims the associated privilege of charging fees as he sees fit, entirely unhampered by rentiers.

This is not to suggest that Ruskin avoids contradictions. Having previously sought to de-monetise literary labour – arguing that 'Whatever in literature, art, or religion, is done for money, is poisonous itself' (28:646) – he now proposes a principle of just payment. Though conceived as a measure to protect and reward all kinds of labour, it sours relations with the very audience he hoped to cultivate: the working men of limited means who complained of unobtainably high prices. Taking refuge in obscurantism, Ruskin responds by citing a 'law of Florence' that 'Eel of the lake shall be sold for three soldi a pound; and eel of the common sort for a soldo and a half' (28:41). A principle of professional worth nevertheless emerges: if 'an annual half-sovereign' cannot be spared 'for my literary labour,' he exclaims, 'in Heaven's name, let him buy the best reading he can for twopence-halfpenny' (28:41). This seems callous from most points of view, but recalls the hard edge, or violent tip, that Ruskin always invests in the nailing operation. When teaching his audience to value their labour, he requires them also to value his own.

Conceived in this way, as a tool, *Fors* re-forms its own audience: as in his lecture 'Traffic', he proposes that 'you will build with stone well, but with flesh better' (18:458). There is a corresponding sense in which these open letters shift the emphasis away from making useless things towards the fashioning of human hearts. In Letter 11 (November 1871), Ruskin takes up that challenge, declaring that 'this whole plan of mine is founded on the very practical notion of making you round persons instead of flat' (27:193). Extending the metaphor, Letter 32 (August 1873) proposes that 'Youth is properly the forming time – that in which a man makes himself, or is made' (27:584). There is simultaneously a humanity in this, and a productivity that entails the violence – 'abuse', even – needed to change the shape of a thing. Ruskin famously writes that 'THERE IS NO WEALTH BUT LIFE' (17:105). Only, the same property of life has then to be worked, either by the human subject, or passively as suggested by the phrasing, 'or is made' (27:584). This attitude to forming flesh can be cavalier, as Frost details in his account of the misadventures befalling the Guild's humbler adherents.[77] Ruskin's unabashed irritation at 'what I have never been able yet to beat, with any quantity of *verbal* hammering, into my readers' heads', bespeaks a related attitude (29:249). He wants his readers to embrace their full humanity as creators, but in the process turns them into creatures, in unwitting realisation of his own image of drivers 'explaining Political Economy to the horses, by beating them over the heads' (27:38).

Despite its author's tendency towards diatribe, and the degree of audience passivity required to perform forging operations in the flesh, *Fors* represents a sincere attempt to cultivate 'companionship' by literary means. As Birch notes, Ruskin's readers 'could be joint partakers in an enterprise, rather than passive consumers'.[78] In 'Notes and Correspondence', he regularly allows his discourse to be interrupted by letters. These interventions are cut short in turn by his own responses, whether indignant or receptive. The work's polyvocal form is genuine, then, and in certain respects reminiscent of a communal working environment, such as a blacksmith's shop. We are not dealing here with the premeditated linearity of the contemporary novel: '*Fors*', Ruskin reminds us, '*is a letter*, and written as a letter should be written, frankly, and as the mood, or topic, chances' (29:197). Thus he strikes while the iron is hot, and avoids 'overworking' the material: 'so far as I finish and retouch it [. . .] it ceases to be what it should be, and becomes a serious treatise, which I never meant to undertake' (29:197). Grotesque, 'obscure', and imperfect, like the Gothic architecture Ruskin loves, *Fors* 'expresses the thoughts that come' to him, 'as they come' (27:293). Instead of polishing towards a complete, coherent, and definitive statement, his prose admits contingency and celebrates a related vulnerability.

The results of this approach can be unnerving. Ruskin alludes mysteriously to 'insectile noise' and, in a curious fusion of the grammatical and the bestial, imagines 'the definite dragon turned into indefinite cuttlefish, vomiting black venom' (27:293). Most disturbingly, he conjures 'a host of pulicarious dragons – bug-dragons, insatiable as unclean' (27:293). More than merely outlandish images, these grotesques distort taxonomies, notably those governing scientific knowledge of the natural world. From forming metal, to forming children, Ruskin turns in this way to malformations. Pondering 'the humorous, [. . .] even slightly mocking and cruel contrivance of the Forming Spirit' (28:278), he wonders why elephants don't build houses with their noses, as birds build nests with their faces' (28:278). Even so, he admits the merits as well as the horrors of these creations. He commits himself in this way to a literary 'workmanship of risk'. As previously quoted, Ruskin resolves to 'submit to all and sundry such chances of error'. Vital marks are captured that would ordinarily be smoothed over in the finishing process, while the dimensions of past, present, and future, resist their usual absorption into the artificial form of a 'work'. Through this conscious refusal of the total vision, Ruskin expresses a preference for writing as process, a procedure more committed to driving nails than to 'seeing nailing'.

He nevertheless hesitates between consigning writing to the field of 'idleness' or 'play', and cultivating a sense of fellowship in labour with his audience. In words, as in coinage, he aims for intrinsic value, for rootedness; but he has a fugitive nature, and hesitates in declaring the writer a craftsman. Indeed, he fears that 'the personal conceit and ambition developed by reading [. . .] led to the disdain of manual labour' (29:483–84). When contemplating the author-function of his own signature, he experiences a related disgust, it being 'only short for "Rough skin," in the sense of "Pigskin"' (27:417). He hardly misses the inflationary potential of his own discourse, then. 'The more I see of writing,' he admits in 1872, 'the less I care for it' (27:294). His despair leads him to Plato's *Phaedrus*, and its warning that 'this art of writing will bring forgetfulness into the souls of those who learn it' (27:295).

Painfully aware of his dependence on such memorial capacities, Ruskin hopes to limit this 'trust in writing'.[79]

The letters of *Fors* pursue an experimental conception that offers something resembling a formal response. They reunite expression with action, while the word emerges less as a testament to thoughts now shrivelled than as a tool that makes its mark. They commit to the action of the moment over the refining process of revision and afterthought. Even mishits are redeemed as the grotesques of a forming process willing to harness the force of chance. Ruskin suffers doubts about the place of writing among his workforce of craftsmen, but alongside the familiar strategy of literalised and reified imagination he grants an immaterial pattern genuine sway. In the end, though, the letters' perceived failure to make this physical impression sends Ruskin into despair. He wonders whether 'All this effort, or play, of personal imagination is utterly distinct from the teaching of *Fors*' (29:385). The implication is that the distortions of the work escape any redeeming purpose, that they conduce to a faithless rather than a faithful grotesque. Ultimately, the poignancy of *Fors* resides in Ruskin's effort to gather unilateral qualities – action, immediacy, independence – that belong to the action of a craftsman with all their materials in front of them. The working predicament of his writing life is more complex, however, as well as more troubled. Isolated from the formal procedures of a given work, it depends not on the manipulation of metal, but on the consensual attention of an audience less easily – or less willingly – hammered into shape.

Hopkins's Poetic Anvil

Hopkins's poetry attracts most attention for its manner of contemplating, and activating, the received beauty of the natural world. There are moments, nevertheless, when a more conspicuously crafted environment comes into view. In 'To Oxford' (1865), the eye notices how 'the mason's levels, courses, all | The vigorous horizontals, each way fall' (2–3).[80] Poetic lines become mortar lines, evoking not just the image of a wall, but an ideal of material observance. A civilisation emerges, as such, from the built fabric 'underneath this chapel-side' (1). In 'Boughs being pruned . . .' (December 1864–January 1865), the particulars of craftsmanship address a paradox of value: 'Enrichèd posts are chamfer'd; everywhere | He heightens worth who guardedly diminishes; (3–4)'.[81] This is not quite Pater's sculptural removal of surplusage, but the poem broaches a familiar mystery of craftsmanship. Before chamfering, an oak post already serves its structural purpose; and it possesses a complete identity. Yet by removing the corner material – wood, paradoxically, that possesses intrinsic value – the craftsman augments the artistic (and therefore intrinsic) value of the whole piece. Its new profile incorporates delicacy, shedding weight without losing strength of support.

These examples show Hopkins reaching closer towards a material aesthetics than anything achieved either by Dickens's re-purposed tools, or Ruskin's combination of force, fortune, and forming. Hopkins in effect realises Coleridgean tenets, in treating words as if they are essentially things.[82] He is aided by a theology that makes physical form holy again, though without any obvious effect in resolving the creative status and legitimacy of his own poetry. Where Ruskin sees craft ethics as the basis of religion – an ultimate pledge to the possibility of intrinsic value – Hopkins senses a reversal of the proper order, a placing of the cart before the horse. The last part of this chapter offers a new approach to the familiar subject of Hopkins's creative doubt, focused less on its theological particulars, than on its neglected engagement with the contemporary philosophy of work and making. In thinking through relations between the human and the divine, he avoids any conception of deputed power. Deterred from creative mimicry, he confines human ingenuity to processes of praise or prayer. In conferring a creative monopoly on God, he also differs from the neo-Thomist craftsmen and theorists discussed in Chapter 6. In that respect, he stands out not only from his Protestant peers, but from the mainstream of modern Catholic thought.

As a young man, Hopkins admired Ruskin, and shared his preoccupation with the spectacle of physical labour. He enjoyed the manual tasks he was assigned as a Jesuit novitiate; and, at Stonyhurst, he relished the 'stirring scene' of 'contractors, builders, masons, bricklayers, carpenters, stonecutters and carvers, all on the spot'.[83] Fred Walker's portraits of manual labour speak to him in similar ways: the 'young man mowing' in *The Harbour of Refuge* (1872), for instance, whom he judges a 'great stroke, a figure quite made up of dew and grace and strong fire'.[84] Catching the rhythm of the scene, he observes 'the sweep of the scythe and swing and sway ri of the whole body'.[85] In each case, a muscular prompt leads to thoughts less sturdy and substantial than light and airy. Hopkins also praises Hamo Thornycroft's *The Mower* (1888–90),[86] a statue whose subject recalls the figure briefly witnessed from a boat in Matthew Arnold's *Thyrsis* (1865). As Catherine Phillips notes, this reified 'glimpse' may have inspired 'Harry Ploughman', and its 'direct picture of a ploughman, without afterthought'.[87] Placing Hopkins at the heart of this intellectual tradition, G. H. Gardner traces his belief in 'the joy of craftsmanship and the dignity of manual labour' to a youthful exercise in copying Brown's pendant sonnet to *Work*.[88] In this way, Hopkins reproduces and transmits a text already engaged in the transcription of visual spectacle. The effect is to query the capacity of poetry to witness and reproduce physical labour. This, in turn, exposes him to ethical quandaries, based in similarities between Brown's labour voyeurism and the perspective of 'Tom's Garland'.

Geoffrey Hill excuses the latter on the grounds that it contains a 'burlesque element'.[89] And yet the two poems are strikingly similar in the way that they profit creatively from spectatorship. Hopkins's contribution resides not in ironical distance, but in a manner of poetic making that fuses subject matter with the handling of words. He takes pains to integrate his poems with their subjects, dwelling where possible on the technical aspects of manual as well as literary labour, and more particularly on their craft. This aspect emerges from several poems, written in the 1860s, that test the limits of 'morticed metaphors' (6).[90] The last phrase comes from '—Yes for a time' (1864), a fragment of *Floris in Italy* (1864) that evokes a persistent reaching after material figures. The result is verse especially amenable to physical alignment. Poetry may resist the neatest fit – such as to 'Shake and unset' (6) these metaphors – but in Hopkins's hands the joinery retains a tight and visible hold.[91] Metallurgical images are also favoured, as where 'those few strokes | That forge her title of inheritance' (4–5) stand for the binding acts of civil power.[92] Arthur's Britain plays host, likewise, to 'The mint of current courtesies, the forge | Where all the virtues were illustrated | In blazon, gilt and images of bronze' (8–10).[93] An allusion to 'The tempered soil where only her flower is found.' (4) anticipates the double purpose – the repurposing, even – of a line from 'Felix Randal':[94] that 'touch had quenched thy tears' (9).[95] A similar transferral of metallurgical terms infuses 'The Alchemist in the City', an early poem that alludes to 'The making and the melting crowds' (3).[96] Hopkins does not remove forging, tempering, and quenching from the blacksmith's hearth; nor does he press artisanal actions into the service of alien expressive aims. On the contrary, these examples foster a process of reintegration, according to which the forms of speech begin to resemble transformations in metal.

Yet such materials alone could never produce a secure weld between the artisan and the poet. For Hopkins, the relationship between human making and divine creation needs to be part of the picture. His thinking in this respect draws on Frederick Faber's *The Creator and the Creature* (1858),[97] a work that understands humanity as 'made' rather than 'making'.[98] Rejecting, as such, the idea of *homo faber* – an idea later popularised by neo-Catholic artists and thinkers – Hopkins argues instead that '*Homo creatus est*'.[99] 'MAN CANNOT CREATE a single speck', he insists, since 'God creates all that is beside himself'.[100] He does not entirely shun analogies with human making: 'every workman', he admits, 'has a use for every object he makes', while God, too, has 'a purpose'. But rather than dwell on continuous or deputed powers of creation, Hopkins claims that God 'meant the world to give him praise, reverence, and service; *to give him glory . . .*',[101] even though '*he does not need it*'.[102] Art remains possible as a form of expression: 'MEN OF GENIUS ARE SAID TO CREATE, a painting, a poem'.[103] Only, they do so strictly as 'creatures of God'. Human creation recedes, meanwhile, to the figure of speech in 'SAID TO'. Poetry, as such, is generative only in the secondary sense: a vehicle for bestowing praise on the creator, not an instance of creation in its own right.

Prompted by his readings in Scotist philosophy, Hopkins pursues a related theme of infinity, and gratuity. '[N]áture', he writes in 'God's Grandeur', 'is never spent' (9).[104] At the same time, he persists in seeing the creation of the world as an act of craftsmanship. The 'azure hills', described in 'Hurrahing in Harvest' (1877), are 'his wórld-wielding shoulder' (9).[105] 'In the Valley of the Elwy', he imagines created things combining to 'build this world of Wales' (10).[106] Hopkins's accounts of 'inscape' bear a related emphasis. Writing to Robert Bridges, he proposes that 'design, pattern or what I am in the habit of calling "inscape" is what I above all in aim at in poetry'.[107] Efforts to capture the inscapes of the world – to honour God through them – search in this way for a kind of maker's mark. This is less a leitmotif than a giveaway sign of the creator at work. As Bernard Bergonzi observes, '"inscape" was the form or design that was unique to a given entity, whether a poem or a flower'.[108] An emphasis on particularity, or *haeccitas*, appeals to this idea of an artisanal first mover. Though unfolding on a grand scale, the constructional qualities of 'land-scape' are retained, as understood in the Germanic sense of *Landschaft*, meaning literally a 'land-making' or 'land-forming'.

In 'The Wreck of the Deutschland' (1875–76), Hopkins itemises a similar process of construction. This time, it arises at the level of the human subject: 'Thou hast bóund bónes and véins in me, fástened me flésh' (5).[109] Here, too, marks of making are part of the poem's landscape. In 'Márk, the márk of mán's máke | And the word of it Sacrificed' (171–72), the opening item issues a Shakespearean summons.[110] 'Márk' might equally suggest a maker's mark of divine provenance; or, a marked condition, an inescapable smear. Such features moderate sin in favour of a divine making in residue. Through its traceability, this creative afterglow keeps humanity close to God's labour. In 'Henry Purcell' (1879), an ability to divine the mark, or 'forgèd feature' (7), becomes a pretext for praise – praise, in effect, of reverent art.[111] As the epigraph has it, Purcell 'uttered in notes the very make and species of man as created both in him and in all men generally'.[112] Elsewhere, such attention becomes a blazon, dedicated to an incarnate process of making. In 'Felix Randal', for instance, an allusion to 'his mould of man, big-bóned and hardy-handsome' (2) activates the senses in 'mould' both of 'character', and cast or 'type'.[113] 'Harry Ploughman', meanwhile, draws a human subject whose lineaments – in 'Hard as hurdle arms' (1) – absorb the processes and products of field labour. And while his 'knee-nave; and barrelled shank –' (3) bespeak butchers' anatomy, they also evoke an ecclesiastical architecture of the human frame.[114]

This emphasis on a constructed and constructing origin brings divine agency and power to the fore, and – as previously seen in Ruskin's notion of 'fors' as 'force' – connects an idea of service to an idea of sub-mission. Bergonzi remarks pertinently that the 'word "instress" implies "force"'.[115] Relatedly, Hopkins's poetry attributes a residual violence to the Fall. His poem 'No Worst' (*c.* 1885–86) gives voice to these tor-ments: 'My cries heave, herds-long; huddle in a main, a chief- | Woe, wórld-sorrow; on an áge-old ánvil wínce and síng –' (4–5).[116] The last phrase assembles the trinity of forge labour, pain, and song tracked across this chapter. It also evokes an explicit violence: a divine blow in fact, of the kind that G. K. Chesterton imagines in his pertinently entitled story, 'The Hammer of God'.[117] Hopkins likewise registers the destructive strokes of his Maker. In 'The Wreck of the Deutschland', for instance, a power of making closely tracks an equivalent power to destroy. Having 'bóund bónes and véins in me' (5), God leaves His crea-ture 'áfter it álmost únmade' (6).[118] The poem thus meditates on the ways of a creator who 'Swings the stroke dealt' (44). As if conflating the hammer rhythms of creation with a merciless lashing out, Hopkins contemplates the 'Stroke and a stress that stars and storms deliver' (45), where the first word doubles as an affectionate caress and a punish-ment.[119] An idea of divine 'strokes' recurs in the companion poem, 'The Loss of the Eurydice' (1878): 'Where she foundered! One stroke | Felled and furled them, the hearts of oak!' (5–6).[120] To borrow Ruskin's phrase, the poetic subjects in both works find themselves at the rough end of an apparently endless 'forming time'. When a salve eventually arrives, it entails glad submission to God's sovereign rule, an austerely generative relief of 'the stress' induced by unreserved fealty.[121]

This emphasis on divine authority unavoidably complicates Hopkins's theorisation of personal creativity. If human beings are barred from acts of primary creation, how should we understand the poet's role? One solution is to cast poetry as a manner of praise, aimed at acts of cre-ation that are already in progress. Prayer can be a flexible instrument, of course: 'It is not only prayer that gives God glory', Hopkins suggests, 'but work', so that 'Smiting on an anvil, sawing a beam, whitewashing a wall [. . .] everything gives God some glory'.[122] But rather than apply this attitude to the conduct of poetry, Hopkins prefers displaced examples. He dwells repeatedly on 'workmanship' in the animal world, as in 'The Windhover' (1877), where 'the mástery of the thing!' (8) recovers prowess from what might seem instinctual behaviour.[123] A similar homage to embodied skill emerges from working-class portraits: Felix Randal, for instance, is 'pówerful amídst péers' (13).[124] In these settings, Hopkins finds mastery in locations remote from his own milieu, albeit that he refers them back to their origin, in God. In so doing, he contains the sense that 'Our make and making break, are breaking, down' ('The Sea and the Skylark' (1877), (13–14)).[125] The universal type, in 'Our make', ensures that breakages are always gathered up, as the poem enrols the hopeless gerund of human 'making' into a divine process that breaks in order to build.

The problem of poetic making persists, however. Discussing the Christian poet and theologian, Charles Williams, Hill defines the 'fundamental dilemma', of 'poetic craft' as 'simultaneously [. . .] an imitation of the divine fiat and an act of enormous human self-will'.[126] In his early years as a Jesuit, Hopkins struggles to differentiate reverent imitation from self-will, and obedience from merely reflexive inscape. He famously burns his poems, in August 1868, on the grounds 'they wd. interfere with my state and vocation'.[127] Even as late as 1883, he confesses to Bridges that 'poets and men of art are [. . .] by no means necessarily or commonly gentlemen'.[128] On fully resuming poetic composition, with 'The Wreck of the Deutschland', he returns to the importance of obedience.[129] Placing his writing at God's service, he hopes to elude the vanity, the dazzle, and the moral danger of fame as described by St Ignatius.[130] '[W]ith things like composition,' he reasons, 'the best sacrifice was not to destroy one's work but to leave it entirely to be disposed of by obedience'.[131] He resolves, then, to wait for 'guidance', in a posture that conceives poetry less as call than as response.[132]

Hopkins's enthusiasm for Scotus eventually presents a way of dampening these anxieties. He 'shews that freedom is compatible with necessity', a doctrine that leaves room for creative action without threatening the principle of absolute deference to God.[133] For Scotus, indeed, 'the singularity of a thing is no impediment to the abstraction of a common concept'.[134] According to this altered form of incarnational thinking, Christ represents not only the point at which God and man are combined, but the realisation and epitome of a more radically unified sensibility running through the whole of nature.[135] Relatedly, Hopkins proposes 'the incredible condescension of the Incarnation',[136] according to which Christ submits to pain and torture, but 'also to the mean and trivial accidents of humanity'.[137] The operations of God in this lowly arena cancel the alienation of the Fall, infusing trivial matters with significance, and freeing human craftsmanship to work in league with a loving condescension. Hopkins retains an interest, this is to say, in 'What makes the man and what I The man within that makes:' (160).[138] But the personal agency he imagines quickly resolves into a deeper conception of divine primacy or 'knowledge'. Thus, according to Scotus, 'Every being other than the first depends upon the latter as upon a cause', just as 'The perfect artisan has a distinct knowledge of everything to be done before he does it'.[139] By definition, the 'perfect artisan' is not the man, but the God who embodies all preceding vision and awareness of what has to be done.

Though Hopkins stays close to these principles whenever questioned, he often struggles to maintain the impression of divine priority in his practice. A personal context for this difficulty arises from the independence of his character, a trait informing not only his conversion to Catholicism in defiance of his parents, but also his subsequent departure from its Aristotelian and Thomist orthodoxies. In this regard, the heterodox complexion of Scotist metaphysics reflects an established tendency to break from the expected course. This does not quite amount to a rebel consciousness: like Barrett Browning's fervent, yet critical, 'Carlyleship', it more closely resembles a form of radical obedience. It is worth, all the same, noting Hopkins's abiding interest in the myth of Prometheus. He offers Bridges generous praise and criticism in response to *Prometheus the Firegiver* (1883),[140] a narrative poem whose famously 'truant' hero has 'ftolen from heaven I The flafh of maftering fire'.[141] In his own poetry, Hopkins reimagines the myth indirectly, at once sharpening the question and softening the sting of disobedience. Discussing a related interest in lightning and electricity, Norman Mackenzie draws out a suggestive field of concern from Hopkins's interest in 'the return stroke'.[142] This, he describes, as 'a tongue of brightness [. . .] running up from the ground to the cloud', which restores the electrical imbalance generated by the first strike.[143] Mackenzie relates this phenomenon to the terrestrial energy evoked in 'God's Grandeur', a lesser-known version of which reads 'like lightening' instead of 'like shining from shook foil'.[144] The emphasis, consequently, is not on stolen fire; instead, we witness an all-encompassing electrical charge, which runs from the human world right up to the heavens. Evidently, this departs from the more passive submission to 'strokes' introduced elsewhere in Hopkins's poetry. By breaking down the distinction between human forge and divine spark, a more active response becomes conceivable. While energy issues first from the heavens, the answering strike articulates a power of return, and with it, a creative role assimilable to poetry.

Hopkins's meditation on 'the random grím fórge' (13) in 'Felix Randal' evokes both the terms and the limits of this reconciliation. What we might call Hopkins's dissident conformity dwells in modes of human creativity that are out of step. This last effect hangs crucially on the adjective, 'random'. Employing a phrase from 'Epithalamion' (1888), we might say that the creative process is 'Built of chancequarrièd' (36).[145] Hopkins's poetry occupies an arena in which the return 'stroke' is guided, but also prone to landing indeterminately. The resulting pattern – of redeemed imperfection – recalls the patina left behind by the polished head of a planishing hammer. No matter how expert the hand, the surface finish is fortuitous, unrepeatable. Hopkins hopes, in effect, to re-purpose and redeem the 'random', just as Ruskin's compositional procedure admits value through risk and hazard. Derived from the Anglo-Norman 'randon, radum', the word's root derives from *rendon* ('speed, haste') and *randir* ('to run fast, gallop'). The *OED* lists 'randall' among English variants occurring right up to the sixteenth century. Etymologically, at least, a self-reinforcing relationship obtains between the forge, the farrier's name, and the title of the poem. Beyond the hinted equine association, 'random' also suggests impetuosity, speed, force, or violence (in riding, running, striking, etc.) (*OED*). As such, it suits the image of a forge in action: timed strokes are required, but so, too, are *timely* strokes. More broadly, it evokes a kind of guided hazard, as in forms of masonry that employ 'stones of irregular sizes' (*OED*), or as in textiles, where the name refers to yarn that contains 'different colours in sequence' (*OED*). 'Random tooling' suggests, similarly, the dressing of a stone 'done in parallel lines with a broad chisel' (*OED*).

This sense of 'random' as a controlled admission of chance exists on the edge of less salutary implications, released by the collocation *'grim* forge'. The adjective's Anglo-Saxon provenance cuts off the flight of 'random' and invites meanings ranging between 'fierce', 'cruel', 'angry', 'harsh', 'ugly', 'uninviting', 'unrelenting', 'merciless', and 'resolute' (*OED*). 'Random' also refers to a 'rush or stream (*of* words, fire, etc.)' (*OED*). In fact it is in this application – rather than as applied to a once powerful farrier – that its significance dwells. Writing to his brother, Everard, on 5–8 November 1885, Hopkins explains that 'Sprung rhythm gives back to poetry its true soul and self'.[146] Poetry, he adds, is 'emphatically speech,' but 'speech [. . .] purged [. . .] ˆof drossˆ like gold in the furnace'. Here, the latter-day sense of 'dross' as 'rubbishy' recalls and re-enacts its primary, metallurgical meaning. This would be 'The scum, recrement, or extraneous matter thrown off from metals in the process of melting' (*OED*). To this method of heating,

Hopkins adds a metallurgical principle of finish: just as 'poetry in general is brighter than ~~prose~~ ^common^ speech', so sprung rhythm 'purges' to 'an emphasis as much brighter, livelier, more lustrous than the ^regular but^ commonplace emphasis of common rhythm'. In this way, the farrier becomes a direct counterpart of the poet. Felix, we read, 'Didst fettle for the great grey drayhorse his bright and battering sandal!', while the poet also removes impurities, as if beating red hot material in pursuit of strength and shine.

In 'The Wreck of the Deutschland', 'the word' simultaneously settles into an essence, and worries over its role, whether as the verb acting or the object acted upon: 'Wording it how but by him that present and past, | Heaven and earth are word of, worded by? –' (229–230).[147] These forms of repetition and verbal play abandon the assumption that language is merely representational. Equally, the beating required to achieve a 'shine' in 'Felix Randal' edges towards a principle of necessary violence, just as it does in *Great Expectations*. Gardner implies this much when arguing that 'Metaphor is often the process of doing exquisite violence to language'.[148] In 'Hopkins', he elaborates, 'the wrench away from an accepted meaning is sometimes so drastic as to cause obscurity'.[149] Hopkins, for his part, is prepared to risk a drastic wrench. He accepts the necessary admission of chance, a guided and energetic strike of the hammer that changes the metal sufficiently to take a polish. The question remains whether this can be achieved without dazzling the eye, or admitting manifestations of the random that are 'unrestrained' or anarchic.

R. C. Trench, the Victorian pioneer of etymological study, makes a helpful distinction between licensed power and given capacity: God, he proposes, 'did not begin the world *with* names, but *with the power of naming*'.[150] Though an admirer of Trench, Hopkins cannot go so far. His Scotist principles insist on the divine referent of legitimate human 'capacity', so that a more fitting summation of this balancing act lies – as previously argued – with the image of the 'return stroke'. In that figure, divine energy does not need to be 'stolen'. As an answering charge, its source in God is clear. Less welcome connotations creep in around the edges of the 'random'. Chance, contingency, or Ruskinian imperfection, are easily construed as worship: in that case, planishing marks or sparks generate beauty, and this applies even as they fall 'at random'. But the divine mark is different: it deals in destruction as well as life. Even a delegated creative faculty is not immune to distortion. And while the admission of chance may be reconciled with Scotism, in an imagined reconciliation of particularity and divine universality, poets working in the temporal world are left vulnerable to misconstruction and verbal hazard. Hopkins in particular fears the dazzle of a creative vanity turned truant from his religious vocation. He suspects, too, the operations of a language whose violence activates versions of the random not easily reconciled with the priority of divine foreknowledge. Influenced, though he is, by the labour romance of Ruskin and Longfellow, his methods assume an inverted or referred idea of action, a prowess based not on stolen tools, nor even stolen fire, but on a guided hand still susceptible to surprise and revelation.

* * *

This chapter has discussed analogies between the forming operations of the blacksmith and the writer. And it has addressed an accompanying anxiety – a self-suspicious anxiety – about the nature of writing. Dickens associates 'song' in the broadest sense with the romance of the forge, but he also reveals its vulnerability to theft, secondary usage, and re-purposing. While these forces condition the operation of hammers, files and manacles, they also recall the linguistic pilfering habitual to authors. Ruskin distinguishes between the craftsman's tools and the phantom planes rented out by capitalists; and he hopes *Fors* will be a tool in the hands of his labouring readers. But he never entirely trusts writing to fulfil that purpose. By contrast with Dickens, Hopkins worries that his poetry is Promethean and pride-inducing precisely because it lies outside his chosen vocation. All three writers connect forming processes – whether mechanical or literary – to acts of violence. And all three hint that this violence is a requisite feature of the creative process. *Great Expectations* dramatises the nightmarish conversion of heartbeats into hammer blows. For Ruskin, geological hammers commence a deranged tapping at cherished beliefs. In Hopkins, the perspective expands beyond these forms of personal threat to encompass a complete scheme of creative destruction.

Amidst this troubled outlook, each reserves a zone of possibility in the connection between blacksmith and writer. And it is this possibility that ensures the conversion of Longfellow's legacy from a mode of edifying spectatorship into a useful bequest. Just as Morris accepts magic and mischief into his conception of artistic cunning, so these writers approach a non-instrumental version of literary craft. Dickens's novel studies a misleading impression of freedom, rather than its fulfilment; but it acknowledges that tools devoted to noble purposes may go astray. And its most writerly passages evoke spots of real time activated by the event of forge work. Ruskin likewise reinterprets the primitive magic of making in positive terms: as a putative tool, *Fors* combines force and conscious timing with an openness to fortune. Ruskin even reconceives textual errors as necessary blemishes on its quick-forged surface. The picture emerges of a literary artefact in spontaneous composition. Hopkins's conception of the 'random' presents a similar conjunction of the timely and the serendipitous. More broadly, he evinces an understanding of words as malleable agents, susceptible to fire welding. The beauty of forge work depends to this extent on the impossibility of minute precision, on the degree of chance admitted by every well-timed strike.[151] Committing, as these writers do, to this workmanship of risk, each also admits a possibility of malformation, and even the occasional monster.

Chapter 6

Modernism and the Maker

Virginia Woolf once observed that 'there is something incongruous, unfit-ting, about the term "craftsmanship" when applied to words'.[1] Spoken as part of a late BBC broadcast on 'Craftsmanship' (1937), her thoughts bear on the legacy of the Arts and Crafts movement, notably the per-sistent comparison of literature to practical activities such as weaving. Gladstone, as we have seen, suppresses the cunning in craft in favour of a manual dexterity reconciled with paternal oversight. For Morris, the 'stones close-fitting' of Odysseus's 'well-builded' (13:340) house symbol-ise a holistic civilisation: 'cunning' he can accept in return for the dramatic fruits of its mischief. Woolf, by contrast, suspects a futility for the writer in eliminating the 'draught between the frames of the windows'.[2] While this seems at odds with her tactile delight in setting up a handpress for the Hogarth venture,[3] and with the equally Morrisian flavour of the painted surfaces created by her friends at Charleston, she evidently senses a threat to truth: '"craft"', she notes '[. . .] means in the first place making useful objects out of solid matter – for example, a pot, a chair, a table', and 'In the second place, [. . .] cajolery, cunning, deceit.'[4] Pressing language into instrumental service, it follows, compromises its most valued function: 'words', she warns, 'never make anything that is useful; and words are the only things that tell the truth'.[5]

Woolf's portrayal of artistic enterprise in *To the Lighthouse* (1927) broadly anticipates this account: Lily Briscoe's abstraction in colour resists both the art-as-toil thesis, and the heroic cast of Mr Ramsay's brain-work.[6] The interrupted dignity of Wagnerian 'hammering' that runs through the opera scene in *The Years* (1937) signals a related ambiv-alence.[7] Woolf was not alone in repudiating the craft ideal: Wyndham Lewis expresses similar sentiments in describing the Omega Workshops as 'Mr Roger Fry's little belated Morris movement'.[8] Indeed, the art and literature of the 1920s tend to evoke intellectualism, a defiant restoration of the mind's independence over the body. In the familiar account, mod-ernist writers installed Bergsonian perceptualism, self-conscious artifice, machine-worship, and abstraction, in place of the Ruskinian 'hand'. The many amputees produced by the Great War complicated the very idea of embodied human agency: the Siemens-Schuckertwerke Universal Arm, for instance, linked worker prostheses directly to the parts of machines.[9] Compelling as it is, this bionic vision should not distract from other kinds of manual persistence. Even the Bauhaus – so often regarded as the epitome of devotion to machine production – achieved its fame with individually crafted prototypes, such as Marianne Brandt's tea and coffee service.[10] David Pye likewise observes that many early machine tools relied, in fact, on foundational acts of craftsmanship.[11] By implication, human discernment and practical skill are not so much extinguished in the modern industrial economy as re-sited.

Recent studies look beyond the dominant Bloomsburyite or Futurist lens, to acknowledge that 'Modernism is not one thing but many'.[12] This perspective presents not just a provincial or global counter to the metropolitan milieu of high modernism, but a longer and broader form of inheritance, drawn from the previous century's art movements.[13] Where the evolution of work is concerned, critics naturally focus on technological change – Morag Shiach's study, for instance, ranges from Taylorism to typewriters.[14] The persistence of the craft idea, and its application to literary experience, tends to receive less attention, however.[15] As Dieter Meindl observes, the early decades of the twentieth century actually witness 'a formidable amount of attention paid to craft'.[16] Even Woolf, who rejects the application of 'craft' to words, attributes renewed power to the idea through her urge to attack it. The threat is potent because it emerges not only from the ethical tradition mapped in previous chapters, but from aestheticist sources more obviously within her purview. As I have discussed elsewhere, Pater's early impressionism plots a route back to Carlyle through his late essay on 'Style' (1889), a commentary on Flaubert's reconciliation of authorial toil with artisanal mystery.[17] In his short story 'The Lesson of the Master' (1888), Henry James rejects the notion that literature is teachable in the manner of an apprenticeship, and he dramatises the abuses of that model. But he inherited sufficient Carlylism from his father to reproduce his self-punishing producerism, as where he exclaims, 'I *did* say to myself "Produce again – produce; produce better than ever, and all will yet be well"'.[18] Not without opposition, Percy Lubbock recruited James as the chief exemplar of his notion that 'the man of letters is a craftsman'.[19] In *The Craft of Fiction* (1921), he turns this Jamesian 'impression' into a physical imprint: not a perceptual or an ethereal event, but a materially *impressed* mark, one 'built into a structure'. Introducing his edition of James's letters, Lubbock includes his friend among 'such deliberate craftsmen as Stevenson or Gustave Flaubert'.[20] Though admitting that the critic 'creates out of life', he argues that 'his work is not the less plastic for that' and must 'proceed in a workmanlike manner'. Even Whistler, whose libel case against Ruskin is often characterised as the nemesis of the ethical tradition, depends on a labour theory of art. His answer to the courtroom query, 'The labour of two days is that for which you ask two hundred guineas!', deserves more attention than it has received.[21] Rather than evading the labour criterion invoked by Ruskin's barrister, Whistler's answer –'No. [. . .] I ask it for the knowledge I have gained in the work of a lifetime' – invokes a different measure of labour. Labour, for him, is not a quantity plotted against manufacturing time: artists, rather, are the human products of individual and collective effort expended over decades. Artistic apprenticeship, and mastership, in effect, become the true site of value (and of time invested). Here, the leading idea is not dilettantism, but a veiled professionalism. Whistler may refer to himself publicly as 'the butterfly', but he characterises himself privately as 'the grinder'.[22] He likewise appraises Venetian painters as masters 'not of technique but in terms of commitment', and persistence.[23] And he sets this persistence in a metallurgical context, reporting how he was 'each day building up and hammering more and more [. . .] just as the coppersmith works out by degrees his beautiful shapes and surfaces.'[24] Instead of disclaiming the idea of work, Whistler combines the artistic labour of a lifetime with the time signature of a moment.

These legacies blend with their mid-Victorian sources to inform modernist encounters with Arts and Crafts precepts. As Meindl registers, one manifestation of this inheritance is a concern with Daedalus, 'the ancient maker turned patron saint of artists'.[25] Here, we can look again to Pater, who writes in 'The Beginnings of Greek Sculpture'[26] that 'The metal-work which Homer describes in such variety is all *hammer-work*, all the joinings being effected by pins or riveting.'[27] This attention to method and construction gives way, in turn, to its 'expressive' contact 'with dextrous fingers', so that 'one seems to trace in it, on every particle of the partially resisting material, the touch and play of the shaping instruments, in highly trained hands, under the guidance of exquisitely disciplined senses – that *cachet*, or seal of nearness to the workman's hand'.[28] Elsewhere in the same essay, Pater indicates that 'Daedal work' (from the Greek artificer, Daedalus) is 'the name of a craft rather than a proper name', and that it means 'to work curiously'. In Arts and Crafts fashion, he even complains of a 'falsifying isolation' of sculptors 'from the work of the weaver, the carpenter, and the goldsmith'.[29] His effort to evoke the 'nearness to the workman's hand' culminates in a Carlylean formulation, according to which 'The heroic age of Greek art is the age of the hero as smith'.[30] This formulation bears most notably on the pledge of James Joyce's Stephen Dedalus to 'forge in the smithy of my soul the uncreated conscience of my race'.[31] 'The artist,' he ventures, is 'like the God of creation'; he 'remains within or behind or beyond or above his handiwork, invisible, refined out of existence, indifferent, paring his fingernails'.[32] Like Pater, Joyce derives this image from Flaubert's published letters,[33] and more broadly from Thomist aesthetics. The familiar assumption – that Stephen intends a supreme articulation of authorial impersonality – is still serviceable, but it obscures the persistent strain of Arts and Crafts thinking running through his Flaubertian materialism. The teenage Joyce – along with Marcel Proust, H.D. (Hilda Doolittle), and Pound – was a keen reader of Ruskin.[34] He may even have derived the Daedalean theme from *Fors Clavigera*. In Letter 23, Ruskin describes the cathedral porch at Lucca, with its sculpture and legend on 'the labyrinth which the Cretan Dedalus built' (27:401). W. B. Yeats's poems are similarly haunted, though they abandon the Ruskinian version of craft in favour of mysticism, and mechanistic perfection.[35] This version of craftsmanship is 'More miracle than bird or handiwork'.[36] 'Sailing to Byzantium' (1927) likewise describes a form of expertise that denies roots in the natural world.[37] If being 'out of nature' is the aim, then the work of 'Grecian goldsmiths' approaches Marx's idea of the commodity fetish: a thing made in the world that lacks detectable human origin.

This chapter addresses the work of three modern writers who take a different path from Yeats, in stressing the persistent imprint of labouring hands. Guided respectively by humanism, Catholicism, and paganism, each embraces anti-capitalism across a broad political spectrum; and each practises a form of spiritual-physical holism that extends from material conceptions of the literary mind to a sanctification of sexual relations.[38] Liz Stanley describes the first figure discussed here – Olive Schreiner – as 'a high modernist before modernism was named or had become a movement'.[39] However this may be, Schreiner was deeply embedded in, and marked by, cultures of late Victorian radicalism. Her dispersed historical placing reflects unusually disparate affiliations, ranging from mid-Victorian labour ethics to early twentieth-century conceptions of social hygiene. Though Schreiner discusses skilled manual labour at length, she rarely associates artisanal images with female advancement in letters. On the face of it, Vernon Lee might be a more compelling case. In *The Handling of Words* (1923), she argues that literature is 'a case of construction, of craft'.[40] Published two years after Lubbock's *The Craft of Fiction*, it may nevertheless have inspired it. As Catherine Maxwell shows, Lee's book absorbs material from a much earlier essay on 'The Craft of Words' (1894).[41] As such, Lee's account seems a possible target of Woolf's counterblast. Only, she confines this sense of 'craft' to a generic or technical appreciation of work well done. And her attention to this quality admits and promotes the idea that good style is 'a teachable practice',[42] explicable in the fashion of the popular writing primers.[43]

Lee, as such, compensates for no theological or class-based unease in placing writing on a material foundation: on the contrary, she insists that 'Writing is an art of emotion'.[44] Schreiner, by contrast, figures intellectual labour – if not writing itself – as a material process; and she posits a pre-history in which women are physically enfranchised by mastering manual skills. In this respect, *Woman and Labour* (1911) runs suggestively against the middle-class tilt of Woolf's 'Professions for Women' (1931). It also pulls against a closing door: as Livesey astutely observes,[45] the Storrington Document (1914) on National Guilds 'combines a unanimous Morrisite commitment to communal craft ideals [. . .] with an irreconcilable rift on the question of women's place in the guild socialist state.'[46] Schreiner resists such developments by placing women's multifaceted labour at the very centre of her socialism. Her re-formulation of an ecstatic word, and a transcendental function, connect her back to Barrett Browning; and, among her contemporaries, to Edward Carpenter, whose labour ethics harness Walt Whitman's rhapsodic holism.

The second part of this chapter addresses the work of the letter cutter, sculptor and typographer, Eric Gill. Gill's attention to letter forms privileges questions of materiality, abstraction, and visibility, as also a renewed conception of the writer-as-worker. In these respects, he was something other, and something more, than a 'proto-Byzantine'.[47] Far from asserting the exclusive primacy of intellect, he pursues a version of what Richard Sennett calls 'craft quality', an attribute founded 'in judgements made on tacit habits and suggestions'.[48] Apart from maintaining a connection between the mind and the hand, he problematises the role of the machine, distinguishing technology fetishism from a more fluid lived reality. His movement from early socialism to Distributism serves as a hinge between the different kinds of anti-capitalism that interact across the chapter, while his paternalistic workshop culture plays a similar role in relation to the different versions of master and apprentice discussed across this book. Not unrelatedly, the abusive nature of his sexual holism – first publicly disclosed in Fiona MacCarthy's biography of 1989 – throws into question a wider field of incarnational and institutional ethics.[49] The last part extends my attention to revived apprenticeship, focusing here on Pound's conception of poetic apprenticeship, as famously evoked by T. S. Eliot's dedication of *The Waste Land*.[50] Discussion returns to the matters of social hygiene raised in relation to Schreiner, a public defender of South Africa's Jews who nevertheless employs anti-Semitic caricature in her fictions. Pound's anti-Semitism is much discussed, but its relation to the interchange between craft and words, and the wider currency of that affiliation, warrants closer scrutiny. This legacy precipitates a moral crisis that bears not only on his own work, but on the cultural solutions he inherits from others.

'My mind strikes work': Olive Schreiner and the Ecstatic Word

Woolf first delivered her famous lecture on 'Professions for Women' at the Women's Service League, a forum evocative of the ways in which previous generations applied mid-Victorian labour theory to 'the Woman Question'.[51] She imagines writing, all the same, as a matter of private concentration rather than self-conscious labour: a 'profession' not a craft or a trade.[52] Though her account differs from Schreiner's less direct commentary on authorial experience, both develop a feminism centrally concerned with women's relationship to work. In this respect, as Maria Antonietta Saracino observes, 'Woolf's thinking owed Olive Schreiner's far more than Woolf herself would be prepared to admit'.[53] In other respects, Schreiner appears more of a rival or opponent than a source of continuity, not least because she pairs female authorship with physical as well as mental labour. In this regard, she emerges as the representative of a counter-factual modernism: an epiphanic thinker whose sympathies are artisanal, a living link between mid-Victorian work ethics and later discourses of feminism and socialism.

On reviewing the edition of letters compiled by Schreiner's husband – Samuel Cron Cronwright-Schreiner – Woolf observes that 'The writer's interests are local, her passions personal'.[54] This impression hints at Schreiner's upbringing in the Cape Colony, and her later years residing in the different territories of what became South Africa.[55] She acknowledges that Schreiner 'came to England', but adds that she 'was at once at the centre of an appreciative group of distinguished men'.[56] In all, Schreiner spent two extensive periods living in London: the first between 1881–89, and the second between 1913–20. She developed friendships with leading intellectual and political figures, including Havelock Ellis, Eleanor Marx, Karl Pearson, Edward Carpenter, J. A. Hobson and W. T. Stead. Far from sitting at their feet, this was an audience pre-formed by the success of her novel *The Story of An African Farm* (1883). Her London years proved formative in this respect, but her South African experiences after 1889 were equally so. Instead of consigning her to marginality, they immersed her in a momentous staging of overlapping labour questions, pertaining to national identity, sexual relations, gender and race. Like May Morris – co-founder and first president of the Women's Guild of Art[57] – Schreiner practised a feminism based in the claims of labour, and in an ethnographic turn that locates sexual injustice in the patriarchal form of the bourgeois family.[58] Her discursive centrality in these debates should not be underestimated. In 'The Woman Question' (1886), for instance, Eleanor Marx and Edward Aveling quote Lyndall's speech ('We were equals once . . .') from *The Story of an African Farm*.[59] Livesey has done much to shed light on these interrelations in a study that encompasses the socialist activism of Schreiner, Clementina Black, Dollie Radford and Isabella Ford.[60] My own treatment concentrates on Schreiner's later, politically hybrid, writings: most notably, her fragmentary manifesto *Woman and Labour*.[61]

Some aspects of Schreiner's life resist an emphasis on physical effort. Her lifelong struggle with asthma rendered her own body a site of pain and discomfort, not ecstatic labour. Equally, her fictional world sometimes eludes the expectations generated by her proselytising. Joseph Bristow observes of the farm in Schreiner's first novel that 'work slumps into the background'.[62] On the other hand, she cultivates an exaggerated respect for physical attributes, not least through a curiously atavistic attraction to Cronwright-Schreiner, whom she dubs a 'real *man*'.[63] Addressing him in 1904, she observes that 'Muscle I admire beyond anything in man or woman'.[64] Schreiner thought of her own body as muscular, too, and would trace this quality through her paternal lineage. Her father, she writes, grew 'to be a strong, stern man', a man in whom 'the blood of his old Puritan ancestors worked mightily'.[65] Carlylean echoes sound even amidst her pacifism, as where she concedes, in speaking of militant suffragettes, that 'I prefer the martyr to the warrior – but I admire the warrior too'.[66] An attraction to hero-worship, equally, informs her first response to Cecil Rhodes, a man whom she later came to loathe. Writing to Havelock Ellis in March 1890 she anticipates 'going to meet Cecil Rhodes the only great man & man of genius S. Africa possesses';[67] four months later, she admits to W. T. Stead that 'The only big man we have here is Rhodes', adding that 'I feel a curious & almost painfully intense interest in the man & his career'.[68] Sturdy statesmen reciprocated her interest: Rhodes was an admirer of *The Story of an African Farm*, and despite its freethinking aspects, so too was Gladstone.

Schreiner's roots in mid-Victorian literary culture sound in her metallurgical (and male) pen name – 'Ralph Iron' – recalling as it does the ferrous preoccupations of *Fors*, then approaching its last year. Towards the end of her career, Ruskin's labour ethics inform her description of a 'great Gothic cathedral' whose 'final form' testifies to the work of generations 'labouring' until 'the work as completed had unity'.[69] This, clearly, is not time travel as conducted by Woolf's Orlando – aristocratic, playful, solitary – but an investigation of social organism in tune with Arts and Crafts principles. Writing to Ellis in December 1885, Schreiner proposes signing a circulating paper in honour of Ruskin.[70] She mentions him again in 1890, and in 1908 draws implicitly on his 'law of help', in promoting 'organised union' between men.[71] Schreiner's unfinished novel *From Man to Man* pays a further compliment to this tradition. Enrolling her heroine, Rebekah, among these 'fellows', she momentarily casts her in the role of builder and founder:

> She rolled up her sleeves and dug a foundation and filled it with stones [. . .] Then she mixed mud [. . .] Then she began to build. She took the bricks in one hand and the trowel in the other; she threw the bricks round in one hand and cut off the rough points with the trowel, as the workmen did. Then she placed each brick carefully on the layer of mortar, and tap-tapped them with the end of the handle of the trowel to see if they were quite straight.[72]

The tactile quality of this primal scene is striking enough, and the Ruskinian joy of intelligent trowel handling palpable. A yet more pressing liberation dwells in the parenthesis that 'She had seen the Kaffirs treading the mud to build the wagon house, but she had never been allowed to help.'[73] Schreiner builds thereby – in a way quite foreign to Woolf's feminism – on a visceral labour yearning inherited from the proto-feminist positions of Jameson and Norton, and the accompanying sense of a communal imperative to work. In *Woman and Labour*, this tradition undergoes an activist transformation, as proposals become demands, and personal duty expands to become a species requirement: '*Give us labour*', the author declares, '*and the training which fits for labour! We demand this, not for ourselves alone, but for our race.*'[74]

Schreiner, crucially, is not focused on the caring professions recommended by Jameson, nor on middle-class professions. 'We seek', she insists, to enter the non-sexual fields of intellectual or physical toil'.[75] Meanwhile, her language becomes elemental, prophetic, and prone to internal colloquy: 'Through all the ages of the past,' she writes, '[. . .] we physically toiled beside man, bearing up by the labour of our bodies the world about us.[76] But while Carlylean positions are initially invoked by this rhetoric, the same impulse verges on parody as a ventriloquised opponent simultaneously denies work to women and proclaims its human necessity: 'You, the child-bearers of the race, have in that one function a labour that equals all others combined; therefore, toil no more in other directions'. A suggestion of imposture neutralises this voice's authority: instead of gaining entry to professions formerly reserved to men, Schreiner adapts the matriarchal ethnology of the period to insist that women have suffered the ancestral wrong of expulsion from domains that always belonged to them.

If Schreiner relies on a Ruskinian fall narrative, her ethnographic emphasis delivers quite different results. In her historical scheme the sexes initially 'laboured free together' in conditions of fulfilled comradeship.[77] Women then performed the manufacturing, building, and agricultural tasks associated with settled society: 'We hoed the earth, we reaped the grain, we shaped the dwellings, we wove the clothing, we modelled the earthen vessels and drew the lines upon them'.[78] They are not then inserted into a pre-existing artisanal history, but cast as original practitioners. By way of an ironical glace at the adherents of Guild Socialism, she writes that 'male hand-workers' have tended to 'exclude women [. . .] even from those ancient fields of textile manufacture and handicraft'. The nature of the injustice shifts, in this respect, from the more familiar idea of exclusion and frustrated opportunity to the injustice of usurpation. This, in turn, becomes the central 'fact which constitutes our modern "Woman's Labour Problem"'.[79] Schreiner's position crystallises in her manner of forging links between intellectual callings and the work of the hands; and in this area, too, she mobilises the insurgent authority of historical precedent. Just as Gladstone bases a theory of statesmanship on his portrait of Odysseus as a carpenter, so Schreiner writes of 'ancient Greece' that 'the King's wife and the prince's daughter do we find [. . .] manufacturing the clothing of their race'.[80] Speaking of her cobbler grandfather, in 'Awl and Last', she imagines 'a philosopher', believing that 'every time the awl went in a great thought flew out'.[81] The origins of this thinking are only partly disclosed by the influence of Carlyle and Ruskin; and only partly by the agenda of social justice implied by Schreiner's socialism.[82] For she envisages a more profound renovation: inspired by the tenets of American Transcendentalism, it gathers form among her social group as the Fellowship of the New Life.

Such 'Puritan' sources work in parallel with Schreiner's own low-church materialism. 'I like the "New Life,"' she writes to Ellis, 'especially the clause on the necessity of combining physical with mental labour.'[83] Her personal route to this apprehension fosters its own eclecticism. James Hinton's otherwise heterodox efforts to reunite spirit and matter return her to the incarnational origins of this thinking, while the likes of Ellis reconcile mind and body in a quasi-spiritual account of reformed sexuality. By 1908, Schreiner was reporting to Carpenter that 'Buddhism is so much more wide & satisfying than Christianity can ever be, because it takes in the animal & world, & *sees* that all life is one', a move that returns transcendentalist thinking to its origins in Hegel's appraisal of Eastern wisdom.[84] From this complex admixture Schreiner develops a convinced belief in the necessity of rethinking intellectual labour. Her independently formulated position falls accordingly within the orbit of Whitman's reformism, and Carpenter's interpretation of it. For the latter, Whitman bears out the principle that 'in every great artist there is something of the manner of the workman'.[85] Relatedly, Carpenter approves Anne Gilchrist's assessment that Whitman's 'lines are like pulsations, thrills, waves of force'.[86] This allowance for bodily ecstasies, as well as bodily work, proves a crucial element in Schreiner's aesthetic scheme. She evangelises Carpenter's ideas when lecturing in South Africa; and the influence of his dynamic holism suffuses a notable passage of *From Man to Man*: 'between mind and matter', it reads, '[. . .] I am able to see nowhere a sharp line of severance, but a great, pulsating, always interacting whole'.[87]

Carpenter's reforming impulse depends on the promise of a same-sex love blended with comradeship and mutual toil. Schreiner draws a different causative force from her experiences as a writer. Finding her work neither easy nor necessarily fulfilling, she pursues compositional models that promise more predictable results. Most tellingly, she combines a transcendental theory of authorship with a material and physical conception of its results. Writing to Ellis, she proposes that 'the brain works hard when one is not conscious of its working'.[88] This thought arises from a dispiriting experience, of sitting but finding 'nothing would come, only a strange blank feeling in my mind' (6–7). That blankness breaks when 'the feeling came to sit down and write' (7–8). Deploying a resonant phrase, she reports that 'suddenly my mind strikes work' (14), as 'all bursts open again, and I find all the thoughts that were half-formed and in confusion when I left work, completed and ready' (15–17). The letter illustrates a secularised version of the vatic theory, according to which the 'given' or 'completed' element of composition comes not from God or the Muses, but from the mysterious mind. She combines this with the excavatory – and pertinently South African – notion of 'striking' work, as diamonds are found in the detail of an unpromising seam. Schreiner uses the same expression four days earlier, on telling Ellis that 'My mind struck work to-day and I have been doing needlework'.[89] The image's implication, importantly, is that the fruits of labour are not continuously plotted against an axis of time – in the manner of a Trollopian quota – but garnered unevenly, as a process open to the chance discovery.

As Schreiner reclassifies literary work, she pushes it away from its official sites. This leads to contradictory emphases. Sometimes the seat of creative life is the body: she claims, for instance, that the brain of the 'great artist [. . .] governs but his sympathetic system does the [. . .] artistic work', so that 'your back gets tired, not your head'.[90] The upshot is that 'I don't do any of my best work in my brain, by the process that is called thinking' (28). At other times Schreiner reconceives literary work as a matter of cerebral process, to be distinguished from the task of setting words down on a page. She writes to Isaline Philpot that 'I get to my work which is sometimes writing, more often walking up and down my room and thinking things out'.[91] This account recalls Cronwright-Schreiner's more frustrated recollection of his wife's manner of pacing when deep in thought. Her concern to relocate literary labour proves a source of enduring confusion for her husband. '[L]etter-writing', he notices, is 'a form of her imperative impulse to express herself to others, and constituted also a mild form of physical exercise'.[92] In his biography, he suggests that 'she often designated "thought" as "work", both in her letters and journals'.[93] This recalls Barrett Browning's subtle critique of the conventional distinctions between epistolary 'distraction', working letters, 'idle' poetry, and literary works. Cronwright-Schreiner instead reaches the uncharitable conclusion that 'she resorted to letter-writing as a justification for postponing her more arduous work'.[94]

Apart from developing accounts of inspiration and composition that combine holistic principles with the lessons of personal experience, Schreiner extends integrative doctrines to her status as a woman writer. Though by no means the first to compare reproductive capacity to authorship – as her attraction to Mary Wollstonecraft testifies – Schreiner's conception of civilisational development, of art, and of women's revived primacy as makers, depends on an authorship-maternity nexus. More than an analogy, the physicality of this conception has a mental bearing. '[T]he passive labour of child-bearing', she explains in a curious phrase, is secondary to a more active process of shaping the next generation.[95] 'Men's bodies', she observes, 'are our women's works of art'.[96] Male children are the focus here, though with the larger aim of restoring female experience to historical positions where it has been marginal, as in war, where men's bodies – 'produced, at an enormous cost' – are 'the primal munition'.[97] A mother, she insists, 'knows the history of human flesh' and 'knows its cost'.[98] Yet the 'knowing' in question is never reduced to a process simply of care, education, or acculturation. In Schreiner's vision, the sinews are always entwined with the cerebrum; and the superstructure resolves back to a 'great, central fact', that 'the entire race passes through the body of its womanhood as through a mould, reappearing with the indelible marks of that mould upon it'.[99]

The physical processes of childbirth are assimilated in this way to the processes of a brickmaker, or potter. A kind of maker's mark has been applied, but one whose effect is physical-intellectual. In an outlandish image, Schreiner proposes that 'the *os cervix* of women, through which the head of the human infant passes at birth, forms a ring, determining for ever the size at birth of the human head'.[100] The individual's pattern is fixed in this way by the exertions of a maternal labour conceived as handicraft. Schreiner also incorporates the possibility of growth between generations, so that the '*os cervix*' of woman expands with 'the course of ages', and with that 'the intellectual capacity, the physical vigour, the emotional depth of woman'.[101] She calls this 'interevolution between the sexes', a kind of virtuous circle activated by the renewal of maternal agency: '[W]ithout the enlarged deep-thinking Eve to bear him,' she reasons, 'no enlarged Adam'; and 'without the enlarged widely sympathising Adam to beget her, no enlarged widely comprehending Eve'.[102] A sharing of attributes between body and brain, as also between male and female, becomes a pre-requisite for the development of the human race.

Schreiner hopes for an intimate mingling and expansion of physical and intellectual characteristics. She remains mindful, all the same, of South Africa's imperilled work ethics. In *The Story of an African Farm*, the unhappy life of Waldo retrospectively exposes Bonaparte Blenkins's casual assertion, '*Work, labour* – that is the secret of all true happiness!'[103] The claim that manual labour consumes 'a man's body so that his soul dies' only gathered authority as the country's extractive industries began to boom.[104] And in this context, ironies lurk in the genealogy of Schreiner's regard for physical labour. An Oxford undergraduate while Ruskin gave his inaugural lecture as Slade Professor on the planting of colonies (20:42), Rhodes influenced an associated convergence of philanthropic and expansionist thinking. In later years, his 'Round Table' discussion group included Alfred Milner, once one of Ruskin's 'amateur navvies', and later Governor of the Cape Colony (1897–1901). In a striking perversion of the dig's original lessons – and of Wedderburn's allusion to 'rough work' at the 'first of the diggers' breakfasts' (20:xlii) – Milner as Governor made the notorious remark that 'We do not want a white proletariat in this country', since national development 'requires a large amount of rough labour'.[105]

Even closer to home, the individualised holism of Whitman and Carpenter transforms into a geo-political holism whose foremost cause becomes the unification of South Africa. A friend of Schreiner, the Boer statesman Jan Smuts was the prime mover in this process. Noting

Smuts's segregationist tendencies, Saul Dubow observes with puzzlement that 'Smuts's approach to politics was shaped by, of all people, Walt Whitman'.[106] In *Holism and Evolution* (1926), Smuts adapts his early graduate work on the poet to claim that 'The ideal personality only arises where Mind irradiates Body and Body nourishes Mind, and the two are one in their mutual transfiguration'.[107] Darwinian theory features here less as a mechanistic or material process than as 'the inner creative factor at the heart of things', a generative force that interacts with a social principle reminiscent of Ruskin's 'law of help'.[108] In passing, Smuts insists, too, on the application of this 'pervasive creative unity' to human creative functions: 'works of art and the great ideals of the higher life', he explains, 'are or partake of the character of wholes'.[109] The reformist agenda of holism and its emancipatory logic are clear, but Smuts's vision of a 'higher race that will succeed the human in the future' evidently broaches a disturbing principle of selection.[110] Liz Stanley, for her part, disputes Schreiner's status as a social Darwinist.[111] The evidence of Schreiner's writings reveal her participation in this discourse all the same. The 'strengthened and expanded race' described in *Woman and Labour* taps the convergence of mind and body envisaged by holistic thinkers. Yet it also employs the biological determinism of Karl Pearson, a member of Schreiner's circle of London friends and later the Galton Chair of Eugenics.[112] This traffic between body and mind interacts with a developing link between biology and politics, between biological types and social types.

Holistic connectivity allows, most notably, for the idea that people become their actions, in a circle of socio-biological reinforcement. In literary matters, Schreiner opposes typological thinking: Ibsen's plays, she observes, 'lack *something*', and 'It's because his persons are so often *types*, not *individuals*; they are not *real*'.[113] But if Schreiner's writing often depicts an isolated inwardness in search of connection to the universe, she also populates the landscape with unnamed representatives of a social position or a race. In *The Story of an African Farm*, the reader is routinely referred to 'the Boer-woman', 'The German', 'the Hottentot', 'the Kaffir maid'.[114] Even if her racial terms passively reflect colonial usage, the impersonal framing is deliberate. The absence of introduction operates here as a fictional strategy. This, in turn, reflects a philosophical position that promotes rapid movement from the level of the individual to that of the social group. At the heart of this socio-biological relation, significantly, is the question of human labour.

From her early time in London, right up to her last years, Schreiner's sense of the good society fixes on the spectre of the parasite, a figure who drains the social body of its vitality by living on the labour of others.

Prostitutes occupy a central place in this vision. As she highlights the female vulnerability engendered by financial dependence, a choice dawns, 'between finding new forms of labour' or sinking into 'passive *sex-parasitism*!'[115] Saracino attributes the roots of this 'indignation' to the conventional morality bestowed by Schreiner's Protestant upbringing.[116] Certainly, Schreiner's picture of 'the active labouring woman' relies on a contrasting picture: an invidious and stigma-dealing vision of 'the effete wife, concubine or prostitute, clad in fine raiment, the work of others' fingers'.[117] If, on one level, sympathy is retained in the portrait of one 'robbed [. . .] of all joy in strenuous exertion', we also see 'the "fine lady," the human female parasite' characterised as 'the most deadly microbe which can make its appearance on the surface of any social organism'.[118] The individuality of the prostitute gives way, ultimately, to her condition as a type, one that 'indicates disease as the pustules of smallpox upon the skin'.[119]

Apart from reproducing the bourgeois notion that social health relies on female virtue, Schreiner's focus on a nexus of female prostitution, female gentility, and civilisational decline, identifies the 'woman question' as the supreme labour question. Her emphasis on behaviour-induced disease introduces the possibility of a social enemy, while the anticipation of fascist diatribe in images of the 'microbe' derives its paranoid force from the degraded action of a kind of anti-work. This connection between work and social health also informs Schreiner's largely sympathetic attitude to South Africa's black population. Female parasitism, she claims, is possible only in societies where 'The males absorbed the intellectual labours of life; slaves and dependents the physical'.[120] Slavery, in this respect, becomes the premise for a counterproductive alienation from manual labour, degrading to slave and master alike. '[T]he native question', it follows, is 'really the labour question complicated & made virulent by the questions of colour'.[121] In *From Man to Man*, equally, the sisters' movement towards emancipated consciousness coincides with a self-acknowledged capacity for oppression, signified by a childhood fantasy of building 'a high wall across Africa' and putting 'all the black people on the other side'.[122]

Schreiner's attitude to the Boer population is also, in its way, a labour question. As Anna Snaith observes, 'Her anti-war position [. . .] involved not only idealizing the Boer lifestyle, but also unifying Boer and English South African'.[123] In this respect, she endorses a multicultural synthesis, the 'very real bond, which unites all South Africans' being '*our mixture of races itself.*'[124] She envisages, all the same, a trade in virtues between these population groups, based once again on typological thinking. If the Boers miss the eighteenth century's 'stern demand for intellectual tolerance', they also miss 'the rise of the commercial system',[125] meaning that 'the Boer [. . .] still believes there are things money cannot buy'.[126] In a further echo of Carlyle, Schreiner's image of Boer frontiersmanship recalls the racially inflected vision of *Latter-day Pamphlets*, in which 'Anglo-Saxon men prove themselves worthy of their genealogy; and, with the axe and plough and hammer, [. . .] are triumphantly clearing out wide spaces' (20:19). Schreiner also points to the role of Boer women in grasping and holding the land;[127] and, in *Woman and Labour*, imagines 'the march of those Teutonic folk, whose women were virile and could give birth to men'.[128]

An estimation of 'honest' labour holds primacy, then, over the advantage accrued by financialism. And again, it is Schreiner's attraction to 'types' as a mode of thought and social analysis that presents problems. Her anti-capitalist pastoralism issues from the Left, but resembles conservative agrarianism. She acknowledges that 'The forefathers of the Boer were slaveholders', but figures slavery as a disease of civilisation in its infancy, rather than an aspect of capitalism.[129] And it is clear, as for Carlyle, that these crimes weigh against the hypocrisies of a liberalism that instigates bondage by financial means. In *The War in South Africa* (1900), Schreiner's associate, J. L. Hobson, observes that 'many organs of British African opinion were already in devoted sympathy with the Jew-Imperialist design that is in course of execution'.[130] Despite being interviewed in this volume, Schreiner's pride in her putative Jewish ancestry[131] and her attacks on anti-Semitism in 'A Letter on the Jew' (1906) suggest that she would not have endorsed this statement.[132] The catch, as Snaith amply demonstrates, is that she recapitulates Hobson's characterisation in *From Man to Man*. Her description of a diamond speculator who takes Bertie to London draws on the full palette of anti-Semitic caricature: 'His face', we read, 'was of a dull oriental pallor, and his piercing dark eyes and marked nose proclaimed him at once a Jew'.[133] Moreover, the moral equation is determined by a labour relation: Schreiner sets out to redeem 'the Jew, persecuted and oppressed' on the basis that being 'incapable in many countries of holding real property [. . .] was driven to finance'.[134] In a parallel move, she restores the idea of the Jew to an artisanal image, in figuring a 'Jewish mother, the wife of a carpenter'.[135] Nevertheless, she refers to the figure of the 'financial Jew' only a few years earlier.[136] Whether intended as a subcategory or a totalising epithet, the political danger in such categories is clear. As *From Man to Man* demonstrates, racial and political types are more or less indistinguishable for as long as rapacious financiers also happen to be cast as Jews.

Schreiner's social vision posits a paradoxical relation between a larger aim of holistic unity, and a reliance on fixed human types, among whom those liable to exclusion are defined by their resistance to the call for a social labour. This raises the question of authors' place in the same scheme, and ultimately her own place. The charge of parasitism, after all, had also been directed at writers and artists. Beyond general references to the learned professions, Schreiner provides strikingly little information on this subject, an omission that reflects her uncertainty about the position of authors within the host of the 'active labouring woman', even as she extends holistic positions to matters of statecraft. When she does raise the subject in *Woman and Labour*, she represents the writing of fiction less as a good in itself than as a stopgap for a 'walled-in' feminine intellect deprived of other intelligent avenues and other 'action'.[137] To add further complication, Schreiner increasingly doubts the complementarity of the mental and the manual. One area of concern arises from the supremacy of intellect in the modern world: as one speaker in 'Three Dreams in a Desert' asserts, 'The Age-of-muscular force is dead'.[138] Her daily routine becomes a focus for these doubts. In an exasperated letter, from 1904, she observes that 'There is no case on record of any cook or housemaid or scullery maid doing any literary or intellectual work of any kind'.[139] Anyone attempting to combine these forms of labour becomes 'a labour machine' (24–25): 'All your brain goes into your hands' (30). Two years earlier, she observes that 'it is all very well for theorists to talk of combining manual labour with mental & if it is mere *mechanical* labour like digging or turning a machine, it *may* be possible to combine both: but complex semiphysical semi-mental labour like house keeping ^if you have no servant^ or attending to children is the death of any intellect'.[140] While this allusion to domestic service reinstates divisions of labour normally rejected by holistic philosophy, she requests more differentiated analysis of the difficult relations between housekeeping and authorial vocation. Neither fits easily into the world of outward work conjured by her public rhetoric, since each shares a corrosive invisibility, and sense of unmarked progress. In this account, the female writer-housekeeper experiences no enlargement of faculties equivalent to the Ruskinian 'Professor of Digging': on the contrary, as she notes in 1902, 'long continued unbroken physical labour kills out the intellectual life'.[141]

The inconsistency between Schreiner's philosophy and practice arises in part because she applies holistic positions to the content of her writing, but not to its compositional origins. Indeed, her discussion of literary labour amounts less to a worked-through theory than a series of isolated reports dispatched to friends from the daily struggle to write. It is true, as Wanne Mendonck claims, that 'Scribbling' is Schreiner's 'only work in life', and that 'she is always alert to its material embeddedness'.[142] Only, her attitude in this respect is so often embattled, and it is burdened, too, by a feeling that authorship is not commensurate with other occupations. Writing, for her, resembles 'a great expenditure of blood pressure'.[143] As a young woman, she imagines a liberty to 'dream, dream, dream, over one chapter for a hundred years till at last it was *perfect*',[144] an instinct that proves obstructive, leaving her 'getting so disgusted with my work'.[145] In her husband's characterisation of these difficulties, we find the most distinct articulation of two writing philosophies. Though a university graduate, Cronwright-Schreiner lived as a farmer, proud of his proficiency with 'the American axe, the spade, the pickaxe and the crowbar, to plough and to reap with the sickle'.[146] Initially imagining a continuity between farm work and literary work, he recalls that 'My relationship with Olive begins with my reading of *The Story of an African Farm*'.[147] By the same token, his despair at Schreiner's failure to meet deadlines reflects deep resentment engendered by the sale of his farm to support their peripatetic life. He implies that Schreiner does not keep her side of the bargain, but the conflict between them might equally be figured as one between different models of production. When a compensatory literary harvest fails to materialise, Cronwright-Schreiner blames his wife's 'impracticability, her inability really to work, or even to see hard facts clearly'.[148] Schreiner's rejection of any correlation between application and output lies at the heart of this standoff. Her husband quotes a letter in which she reveals that 'I dare not touch my work at a lower mood than the mood I wrote it in, or I shall spoil it'.[149] These words eloquently express restlessness, a sense that literary production requires not regular workshop hours, or a seasonal yield, but the right mood, the right place, the right time, the right vision, in an ever-shifting interchange of intention and contingency.

Schreiner's entire social and intellectual vision connects human flourishing to the availability of healthy labour. To a great extent, this idea models primordial or pre-capitalist conditions. Women, in particular, would reclaim their ancient domains of housebuilding, agriculture and pottery. And, in a virtuous circle of physical-intellectual expansion, they would use their reproductive capacities to shape the brains of the next generation. A number of analogies between physical labour and the work of writing affirm this agenda, most notably Schreiner's allusion to having mentally 'struck work', in a process that rewards chance revelations rather than steady effort. And there are other circumstances that make Schreiner a distinct case. Like Barrett Browning, she revives aspects of the vatic theory of composition. Both writers defy the male coding of writerly yearning for manual expression, and both appeal to forms of transcendence, possibly encouraged by the imprisoning physical circumstances of chronic sickness. This lack of control also explains

Schreiner's tendency to exempt her own labour from the wider scheme of physical-intellectual shaping, as also her failure to theorise or historicise literary labour as she does the trades and professions. At the level of practice, moreover, she shares a concern to reclassify and redescribe the moment of composition: preparatives like 'thought', or ancillary devices like letters, become the main event, in a way that challenges commodified and reified versions of production.

Barrett Browning's tight control of the sick room differs, even so, from Schreiner's restless search for the right writing conditions. Her capacity to work seems unusually subservient to passing mood, and suitable environment, though always in anticipation of some mental and physical reunion, an ecstatic apprehension or total vision. In this respect, Schreiner's literary holism is less an ongoing state, than an ideal whose activation is rare and erratic. At the level of formal habit, the structuring device of the waking vision musters a response to these conditions. The 'Times and Seasons' chapter of *The Story of an African Farm* pioneers this method: Waldo's response to the ancient landscape interacts not only with his perception of deep time, but with novelistic time-values which, until that scene, have respected conventional modes of narration.[150] Joseph Bristow and Jane Marcus note the influence of these experiments on Woolf's *The Years*.[151] Traced through this modernist lineage, the epiphanic mode shrugs off Schreiner's holistic yearning for a reunion with matter, only to emerge as a harbinger of works more lopsidedly given to the ecstatic.

A further loose end concerns the political effect of a holistic aesthetics that simultaneously privileges unification, diversity, and a connection between character and acts, mind and body. These affinities would lead Schreiner to a conception of social hygiene continuous with her aesthetic philosophy. The lineaments of this position prepare the ground for a closing discussion of Pound's correspondingly anti-capitalist pastoralism. Schreiner's biological types are themselves perilously close to her social types, and like Pound she resorts to an underpinning belief in socially healthy labour. And yet the link to authorship is not so clear in her case. An unspoken exemption of the writer from this scheme distinguishes her from the more self-conscious forms of modernist producerism. And curiously – given this chapter's initial trajectory – it aligns her closely with Woolf, in privileging a quiet writing environment facilitated by the domestic labour of servants. Her lived experience as a writer explains this discrepancy: Schreiner relishes the thought of women reunited with their ancestral trades, yet excludes her own authorial work from that vision of 'Woman and Labour'. In her experience, literary composition does not fit naturally into the wider world of joyous communal effort. Rather, it obliges her to walk, think, and write at home, in an environment fitted out for other purposes. Instead of harbouring a truly multifarious cottage economy, Schreiner's domestic life tilts her away from intellectual ends, and correspondingly away from the holistic logic of her own social writings.

Gill's Letter-Craft

A craftsman of the material letter rather than of literature in the compositional sense, Eric Gill nevertheless expressed views on authorship that go beyond the limits of his workshop practice. 'Writing', he muses, 'is the only child of our time unspoiled by instrumental delivery', and therefore seems a rare survival.[152] Gill believed, for instance, that modern novelistic methods had settled into a harmful independence – at least, at the level of pen and page – and that this hindered the emergence of a more social literary art. Though celebrating Joseph Conrad and Henry James as the 'modern of moderns', he finds that they will 'collaborate with no one'.[153] If 'collaboration' is a source of literary 'trammels' – a net to fly – it proves by contrast a source of 'help' to craftsmen.[154] For Gill, this difference reflects an artisanal concern with 'will', which in turn reflects a commitment to 'doing' and 'making', as distinct from matters of pure intellect.[155] He develops a less defensive position when promoting the writer's renewed visibility as a worker, and it is in this regard that Gill's literary reputation as a footnote to the career of his pupil, the artist and poet David Jones, warrants re-examination. Unlike Brown – who makes authors visible by depicting their bodies – Gill rescues literary activity by making its means of production legible at the level of text and alphabet. In this way, the chisel and the printing press become intimate again with the authorial pen. As a Catholic convert, he extends the theological sweep already observed, not only beyond Calvinist models, but beyond Hopkins's more imperilled poesis. In his case, though, boundaries are pushed dangerously: not only through the collapsed binaries of Gill's private and working lives, but also through his interpretation – and translation – of Catholic doctrine. These effects are most evident in his account of God's creative gratuity, and of the human maker's access to it.

In common with Schreiner, Gill is a transitional figure, and as such enacts the movement between late Victorian and modernist conceptions of artistic labour that this chapter tests. His complex placing matters less in itself than for what it can tell us about the reception and dissemination of the artisanal ideas under discussion. Gill himself insisted, with revealing self-consciousness, on the necessity of a break with the

Edwardian past, most notably in 'The Failure of the Arts and Crafts Movement' (1909).[156] As MacCarthy observes, he was 'at least partly in the avant-garde' by the 1930s: indeed, she cites his links with Serge Chermayeff, Eric Mendelsohn and Maxwell Fry.[157] The most secure token of Gill's modernity is his commitment to rationalism, a tenet that causes him to rail against 'Art-Nonsense', and to favour 'the new electrical switchboard' in a 'sham-gothic building' over its architectural surroundings.[158] When discussing lettering, he questions the view 'that art and reason are poles asunder, that the artist is the irrational person and all his works the produce of caprice and emotional temperament'.[159] Thus 'fine lettering' is 'in the first place rational lettering'.[160] In certain contexts this respect for 'reason' leads Gill to abandon direct making. The typefaces he produces for the Monotype Corporation, for instance, assume machine punch-cutting, with 'as much as possible mathematically measurable'.[161] Eclectic loyalties inform this self-image. Like Whistler, he attributes early art enthusiasm to a most un-Ruskinian passion for steam engines, having 'supposed I was training myself to be an engineer'.[162] Even his love of lettering begins in a project connected to 'Engine Names', submitted to the Art School, at Chichester.[163] Lettering, in this respect, remains connected in his mind with a function, and an occasion – a moment as well as a means of production.

W. R. Lethaby thought that Gill was 'crabbing' his 'own mother' in denouncing the Arts and Crafts movement.[164] The bare facts of his early career confirm this impression, among them his calligraphy classes under Edward Johnston at Lethaby's impeccably Morrisian Central School of Arts and Crafts;[165] his showing at the 1906 Arts and Crafts Exhibition Society;[166] and his early residence among well-connected Arts and Crafts households in Hammersmith.[167] Following Morris, Gill styled himself as a workman: dressing first in a mason's smock, and latterly in a monkish habit. And he likewise believed in a holistic union of art and craft, household and work, in 'reuniting what should never have been separated: the artist as man of imagination and the artist as workman'.[168] The irony, moreover, is that Gill's modernist credentials sprang from the same sources. If his sculptures attracted attention for their primitivism, this quality was owing as much to a lack of formal training. He starts from scratch in the Morrisian manner, looking back to the Middle Ages in the spirit of a Pre-Raphaelite modernity. A similarly mixed meaning applies to Gill's signature technique of direct carving, which dispenses with clay models, as well as intermediary hands. Though a feature of most modernist sculpture – ranging from Jacob Epstein and Gaudier-Brzeska to Barbara Hepworth – it originates in the Arts and Crafts emphasis on combining the making with the mental conception. Gill later employed assistants to execute commissions, but rather than contracting work out to a third party, he adapted the late medieval employment of workshop apprentices under the master's eye.[169] This preserved the sense of intellectual and moral succession, while extending the chain of responsibility. Even his principle of rationality in design derives from the Arts and Crafts insistence on functional ornament and the rejection of 'sham'. Far from depersonalising the process, his recourse to mathematical accuracy restores artistic integrity and responsibility by eliminating barriers between the maker (here, the designer) and the product.

It follows that Gill cared less about the fact of mechanised or manual production than about a principle that the 'maker or doer is responsible'.[170] Just as this principle reflects the ongoing influence of the Arts and Crafts movement, so it also reflects deeper origins in a sterner, mid-Victorian morality. The Calvinism that Gill's father absorbed from the Countess of Huntingdon's Connection makes its way into the family home in the form of an object on the wall, above where the family breakfasted: 'a large coloured and very "natural" representation of an eye – all by itself on a card'.[171] Called '"father's eye"', it illustrates the text "thou God seest me"'.[172] Such monitory visual attention inaugurates Gill's awareness of the connections between responsibility, accountability, and visibility. Even the naming of Gill's siblings – Stephen Romney Maurice, Vernon Kingsley, and Kenneth Carlyle – evokes low-church morality and Victorian Sage literature. Gill might have been anxious to throw all this off, but he reports reading Carlyle's *Sartor Resartus*, and *Past and Present*, with some eagerness in his first digs at Clapham.[173] Later in life, in an address to the English Speaking Union (1934), he draws out the cultural significance of his father's habits of surveillance, here playfully reformulated as 'Thou Ruskin seest me' in acknowledgement of an intellectual influence, and the responsibilities conferred and created by vision.[174]

Gill presented his conversion to Catholicism in 1913 as a kind of year zero. But his personal and institutional trajectory tells a different story. Far from superseding his Arts and Crafts philosophy, Gill's new allegiance to Rome offered a way of defending working practices that he already favoured. In essence pre-modern, his methods could be embraced without apology because buttressed by the ancient edifice of Western Christianity. Modern economic life, by contrast, he associates in Morrisian fashion with machine-minding, with 'a sort of dishonesty or a detachment of mind', and 'an acceptance of that lack of integrity, that lack of *integralness*'.[175] Unlike the artists' collectives proposed by the Pre-Raphaelites, however, Gill's Catholic communities entail genuinely shared lives. Initially co-founding the Guild of St Joseph and St Dominic at Ditchling, Sussex, he later sets up a Catholic craft community at

Capel-y-Ffin, Wales.[176] Work, here, becomes a binding agent: the main source of collective meaning. The Constitution of the Guild of St Joseph and St Dominic requires that its members be 'Earning their living by creative manual work' as 'practising Catholics'.[177] In phrasing redolent of Carlyle's *Past and Present* – which honours the monkish principle of *Laborare est orare* (10:233) – the Guild holds that 'all work is ordained to God and should be Divine worship'.[178] The same document identifies the importance of owning the means of production: 'workers should own their own tools, their workshops and the product of their work', in a ring of independence that protects the community from the world, and the individual within the community.[179] Gill reasons that 'if men are to control a trade and be independent of middle-men they must be banded together in unions or guilds'.[180] Here, too, his phrasing discloses an intellectual lineage, with its echo of the 'Banded-workshops' (16:46) in Morris's *News from Nowhere*. Indeed, Gill's model of the workshop overseen by a master-craftsman continues and realises a logic that runs back through Morris's role at his own firm to Carlyle's paternalistic Captains of Industry.

These communal and medievalist structures were hardly new, then; but Gill found fresh corroboration of them in the pages of *The New Age*, a literary review whose assault on monopoly capitalism applied Guild Socialist precepts in conceiving its challenges soluble by artists and writers. In this respect, and as a contribution to the period's complex swirl of heterodox economics and aesthetics, *The New Age* forms the epicentre of the legacies tracked by this chapter. While the magazine's influence coincided with the birth of a British modernism – its contributors include T. E. Hulme, Herbert Read, Katherine Mansfield, Edwin Muir and Ezra Pound – this circumstance should not distract from its roots in the past. Its editors, for instance, emerged from the world of Morrisian London: A. R. Orage's first wife had been an embroideress at Morris & Company,[181] while Holbrook Jackson was the author of a book about Morris as socialist and craftsman.[182] *The New Age*'s combination of medievalism and modernism is perhaps best epitomised by its serial publication of A. J. Penty's *The Restoration of the Gild System* [*sic*] (1906), a work that proposes a reconstituted form of economic competition based not on price, but on quality, understood here in the light of a social benefit.[183]

Gill took similar bearings from Pope Leo XIII's *Rerum Novarum* (1891), an encyclical that rejects socialism, yet calls for 'collaboration' inspired by '[t]he good done by the old guilds of artisans'.[184] In the hands of Hilaire Belloc, G. K. Chesterton and Fr Vincent McNabb, this legacy developed into Distributism. The result, in Gill's case, was an effort to foster and describe relations between the craftsman and God, the craftsman and work, and the craftsman and the things of creation, a key proposition being that 'all men are artists'.[185] Defining humanity in relation to making, he echoes Carlyle's 'Man is a tool-using Animal' (1:32), while developing his own formulation: 'man is essentially a tool-using animal'.[186] Far from being a cog in the industrial system, this reborn maker wields rather than embodies the tool or cutting edge.[187] The liberty implied by this prowess knows certain limits, in that the Guild requires service and obedience. But it also redefines restriction as an enabling pretext. In the paternalistic judgements 'of a father to a son or of a master workman to his journeyman and apprentices', Gill identifies a freedom missing from the life of the 'factory workman'.[188] He likewise contends that 'art is collaboration with God in creating'.[189] He drew this notion from readings in the neo-Aristotelian philosophy of Jacques Maritain, the first English edition of whose *Art and Scholasticism* appeared in a translation by Father John O'Connor that Gill himself introduced.[190]

Maritain argues that 'artistic creation does not copy God's creation, but continues it',[191] and Gill likewise avers that the 'act of creation is a gratuitous act' and its 'song' 'pure and purposeless'.[192] Conferring an active role on the artist, in a universe where creative energy is liberally dispersed, he imagines something closer to a sacrament than simple worship. 'As the priest brings God to the marriage', Gill explains, so 'the artist brings God to the work'.[193] In Wildean fashion, he suggests that 'Art improves on Nature', and that this is 'what it is for'.[194] This sense of an empowered and unmediated role informs Gill's heterodox notion that the artist 'will always be somewhat of a PELAGIAN in practice and will act as though man has never 'fallen' – [. . .] and all work were play'.[195] The doctrinal justification for these statements presumes that God holds power absolutely and yet shares it in an act of love. 'Just as God's creation was gratuitous', Gill explains, so 'Man also is able to make gratuitously'.[196] And while the maker operates in the material sphere, he can see beyond it, as if from a vantage point: 'Man is therefore [. . .] able to comprehend, though not fully, the spiritual significance of the material'.[197] The artist's deputised power, in this account, is considerable, checked only by the wording in 'not fully'.[198] Wary, perhaps, of affirming a brazen heterodoxy, Gill cautions that 'God is the end' – as 'the cause of all things made' – so that 'things that do not envisage God as their end are like arrows not even aimed at their target'.[199] In phrasing that recalls Carlyle's fascination with the stone span (and ghostly reach) of an arch, Gill notes elsewhere that 'that man is a bridge connecting the material and the spiritual'.[200] He concedes, too, that 'the artist is not precisely a God', as 'He does not create out of nothing'.[201] The word 'precisely' nevertheless signals a curiously double-edged concession: if not a god, this conception of the maker stops not far short of one, suggesting perhaps an 'imprecise' god.

Discussing these matters in *Grace and Necessity* (2005), Rowan Williams attributes an 'unavoidably theological element to all artistic labour'.[202] He addresses Gill's position, but draws out the hazardous allurement of 'a "promethean" enterprise'.[203] This enterprise crystallises in 'the magical fallacy', where the artist becomes a kind of necromancer, or where the artist succumbs to a 'will to power' or 'cult of personality'.[204] According to Williams, Maritain's attention to this possibility affirms the same cautionary principle. It follows, for him, that 'what theology might have to say to the artist is not exactly that human creativity imitates the divine but almost the opposite of this – that divine creativity is not capable of imitation',[205] because we ourselves are 'timebound'.[206] This analysis is convincing on its own terms: indeed, O'Connor's translation bears out Gill's own reservations, in having Maritain cast art as produced 'doubtless not out of nothing, but out of pre-existing matter'.[207] And it diligently qualifies the authority of the master craftsmanship, in stating that the artist 'must be God's pupil, for God knows the building rule of the beautiful works'.[208] But perhaps such disclaimers are only necessary because the text sails in the first place so close to the wind.

Gill's self-piloted – even Promethean – artistic theology finds most obvious refuge in O'Connor's rendering of the claim that 'the feeling in the artist of his especial dignity' is 'like a partner with God in the making of beauteous works'.[209] This conception of partnership closely tracks the original French, which reads: '*De là provident en l'artiste le sentiment de sa dignité particulière*' and '*Il est comme un associé de Dieu dans la facture des belles oeuvres*'.[210] If the '*comme*' ('like', 'as') signals a step short of actual partnership, it also seems the least possible check on the artist's special status. Equally striking is Maritain's view that 'Artistic creation does not copy Divine creation, it carries it on' ('*La création artistique ne copie pas celle de Dieu, elle la continue*').[211] Although the maker only has a 'feeling' of dignity ('*le sentiment*'), in 'developing the powers put into him by the Creator',[212] the stress falls nevertheless on an idea of association rather than service. Gill even compares the office of the artist to 'a spiritual marriage',[213] a phrase that inadvertently anticipates the illicit forms of sexual union that Gill practised in his own life, ranging from opportunistic sexual encounters with strangers to bestiality, incest, and abuse of his own children.[214] The link between these areas of concern is not necessary or inevitable; but, as MacCarthy demonstrates, his fluid conceptions of association, or 'integration', relate to his violation of personal and sexual boundaries within and outside the family group.[215] In this respect, Gill reinterprets – and perverts – Arts and Crafts and principles of the integrated life. In particular, he finds a justification for unacceptable forms of licence in the artist's role as a 'bridge'.

Other kinds of latitude – apparent in the O'Connor translations that Gill sponsors – complicate the more specific question of the maker's powers. These emerge from the way that they eliminate the distinction between liberal and menial occupations. Maritain's own position is less amenable to such notions than their translation of him implies. Most notably, he maintains a distinction between the rarefied contemplation of 'art' and simple making.[216] This discrepancy is most apparent in Gill's blithe introductory claim that 'Art embraces all Making and there should be no need to talk about it', which contrasts markedly with Maritain's warning that 'Art has to defend itself [. . .] against the allurement of manual dexterity'.[217] The O'Connor edition disguises these tensions in several ways. First, it renders the French word '*l'artisan*' as 'craftsman'. 'Craftsman' is properly idiomatic, but it diminishes Maritain's play on 'artist' in the originary 'artisan', and produces a third occupational category not envisaged in the original language. By contrast, the Scanlan translation of 1930 opts for 'artisan'.[218] A habit of re-emphasis produces a similar effect at the level of the formatting. Footnote 42 of the original French explains how the figure of the artist has parted from the artisan, and now looks down on him. Rather than reproduce the note in that form, O'Connor's translation promotes it to the status of an appendix ('Appendix A'). And a new title is inserted: 'ARTIST AND CRAFTSMAN'. Combined with this structural adjustment, the subtle linguistic shift to 'craftsman' amplifies the manual implication and diminishes the conditional form of the original French.

This refocusing of Maritain in translation – away from philosophical-aesthetic concerns and towards the fortunes of practical craftsmanship – bears crucially on Gill's theory of cultural production. Supplied with authority by a Catholic theologian, the artist can be viewed as a species of maker, just as Gill's Arts and Crafts education demands. As Jones later states, the 'activity of art' is not 'a branch activity': 'the artist is not [. . .] "out on a limb"', but an artisan among artisans.[219] It is evidently harder to place the writer in this happy continuum, though one imagines that literature will belong to 'the Practical Order' once certain conditions are satisfied.[220] Flannery O'Connor, herself an admirer of Maritain, frankly concludes that 'When I write I am a maker'.[221] Jones, similarly, approves Joyce's observation that 'practical life' or 'art' must comprehend all our activities, from boat building to poetry'.[222] Though not primarily concerned with the problems of literary life, Gill's typographic activities promulgate a revised notion of what a 'writer' might be. While the alphabet's abstraction has grown in the digital age, today's immaterial letter relies on earlier habits and practices, which have conditioned our tendency to see writing as an aspect of mind. For Gill, equally, letters are removed from reality: they are 'not pictures or representations',[223] being 'more or less abstract forms' that exercise 'special and peculiar attraction for the "mystical mug" called man'.[224] He knows the origin of the Roman letters in pictographic forms, but concentrates on their latter-day conversion into 'conventional signs', according to which 'pictures are used to signify *words* and not simply *things*',[225] and finally 'single sounds'.[226] This sense of writing slipping the net of the created world – becoming if not spiritual, then certainly immaterial – prompts Gill's interest in restoring to writing its material heft. Thus Jones observes, on celebrating his deceased teacher, that 'the Word is made stone'.[227]

Gill, as we have seen, achieves this convergence by combining designing with making. And like other cases discussed in this book, he derives sustenance and authority from a correspondent shift in his working identity. If the word can become stone, then the artist can be a maker or a mason. But this is also, in its own individual way, a 'labour of mind'. Insisting on a re-materialisation of abstract letter forms, he achieves that end by disrupting the semantic and formal conventions that suppress the alphabet's incisions and shadows. This sense – that there might be a value in signal distortion or resistance – reflects his original slowness in learning to read,[228] his difficulty with foreign languages, and an enduring dyslexic tendency.[229] Reconfigured as gifts, these traits afford an awareness of shape and literal meaning, which cuts the craftsman loose, albeit temporarily, from what Jones would call 'the trip-wire of sign', the 'entanglement of signs'.[230] Gill observes, more proactively, that 'the letter cutter's business is not symbolism but letter cutting',[231] and that 'letters are things, not pictures of things'.[232] In this way, he resolves superstructural elements into a tangible infrastructure. Williams notes in related fashion that 'a painting must be a thing and not the impression of something', and is therefore comparable to 'what the Church has said of the Mass'.[233] Removing letters from the realm of abstraction, it follows, does not limit them. Rather, it activates the lively awareness of a double sense, and by that means generates what Jones calls 'a praxis which is also a poesis'.[234]

The 'interference' enacted by a newly substantial writing does not entail a worship of the graven image – nor a cult of the graven letter. Letters themselves are not 'debased'; nor are they divorced from the spirit. Rather, they are seen as incarnational. Shorn of abstract symbolism, they neither revert to the old pictorial symbolism, nor become ethereal. They reveal a presence of things out of reach or beyond sight. Jones takes this notion further after Gill's death, in painted 'inscriptions' that reunite meaning with materiality. In '*Quia per incarnati verbi mysterium*' ('For by the mystery of the Word made flesh') (1953), a red highlight on '*verbi*' [word] evokes both sanguinary presence, and the enduring entanglements of typographic convention [Figure 6.1].

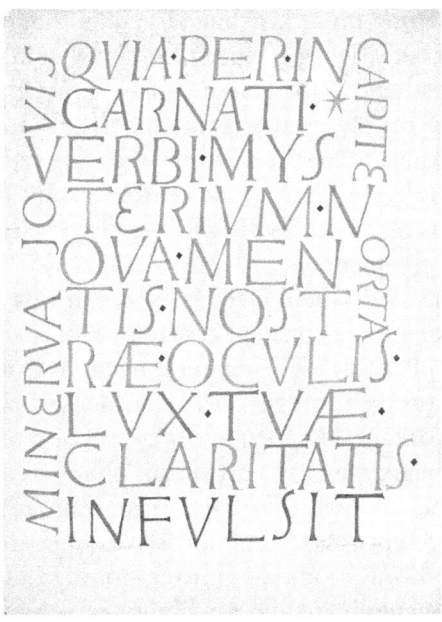

Figure 6.1 David Jones, *Quia per Incarnati* . . ., c. 1953, watercolour and graphite on paper. © Kettle's Yard, University of Cambridge / Bridgeman Images

However, the medium applied here – watercolour on paper – *represents*, rather than embodies, an inscribed Roman alphabet. With its serifs, chisel-sharp interpuncts, and ligatures, the design resembles the incised forms that Gill might cut in Hoptonwood stone. Even the use of watercolours echoes this context, since once evaporated they would bestow their pigments along the 'v'-cut of Gill's illuminated inscriptions.[235] But Jones's letters simultaneously flout the classic Trajan forms, as well as their usual lateral relations. Moreover, the script's flex towards the uncials of early manuscript culture hint at a medium in transition. Crucially, neither an artisanal nor a scribal identity wins out: we recognise the form of the serif, but instead of tracing the home-going path of a chisel, a flat field of colour keeps us guessing on the surface. In this way, Jones's late lettering expresses a yearning for substance that is knowingly elegiac. This applies in as much as a gap between suggestion and realisation reflects his sense of being marooned in a culture whose conception of the poet is no longer 'by profession the custodian, rememberer, embodier and voice of the mythos'.[236] Instead of casting out doubt, Jones makes loss his subject. His vision of 'man as a maker of things', and his comparison of the artist to a carpenter, insist on the possibility of making meanings, and making signs.[237] So

the constructive work proceeds, but largely as haunted by lost substance, lost materiality, lost presence.[238] Gill, by comparison, asserts a
revived role as aesthetic priest. He imagines himself actually bridging
the divide between the material and the spiritual, as if realising humanity's 'amphibious' nature, or the status of a go-between. In this respect,
the distinction between Gill and Jones marks a transition, between the
confident solutions proposed by the writers discussed in this book, and
a later emphasis on lament.

  Though a visual artist, Gill claims a place in this book because he
lays the foundations for a changed conception of literary work and of
the writer. To employ Carlyle's spanning metaphor once again, I have
argued for his status as a bridge – between the Arts and Crafts idea of
a self-styled art-worker and an emergent conception of the maker's role
within modernism. As the next part of this chapter confirms, the intellectual milieu associated with *The New Age* instantiates the last conception. But Gill represents more than a case study in staggered influence
and intellectual hybridisation. His starting-point as a letter cutter alerts
him, more fundamentally, to the possibility of a 'writing' that is also
manifestly a making. Direct carving becomes in this respect a repudia-
tion of art mediated as design, a method that restores a finality more
usually associated with the pen on paper. Gill's contribution to literary
affairs resides in three areas. First, he posits the possibility of a writer,
and a writing, whose methods are 'collaborative' in the manner of a
craftsman operating in a trade guild. This social ideal allows him to contribute to the theologies of composition discussed previously. Maritain's
comparison of the artisan to an '*associé*', most notably, smuggles in the
sense of an elect figure that artisanal analogies usually extinguish. These
connotations are to some extent mitigated by the accompanying sense
of gratuity, of a shared creative energy not subject to scarcity. Second,
he develops a theology of the material letter that incorporates a double-
ness, operative not so much at the more familiar level of textual meaning, than at the level of the text's deeper existence. The result is a writing
susceptible to making, but also, in a fundamental way, mysterious, as
an incarnation of the scriptor's eternal nature. Finally, it transpires that
this insistence on the material letter draws not only on the paradox of
spiritual substance, but also on a mental operation, one that bears on a
perceptual psychology of reading. Gill, in this respect, locates the work
of incarnational writing in a mode of interference or distortion. This
cuts through visual habit, and in that way delivers an apprehension of
writing capable of including a maker's mark.

  Though not a conscious advocate of holism, Gill shares with Schreiner
a tendency to cycle between – and ultimately to combine – a material and

a higher dimension of literary experience. Whereas Schreiner's philosophical pluralism has recourse to fixed social types, Gill runs into difficulties through a kind of overreaching. This is evident first in the way that he extends the 'associate' powers of the artist to wider spheres of experience. Most notably, he seeks self-justification for sexual crimes in terms indebted to the same forms of spiritual marriage and incarnation. Indeed, a yearning for 'justification' acquires a structural significance in Gill's ethical code, perhaps not unrelated to the surveillance mechanism suggested by his father's artificial eye. As in previous chapters, a preoccupation with professional status emerges, here centred on the justification conferred by a stable trade identity. Jones possesses a keen sense of words in their unavoidable origins, and of the poetic profession as committed to memory. Gill, by contrast, focuses on creative potency. And he seeks to stabilise an uncertainty. As his role in the O'Connor translation demonstrates, he finds a warrant for this approach in a convenient superimposition: it is the 'craftsman', this is to say, who eliminates the tricky abstractions of 'art' still latent in the French *'l'artisan'*, and the maker who bridges the interval between human limits and a divine creative power.

Rusty Chisels: Pound, Prejudice, and Poetic Apprenticeship

The last part of this chapter addresses the question of poetic 'profession', here understood in the sense of teaching (or, 'professing') as well as working. Its scope extends beyond the ground occupied by the preceding transitional figures, and into the domain of high modernist poetics. The focus shifts as such, away from theology towards the Poundian effort to rebuild, and ultimately police, a collective body before whom the poet as revived 'custodian' might speak. In Pound's hands, as in previous cases, apprenticeship regulates artistic training, and more specifically the training of poets; but he also enunciates a conception of the guild based in technical, professional, and social discipline. These organisational principles apply equally to his forays, later, into economic thinking. Apart from revisiting the forms of social hygiene explored in relation to Schreiner, such questions bear on Pound's anti-Semitic discussion of craftsmanship in *The Cantos*.

Robert Casillo's *The Genealogy of Demons* (1988) marks the beginning of modern critical debate over the sources of Pound's anti-Semitism and its influence on his greatest poem. Though acknowledging the influence of Ruskinian medievalism and Social Credit in formulating his opposition to usury,[239] Casillo finds its source in 'religion, cultural tradition, racist theory', and 'hatred of monotheism'.[240] Attempts to settle this question do not take us very far – the likelihood being that the two tendencies are closely entangled. Tim Redman offers a suggestive opposing view, in stating that Pound 'began his conversion to fascism through the pages of a socialist newspaper' – that is, *The New Age* – and that he 'first encountered the linking of anti-Semitism and usury in that British intellectual milieu'.[241] My analysis builds on this observation, as well as on Serenella Zanotti's related claim that Pound's fascism was rooted in 'his faith in the public function and utility of art'.[242] While the relations between craft ethics and Italian fascism are not straightforward, Pound evidently found them to be so, and a continuum emerges between his literary work ethics and racialised economics. Having assessed this question from the point of view of a history of ideas, the remainder of the chapter applies close textual analysis to *The Cantos*. This approach displaces the instrumentality of Poundian intention to reveal a verbal texture less easily harnessed to a politics of prejudice: far from infiltrating a stable social body, the 'unnatural increase' that Pound views as a threat to poetic craftsmanship turns out to be an intrinsic quality of his own poetry.[243]

Pound owes his best-known evocation of the poet-as-craftsman to his friend, T. S. Eliot. Thanking him for editorial advice given on early drafts of *The Waste Land*, Eliot dedicates the poem's 1925 edition, 'For Ezra Pound: *il miglior fabbro*' ['the better craftsman']. Critical commentary on this gesture largely addresses the influence of Pound's cuts and emendations. Or, as Aaron Jaffe suggests, it explores Pound's role as co-originator: a 'predecessor, forerunner of the forerunner, inventor [. . .] *il miglior fallo*'.[244] Less attention is paid to the implications of calling a poet an ironsmith or a craftsman. Michael Alexander comes closest in tracking the medievalism of this gesture through a 'phrase from Dante's *Purgatorio* Canto XXVI, line 117: "fu miglior fabbro del parlar materno" – "*He* was the better maker in the mother tongue"'.[245] Though he ponders the effect of the additional '*il*' in rendering a superlative, a more pressing question for my purposes concerns the word '*fabbro*'. In revealing a concerted view of the poet as ποιητής (poiētēs) ('maker'), it works more literally and with greater amplitude than Stephen Dedalus's resolution to 'forge in the smithy of my soul'. As Eliot explains, he did not mean to imply 'that Pound was only that'.[246] Rather, he 'wished [. . .] to honour the technical mastery and critical ability in his own work'.[247] Pound, for his part, might have appreciated this more direct appeal to a material intelligence: in *ABC of Reading* (1934), he applies a similar thought on observing that 'The best smith, as Dante called Arnaut Daniel, made the birds sing IN HIS WORDS'.[248]

Judging from these evocations of poetic 'craft', the artisanal medi-evalism of the late nineteenth century continued to live in the 1920s and 1930s, even within the main current of modernism. Such connections cast fresh light on Pound's involvement with *The New Age*: as early as 1914, Penty claimed that 'the discovery that the artist and the craftsman should be one was the greatest discovery of the nineteenth century'.[249] Pound's spiky rhetoric certainly complicates this picture: he describes Ruskin as 'well-meaning but a goose',[250] and in a classic swipe at High Victorianism, writes in 1920 that 'Gladstone was still respected, | When John Ruskin produced | "King's Treasuries"; | Swinburne and Rossetti still abused.'[251] But Pound still appears a moralist and a medievalist: in his own way, as well as in received ways. It seems credible, as Giovanni Cianci and Peter Nicholls claim, that for him 'Ruskin's relentless prob-ing of the relations between aesthetics and ethics retained an irritating authority'.[252] As time passes, however, this anxiety of influence begins to abate. In 1931, Eliot declares, 'We need another Ruskin'.[253] Casillo identifies a similar recovery of discarded thinking on observing Pound's increasing profession of Ruskinian 'craft ideals and the guild organiza-tion of society'.[254] This medievalism is based, it is true, on a dream of labour properly rewarded. Writing in 1937, he asserts that 'The just price is a canonist concept'.[255] And, in common with Gill, and Schreiner, he rejects the dualistic separation of mind and matter in favour of a liber-ated sex act, for him epitomised by pagan or Greek physical joy. Pound even recognises Distributist tenets, wondering whether the encyclicals *Rerum Novarum* and *Quadragesimo Anno* (1931) might bring about 'a new ascension' of Christianity.[256] Though he favours solutions derived from Eastern philosophy, he shares with Ruskin and Gill a recognition that cultural activity requires 'labour', and that this might range from stonemason's work to sculpture and poetry. As a follower of Pound, Bunting poses similar questions. But what sets Pound apart are the rem-nants of a discriminating moralism, derived in part from mid-Victorian sources: in *ABC of Reading*, he condemns 'the desire to get something for nothing or to learn an art without labour'.[257] In 'The serious Artist', he anatomises 'several kinds of honest labour'.[258] Both statements posit an ethical labour theory of value defined in opposition to unearned or unscrupulous gains.

Pound thinks mainly in absolute rather than strictly historical terms; and, unlike Jones, focuses on revival rather than elegy. In the words of the eponymous 'Hugh Selwyn Mauberley', he 'strove to resuscitate the dead art | Of poetry'.[259] And this resolution entails a certain self-definition. As Redman observes, the early Pound is an 'artist convinced of the superior-ity of his calling over those more common in society'.[260] He expresses this 'superiority' in terms reminiscent of Shelley, on observing that 'governor and legislator cannot act effectively or frame his laws, without words'.[261] And it is with a certain irony that he reports the 'solidity and validity of these words' to be '[. . .] in the care of the damned and despised *litterati*'.[262] The whole edifice of capitalist society depends as such on a group that operates by a different rule book: far from privileging accumulative efficiency, writers are always 'detaching the idea of work from the idea of profit'.[263] The result is a dissident definition of work, one that trumps a bourgeois emphasis on returns, yet draws on the equally middle-class morality of religious Non-conformity. Pound required a shock, all the same, to move from this stance of entitled vocation to a mode of action and activism. It arrived in the shape of the First World War, a cataclysm that simultaneously wiped out his friend Gaudier-Brzeska and his hopes of artistic and literary revival.[264]

The War made Pound receptive to anti-capitalist arguments that connect artistic discontents to the unequal spoils of conflict.[265] 'The artist, the maker', he opines, 'is always too far ahead of any revolution, or reaction [. . .] for his vote to have any immediate result'.[266] He feels, all the same, that something has to be done, and that effective action entails refining the processes by which cultural leaders are selected: 'Blessed', he proclaims, 'are they who pick the right artists and makers'.[267] While this formulation recalls Gill's redefinition of artistic activity as a calling towards fabrication, or making, it also steps back from the *homo faber* ideal in imagining an elect artistic cadre. New criteria apply in picking winners, among which Pound specifies 'technique', the body of skill that should underpin the practice of poetry: not so much an attitude, then, but a form of tacit knowledge manually felt and materially expressed. The principles and institutions of craftsmanship loom large in these accounts, and they are ethically charged in the Ruskinian manner.[268] 'Labour on the technique of singable words', Pound insists, 'is honourable labour'.[269] 'Technique', meanwhile, means 'not only suavity of exterior', but 'the clinch of expression on the thing intended to be expressed'.[270]

Pound's awareness of a language relating to fabrication finds pertinent articulation through the practice of 'clinching', a word that recovers literal meaning in the process by which a nail driven through two pieces of wood secures them when hammered over at the protruding end.[271] Elsewhere, Pound asks readers to imagine that 'words are like great hollow cones of steel of different dullness and acuteness'.[272] If technique is a spatial and substantial matter, the depths are quickly reconciled with the surfaces. There are precedents for this in Henry James's conception of 'doing' – as Hugh Kenner observes – and in literary critical trends that understand the novel as having 'a *structure*, being more like a building than a statement'.[273] Pound's imagism likewise emphasises concretion, through 'Direct treatment of the thing'.[274] In later years, his 'images' became less conceptual, and more obviously graven. He takes his 'bearings',[275] as Donald Davie observes, 'from the art of sculpture', while testing the limits of the '"marmorial" or "stony"'.[276] Stone here represents a compromise between malleability and durability, a workable medium fixed in time as well as space. Though he does not perform manual labour himself, Pound recognises stone-built edifices as an arena in which forms and letters are incised in the moment, according to a definite will that allows no hesitation or rubbing out. Reaching beyond 'the "sculpture" of rhyme' ('Hugh Selwyn Mauberley'), he discovers fully incised affinities, a literalisation of the principle that 'Rhythm is a form cut into TIME, as a design is determined SPACE'.[277] 'Good writers', likewise, 'are those who keep the language efficient', who 'keep it accurate, keep it clear'.[278] Though she does not mention Pound, Denise Riley charts a 'lapidary style' whose nature resides in the cultural and technical valence of incised letters, and whose qualities range between concision, brevity, stillness, 'petrified memory', and an associated authority and power to admonish.[279] The last two categories are especially pertinent, in clarifying the Poundian link between matters stylistic, legal and institutional.

A corollary of poetry's renewed association with craft, and the stringency of an unforgiving material, is – relatedly – its accountability to shared professional standards. Vague or ill-defined lines become reprehensible failures of workmanship. Thus Pound intones approvingly that 'Mr Joyce writes a clear, hard prose',[280] and commends 'Mediterranean sanity' in giving 'churches like St Hilaire, San Zeno, the Duomo di Modena, the clear lines and proportions'.[281] A suspicion of the unserious artist goes along with such talk, as does the Whistler-like conviction that 'The mastery of any art is the work of a lifetime'.[282] Pound hopes this will promote a 'general understanding of the fact that poetry is an art and not a pastime'.[283] Discussions of professional discipline meanwhile feed a broader set of attitudes bearing on the exercise of freedom. 'Eliot has said the thing very well', he famously recalls, in claiming that '"No *vers* is *libre* for the man who wants to do a good job"'.[284] Though directed towards controversies in prosody, its wider implication is that great art entails submission.[285] For all the emphasis on craft tradition, Pound's rhetoric cycles opportunistically between different organisational contexts, as if searching for the right fit: his writings hesitate revealingly between addressing 'the candidate'[286], or the 'student',[287] and inducting readers into the mysteries of a trade.

The 'neophyte', he proposes, 'should 'know assonance and alliteration, rhyme immediate and delayed, [. . .] and all the minutiae of his craft'.[288] Pound is aware all the while that apprentice poets are on their own. For all his talk of training, no collective body offers education or enforces standards. This encourages him to fill the breach, in 'weaning young poetesses' or '[c]onducting a kind of literary kindergarten for the aspiring'.[289] Acknowledging Pound's contributions in the matter of 'training', Eliot announces his own 'insistence upon the immensity of the amount of *conscious* labour to be performed by the poet'.[290] His doctrine of impersonality likewise connects 'technique' to the question of self-exposure, in an implied link to the craft guild or *scuola*. In these institutional contexts, the master's way of being entails high standards and a 'selfless' commitment to passing down understanding. This is not a bilateral exchange, but a communal enterprise aimed at cultivating and perpetuating bonds between past and future craftsmen. A similar principle informs Sennett's observation that 'the demioergoi were frequently addressed in public by the names of their profession', and as such known impersonally.[291] The qualities of the individual are subsumed, accordingly, into the corporate life of an intergenerational community.[292]

The Cantos seek at once to embody these principles, and to report on the history of their formation and failure. Canto XLVI, for instance, quarantines objects of value within a specific epoch, or golden age, effectively mimicking the Ruskinian conceit of an absolute historical cut-off: '1527. Thereafter art thickened. Thereafter design went to hell, | Thereafter barocco, thereafter stone-cutting desisted.'[293] The 'act of direct carving', as Clive Wilmer notes, 'adds value to a material that is already an object of value'.[294] In the Poundian universe, the decline of 'stone-cutting' maps directly on to the birth of a usurious civilisation, and in the process eliminates the foundation of artistic value in material value. Canto XLV declares similarly that from usury 'came no church of cut stone signed: *Adamo me fecit*',[295] a reference that several critics trace to an inscribed capital in the Church of San Zeno, Verona.[296] In *The Stones of Venice*, Ruskin writes of this same stone that 'Its workman was proud of it [. . .] (the goodly stone proclaims for ever, ADAMINUS DE SANCTO GIORGIO ME FECIT)' (9:379), and includes a drawing that shows the inscription side-on, but catching the light [Figure 6.2].

Alluding to this wording in a wartime radio broadcast, Pound invokes a broader context of deliberate and deliberated words, in linking 'real versification' with 'Order in stone work, in paintin', *Adamo me fecit*'.[297] From there he commends the same church at Verona whose 'architect had cut that column by HAND, by his own hand', and thereby enshrined

Figure 6.2 John Ruskin, 'Capitals – Concave', Plate XVII to Volume 1 of *The Stones of Venice*, 1851 (*Library Edition*), photogravure from mezzotint. By permission of the Master and Fellows of Magdalene College, Cambridge

an 'INTEGRAL totalitarian interest in the job of buildin". This move-ment between versification, stonework, handiwork, personal signatures, and integrated building, is at one level baffling. But the link resides in an attachment to a connectedness so total that no conflict is felt between the individual will and the common good.

Ruskin reads a similar synthesis of civic pride and personal pride into the mottos on the twenty-first capital of the Doge's Palace in Venice. The first side shows an old man 'beating in a kind of mortar with a hammer' (10:420). Inscribed 'LAPICIDA SUM' [I am a stonecutter], it forms a pair with the eighth side depicting 'A smith forging a sword or scythe-blade' (10:420). Discussed previously in Chapter 5, this fig-ure '[. . .] beats with a large hammer on a solid anvil; and is inscribed "FABER SUM"' [I am a maker] (10:420). For Pound, as for Ruskin, a seamless connection prevails between the face of a civilisation and its generative methods. Individuals unashamed to make their mark lodge tangible value in tangible things. The recipients of these things resemble what Major C. H. Douglas calls 'a "tenant-for-life"', a beneficiary of 'the cultural heritage handed down', whose vital interest is 'to preserve and enhance it'.[298]

This model of inheritance indicates a further means by which Pound collectivises the creative act. On wartime radio, he intones that 'It takes a Whistler to reply to old Eden's lawyers, "No, not for an half hour's work, for the knowledge of a lifetime."'[299] Praising this defence of 'anterior work that piles up into SKILL (material skill, handcraft, hand sleight, knowledge, discrimination.)',[300] he addresses Ruskin in imagining not just Whistler's work performed over a lifetime, but also 'the WORK done by men, now dead'.[301] Synthesising the message of these courtroom opponents, Pound lodges 'the craftsman's pride' in an 'instinct for the justice of the claims of ANTERIOR work'.[302] This form of 'family pride' turns the individualism of Whistler's protectionism on its head.[303] Instead of viewing work as the expression of a unique or time-seasoned self, Pound lodges it in the action of dead (and deft) hands. These hands co-operate unconsciously, but also cumulatively – rather as Eliot understands 'tradition' in relation to 'the individual talent'.[304]

More than an aesthetic or professional preference, Pound's promotion of clean lines offers a commentary on the individual rectitude and 'health' of the maker. Contributors to *The New Age*, many of them members of the old Arts and Crafts Left, likewise flirted with the syndicalism of a new Right. Cianci understands the assembly and interaction of these diverse sources as part of a *'rappel à l'ordre'* [the return to order], a distinctive 'stage of modernism' that combines neo-classicism with 'the tradition of the medieval brotherhood of artisans'.[305] Hilaire Belloc's *The Servile State* (1912), Giorgio De Chirico's manifesto 'Il Ritorno al Mestiere' (1920) [The Return to Craft], and Walter Gropius's resurrection of the Gothic *Einheitskunstwerk* [unified work of art], reveal the European reach of these ideas. More locally, John Hargrave's Kibbo Kift (meaning 'strength or Proof of Great Strength') combined craft ethics with messianic leadership and dreams of mass mobilisation based in 'the formation of Craft Training Groups for senior boys and girls', and 'Craft Guilds.'[306] In the wake of the monetary crisis, Social Credit became a convenient rallying point for Hargrave, as for Pound, even though the latter's economics cleave closer to Ruskin's 'House-law (*Oikonomia*)' (17:19) and his conception of a 'National Store' than to Douglas's worries over 'underconsumption'. As Tim Armstrong shows, Social Credit appealed because of 'its striving towards an aesthetic arm', a tendency declared by the 'printed endorsements from artists and authors' on its pamphlets.[307] Even more pertinently, Social Credit addressed the vexing problems of artistic life by organising it along the lines of a 'handicraft'.[308] Adapting Marx for the management class, Douglas finds 'nothing inherently absurd in a man being a bricklayer in the morning, and a company director in the afternoon'.[309] All this speaks to Pound's enduring dream of applying dissident economic thought to benefit the cultural sphere. In 1938, he called for 'A guild nucleus' for 'writers', accepting applicants 'according to its own criteria'.[310] '[S]uch centred groups', he explains, might eventually 'be correlated into a *sindicato* which would have some vitality'.[311] At this point, the medievalism of his ideal collective order is unmistakable.

Within the cultural milieu of *The New Age* – as elsewhere in Europe – medievalist anti-capitalism ran together with opposition to usury. The sources in this respect – Arthur Mackmurdo's *The Immorality of Lending for Payment of Interest, or Any Other Usurous Gain* (1878), Ruskin's *Fors Clavigera*, and R. G. Sillar's *Usury and the English Bishops* (introduced by Ruskin) (1885) – revived the principles of medieval canon law, in new alignment with notions of a Just Price.[312] Another common theme was hostility to English financial liberalism: what Jeremy Bentham, in *A Defence of Usury*, terms 'the *liberty of making one's own terms in money bargains*'.[313] Guild Socialists as well as Distributists absorbed and developed this thinking. Gill, for instance, admired the 'medieval conception of life', according to which 'Usury was not only illegal but execrated'.[314] The rise to 'supremacy of the financier', he complains, leads to 'the degradation of the small trader and the small craftsman', a change 'accompanied by a degradation of the whole idea of labour and craftsmanship'.[315] Like Pound, he blamed the War on the self-interested machinations of 'men of business'.[316] 'Christ and the Money Changers' (1919), a woodcut from his rejected scheme for the Palace of the League of Nations, urges the League towards 'the ridding of Europe and the World of the Stranglehold of finance'.[317] Gill even advocated Social Credit, having inherited from Guild Socialism and Distributism the scholastic view of usury as a threat to the body politic.

While anti-usury need not mean prejudice, anti-Semitism pervades much of this intellectual ecology.[318] G. K. Chesterton's Christian ethics are infiltrated by it, and Eliot's reliance on anti-Semitic caricature is well known.[319] To complicate matters, there are some in the 1920s – Hargrave among them – who appear fascist on the level of symbol and insignia without actually being so. The Roman salutes and carved swastikas employed by the Kibbo Kift work within a parallel system of meaning. Even after the organisation became the Green Shirts, Hargrave presented Social Credit as a separate enterprise, or 'the "third resolvent force"'.[320] His Jewishness, his opposition to anti-Semitism, and his internationalism likewise resist the profile of a fascist. In 1931, Edith Hope Scott improbably compared the land management experiments pursued by the Guild of St George to Mussolini's '"bonifiche" movement for draining the Roman Campagna'.[321] Pound exploits such confluences on wartime radio in lamenting how 'good sense got lost', when 'The guilds, the anti-trade organizations, with their grades of apprenticage, got chucked into the discard'.[322] This prompts the extraordinary claim that the Allies were fighting 'All the hopes of Ruskin and William Morris'.[323] Notwithstanding its chaotic referentiality, the intellectual genealogy Pound proposes is not entirely fanciful. Just as Guild Socialism eventually tilted towards Italian fascism, so accounts of guild history turned to statist and absolutist approaches.[324] In this period, as Gervase Rosser shows, Otto von Gierke's static conception of the guild, or 'free union' (*freie Einung*) – positioned between 'the communitarian (*genossenschaftlich*) and the hierarchical (*herrschaftlich*)' – underwent a transformation towards the latter.[325] This is apparent in treatments ranging from the Prussian statism of Georg von Below to the organic communitarianism of Ferdinand Tönnies.[326] Rosser insists that 'Tönnies' move [. . .] towards support for an all-powerful national socialist state was not a natural development of his views in *Gemeinschaft und Gesellschaft* (1887)'.[327] But, evidently, Tönnies was not alone in discovering a case for 'strong government' in the lessons of war. Nor, from the point of view of Pound's reading, was the allusion to Morris a flash in the pan: Hilda Doolittle dwells on Pound's early enjoyment of Morris, as also his influence on Pound's symbolic nexus of the economic, the literary, and the familial.[328] Indeed, she recalls Pound's father – named 'Homer' – showing them 'gold bars' when he worked as 'government essayer at the Philadelphia Mint', an incident that helps her explain 'later compulsions', including his being 'obsessed' with the word '*Usura*'.

Redman is right, of course, that 'the radical syndicalism of continental Europe' differs from the 'English craft tradition' associated with Ruskin and Morris.[329] In Letter 76 of *Fors Clavigera*, Ruskin writes that 'The St George's creed includes Turks, Jews, infidels, and heretics; and I am myself much of a Turk, more of a Jew' (29:92). Equally, the earlier historiography of associationalism runs against Pound's analysis. Morris, for one, understood guilds as incubating democratic values, and as fostering a creative disruption of feudal structures (16:389).[330] 'By the beginning of the fourteenth century', he contends, 'the supremacy of the craft-gilds [*sic*] [over the earlier merchant gilds] was complete, and at that period at least their constitution was thoroughly democratic' (22:304). In such matters he takes his bearings not from Carlyle, but from E. T. Kemble's Anglo-Saxon constitutionalism – according to which the guilds were 'the nursing-cradles of popular liberty' –[331] and from Edward Freeman's assertion that 'freedom is everywhere older than bondage', and that 'toleration is older than intolerance'.[332] Rosser tracks an associated liberal tradition through Wilhelm Wilda's *Das*

Gildenwesen im Mittelalter (1831) and the 'mutuality' championed by Joshua Toulmin Smith.[333] Such connections prevail up to the point of G. D. H. Cole's *Social Theory* (1920), a work that commends 'the liberty of associations' as a matter of 'their democratic character'.[334] A counter-manding strain of English liberalism likewise characterises the Arts and Crafts tradition. The potter Bernard Leach spoke of the 'dire need for a unifying culture', but distanced himself from the 'totalitarian concep-tion of national life'.[335] Relatedly, Gill's meeting with Pound in Rapallo was not entirely a success, as MacCarthy shows: 'Pound had drawn the [mistaken] inference that Gill's belief in monetary reform made him a Fascist'.[336] Bunting shared Pound's belief in 'the objective workabili-ties of objective materials (words)',[337] but expressed disgust at learning of the 'anti-semite bile' contained in a letter sent to Louis Zukofsky.[338] While the gates of Auschwitz notoriously proclaim a persistence and perversion of the nineteenth-century labour ethic – 'Arbeit Macht Frei' [Work Makes You Free] – neither Mussolini nor Hitler were especially interested in artisanal traditions. It is equally apparent, as Leon Surette notes, that neither had much interest in Social Credit either.[339]

Many of Pound's contemporaries renounced their sympathy for syn-dicalism once political fascism began to advocate aggressive racial war. Pound, by contrast, grew only more adamantly in favour. In 1934 – as Alex Houen shows – he began to express a 'compound theory of pervasive Jewish contagion'.[340] By 1937 he was claiming that Jews are 'the GREAT destroyers of value | the *obliterators* of all demarcations | the shifters of boundary stones'.[341] Victorian commentaries on usury continue, even so, to have a significant bearing on Pound's conceptions of literary labour. Just as he understands poetry as a form of making, so usury is described as 'a charge for the use of purchasing power, levied without regard to pro-duction'.[342] This in turn reflects a medievalist concern about 'the decline of Christian ethics'.[343] But while Hopkins worries about a Promethean drift in creative acts, Pound considers them immaculate. It is usury, in his account, that corrupts and frustrates artistry. In the Dantean scheme, he insists, 'Usury' is judged '"contrary to natural increase", contrary to the nature of live things (animal and vegetable) to multiply',[344] and a standing insult to the sacrifices involved in human or divine labour. This same com-plaint informs his views on paper money and the system of private central banks. Though he worries about the private profits made in lending to the Treasury on a public licence, he worries more about the mechanism by which those gains are achieved.

These concerns are unbridled in their reach, and as such difficult to summarise, but they divide broadly into those applicable to the banking system and those applicable to language. Under the first heading, Pound addresses a case of aboriginal overreach supposedly perpetrated by the Bank of England's founder, William Paterson. In 'What is money for?', he has Paterson tell his shareholders that "'the bank hath profit on the increase of all the moneys which it creates out of nothing'".[345] Pound evokes this appropriation of divine creative functions through a reversal of the classical adage *ex nihilo nihil fit*[346] (and King Lear's 'nothing will come of nothing' (I. 1. 90)).[347] But the formulation attributed to Paterson seems to be apocryphal. It does not appear in the Bank's founding Royal Charter; nor is it in *A Brief Account of the Intended Bank of England* (1694).[348] As Meghnad Desai suggests, Pound probably got it second hand, from an unsubstantiated – and it turns out, elusive – reference in Christopher Hollis's *The Two Nations* (1934).[349] The unintended irony of this shoddy attribution crystallises in Canto XLV, a work that elaborates usury's economic effects into a connection between financial instruments and craftsmanship. Usury, we read, precludes the solidity of 'a house of good stone | each block cut smooth and well fitting'.[350] Insistent itemisation suggests proliferating harm, running through the entire social body:

> Stonecutter is kept from his stone
> weaver is kept from his loom
> WITH USURA
> wool comes not to market
> sheep bringeth no gain with usura
> Usura is a murrain, usura
> blunteth the needle in the maid's hand
> and stoppeth the spinner's cunning.

Usury, in this account, produces a 'murrain', or plague: a seemingly natural event that exacts retribution for impiety. As a visitation, it has a cruel and ironical edge: it disperses and interrupts the very folk community whose processes are initially deemed innocent. More particularly, usury attacks the holy trinity of skilled application, comprising tool, medium, and operative: 'Usura rusteth the chisel | It rusteth the craft and the craftsman'. Archaic endings, and an emphasis on rural production, enact a frustration of homely rhythm, ordained as if by Scripture. Crucially, Pound characterises usury not just as a destroyer of well-made objects, but a threat to the regeneration of that order: 'It gnaweth the thread in the loom'; while under its sway, 'None learneth to weave gold in her pattern'.[351] Usury spells the death of apprenticeship, whether of weaver, blacksmith or poet, portending the collapse of the whole artisanal order.

Poundian craftsmanship aligns in this way with the natural increase of an agrarian order, a position most vividly illustrated by the paeon to the Monte dei Paschi di Siena in *The Fifth Decad of Cantos* (1937). Having identified this 'species of bank', or 'damn good bank',[352] as a 'fund', he upgrades it to a 'BANK of the grassland'.[353] Canto XLIV confirms that the bank's effect 'has been to keep bridle on usury', to privilege 'use' over its slippery cousin.[354] This tendency reflects American as well as European political traditions. Rather as Thoreau praised Carlyle for writing that resembles 'the plough, and cornmill',[355] so Pound hails the Founding Father John Adams as 'capable of holding the plough'.[356] In his propaganda broadcasts, Pound likewise develops an opposition between modern finance and a Jeffersonian natural economy.[357]

A second focus of Poundian usury – its concern with language – understands the written word as a physical tool. Speaking on Italian radio in March 1942, he expands the scope of a 'day's work' to include 'physical' labours and those performed by the 'mind'.[358] Economic questions are never far from the literary ones that bend them out of shape. Pound's hatred of usury likewise operates at the closest textual level, in the figures and phrasing that declare a text's moral nature. 'No man', he insists, 'will ever be a great writer, not even a good writer, a useful craftsman of letters if he persists in misusin' words'.[359] In his account, poetic goods are not necromantically conjured 'out of nothin'', but fashioned according to the laws of honest labour, if not Just Price.[360] And it is at this point – at the level of poetic language – that anti-Semitic currents return most angrily to the surface. Aesthetic concretion extends to an insistence that Jewish culture invented the 'invisible and immaterial God', and the codes and hermeticism that promote abstraction.[361] From here, he is led to the basic abstraction of usury, a practice that turns money into a 'symbol'.[362] The result, Pound concludes, is 'vagueness in communication'.[363] He argues, accordingly, that 'the greater the component of tolerance for usury the more blobby and messy the work of art'.[364] Armed with this preconception, he elucidates connections between the purportedly usurious qualities of vagueness or metaphor, and the lost craftworld of a poetry separated from its normally slippery apparatus.

While this alarm about metaphor might seem strange in a writer, anxiety about the moral character of poetic language is not in itself unusual. Ruskin harbours not dissimilar anxieties, alluding as he does to Plato's foundational discussion of writing and deception in *Phaedrus*.[365] Pound belongs, though, to a smaller group of modern figures who downplay or suppress the trickier aspects of language. Gladstone, as discussed in Chapter 4, comes closest in ruling out a generative role for deception amidst the Odyssean brand of craftsmanship. Woolf, as previously noted, is so worried about the 'cajolery, cunning, deceit' in craft that she excludes it from literature entirely. Morris, as demonstrated, takes a different view. For him, artifice, cunning and magic, are not easily excluded from the workings of the craftsman: indeed, the same qualities that destroy civilisations – as revealed by the Arthurian legends and the *Volsunga Saga* – turn out to be essential to great art. He admits the trickster and the mischief maker: not only Odysseus, but also Tom Sawyer and Br'er Rabbit. In his vision, we cannot expect delight without damage, or love without pain. Morris's legacy thereby confounds Pound's effort to co-opt him: he resists moving from the trained hand or the ordered workshop to the ordered society and the 'clean' work of art.

Instead of accepting a connection between art and impetuosity, Pound doggedly distinguishes the creative acts of the financier and poet. Whereas Gill evades Promethean guilt through 'associate' status, Pound shuffles it off in the form of a scapegoat, sustaining all the while an unbridgeable opposition between art and usury. This position leads him into several suggestive contradictions. The first concerns the place of usury within his own poetry, which in making its point rehearses and mimics the very usurious production that he casts as an existential threat. *The Fifth Decad of Cantos* is consumed by this paradox. Even as it condemns usury, it revels linguistically in the potency of unnatural increase. Canto XLV's rhetorical pattern of ramifying negation is illustrative.[366] Pound aims, seemingly, to enact and condemn usury's *ex nihilo* methods: to show how the things conjured by usury suffer cancellation. But we linger on the substance more than we do the results. The craft values supposedly under attack endure in the 'well fitting' masonry, the 'painted paradise', the 'halo' projecting from an 'incision'.[367] These clear visions are summoned into being, materially, at the point of negation rather than before; indeed, their existence barely precedes their ritual destruction. And this is a process owing, of course, to poetic method rather than financial tricks. The lineation, too, practises a kind of magic: recurrent isolation of 'with usura' only adds to the peculiarly positive charge, the sense of a spell that miraculously recovers positive effect from negative ingredients.

By identifying usury as 'CONTRA NATURAM', Pound implies that 'honest' crafts, including poetry, are natural and wholesome.[368] Two cross-currents emerge, however. Though shaded by a language of biblical wrath, the agents of usurious effect that Pound employs – rust, canker, palsy, the gnawing of mice – are, themselves, temporal. This natural order of decay undermines the singularity of usury's supposed threat. Moreover, the poem strays beyond the bounds of nature. Its rhetorical method, in conjuring illusory or defeated substance, illustrates the action of poetry as much as it does usury. And its persistent vitality as a work of art defies the instrumental message. We read, for instance, that 'usura | blunteth the needle in the maid's hand | and stoppeth the spinner's cunning'.[369] But the needle, and a subsequent reference to 'cramoisi [. . .] unbroidered' conjure thoughts of Penelope. Penelope relies on a deception legitimised by loyalty, and the result of her unpicking is unnatural decrease.[370] Blunt tools are not part of the equation. Equally, the 'cunning' of the spinner contains obvious ambiguity. Usury here obstructs the positive 'cunning' of skilful hands, but as a stock term 'cunning' also applies to the financial wiles that Pound condemns. By welcoming usury into the poem, Pound enlivens what otherwise he seeks to repress – namely, the unlicensed affinities between usury and poetry, both of which deal in immateriality and representational processes removed from work-a-day reality. In this respect, his brand of classicism also makes him vulnerable. In contrast to Gladstone's monotheistic world-view, Pound's polytheism unwittingly favours polytropism ('many turns') and opportunism. As Lewis Hyde discusses, these are the same qualities that render the trickster (and his Odyssean epitome) the archetypal boundary crosser, a figure who navigates the gulf between gods, mortals, and worlds.[371] He even emerges as an irregular maker, one whose manner of invention undertakes a 'disjointing' that is also a 'rejointing'.[372]

While Pound initially encounters these contradictions within the formal boundaries of his poetry, they come to a head – revealingly – when he violates the same boundaries. This effect transpires when 'replaying' *The Cantos* in the altered context of wartime radio, and most dramatically in his radio broadcast of 12 February 1942. Eventually setting aside the manic chatter of his wireless personality, he reads out the whole of Canto XLVI (1937). Its subject '*Hic Geryon est*' refers to the Greek giant Geryon, identified in Dante with 'extra strong usury' or 'super usury'.[373] The poem transforms Pound's case against central banks into an incantation, mixing journalistic reportage with the language of the law and the King James Bible: 'Said Paterson: | Hath benefit of interest on all | the moneys which it, the bank, creates out of nothing'.[374] This quotation, as noted, is apocryphal; but here it arrives culled from Pound's polemical writings, in which form it enters a third level of remove, as the language of the Canto submits to the political diatribe and the commentary of the broadcast.[375]

In as much as the framing discourse of a radio personality keeps Canto XLVI within instructional limits, Pound employs it as a thing of use in the world, a tool of enlightenment. Only, this need to mediate between poem and audience – by 'feedin' you the footnotes first' – unintentionally implies irregular uses, and less controlled possibilities.[376] Lured initially into a four-paragraph moraine of explanatory literary criticism, he issues the unconvincingly blunt resolve, 'All right, now I am going on with Canto 46'. It seems that poetry, after all, is not simply a negation of usury, nor simply an instrument in the hands of the propagandist, but a medium requiring some negotiation of meanings and contexts. It might be true, as Casillo observes, that Pound follows Ruskin in understanding 'that literature, like any drug, can poison', that it 'distorts intrinsic value'.[377] But this lesson is not necessarily clear from the effort to harness Canto XLVI. Casillo adds, moreover, that 'bad writing is linked to usury', while '[m]etaphor is a kind of usurious "borrowing"'.[378] Here he misses an important distinction between the examples of Ruskin and Pound. Like Plato, Ruskin worries that all poetry, indeed all writing, is inflationary. Pound, by contrast, believes that good writing – writing produced by apprenticed poets – would not exhibit these characteristics; indeed, that illusions, idolatries and falsehoods are not a feature of genuine art.

This position finds itself undone by Pound's own poetic practice. His radio performance precipitates an unnerving generic encounter between past and present modes, which exposes a quality already present in the original Canto: namely, a fluid relation to other works, and other genres, and an acquisitive energy not itself especially respectful of dividing lines. This simultaneously compromises the subtlety of the pre-War Canto and highlights the propagandist energies at work within it. Two larger effects follow, the first of which arises through an interruption of the poem's agrarian seclusion. A promiscuous hunger for borrowed words shows through its fabric – and a habit of repurposing that defies the stated separation of town and country, of good banks and bad, of true and false writing. The second bears on Pound's stylistic preference for the marmoreal, including the ways in which broadcast propaganda restages lapidary admonition only to cut against the usual association with permanence and considered wisdom. Pound's earlier accounts imply a 'nonironic lapidary', but that confidence seems misplaced: just as Riley notes how 'Irony will establish itself in the self-noticing word', so Pound's style speaks here in unlicensed ways.[379] Evoking not just the lapidary turned aerial, it constitutes an ironic instance of unselfnoticing, a lurching relation between stony concision and rambling polemic.

A customary anti-Semitism shadows much of the declared opposition to usury in Guild Socialist, Distributist, and Social Credit circles. Each group draws heavily on the institutional freight of medievalism, in promoting fixed social bonds, discipline, authority, and mastership. This mixed and conflicted inheritance is not identical to European fascism. But the connected facts of Pound's trajectory are not in doubt: he moves smoothly from dreams of 'a utopian state where writers would not have to struggle to exist' to a fully racialised aesthetics and economics.[380] He amplifies the existing links between a racialised conception of usury and a civilisational view of craftsmanship, according to which money loaned at interest rusts the chisel and weakens the stanza. And, in so doing, he strengthens associations that are loose or marginal in earlier anti-capitalist discourses. Though not typical, his case presents a far-reaching problem: he is not only an eminent and articulate advocate of these literary applications, but a great poet. For writers wishing to uphold a work of words based in communal relations, and material value, his legacy presents a grave ethical challenge.

The last phase of this discussion does nevertheless suggest alternative directions. Embedding Canto XLVI in the propagandistic discourse of wartime radio, Pound unwittingly exposes his poetry to a process of corrosion. This strengthens the poison of its prejudice, and realises his own worst fears, in conceiving literature as a source of dissolution rather than determinacy. But by exhibiting the inflationary qualities otherwise attributed to usury, it also challenges the distinction between good writing and everything else. These problems are exposed not only at the point of intersection between propaganda broadcasts and finished poems, but also within the poetry itself. Pound's need to dramatise unnatural increase reveals his grasp of similar powers, so that a clear distinction between artistic rhetoric and financial instruments falls away. The fugitive qualities attributed to usury turn out to be a characteristic of literature itself. Having reached this impasse, more accommodating and less exclusive versions of the craft analogy slide into view: notably, those based on working processes and communities rather than social or racial types. Morris, in particular, comes back to haunt Pound, but not in the way implied on wartime radio. Rather, his legacy subverts the continuum between prejudice and poetry that Pound defends. Morris likewise aligns poetry with craft, but he grants that word its full import, its range between values, standards, and illusion, as also an unavoidable creative intimacy between poetry and trickery, poetry and cunning.

* * *

All three writers discussed in this chapter sanctify and reform 'work' as a route to enhanced social relations. Schreiner reclaims manual toil and craft as possessions of the active, female labourer, and she imagines women guiding a physical process of intellectual advancement beneficial to the whole human race. However, her uncertainty about the writer's place within this programme sets her apart from the Promethean agency claimed by Gill and Pound. Gill's conception of the material letter, and his attraction to guilds and apprenticeship, bear most obvious comparison with Pound's thoughts on concretion and poetic apprenticeship. He, like Jones, worries over the poet's disempowerment, but shares with Gill a sense of entitlement in recovering an audience and a position from which to speak. All three writers yearn nevertheless for professional and moral justification. Schreiner pursues this in her letters, proposing a literary production relocated from writing to a scene of walking or thinking. Gill, as discussed, mediates between his craft and the public, in the form of lectures, but also at the level of doctrine, as he inserts into Maritain's translated prose an adapted idea of the craftsman. He, like Pound, builds new forms of collaboration into artistic experience, which are underpinned by authority and discipline.

The most striking common thread is medievalist anti-capitalism, apparent in the means by which each figure circumvents mercantile values by connecting literary values with artisanal ones. This prompts a positive message, focused on the possibility of an art-practice untrammelled by the tyranny of the market. But it also introduces a social organicism that leads each, in different ways, on to dangerous ground. Pound's virulent prejudice distinguishes him from Schreiner and Gill, but in all three cases a problem emerges: a sense that work, when taken as a founding value, does violence to social and literary complexity, and that crossing boundaries can also mean violating them. We should by the same token register the singularity and complexity of these examples. Avoiding the teleological fallacy in the history of ideas is easiest when alternative directions, and counter currents, are kept to the fore. Schreiner's humanitarianism does not entirely succumb to her social typology. Jones's conception of *homo faber* – as applied to poetry as much as to boat-building – survives Gill's abuses of power. And while Morris also succumbs to social organicism, his conception of the good society, and of literary value, admits an idea of mischief and impetuosity that respects a changeful and impetuous human spirit.[381] Even Pound's poetry – at the level of verbal texture, rather than authorial intent – unsettles instrumental purity, pitting the flexibility and unpredictability of the written word against authorial protocol and prejudice.

Conclusion: Writing as Working

The examples collected in this book address a literary *rapprochement* with the idea (and the practice) of skilled manual labour. Initially inspired by classical principles of united sensibility, its early Victorian form arises in Dissenting cultures of visible effort, neo-Lockean conceptions of property, prescriptions against occupational disease, and gymnastic ideas of self-culture; thereafter, it develops into a project of cerebral-physical integration, which assumes various shapes, before culminating in the Arts and Crafts (and latterly, modernist) vision of a craftsmanship that unites physical making with the mental conception. What comes into view is a sustained attempt to resolve and renovate the status of writing, a determination to make writer and writing accountable, to forge a physically legible 'labour of mind'. The writers in question effect this outcome in different ways: through testamentary or material visualisations of literary work, writerly performances of agricultural labour or handicraft, as well as through craft-based theories of composition, literary association, linguistic tooling, and direct carving in prose.

Tracking these experiments across a hundred years illuminates a striking longevity of ideas and practices, as well as connections between apparently disparate contexts. Links emerge between Carlyle's Teufelsdröckh on 'Man' as 'a tool-using Animal' (1:32) and Gill's notion that 'the tool is from the beginning that of the artist, no less than the labourer'.[1] Others are apparent between Whistler's rejection of hours counted at the canvas and Pound's incongruous allusion to apprenticeship in his wartime broadcasts; between vaticism and artisanal approaches; and between the differing conceptions of an artist's relation to a working God held by Barrett Browning, Hopkins and Gill. Meanwhile, Gladstone, Ruskin, Schreiner and Pound share an agrarianism focused both on labour value and an idea of poetic participation.[2] As previously stated, the cases discussed are determined less by political loyalties, or a particular literary tradition, than by an evolving occupational strategy, one that responds to an inherited problem of value. In this respect, it is better to think in terms of loose formations than of a lineage or succession, though the textual and personal connections can be compelling, as suggested by Pound's recourse to Whistler, Ruskin and Morris. Equally, this book has sought to instantiate and test a history of ideas at the level of close textual readings: without conceiving authors as mere siphons for notions in transit, these chapters track patterns that cut across generic and generational boundaries, some of which are brought to full consciousness, some of which remain latent.

It is equally possible to identify dividing lines. One such concerns the movement from early Victorian accountancies of labour based on visual scrutiny towards an emphasis on artisanal vocation, being, and community. Carlyle's influence endures, perhaps, because he establishes a relationship between the strenuous and the skilled, the material and the poetic: but equally, his self-appointed disciples continuously mediate and adapt such precepts, strengthening or weakening the concentrations of certain elements according to their circumstances. As argued in the last chapter, Morris presents the most serious check on political 'Carlyleship', in that his medievalism – and his conception of a guild or craft community – takes its bearings from a liberal rather than authoritarian constitution. Other ripples originate from anxieties about creative pride, or about a literary pollution of the innocence associated with the craft community. While these concerns are consonant with Carlylean anxieties about 'anarchy', they are not resolved by an appeal to social control. Dickens and Hopkins invest in an idea of apprenticeship that simultaneously tests its vulnerability to abuse and disappointment. What unites these cases, all the same, is an apprehension of skilled manual labour as desirable, and a yearning sense – even if defeated or sceptical – that it might reshape the work of authorship.

Three persistent conceptual problems cut across the pairings and positions that populate these chapters. They apply to matters of theology and performance; of instructional and institutional authority; and of worked form or texture. The first takes root in a kind of social strain, whereby literature resorts to theatricality or metaphor in staking its claim to labouring identity. This sense of 'unnatural' performance runs through Carlyle's resolution to make the 'idle tattle' of literature into mason's work; it informs Brown's composition of navvy labour, as well as Ruskin's Ferry Hinksey road dig; and it conditions Gladstone's heavily mediated guise as a woodman. This need to 'show' work reflects an enduring practical difficulty in proving the action of thought; but it is also a theological conception, drawn from the Calvinist emphasis on performing personal election, and from the overlapping discourses and philosophies discussed in the Introduction. The same inheritance, equally, penalises inauthentic utterance as ritualistic or insincere, so that an obvious irony accompanies the staged transformation of immaterial forms into working substance. Carlyle, accordingly, is as impatient with himself as with those cultural artificers – including poets and painters – who seem to privilege appearance over action.

Barrett Browning's role-playing responds to this concern, in that she moves from a mobile poetic identity to one that locates authentic being in the testament of the body. She also shares Carlyle's idealist infusion of matter with spirit, though in her case the prophetic enters into a paradoxical relation with poetic labour. Her effort to recast and transform bodily limit invites comparison with Schreiner, whose ecstatic poetics recruit to the future an ancient vision of woman as mason and potter. These cases represent significant stirrings within a tradition that tends to assume that a return to the body will be a return to the male body. They also broaden the scope of what literary composition might mean. Schreiner develops an analogy with birth labour, which aligns maternity not only with cultural production, but with revolutionary world-making; she also accords working status to thought – whether visionary or compositional – and to letters. Each of these 'irregular' cases takes its place at the frontline of a struggle for visibility, encompassing not only intangible forms, but a gendered division of labour. Theological resonances arise, finally, in debates about the appropriate connection between divine labour and human labour. A tension exists between Hopkins's conception of making as praise, and Gill's conception of co-partnership in the creative process, where *homo faber* acquires facets of divinity. In most cases – notably in Dickens, Ruskin and Hopkins – a persistent connection emerges between use and abuse, between the roles of creator and creature.

The last opposition activates a second set of problems. These concern reforms to the circumstances in which writers operate, often drawing on medievalist workshop or guild templates. Distributed evenly across Tory Radicals, liberals, and socialists, this institutional medievalism encompasses the social and cultural critique practised by Carlyle and Ruskin alongside the hierarchies entrenched in inherited principles of apprenticeship and mastership. For James – as briefly discussed in relation to 'The Lesson of the Master' – conceiving the writer as a guild member represents a category error. Many other writers are attracted by the possibility of common standards, and a working community, otherwise lacking in literary life. The question of authority and its proper limits recurs amidst these debates. Ruskin models the governing office of Master, in his Guild of St George, on a version of the obedience expected of apprentices, though in class terms it interacts confusingly with the equally medieval, but differently inflected, role of a collegiate Head of House. Gladstone instead refers authority to the figure of a craftsman king; and his versions of subservience hesitate radically between class harmony and the agricultural economy of his father's slave estates (where the word 'master' acquires yet another resonance). The final chapter extends this theme to discourses of failed authority, moral panic, and prejudice, centred on perceptions of social parasitism and financier capitalism.

Such forces come into focus at the book's close. Certainly, they are explicable within an intellectual scheme activated by a longing for roots, solidities, intrinsic values, and a narrowly defined idea of community. There remains a risk in allowing this total reading – compelling as it is – to flatten out the moral complexities governing individual cases; or to diminish the ever-shifting combinations of hope, potential, idealism, anxiety, and personal advantage, which they evoke. As discussed in relation to Gladstone, Morris and Pound, the insurgent life of craft as cunning places an important check on dreams of order. Equally, this book looks beyond the identity of the writer or the context in which writing appears, to consider its worked substance as a source of complexity and surprise, revealed through the technical means by which texts register the labour or craft usually deemed foreign to their fabric. Barrett Browning's letters, and Brown's diary, are so much more than historical sources pertaining to artistic identity: they reveal a history of forms, and of formal possibilities. And they disclose the relations between forms. Brown's diary, as discussed, is haunted by the oral mode of the confession; yet it strives simultaneously toward the official compact of a ledger. Barrett Browning's letters, in curious ways, perform actions normally reserved to the body, while absorbing and redeeming the 'idle' characteristics often levelled at poetry.

Fluid relations emerge, equally, between literature and the visual arts, a cognate field prone to similar productive difficulties and a related stigma. If, for writers, the visual field dispenses with accountancies of effort, in speaking for itself, artists discover in the word a solution to anxieties about speechless acts, ensuring a union of things and thoughts. In this regard, Gill's attention to the incarnate letter stands as a resolution of the hesitation between writerly and artistic labour. Moving from genre to worked substance, Ruskin's double-sense of *Fors* – indicating either force or fortune – extends the unpredictable implications of cunning into the realm of guided chance. The stony, the marmoreal, the lapidary, are less susceptible to this analysis than metallurgic materials; but here, too, an impression of fixity and admonition undergoes transformation, whether through Ruskin's adaptation of the merchants' law inscribed on San Giacomo di Rialto, or the unlicensed means by which *The Cantos* dislodge Pound's own 'boundary stones'.[3]

* * *

An important impetus for writing this book has been a desire to think through topical problems in a refracted historical context. Far from confirming a bias towards intractability, present discontents contain surprises when traced back: in their structure, forgotten responses model alternative, even counter-factual, versions of the creative process; in their audacity they suggest the possibility of more successful manipulations. In all these respects, the situational and aspirational otherness of the past is instructive. At the close, it repays to widen the view yet further, to include the submerged route to our own historical moment. What became of the argument that writing bears a relation to physical craftsmanship? Does the idea retain any currency that words are tangible raw materials, requiring laborious lifting, strenuous hewing, or dexterous manipulation?

At the limit of its chronological span, *The Work of Words* registers a transition of sorts. The Second World War inaugurated a technological sublime – epitomised by Hiroshima and a new scale of mass production – that made talk of apprenticeship seem quaint and outmoded. In literature and philosophy, the subsequent rise of existentialism, the 'Angry Young Man', and the Movement poets, announced a turn towards lived experience and alienation that pushed aside the technical and artistic self-consciousness of the pre-War era. Postmodernism completed this process: first emerging in architectural contexts, it spurned the deep structure and united sensibility that modernist buildings inherited from Arts and Crafts principles. More than a fashion in art, its preference for surface, allusion, and irony informs more general assessments of the West's civilisational condition, defined variously as 'late capitalism'[4] or 'liquid modernity'.[5] The neo-classical economists of the late 1970s and 1980s famously rejected Keynesian demand management in favour of supply-side solutions; but they also sought to purge their discipline of its roots in moral philosophy.[6] Favouring the perceived scientism of utility-based models over this metaphysical residue, they completed the long departure from labour-based theories of value, and related searches for value's 'origin'. An associated de-coupling from attitudes privileging production – and the intrinsic value smuggled in behind it – occurred in the political sphere. From the 1990s, policy makers construed an associated turn towards pure design, and conceptual art, as a chance to de-emphasise practical skills, most notably in secondary schools:[7] crudely put, the technical education of Harold Wilson's 'white heat' fell away in favour of a new 'knowledge economy' embraced by politicians anxious to justify deindustrialisation.[8]

Peter Dormer's *The Art of the Maker* (1994) delivers one of the earliest checks on this gathering orthodoxy, in challenging the idea 'that conception and execution are separate activities and that execution – mere making – can take care of itself'.[9] He attributes this failure to a conceptual misstep, in an analysis that leans on Ruskin, but also the Austrian philosopher, Allan Janik. Janik argues that serious thinkers have failed 'to take working life seriously', with the significant exceptions of Marx, Wittgenstein and Tolstoy.[10] Though illustrious, this list invites expansion. A meaningful and enduring counter-current informs the example of Dormer himself, as also David Pye;[11] equally, a history of interest in the writer-worker runs almost uninterrupted across the twentieth century. The idea of a 'Practical Criticism' influenced the teaching of English Literature through much of this period. Though drawn from I. A. Richards's scientificism, and his search for 'exercises not too difficult for practical application in education', it soon posited the cultural benefits of 'workshop' practice in the classroom.[12] The physicality of such tooling is inescapably metaphorical, of course – as it would also be for Joan Littlewood's 'Theatre Workshop', and the workshop theatres that proliferated across university literature departments in the 1960s and 1970s. Similar analysis might be applied to the more recent boom in Creative Writing instruction – in America as well as in Britain – where the 'workshop' serves as the principal model of tuition. Rather than marking a break, though, the very awkwardness of this institutional strain towards materiality recalls the tenor of nineteenth-century experiments.

A different kind of survivor, Basil Bunting, was discussed in the Preface. By contrast with the eponymous and ineffectual 'Tom',[13] the bardic speaker of his late-flowering epic *Briggflatts* (1966) declares, 'Pens are too light. | Take a chisel to write.'[14] As if recalling the philosophy of a similarly belated peer, David Jones, the poem redescribes the act of writing from within the bounds of the act itself as a materially witnessed and witnessing word. All this seems a long way from post-War youth culture; but even that recalls something older. Although accounts differ,[15] most critics trace the 'Angry Young Man' label of the 1950s to a memoir of the same name by Leslie Paul.[16] Far from addressing the disaffected of that decade, Paul focuses on the 1920s and 1930s, when he left Hargrave's Kibbo Kift to found the Left-leaning Woodcraft Folk.[17] This process develops his 'rebel' consciousness,[18] but also consolidates his pacifism, his desire for 'a new education on woodcraft lines', and his Morrisian advocacy of Craft Guilds.[19] The link between uniformed youth movements and the insurgent aspirations of 1950s teenage culture may not be immediately clear; but a peculiar lineage stretches from Paul's bodily forms of self-actualisation to the more unsettled heroism of John Osborne, and the sculpted motorcyclists of Thom Gunn's *The Sense of Movement* (1957).[20] The War, as such, seems less a terminal break than a suspension.

The idea of a physical literature – and more particularly, a working literature – is not confined to these strange survivals, nor to the 'Angry Young Man'. In the experience of a generation abruptly removed from industrial roots, the possibility that writing might still be working exercises instinctive appeal. Drawn from working-class backgrounds into educational opportunity, Richard Hoggart's 'scholarship boy' lacks 'the compensations of a craftsman'.[21] On the contrary, his dilemma of uprooting leads to 'an unconvincing pride in his own gaucheness at practical things', based in a conviction that '"brain-workers" are never "good with their hands"'.[22] Three talented poetic products of that educational experiment – Seamus Heaney, Tony Harrison and Geoffrey Hill – comment on the class dynamics of a working literature in ways conspicuously owing to nineteenth-century precedents. As if recalling Carlyle's resolution to write his books as his father built his houses, Heaney's 'Digging' (1966) famously pictures his father 'Stooping in rhythm through potato drills.'[23] The final stanza ventures an equivalence between the spade and the 'squat pen' that is at once moot and the beginning of a productive challenge as the speaker declares, 'I'll dig with it.'[24] In 'v.' (1985), Harrison imagines a place for himself among occupations of 'the family dead': 'butcher, publican, and baker, now me, bard | adding poetry to their beef, beer and bread.'[25] Supplementing these perishable professions with manufactured value, he conjures an alternative past from headstones suggesting that 'Wordsworth built church organs, Byron tanned | luggage'.[26] In *Mercian Hymns* (1971), Hill sceptically reviews the exhibition of nailing in *Fors Clavigera*.[27] He later confesses a yearning respect for Ruskin's evocations of intrinsic value,[28] and enters a related self-description in *Without Title* (2006): 'I also am a worker in iron'.[29] As if re-opening poetry's relation to the manual, he finally dedicates *Broken Hierarchies* to his working-class forebears, quoting in the process Psalm 90's entreaty to 'establish' the 'work of our hands upon us'.[30] These preoccupations live on, and undergo transformation, in recent poetry. As previously noted, Denise Riley reads the so-called lapidary style as a '*cutting gesture*', an 'enacted verb of incising'.[31] She enters a pertinent gloss, on explaining that such writing 'runs closer to control and craft than to style considered as a demonstration of the author's sensibilities'. Alice Oswald likewise explores a marmoreal basis for poetry, based less in expression than in physical presence – a sense dynamically present in *The Thing in the Gap-Stone Stile* (1996),[32] and her suggestive model of classical translation as a process of 'excavation'.[33]

When embracing a liberal education and a professional career, the 'scholarship boy' (and 'girl') typically worries over a class heritage left behind. In a collective development of this predicament, the Global Financial Crisis of 2008 prompted soul searching about what whole

234 The Work of Words

societies – the post-industrial societies of Great Britain and America – might be leaving behind in rushing headlong towards a service-based economy. In the long shadow of these events, it is not just the writer who seems haunted by a lost world of material production. By taking the long view on efforts to make composition physical, this book sheds light on recent anxieties about the distinction between tangible and intangible value, and the weight and worth of the humanities. Corresponding attempts have been made by historians to re-examine and grasp such concepts as 'craft' and 'apprenticeship'. Accounts of Germany's *Wirtschaftswunder* ('economic miracle'), and more recent economic strength, often point to a singular reliance on industrial training.[34] In the cultural arena, works by Schaffer and Sennett signal a related turn.[35] The question remains whether these debates hold lessons for literary writers, less for matters of content, than at the level of professional process. The Poundian example, evidently, reveals the danger in aligning writing with social hygiene, or making it a bulwark against financial crises supposedly stirred by fugitive elements.

Several decades into the digital age, writing feels more than ever remote from physical labour, notwithstanding the repetitive strain of keyboard and mouse. Generated virtually, for the most part, as 'word processing', the materiality of text rarely figures as a compositional reality; web-based publication, equally, dissevers the word from the printed impression. Even so, nineteenth-century debates continue to pose productive questions. D'Israeli's foundational complaint, that intellectual processes are 'rarely [. . .] palpable to [. . .] observers', recalls an enduring link between visibility and value. And his bold proposition, that 'writing should be called working', issues a still potent challenge.[36] Responses that appease materialist outlooks – and in the process install a merely conventional visibility – are likely to be counter-productive, because they suppress methodological difference, and sacrifice the main event to appearances. An opportunity dwells, all the same, in the query. The optimism of past attempts to turn the tables might, for instance, inspire revision of the class-based divisions of labour that still separate manual tasks from intellectual ones. Literary composition, meanwhile, could align more closely with what Michael Polanyi calls 'tacit knowledge', so as to restore expertise to the thinking and feeling body.[37] This would allow writing to be re-imagined and reworked as a kind of event, during which hard-won technique interacts with vital thought. Without exactly replicating Pye's 'workmanship of risk', where the workpiece can be irrevocably spoilt by a mistake or misstep,[38] this model proposes an action at once practical and meditative. It trades predictability for opportunity; it makes and converts its chances, through the application, and the work, of a lifetime.

Notes

Preface

1. Basil Bunting, 'What the Chairman Told Tom', in *Complete Poems*, ed. by Richard Caddel (Newcastle: Bloodaxe, 2000), pp. 140–41 (p. 140).
2. Keith Alldritt attributes the poem to the experiences of Tom Pickard, who was 'trying to obtain funding from local government in order to write his poetry' (*The Poet as Spy: The Life and Wild Times of Basil Bunting* (London: Aurum Press, 1998), p. 167).
3. W. B. Yeats, 'Adam's Curse', in *W. B. Yeats: The Major Works*, ed. by Edward Larrissy (Oxford: Oxford University Press, 2001), pp. 37–38.
4. Vladimir Mayakovsky, 'The Poet Worker', in *'Vladimir Mayakovsky' and Other Poems*, trans. by James Womack (Manchester: Carcanet, 2016), pp. 91–92 (p. 91).
5. Cf Mary Poovey, *Uneven Developments: The Ideological Work of Gender in Mid-Victorian England* (Chicago: Chicago University Press, 1988), p. 105.

Introduction

1. Isaac D'Israeli, *The Literary Character, Illustrated by the History of Men of Genius, Drawn from their Own Feelings and Confessions*, rev. edn (London: John Murray, 1818), p. 127.
2. Stefan Collini, *Absent Minds: Intellectuals in Britain* (Oxford: Oxford University Press, 2006), pp. 279–300, p. 413, p. 454. See also Helen Small, 'Introduction', *The Public Intellectual*, ed. by Helen Small (Blackwell, 2002), pp. 1–18.
3. Martha Woodmansee, 'The Cultural Work of Copyright: Legislating Authorship in Britain, 1837–1842', in *Law in the Domains of Culture*, ed. by Austin Sarat and Thomas Kearns (Ann Arbor: University of Michigan Press, 1998), pp. 65–96 (p. 68).
4. Brad Sherman and Lionel Bently, *The Making of Modern Intellectual Property Law* (Cambridge: Cambridge University Press, 1999), p. 16.

5. Deirdre David, *Intellectual Women and Victorian Patriarchy: Harriet Martineau, Elizabeth Barrett Browning, George Eliot* (London: Macmillan, 1987), p. 11.

6. Walter Houghton, *The Victorian Frame of Mind, 1830–1870* (New Haven: Yale University Press, 1957), pp. 242–62; Asa Briggs 'Samuel Smiles and the Gospel of Labour', in *Victorian People: A Reassessment of Persons and Themes 1851–67* (1955; Harmondsworth: Penguin Books, 1971), pp. 124–47.

7. The motto of the Great Exhibition declares that 'The workers, of all types, stand forth as the really great men'. The interior of Leeds's Victorian Town Hall (Cuthbert Brodrick, 1853–58) is likewise emblazoned with the motto 'industry overcomes all things', along with its Virgilian source, 'labor omnia vincit'.

8. See Ruth Danon, *Work in the English Novel: The Myth of Vocation* (London: Croom Helm, 1985); *The Voice of Toil: Nineteenth-Century British Writings About Work*, ed. by David J. Bradshaw and Suzanne Ozment (Athens: Ohio University Press, 2000); Carolyn Lesjak, *Working Fictions: A Genealogy of the Victorian Novel* (Durham, NC: Duke University Press, 2006); and John Hughes, *The End of Work: Theological Critiques of Capitalism* (Oxford: Blackwell, 2007).

9. Raymond Williams, *The English Novel from Dickens to Lawrence* (London: Chatto & Windus, 1970); Catherine Gallagher, *The Industrial Reformation of English Fiction: Social Discourse and Narrative Form, 1832–1867* (Chicago: Chicago University Press, 1985).

10. Lesjak, *Working Fictions*, p. 10.

11. Herbert Sussman, *Victorian Masculinities: Manhood and Masculine Poetics in Early Victorian Literature and Art* (Cambridge: Cambridge University Press, 1995); Martin Danahay, *Gender at Work in Victorian Culture: Literature, Art and Masculinity* (2005; London: Routledge, 2016), p. 74; Tim Barringer, *Men at Work: Art and Labour in Victorian Britain* (New Haven and London: Yale University Press, 2005).

12. John Ruskin, *Sesame and Lilies*, in *The Library Edition of the Works of John Ruskin*, ed. by E. T. Cook and Alexander Wedderburn, 39 vols (London: George Allen, 1903–12), XVIII, pp. 1–192 (p. 122, p. 123). Subsequent references to this edition are given parenthetically in the text.

13. Richard Salmon, *The Formation of the Victorian Literary Profession* (Cambridge: Cambridge University Press, 2013); Daniel Hack, *The Material Interests of the Victorian Novel* (Charlottesville: University of Virginia Press, 2005). [Charles Dickens], *Prospectus of a New Endowment in Connexion with an Insurance Company, for the Benefit of Artists and Men of Letters* (Whitefriars: Bradbury and Evans, 1851), p. 3; Charles Dickens, 'The Guild of Literature and Art', *Household Words*, 3.59 (10 May 1851), 145–47 (p. 146).

14. Daniel Hack, 'Literary Paupers and Professional Authors: The Guild of Literature and Art', *Studies in English Literature 1500–1900*, 39.4 (1999), 691–713 (p. 695).

15. Salmon argues that a discourse of consecration nevertheless persists (*The Formation of the Victorian Literary Profession*, p. 9).

16. Clare Pettitt, *Patent Inventions: Intellectual Property and the Victorian Novel* (Oxford: Oxford University Press, 2004), p. 8.

17. See J. W. Saunders, *The Profession of English Letters: A Study of the Relation of Author to Patron, Publisher, and Public, 1780–1832* (London: Routledge and Kegan Paul, 1964); John Gross, *The Rise and Fall of the Man of Letters: Aspects of English Literary Life Since 1800* (London: Weidenfeld & Nicolson, 1969); Philip Waller, *Writers, Readers, and Reputations: Literary Life in Britain, 1870–1918* (Oxford: Oxford University Press, 2006); Dustin Griffin, *Literary Patronage in England 1650–1800* (Cambridge: Cambridge University Press, 2008); Amy Prendergast, *Literary Salons Across Britain and Ireland in the Long Eighteenth Century* (Basingstoke: Palgrave Macmillan, 2015).

18. William Blake, 'To Mr Butts', 25 April 1803, in *The Complete Poetry & Prose of William Blake*, ed. by David V. Erdman, rev. edn (Berkeley and Los Angeles: University of California Press, 1982), pp. 728–29 (p. 729). See M. H. Abrams, *The Mirror and the Lamp: Romantic Theory and the Critical Tradition* (Oxford: Oxford University Press, 1971), p. 216.

19. Thomas Carlyle, 'Lecture V. The Hero as Man of Letters', *On Heroes, Hero-Worship and the Heroic in History* [hereafter, *On Heroes*], in *Centenary Edition of The Works of Thomas Carlyle*, ed. by H. D. Traill, 30 vols (London: Chapman and Hall, 1896–99), V, pp. 154–95. Subsequent references to this edition are given parenthetically in the text.

20. Mary Sanders Pollock, *Elizabeth Barrett Browning and Robert Browning: A Creative Partnership* (Farnham: Ashgate, 2003), p. 16; Percy Bysshe Shelley, 'A Defence of Poetry', in *Percy Bysshe Shelley: The Major Works*, ed. by Zachary Leader (Oxford: Oxford University Press, 2003), pp. 674–701.

21. Danahay, *Gender at Work in Victorian Culture*, pp. 23–24.

22. Barringer, *Men at Work*, p. 73.

23. Pettitt, *Patent Inventions*, pp. 7, 9.

24. Ibid., p. 12.

25. Salmon, *The Formation of the Victorian Literary Profession*, p. 67.

26. Ibid., p. 32.

27. Christopher Frayling, *On Craftsmanship: Towards a New Bauhaus* (London: Oberon Books, 2011), pp. 84–85.

28. Jean Baudrillard, *The Mirror of Production*, trans. by Mark Poster (St Louis: Telos Press, 1975), p. 98.

29. Ibid., pp. 98–99.

30. Clifford Siskin, *The Work of Writing: Literature and Social Change in Britain, 1700–1830* (Baltimore: The Johns Hopkins University Press, 1998), p. 35.

31. Hack, *The Material Interests of the Victorian Novel*, p. 36.

32. William Hogarth, *The Distrest Poet*, c. 1736, oil on canvas, Birmingham Museum and Art Gallery, Birmingham; see also Thomas Love Peacock, 'The Four Ages of Poetry', in *Peacock's Four Ages of Poetry, Shelley's*

Defence of Poetry, Browning's Essay on Shelley, ed. by H. F. B. Brett-Smith (Oxford: Basil Blackwell, 1937), pp. 3–19.

33. Charles Dickens, *Bleak House*, ed. by Nicola Bradbury and Terry Eagleton (Harmondsworth: Penguin Books, 2003), p. 90.

34. George Eliot, *The Mill on the Floss*, ed. by Gordon S. Haight (Oxford: Clarendon Press, 1980), p. 202.

35. Adam Smith, *An Inquiry into the Nature and Causes of the Wealth of Nations*, ed. by W. B. Todd, 2 vols (Oxford: Clarendon Press, 1976), I, p. 148.

36. Ibid., p. 330.

37. See, for instance, Charles Leadbeater, *Living on Thin Air: The New Economy* (London: Penguin, 2000).

38. Henry William Spiegel, *The Growth of Economic Thought*, 3rd edn (Durham, NC: Duke University Press, 1991), p. 239.

39. Hannah Arendt, *The Human Condition* (Chicago: University of Chicago Press, 1958), p. 80.

40. Ibid., p. 86.

41. Ibid., p. 86.

42. Catherine Gallagher, *The Body Economic: Life, Death, and Sensation in Political Economy and the Victorian Novel* (Princeton: Princeton University Press, 2006), p. 25.

43. Smith, *The Wealth of Nations*, I, p. 330.

44. Ibid., p. 331.

45. Isaac D'Israeli, *The Literary Character, Illustrated by The History of Men of Genius, Drawn from their own Feelings and Confessions* (1795), 3rd edn, 2 vols (London: John Murray, 1822), I, p. 7.

46. Shelley, 'A Defence of Poetry', in *Percy Bysshe Shelley: The Major Works*, p. 694.

47. William Hazlitt, 'The Indian Jugglers', in *The Selected Writings of William Hazlitt*, ed. by Duncan Wu (London: Pickering & Chatto, 1998), 6, pp. 67–77 (p. 68).

48. Jeremy Bentham, *The Rationale of Reward* (London: Robert Heward, 1830), p. 206. See also Ross Harrison, *Bentham* (London: Routledge and Kegan Paul, 2011), p. 4. Cf Bentham's 'Present System of Education', *The Westminster Review*, IV (July–October 1825), pp. 147–76 (p. 166), which concedes that 'solid literature' is 'still a trade', 'acquired by persevering industry' (p. 168).

49. John Whale, *Imagination under Pressure, 1789–1832* (Cambridge: Cambridge University Press, 2000), p. 193.

50. Salmon, *The Formation of the Victorian Literary Profession*, p. 1.

51. Ibid., p. 5.

52. Carolyn Steedman, *Dust* (Manchester: Manchester University Press, 2001), pp. 20–33.

53. A. D. Nuttall, *Dead from the Waist Down: Scholars and Scholarship in the Popular Imagination* (New Haven: Yale University Press, 2003), p. 1.

54. Robert Browning, 'A Grammarian's Funeral', in *The Poetical Works of Robert Browning*, ed. by Ian Jack and Robert Inglesfield, 15 vols (Oxford: Clarendon Press, 1995), V, pp. 454–62 (p. 462); George Eliot, *Middlemarch*, ed. by David Carroll (Oxford: Oxford University Press, 2008).

55. Dinah Birch, 'Critical Opinion: The Scholar Husband', *Essays in Criticism*, LIV, No. 3 (July 2004), 205–215 (p. 208, p. 210).

56. In October 1872, Eliot confided to Harriet Beecher Stowe that 'the Casaubon-tints are not quite foreign to my own mental complexion' (Gordon S. Haight, *The George Eliot Letters* (Oxford: Oxford University Press, 1956), V, p. 322).

57. Eliot, *Middlemarch*, p. 39; Eliot annotated her 1813 edition of Burton's *The Anatomy of Melancholy* with linings and notes (see William Baker, *The George Eliot-George Henry Lewes Library: An Annotated Catalogue of Their Books at Dr Williams's Library, London* (New York: Garland Publishing, 1977), p. 32).

58. Eliot, *Middlemarch*, p. 266.

59. George Henry Lewes, *The Physical Basis of Mind: Being the Second Series of Problems of Life and Mind* (London: Trübner & Co, 1877).

60. The following relevant titles are listed in *The George Eliot-George Henry Lewes Library*: John Abercrombie, *Pathological and Practical Researches on Diseases of the Brain and the Spinal Cord* (Edinburgh, 1836); Henry Charlton Bastian, 'On the Various Forms of Loss of Speech in Cerebral Disease', offprint from *British and Foreign Medico-Chirurgical Review* (January 1869), 1–28; and Antoine Laurent Jesse Bayle, *Traité des maladies du cerveau et de ses membranes. Maladies mentales* (Paris, 1826). See also Joseph Althaus, *Diseases of the Nervous System, their Prevalence and Pathology* (1877); Claude Bernard, 'Étude sur la physiologie du coeur', *Revue des Deux Mondes*, 56 (1865), 236–52; Claude Bernard, *Leçons sur la physiologie et la pathologie du système nerveux*, 2 vols (Paris, 1858); Sir George Burrows, *On Disorders of the Cerebral Circulation, and on the Connection between Affections of the Brain and Diseases of the Heart* (London: Longman, Brown, Green, and Longmans, 1846); Louis Florentin Calmeil, *Traité des Maladies Inflammatoires du Cerveau, où Histoire Anatomo-Pathologique*, 2 vols (Paris, 1859); and Rudolph Leubuscher, *Die Krankheiten des Nervensystems* (Leipzig, 1860); and Alexander Bain, *Mind and Body. The Theories of their Relation* (London: Henry S. King & Co., 1873).

61. Samuel Auguste Tissot, *Traité des Nerfs* (Genève, 1785).

62. S. A. Tissot, *A Treatise on the Diseases Incident to Literary and Sedentary Persons* (Edinburgh: A. Donaldson, 1772), p. 27.

63. C. Turner Thackrah, *The Effects of the Principal Arts, Trades, and Professions, and of Civil States and Habits of Living, on Health and Longevity* (London: Longman, Rees, Orme, Brown, and Green, 1831).

64. *The Cyclopædia of Practical Medicine*, ed. by John Forbes, Alexander Tweedie and John Conolly, 4 vols (London: Sherwood, Gilbert, and Piper, and Baldwin and Cradock, 1833), vol. 1.

65. According to Anne D. Wallace, pre-Romantic representations of 'pedestrian process' were largely allegorical (*Walking, Literature, and English Culture* (Oxford: Clarendon Press, 1993), pp. 52–53). See, also, Manfred Kuehn on Immanuel Kant's daily promenade (*Kant: A Biography* (Cambridge: Cambridge University Press, 2001), p. 14); and Jean-Jacques Rousseau, *Reveries of the Solitary Walker*, trans. by Charles E. Butterworth (Indianapolis: Hackett Publishing, 1992). William Hazlitt speaks of

how Coleridge 'liked to compose in walking over uneven ground', while 'Wordsworth always wrote (if he could) walking up and down a straight gravel-walk' ('My First Acquaintance with Poets', in *The Selected Writings of William Hazlitt*, IX, pp. 95–109 (pp. 105–6)).

66. Thackrah, *The Effects of the Principal Arts, Trades, and Professions*, p. 90.
67. Forbes, *The Cyclopædia of Practical Medicine*, pp. 149–160.
68. Thackrah, *The Effects of the Principal Arts, Trades, and Professions*, p. 97.
69. Ibid., pp. 15–18.
70. Tissot, *A Treatise on the Diseases Incident to Literary and Sedentary Persons*, p. 122.
71. Thackrah, *The Effects of the Principal Arts, Trades, and Professions*, p. 87.
72. Hamerton, *The Intellectual Life*, 2nd edn (London: Macmillan, 1875), p. 30.
73. Samuel Smiles, *Life and Labor, Or, Characteristics of Men of Industry, Culture and Genius*, (1887; London: J. Murray, 1897), p. 12.
74. Eliot, *Scenes of Clerical Life*, ed. by Thomas A. Noble (Oxford: Oxford University Press, 2015), p. 109.
75. Samuel Butler, *The Way of All Flesh* [posthumously published, 1903] (Harmondsworth: Penguin, 1986), p. 173.
76. Ibid., p. 173.
77. Eliot, *Middlemarch*, p. 268.
78. Ibid., p. 269.
79. Ibid., p. 268.
80. *Oxford Book of Work*, ed. by Keith Thomas (Oxford: Oxford University Press, 1999), p. xvi.
81. Arendt, *The Human Condition*, p. 7.
82. Ibid., p. 7, p. 79.
83. Ibid., p. 7, p. 136.
84. Richard Sennett, *The Craftsman* (London: Penguin Books, 2009), p. 7.
85. William Morris, 'Useful Work *versus* Useless Toil', in *The Collected Works of William Morris*, ed. by May Morris, 24 vols (London: Longmans, Green, and Company, 1910–15), XXIII, pp. 98–120. Subsequent references to this edition are given parenthetically in the text.
86. Raymond Williams, *Keywords: A Vocabulary of Culture and Society*, rev. edn (New York: Oxford University Press, 1983), p. 177.
87. Ibid., p. 177, p. 335.
88. Siskin, *The Work of Writing*, p. 7.
89. Thomas Hood, 'The Song of the Shirt', in *Selected Poems*, ed. by Joy Flint (Manchester: Carcanet, 1992), pp. 103–5 (p. 103); see also Herbert Tucker, 'Over Worked, Worked Over: A Poetics of Fatigue', in *The Feeling of Reading: Affective Experience and Victorian Literature*, ed. by Rachel Ablow (Ann Arbor: University of Michigan Press, 2010), pp. 114–30.
90. J. S. Mill, 'The Negro Question', *Essays on Equality, Law, and Education*, in *Works*, XXI, pp. 85–95 (p. 90). Originally published as J. S. Mill, 'The Negro Question', *Fraser's Magazine*, XLI (January 1850), 25–31.

91. Chris Louttit, *Dickens's Secular Gospel: Work, Gender, Personality* (London: Routledge, 2009); Rob Breton, *Gospels of Grit: Work and Labour in Carlyle, Conrad, and Orwell* (Toronto: University of Toronto Press, 2005), p. 4.

92. See 'The Victorian Ethos: Before and After Victoria', in Gertrude Himmelfarb, *Victorian Minds* (New York: Alfred A. Knopf, 1968), pp. 275–99.

93. Max Weber, *The Protestant Ethic and the Spirit of Capitalism* (1930), trans. by Talcott Parsons (Oxford: Routledge, 1992); R. H. Tawney, *Religion and the Rise of Capitalism* (1922) (Harmondsworth: Penguin Books, 1964), p. 242; E. P. Thompson, 'Time, Work-Discipline, and Industrial Capitalism', *Past and Present*, 38 (1967), 56–97; P. D. Anthony, *The Ideology of Work* (London: Tavistock, 1977), p. 46.

94. Susan Manning, *The Puritan-Provincial Vision: Scottish and American Literature in the Nineteenth Century* (Cambridge: Cambridge University Press, 1990), p. 3.

95. John Hughes, *The End of Work: Theological Critiques of Capitalism* (Oxford: Blackwell, 2007), p. 35.

96. Q. D. Leavis, *Fiction and the Reading Public* (1932; London: Chatto & Windus, 1965) p. 103; Thompson, *The Making of the English Working Class* (1963; Harmondsworth: Penguin Books, 1968) p. 391, p. 393, p. 441; Valentine Cunningham, *Everywhere Spoken Against* (Oxford: Oxford University Press, 1975), pp. 107–9.

97. Manning, *The Puritan-Provincial Vision*, p. 3.

98. James Aho, *Confession and Bookkeeping: The Religious, Moral, and Rhetorical Roots of Modern Accounting* (Albany: SUNY Press, 2012), p. 3, p. 63.

99. Weber, *The Protestant Ethic and the Spirit of Capitalism*, p. 5; see Carlyle (11:1).

100. Samuel Smiles, Preface, *Self-Help*, 2nd edn (1866; London: John Murray, 1897), p. vii; See Briggs, *Victorian People*, p. 124.

101. See Briggs, *Victorian People*, p. 124.

102. Anne Janowitz, *Lyric and Labour in the Romantic Tradition* (Cambridge: Cambridge University Press, 1998), p. 143.

103. Leavis, *Fiction and the Reading Public*, p. 116; Thompson, *The Making of the English Working Class*, p. 391, p. 433; Cunningham, *Everywhere Spoken Against*, p. 96.

104. John Locke, *Two Treatises of Government*, ed. by Peter Laslett (Cambridge: Cambridge University Press, 1988), pp. 289–93.

105. David Ricardo, *On the Principles of Political Economy, and Taxation*, ed. by R. M. Hartwell (London: Penguin Books, 1971).

106. Ian Haywood, *Working-class Fiction: From Chartism to Trainspotting* (Plymouth: Northcote House,1997), p. 1.

107. John Cazenove, *Outlines of Political Economy: Being a Plain and Short View of the Laws Relating to the Production, Distribution, and Consumption of Wealth* (London: Pelham Richardson, 1832), p. 22.

108. Hughes, *The End of Work*, p. 7.

109. Karl Marx, *Economic and Philosophic Manuscripts of 1844*, trans. by Martin Milligan (New York: International Publishers, 1972), pp. 112–13.

110. In *Report to the County of Lanark, of a Plan for Relieving Public Distress and Removing Discontent, by Giving Permanent, Productive Employment to the Poor and Working Classes* (Glasgow: University Press, 1821), Owen proposed 'That manual labour, properly directed, is the source of all wealth, and national prosperity', p. 1.

111. Smith, *The Wealth of Nations*, I, p. 47.

112. Cunningham, *Everywhere Spoken Against*, pp. 107–09.

113. Anthony Trollope, *An Autobiography*, ed. by Nicholas Shrimpton (Oxford: Oxford University Press, 2014), p. 78.

114. Ibid., pp. 78–82.

115. Nigel Cross, *The Common Writer: Life in Nineteenth-Century Grub Street* (Cambridge: Cambridge University Press, 1985), pp. 126–63; Janowitz, *Lyric and Labour in the Romantic Tradition*, p. 31, pp. 159–94. For more recent studies, see Mike Sanders, *The Poetry of Chartism: Aesthetics, Politics, History* (Cambridge: Cambridge University Press, 2009); *Class and the Canon: Constructing Labouring-Class Poetry and Poetics, 1780–1900*, ed. by Kirstie Blair and Mina Gorji (Basingstoke: Palgrave, 2012); Salmon, *The Formation of the Victorian Literary Profession*, pp. 138–51.

116. Edward Paxton Hood, *The Literature of Labour: Illustrious Instances of Poetry in Poverty* (London: Partridge & Oakley, 1851).

117. Richard Salmon, 'The Literature of Labour: Collective Biography and Working-Class Authorship, 1830–1859', in *The Labour of Literature in Britain and France, 1830–1910: Authorial Work Ethics*, ed. by Marcus Waithe and Claire White (London: Palgrave Macmillan, 2018), pp. 43–59 (p. 49).

118. For the 'literary advice' industry that grew up around this one-directional flow, see Waller, *Writers, Readers, and Reputations*, pp. 69–115; and Christopher Hilliard, *To Exercise Our Talents: The Democratization of Writing in Britain* (Cambridge, MA, and London: Harvard University Press, 2006).

119. E. P. Thompson, *The Making of the English Working Classes* (Harmondsworth: Pelican, 1968), p. 259, p. 266.

120. Interview with Richard Burton, The Dick Cavett Show, 08/04/1980, https://www.youtube.com/watch?v=708q7LjMGso&t=916s [accessed 28 June 2022].

121. Lesjak, *Working Fictions*, p. 17.

122. See, for example, Richard Sennett, *The Craftsman* (London: Penguin, 2009); Glenn Adamson, *Thinking through Craft* (London: Bloomsbury, 2013); Matthew Crawford, *Shot Class as Soulcraft: An Inquiry into the Value of Work* (New York: Penguin, 2010).

123. See Linda H. Peterson, *Becoming a Woman of Letters: Myths of Authorship and Facts of the Victorian Market* (Princeton: Princeton University Press, 2009); see also Jennie Batchelor, *Women's Work: Labour, Gender,*

Authorship, 1750–1830 (Manchester: Manchester University Press, 2010), p. 90; and *What is a Woman to Do? A Reader on Women, Work and Art, c. 1830–1890*, ed. by Kyriaki Hadjiafxendi and Patricia Zakreski (Oxford: Peter Lang, 2011), p. 8.

124. Talia Schaffer, *Novel Craft: Victorian Domestic Handicraft and Nineteenth-Century Fiction* (New York: Oxford University Press, 2011), p. 21; see also *Crafting the Woman Professional in the Long Nineteenth Century: Artistry and Industry in Britain*, ed. by Kyriaki Hadjiafxendi and Patricia Zakreski (London: Routledge, 2013).

125. [Craik], *A Woman's Thoughts about Women* (London: Hurst and Blackett, 1858), p. 66.

126. '[Martineau], "Female Industry", *Edinburgh Review*, 109 (1859), 293–336', in *What is a Woman to Do?*, ed. by Hadjiafxendi and Zakreski, p. 61.

127. See Zoë Thomas, *Women Art Workers and the Arts and Crafts Movement* (Manchester: Manchester University Press, 2020).

128. Margaret Oliphant, 'The Great Unrepresented', *Blackwood's Magazine*, vol. 100 (1866), pp. 367–79 (p. 379).

129. See David Sprague Herreshoff's *Labor into Art: The Themes of Work in Nineteenth-Century American Literature* (Detroit: Wayne State, 1991); Nicholas K. Bromell, *By the Sweat of the Brow: Literature and Labor in Antebellum America* (Chicago: University of Chicago Press, 1993); Cindy Weinstein, *The Literature of Labor and the Labors of Literature: Allegory in Nineteenth-Century American Fiction* (Cambridge: Cambridge University Press, 1995).

130. *The Labour of Literature* ed. by Waithe and White.

Part I

1. Ford Madox Ford (né Hueffer), *Ford Madox Brown: A Record of his Life and Work* (London: Longmans, Green, and Company, 1896), p. 48.
2. Ibid., p. 196.
3. Ibid., p. 94.

Chapter 1

1. J. S. Mill, 'The Negro Question', pp. 85–95 (p. 90).
2. Ibid., p. 91.
3. Ibid., p. 87.
4. Among Carlyle's close friends was the society hostess, Lady Harriet Ashburton.
5. Thomas Carlyle, *Two Notebooks of Thomas Carlyle from 23rd March 1822 to 16th May 1832*, ed. by Charles Eliot Norton (New York: The Grolier Club, 1898), pp. 176–7.

6. Ian Campbell, *Thomas Carlyle* (London: Hamish Hamilton, 1974), p. 7.

7. David DeLaura, 'Carlyle and the "Insane" Fine Arts', in *The Carlyles at Home and Abroad: Essays in Honour of Kenneth J. Fielding*, ed. by David Sorensen and Rodger Tarr (Aldershot: Ashgate, 2004), pp. 27–37 (p. 32).

8. Chris R. Vanden Bossche, *Carlyle and the Search for Authority* (Columbus: Ohio State University Press, 1991), p. 26, pp. 38–9.

9. For a different study of Carlyle's verbal evocations of work, see James Treadwell, '*Sartor Resartus* and the Work of Writing', *Essays in Criticism*, 48.3 (1998), 224–43. Treadwell explores 'the dangerously Romantic notion that writing displaces or even *replaces* labour' (p. 241). Campbell, *Thomas Carlyle*, p. 7.

10. Thomas Carlyle, 'James Carlyle', in *Reminiscences*, ed. by Ian Campbell and K. J. Fielding (Glasgow: Kennedy & Boyd, 2009), pp. 1–33. Subsequent references to this edition are given parenthetically in the text.

11. Cf Ruskin's 'Traffic': 'you will build with stone well, but with flesh better' (18:458).

12. Carlyle, 'To C. A. Ward' (6/VII/1854), *The Carlyle Letters Online* [hereafter, *CLO*], ed. by Brent E. Kinser (Durham, NC: Duke University Press) <http://carlyleletters.org> (para. 2 of 3).

13. Arendt, *The Human Condition*, p. 207.

14. As Vanden Bossche notes, this assertion revises Carlyle's previous claim, in *Sartor Resartus*, that 'the author of a book has "built what will outlast all marble and metal"', *Carlyle and the Search for Authority*, p. 39.

15. 'To Sarah Austin' (13/VI/1833), *CLO* (para. 4 of 7).

16. See Richard Salmon, 'Thomas Carlyle and the Idolatry of the Man of Letters', *Journal of Victorian Culture*, 7.1 (2002), 1–22.

17. Carlyle, *Two Notebooks*, p. 184.

18. 'To The House of Commons' (7/IV/1839), *CLO* (para. 1 of 11).

19. Ibid. (para. 4 and para. 8 of 11).

20. Carlyle, *Two Notebooks*, p. 214.

21. 'To John Stuart Mill' (28/VIII/1832), *CLO* (para. 2 of 8).

22. 'To Edward Strachey' (20/XII/1848), *CLO* (para. 2 of 2).

23. 'To Elizabeth Gaskell' (8/XI/1848), *CLO* (para. 2 of 3).

24. See Waithe, 'Hill, Ruskin and Intrinsic Value', in *Geoffrey Hill and his Contexts*, ed. by Piers Pennington and Matthew Sperling (Oxford: Peter Lang, 2011), pp. 133–49.

25. 'To Alexander Carlyle' (12/I/1822), *CLO* (para. 1 of 5).

26. 'To James Carlyle' (2/IV/1823), *CLO* (para. 1 of 4).

27. Cf Henry D. Thoreau: 'the style is no more than the *stylus*, the pen he writes with' ('Thomas Carlyle and his Works', in *Early Essays and Miscellanies, The Writings of Henry D. Thoreau* (Princeton: Princeton University Press, 1975), pp. 219–67 (p. 232)).

28. See, for instance, Kristen Guest, 'Dyspeptic Reactions: Thomas Carlyle and the Byronic Temper', in *Nervous Reactions: Victorian Recollections of Romanticism*, ed. by Joel Falflak and Julian Wright (Albany: State University of New York Press, 2004), pp. 141–61.

29. 'To Alexander Carlyle' (12/I/1822), *CLO* (para. 1 of 5).

30. The First Draft of *Past and Present* (British Library ms. 41641) exhibits many re-workings. See Grace Calder, *The Writing of Past and Present: A Study of Carlyle's Manuscripts* (New Haven: Yale University Press, 1949), p. 154.
31. Carlyle had earlier described his literary endeavours as an 'apprenticeship' ('To Alexander Carlyle' (1/III/1820), *CLO* (para. 2 of 4)).
32. 'To Jean Carlyle Aitken' (9/IV/1835), *CLO* [para. 4 of 5]; Carlyle, *Two Notebooks*, pp. 208–9.
33. See Houghton, 'The Worship of Force', in *The Victorian Frame of Mind*, pp. 196–217.
34. An earlier version of this discussion was published as 'The Pen and the Hammer: Thomas Carlyle, Ebenezer Elliott, and the "active poet"', in *Class and the Canon: Constructing Labouring-Class Poetry and Poetics, 1780–1900*, pp. 116–35.
35. Carlyle, *Two Notebooks*, p. 255; 'To Macvey Napier' (6/II/1832), *CLO* (para. 4 of 6).
36. Karen Wolven, 'Ebenezer Elliott, The "Corn-Law Rhymer": Poor Men Do Write – The Emergence of Class Identity within a Poetry of Transition', in *Victorian Keats and Romantic Carlyle: The Fusions and Confusions of Literary Periods*, ed. by C. C. Barfoot (Amsterdam: Editions Rodopi, 1999), pp. 235–46 (p. 238).
37. Anon. (VII-X/1829) 'Art. VII. – *The Village Patriarch* A Poem. pp. 198. Bull.', *Westminster Review*, XI, 92–6 (p. 93); Elliott, Preface, *The Village Patriarch: A Poem* (London: Edward Bull, Holles Street, 1829), p. v.
38. Ibid., p. 92.
39. Southey and Elliott first corresponded in 1808.
40. Charles Dickens, 'Ebenezer Elliott', *Household Words*, II (Leipzig: Bernard Tauchnitz, 1851), pp. 232–8 (p. 237).
41. Elizabeth Gaskell, *Mary Barton*, ed. by Shirley Foster (Oxford University Press, 2006), pp. 37–8; Elliott, *The Splendid Village: Corn Law Rhymes; and Other Poems* (London: Benjamin Steill, 1833).
42. January Searle, *The Life, Character and Genius of Ebenezer Elliott, the Corn Law Rhymer* [hereafter, *LCG*] (London: Charles Gilpin, 1850); John Watkins, *Life, Poetry, and Letters of Ebenezer Elliott, The Corn-Law Rhymer* [hereafter, *LPL*] (London: John Mortimer, 1850).
43. J. W. King, *Ebenezer Elliott: A Sketch, with Copious Extracts from his Descriptive Poems* (Sheffield: S. Harrison, 1854).
44. 'To John A. Carlyle' (13/I/1852), *CLO* (para. 2 of 2); Searle, *LCG*, p. 15 and p. 17.
45. Searle, *LCG*, p. 17, p. 148.
46. King, *Ebenezer Elliott*, p. 4 and p. 17.
47. Searle, *LCG*, p. 18.
48. [Ebenezer Elliott] (1831) *Corn Law Rhymes*, 3rd edn (London: B. Steill). Carlyle also refers to *The Village Patriarch* (1829 and 1831). See *Selected Poetry of Ebenezer Elliott*, ed. by Mark Storey (Cranbury, N.J.: Associated University Presses, 2010), p. 33.
49. Ibid., p. iv.

50. [Edward Bulwer], 'A Letter to Doctor Southey, &c. &c. Poet Laureate, Respecting a Remarkable Poem by a Mechanic, 19 March 1831', *New Monthly Magazine*, 31.124 (IV/1831), 289–95 (p. 290); [Elliott], *The Village Patriarch* (1829), p. viii.

51. Responding to criticism of his use of the Dorsetshire dialect, William Barnes replied similarly: 'I cannot help it' (Preface, *Poems of Rural Life in the Dorset Dialect*, third collection (London: John Russell Smith, 1862), p. iii).

52. [Elliott], Preface, *Corn Law Rhymes*, 3rd edn (1831), p. iv.

53. According to Carlyle, Elliott was 'one of the lower, little removed above the lowest class.' (28:138). Elliott himself asks 'is it of no importance what a man of the middle class – hardly raised above the lowest, thinks – when the lowest are beginning to think?' (Preface, *Corn Law Rhymes*, 3rd edn (1831) p. vii).

54. Watkins, *LPL*, p. 133.

55. Elliott's closest approach to poverty followed his bankruptcy in 1816, when he accepted help from Earl Fitzwilliam (Keith Morris and Ray Hearne, *Ebenezer Elliott: Corn Law Rhymer & Poet of the Poor* (Rotherham: Rotherwood Press, 2002), pp. 16–19 (p. 28)). The phrase 'jobbing merchant' appears in *Holden's Dollar Magazine*, 5.4 (IV/1850), p. 225.

56. Elliott recalls his father working 'for a salary of sixty or seventy pounds a year, with house, candle and coal!' (Elliott, 'Autobiography' (21/VI/1841), in Watkins, *LPL*, pp. 2–29 (p. 7)).

57. Elliott, 'Autobiography', p. 5.

58. Morris and Hearne, *Ebenezer Elliott*, pp. 16–19; Elliott, 'Autobiography', p. 16.

59. Watkins, *LPL*, p. 26.

60. Ibid., p. 33.

61. Ibid., p. 33.

62. Carlyle writes to Macvey Napier on 8 April 1832, promising to deliver the review within two weeks (*CLO* (para. 2 of 3)); by 18 May 1832, he was writing to J. S. Mill with the news that 'the Corn Law Rhymer has got his *Article*' (para. 4 of 7); see also 'To Macvey Napier' (22/VI/1832) (para. 2 of 5).

63. It was J. S. Mill who misinformed Carlyle, both as to Elliott's name and his occupation (Letter 51, 'To Thomas Carlyle' (29/V/1832) in *The Earlier Letters of John Stuart Mill 1812–1848*, ed. by Francis E. Mineka (London: Routledge & Kegan Paul, 1963), pp. 102–7 (p. 104)).

64. Simon Brown, 'Ebenezer Elliott and Robert Southey: Southey's Break with the Quarterly Review', *The Review of English Studies*, 22.87 (VIII/1971), p. 308.

65. Morris and Hearne, *Ebenezer Elliott*, p. 25. Elliott's advertisements in the local press indicate the scale of his operation: one offers 'a constant and complete assortment of IRON and STEEL' (*The Sheffield Independent* [hereafter, *SI*], 4 February 1832); another offers to let 'four chambers' on Gibraltar Street to a 'Factor or Merchant, in extensive business' (*SI*, 2/VI/1831).

66. Letter 'To Mr Tait' (Watkins, *LPL*, p. 82). According to King, Elliott set up business on Gibraltar Street with capital of £150, raised 'by the affectionate generosity of his wife's sisters', 'which accumulated something handsome, it is said a fortune!' (*Ebenezer Elliott*, p. 17).

67. Watkins, *LPL*, p. 82.

68. See the petitions to Thomas Aline Ward, Esq. to serve as M.P. for Sheffield (*SI*, 17/IX/1831), and to the Master Cutler requesting a mechanics' educational institute (*SI*, 13/X/1832). Elliott was also a special constable (*SI*, 25/IV/1829).

69. Brown, 'Ebenezer Elliott and Robert Southey: Southey's Break with the Quarterly Review', p. 308; E. R. Seary, 'Robert Southey and Ebenezer Elliott: Some New Southey Letters', *The Review of English Studies*, 15.60 (X/1939), 412–21.

70. [Elliott], *The Vernal Walk* (Cambridge: B. Flower, 1801); Elliott, *The Soldier and Other Poems* (Harlow, 1810); Elliott, *Night: A Descriptive Poem* (London; Rotherham, 1818); Elliott, *Peter Faultless to his Brother Simon: Tales of Night, in Rhyme, and Other Poems* (Edinburgh: Archibald Constable & Co., 1820); and Elliott, *Love, a Poem in Three Parts to which is Added, The Giaour, a Satirical Poem (Addressed to Lord Byron)* (London: C. Stocking, 1823).

71. James Sowerby, *English Botany; or, Colour Figures of British Plants, with Their Essential Characters, Synonyms and Places of Growth* (London, 1870).

72. [Elliott], *The Vernal Walk*, p. 11 and p. 6. Elliott included an extended defence of the Lake Poets in *Love, a Poem in Three Parts to which is Added, The Giaour*, pp. 133–80 (p. 136).

73. Ibid., p. 25 and p. 39.

74. See *Peter Faultless* (1820) (addressed to 'a living pedant', p. 3), and the anti-Byronic *The Giaour* (1823).

75. [Elliott] (1831), 'The Tree of Rivelin', *Corn Law Rhymes*, pp. 54–55 (p. 54).

76. Wolven, 'Ebenezer Elliott, The "Corn-Law Rhymer": Poor Men Do Write – The Emergence of Class Identity within a Poetry of Transition', p. 236.

77. Ibid., pp. 54–55 (p. 54).

78. Watkins, *LPL*, pp. 127–28.

79. Searle, *LCG*, p. 159.

80. [Elliott], Preface, *Corn Law Rhymes* (1831), p. vii.

81. The sentence begins, 'But when suicidal anti-profit laws speak to my heart [. . .]', [Elliott], Preface, *Corn Law Rhymes* (1831), p. vii.

82. Elliott's first articulation of a class position coincides with his satirical attack on Lord Byron: 'I have no gold, impartial praise to buy, | No rank' (Elliott, *The Giaour*, p. 170).

83. Raymond Williams, *Culture and Society 1780–1950* (1958; Harmondsworth: Penguin, 1963), p. 60.

84. [Elliott], 'Song', *Corn Law Rhymes* (1831), pp. 69–70 (p. 69).

85. [Elliott], 'Drone v. Worker', *Corn Law Rhymes* (1831), pp. 55–57. See Jeremy Prynne on 'the exertion of a field-worker [. . .] who *also* sings, as a comfortable discharge of customary practice' (*Field Notes: "The Solitary*

Reaper" and Others (Cambridge: Barque Press, 2007), pp. 11–20). See also an early and unidealised example of this convergence in 'The Thresher's Labour' by Stephen Duck (d. 1756) (Southey, 'An Introductory Essay' in *Attempts in Verse by John Jones, an Old Servant* (London: John Murray, 1831), pp. 1–168 (pp. 96–105)).

86. A correspondent, signing himself 'Agricola', counters that 'the agricultural labourer, and the farmer himself, is obliged to live and is satisfied with the very refuse of what their [Sheffield operatives] appetites refuse' (*SI*, 15/VI/1833, p. 1); [Elliott], 'Rogues v. Reason', *Corn Law Rhymes* (1831), pp. 61–62 (p. 61).

87. [Elliott], *Corn Law Rhymes* (1831), pp. 74–76 (p. 75).

88. Elliott reflects that even in youth 'I was a free-trader, though I knew it not.' (Watkins, *LPL*, p. 12).

89. See Searle: 'Elliott was a redoubted champion of competition' (*LCG*, p. 131).

90. After the Chartists repudiated Corn-Law Repeal, Elliott resigned from the Sheffield Working Men's Association, complaining that the real enemy was landed 'aristocracy' (Watkins, *LPL*, pp. 130–31).

91. Carlyle, 'Corn-Law Rhymes', in *Works*, XXVIII, p. 149.

92. Carlyle seems not to have noticed Elliott's dedication to Jeremy Bentham in the 1833 edition (*The Splendid Village: Corn Law Rhymes; and Other Poems* (London: Benjamin Steill, 1833), p. 45).

93. Elliott lived at Upperthorpe, Sheffield, between 1834 and 1841, with three acres of walled garden, and two servants, in a house originally built for John Blake, the Master Cutler. He moved to Great Houghton in 1841, having purchased a house with ten acres (Morris and Hearne, *Ebenezer Elliott*, p. 38).

94. Ruskin founded the St George's Museum in 1875 to foster 'the liberal education of the artisan' (30:39), and to preserve 'memorial studies' of Venice (24:424). See Marcus Waithe, *Ruskin at Walkley: Reconstructing the St George's Museum* <http://www.ruskinatwalkley.org>.

95. Carlyle, 'Corn-Law Rhymes', in *Works*, XXVIII, p. 165.

Chapter 2

1. Thomas Plint, 'To Ford Madox Brown' (24/XI/1856), in Ford, *Ford Madox Brown*, p. 112.

2. Ibid., p. 176.

3. Ford Madox Brown [hereafter, FMB], *The Exhibition of Work, and Other Paintings, by Ford Madox Brown, at the Gallery, 191 Piccadilly* (London: McCorquodale, 1865).

4. Ibid., p. 27.

5. Ibid., p. 26.

6. Ibid., p. 28.

7. Danahay, *Gender at Work*, p. 97.

8. Ibid., p. 97.

9. Isaac D'Israeli, *The Literary Character; or, The History of Men of Genius, Drawn from their Own Feelings and Confessions*, 4th edn, 2 vols (London: Henry Colburn, 1828), I, p. 238.

10. Horace Bushnell, *An Oration Delivered Before the Society of Phi Beta Kappa at Cambridge, August 24, 1848* (Cambridge: George Nichols, 1848), p. 18.

11. Barringer, *Men at Work*, p. 53.

12. Norbert Wolf, *Painting in the Romantic Era* (Cologne: Taschen, 1999), p. 91.

13. Larry D. Lutchmansingh, 'Brown, Ford Madox (1821–1893)', in Sally Mitchell, *Victorian Britain: An Encyclopaedia* (Oxford: Routledge, 2012), p. 98.

14. Editorial introduction to Carlyle, *Past and Present*, ed. by Chris Vanden Bossche, Joel J. Brattin, and Dale J. Trela, (Berkeley: University of California Press, 2005), p. lx.

15. Barringer, *Men at Work*, pp. 30–31.

16. Ibid., p. 37.

17. FMB, *The Exhibition of Work*, p. 21.

18. Ibid., p. 28. Cf Coleridge's proposal for a 'nationalized, learned order' in *On the Constitution of Church and State* (London: William Pickering, 1839), p. 70.

19. FMB, *The Exhibition of Work*, p. 28.

20. Colin Trodd, 'The Laboured Vision and the Realm of Value: Articulation of Identity in Ford Madox Brown's *Work*', in *Re-Framing the Pre-Raphaelites: Historical and Theoretical Essays*, ed. by Ellen Harding (Aldershot: Ashgate / Scolar Press, 1996), pp. 61–80 (p. 63).

21. Art. II 'Mental Hygiene. By William Sweetser, MD' *A Theological and Literary Journal*, 6:25 (London: John Chapman, 1844), pp. 255–66 (p. 255).

22. William Sweetser, MD, *Mental Hygiene, or An Examination of the Intellect and Passions* (New York: J. & H. G. Langley, 1843).

23. Calvin Colton, *Public Economy for the United States*, 2nd edn (New York: A. S. Barnes & Co, 1849), p. 274.

24. See *Embodied Selves: An Anthology of Psychological Texts, 1830–1890*, ed. by Sally Shuttleworth and Jenny Bourne Taylor (Oxford: Clarendon Press, 1997).

25. Henry Maudsley, *The Physiology and Pathology of Mind*, 2nd edn (London: Macmillan and Co., 1868).

26. Elaine Scarry, *Resisting Representation* (Oxford: Oxford University Press, 1994), p. 68.

27. Ford, *Ford Madox Brown*, p. 94.

28. John A. Walker, *Work: Ford Madox Brown's Painting and Victorian Life* (London: Francis Boutle, 2006), p. 65.

29. FMB, *Chaucer at the Court of Edward III*, oil on canvas, 1847–51, Art Gallery of New South Wales, Australia.

30. FMB, *The Seeds and Fruits of English Poetry*, oil on canvas, 1845–53, Ashmolean Museum, Oxford.

31. FMB, *Wilhelmus Conquistador (The Body of Harold)*, oil on canvas, 1844–61, Manchester Art Gallery, Manchester.

32. Max Weber quotes the same line when discussing Benjamin Franklin's strict Calvinist father (*The Protestant Ethic and the Spirit of Capitalism*, p. 19).

33. Gregory Dart, 'The Reworking of Work', *Victorian Literature and Culture*, 27.1 (III/1999), 69–96 (p. 81).

34. FMB, *The Exhibition of Work*, p. 26.

35. Barringer, *Men at Work*, p. 74.

36. Mill, *Principles of Political Economy*, in *Works*, II, p. 25.

37. Carlyle to Brown, (5/V/1859), *CLO* (para. 1 of 1).

38. FMB, *The Exhibition of Work*, p. 29.

39. W. M. Rossetti, 'Mr Madox Brown's Exhibition, and its Place in Our School of Painting', *Fraser's Magazine*, 71 (V/1865), 598–607 (599–600).

40. Dart, 'The Reworking of Work', p. 71.

41. See, for example, Joanna Woodall, 'Trading Identities: The Image of the Merchant', Gresham College lecture <https://www.gresham.ac.uk/lectures-and-events/trading-identites-the-image-of-the-merchant> [accessed 28 June 2022].

42. W. J. T. Mitchell, *Blake's Composite Art: A Study of the Illuminated Poetry* (Princeton: Princeton University Press, 1968).

43. FMB, *The Hayfield*, oil on mahogany, 1855–56, Tate Britain, London.

44. Carlyle, *Two Notebooks*, p. 172.

45. '26/VIII/1854', *The Diary of Ford Madox Brown* [hereafter, *DFMB*], ed. by Virginia Surtees (New Haven and London: Yale University Press, 1981), p. 86.

46. Paula Gillett, *The Victorian Painter's World* (Gloucester: Alan Sutton, 1990), p. 14.

47. Walker, *Work*, p. 15.

48. Ford, *Ford Madox Brown*, p. 11, p. 59.

49. Ibid., p. 11, p. 59.

50. Lionel Bently, 'Art and the Making of Modern Copyright Law', in *Dear Images: Art, Copyright and Culture*, ed. by Daniel MacClean and Karsten Schubert (London: Ridinghouse, 2002), pp. 331–33.

51. Ford, *Ford Madox Brown*, p. 176.

52. Samuel Smiles, *Self-Help; With Illustration of Character and Conduct* (London: John Murray, 1859), pp. 101–31.

53. Philip Gilbert Hamerton, *Thoughts about Art*, rev. edn (1862; London: Macmillan and Co., 1873), p. 264.

54. Smiles, *Self-Help*, p. 101.

55. Sir Joshua Reynolds, 'Discourse IV', *The Discourses of Sir Joshua Reynolds* (London: Joseph Carpenter, 1843), p. 52.

56. Reynolds, 'Discourse I', *Discourses*, p. 14.

57. Reynolds, 'Discourse IV', *Discourses*, p. 52.

58. Barringer, *Men at Work*, p. 79, p. 81.

59. The critic for *The Illustrated London News* (1306. XLVI (18/III/1865), p. 266) observes 'aggregations of a life's labour to an eminent degree'. The critic for *The London Review* ((10–18/III/1865), p. 299) argues that 'Art

is not a matter of this hodman kind of labour in any form' (p. 299). *The Pall Mall Gazette* ('Mr Madox Brown's Exhibition', 20.44 (29/III/1865), pp. 6–7 (p. 6)) praises *Work* as a painting 'singularly rich in thought both deep and humorous' (p. 6).

60. Giles Waterfield, *The People's Galleries: Art Museums and Exhibitions in Britain 1800–1914* (New Haven and London: Yale University Press, 2015), p. 192.
61. Ford, *Ford Madox Brown*, p. 210.
62. Ibid., p. 211.
63. Ibid., p. 211.
64. Ibid., pp. 211–12.
65. Ibid., p. 91.
66. Barringer, *Men at Work*, p. 44.
67. Ford, *Ford Madox Brown*, p. 76.
68. FMB, *Study of Rev. F. D. Maurice and Carlyle for 'Work'*, 1859, pencil on paper, Manchester City Art Gallery.
69. Ford, *Ford Madox Brown*, p. 164.
70. Charles Thompson, *Thomas Carlyle*, Photograph, 12/V/1859, Birmingham Museums and Art Gallery; 'To Ford Madox Brown' (10/V/1859), *CLO*.
71. Ford, *Ford Madox Brown*, p. 165.
72. '16/III/1857', *DFMB*, p. 194.
73. '17/I/1858', *DFMB*, p. 199.
74. Charles Dickens, *Our Mutual Friend*, ed. by Michael Cotsell (Oxford: Oxford University Press, 2008), p. 78.
75. '17/I/1858', *DFMB*, p. 198.
76. FMB, *The Exhibition of Work*, p. 31.
77. '26/VIII/1854', *DFMB*, p. 86.
78. '4/IX/1847', *DFMB*, p. 1.
79. Manning, *The Puritan-Provincial Vision*, p. 11.
80. Ibid., p. 11.
81. Augustine, *Confessions*, trans. by F. J. Sheed, 2nd edn (Indianapolis: Hackett, 2006).
82. James Aho, *Confession and Bookkeeping: The Religious, Moral, and Rhetorical Roots of Modern Accounting* (Albany: State of New York Press, 2005), p. 2.
83. '4/IX/1847', *DFMB*, p. 4.
84. Ibid., p. 4.
85. Ibid., p. 4.
86. Ibid., p. 4.
87. Weber, *The Protestant Ethic and the Spirit of Capitalism*, p. 71.
88. James Hogg, *The Private Memoirs and Confessions of a Justified Sinner*, ed. by John Carey (Oxford: Oxford University Press, 1981).
89. '5/IX/1847', *DFMB*, p. 4.
90. '25/IX/1847', *DFMB*, p. 7.
91. '7/X/1847', *DFMB*, p. 9.
92. Robert Louis Stevenson, *The Strange Case of Dr Jekyll and Mr Hyde* (Oxford: Oxford University Press, 1998).

93. 'To Crom Price', (18/I/1863), in *The Collected Letters of William Morris*, ed. by Norman Kelvin, 4 vols (Princeton: Princeton University Press, 1984–85), I, p. 23.

94. Q. D. Leavis, *Fiction and the Reading Public* (1932) (London: Chatto & Windus, 1965), pp. 103–04.

95. Daniel Defoe, *The Complete English Tradesman*, in *Religious and Didactic Writings of Daniel Defoe*, ed. by John McVeagh, 8 vols (London: Pickering & Chatto, 2007), VII, p. 44.

96. Ibid., p. 207.

97. Weber, *The Protestant Ethic and the Spirit of Capitalism*, p. 77.

98. Defoe, *The Complete English Tradesman*, p. 208.

99. '10/XI/1847', *DFMB*, p. 14.

100. '18/IV/1848', *DFMB*, p. 39.

101. '2/XI/1847', *DFMB*, p. 12.

102. '14/XI/1847', *DFMB*, p. 14.

103. '27/XI/1847', *DFMB*, p. 17.

104. '26/VIII/1854', *DFMB*, p. 86.

105. '7/XI/1847', *DFMB*, p. 13.

106. '6/XI/1847', *DFMB*, p. 13.

107. '6/IX/1847', *DFMB*, pp. 4–5.

108. Manning, *The Puritan-Provincial Vision*, p. 11.

109. Defoe, *The Complete English Tradesman*, p. 44

110. Aaron Brown, *Financial Risk Assessment for Dummies* (New York: John Wiley, 2015), p. 294.

111. See Marcus Waithe, 'Empson's Legal Fiction', *Essays in Criticism*, 62.3 (VII/2012), 279–301.

112. Brown, *Financial Risk Assessment for Dummies*, p. 294.

113. Ibid., p. 294.

114. '24/IX/1854', *DFMB*, p. 94.

115. '2/I/1855', *DFMB*, p. 114.

116. '3/I/1855', *DFMB*, p. 113.

117. '29/IV/1855', *DFMB*, p. 135.

118. John Haffenden, *Viewpoints: Poets in Conversation with John Haffenden* (London: Faber & Faber, 1981), p. 83.

119. '5/I/1855', *DFMB*, p. 114.

120. Anthony Trollope, *An Autobiography*, p. 78.

Part II

1. Maria H. Frawley, *Invalidism and Identity in Nineteenth Century Britain* (Chicago: University of Chicago Press, 2004), p. 4.

2. William Morris, 'The Lesser Arts', in *The Collected Works of William Morris*, ed. by May Morris, 24 vols (London: Longmans, Green, and Company, 1910–15), XXII, pp. 3–27 (p. 4). Subsequent references to this edition are given parenthetically in the text.

Chapter 3

1. Elizabeth Barrett Browning [hereafter, EBB], 'To Robert Browning' [hereafter, RB] (17/III/1846), *The Browning Letters* [hereafter, *BL*], Wellesley Special Collections and Armstrong Browning Library (Baylor University Digital Collections), <https://digitalcollections-baylor.quartexcollections.com/abl-collections/the-browning-letters> p. 2 of 4 [accessed 28 June 2022]. Most citations from the letters are taken from this online edition.

2. 'To Mary Russell Mitford' ([27–28]/III/1842), in *The Letters of Elizabeth Barrett Browning to Mary Russell Mitford 1836–1854*, ed. by Meredith B. Raymond and Mary Rose Sullivan, 3 vols (Winfield, KS: Armstrong Browning Library of Baylor University, 1983), I, pp. 373–81 (p. 378).

3. Rosalie Mander, *Mrs Browning: The Story of Elizabeth Barrett* (London: Weidenfeld & Nicolson, 1980), p. 30.

4. 'To RB' (27/II/1845), *BL*, p. 2 of 10.

5. Rosemary Ashton, *Thomas and Jane Carlyle: Portrait of a Marriage* (London: Chatto & Windus, 2002), p. 225.

6. 'Thomas Carlyle', in *A New Spirit of the Age*, ed. by R. H. Horne, 2 vols (London: Smith, Elder and Co., 1844), II, pp. 253–80 (p. 267).

7. 'To Henry Fothergill Chorley' (7/I/1845), *BL*, p. 5 of 13. For instance, Carlyle is not mentioned in Anne D. Wallace, '"Nor in Fading Silks Compose": Sewing, Walking, and Poetic Labor in *Aurora Leigh*', *ELH*, 64.1 (Spring 1997), 223–56 (p. 225).

8. Barbara Dennis, *Elizabeth Barrett Browning: The Hope End Years* (Bridgend, Mid-Glamorgan: Poetry Wales Press, 1996), p. 128.

9. Angela Leighton, *Elizabeth Barrett Browning* (Bloomington: Indiana University Press, 1986), p. 12, p. 25.

10. Beverly Taylor, 'Carlyle, Barrett Browning, and the Victorian Poet', in *On Heroes, Hero-Worship, and the Heroic in History*, ed. by David R. Sorensen and Brent E. Kinser (New Haven: Yale University Press, 2013).

11. Marjorie Stone, *Elizabeth Barrett Browning* (Basingstoke: Macmillan, 1995), p. 147. See also David, *Intellectual Women and Victorian Patriarchy*, p. 116, p. 156.

12. Stone, *Elizabeth Barrett Browning*, p. 138, p. 149. Salmon agrees that 'Carlyle's "gospel of work"' aids the eventual reconciliation of Aurora and Romney, but focuses for his part on a form of vitalism that sees Aurora turning cold stone into 'a *moving* statue' (*The Formation of the Victorian Literary Profession*, p. 209).

13. 'To RB' (17/II/1845), *BL*, p. 13 of 18.

14. See James Thorpe, 'Elizabeth Barrett's Commentary on Shelley: Some Marginalia', *Modern Language Notes*, 66 (1951), 455–8. See also her praise of Wordsworth 'as poet-hero' and 'poet-prophet', 'The Book of the Poets' (*The Athenæum*, 1842), in *Essays on the Greek Christian Poets and the English Poets* [hereafter, *GCPEP*] (New York: James Miller, 1863), pp. 119–233 (p. 222).

15. Barrett Browning, *GCPEP*, p. 177.

16. 'To Anna Brownell Jameson' (7/VIII/1855), *BL*, p. 2 of 6.
17. Cf Robert Macfarlane's argument that 'two alternative visions of creativity [. . .] run through nineteenth-century poetics' (*Original Copy: Plagiarism and Originality in Nineteenth-Century Literature* (Oxford: Oxford University Press, 2007), p. 41). See also Leighton, *Elizabeth Barrett Browning*, p. 13; and, Mary Sanders Pollock, *Elizabeth Barrett Browning and Robert Browning: A Creative Partnership* (Farnham: Ashgate, 2003), pp. 16–17.
18. 'To RB' (3/II/1845), *BL*, p. 10 of 18.
19. Alethea Hayter, *Mrs Browning: A Poet's Work and its Setting* (London: Faber & Faber, 1962), p. 13.
20. 'To EBB' (10/I/1845), *BL*, p. 1 of 6.
21. 'To RB' (18/I/1846), *BL*, p. 2 of 8.
22. Ibid., p. 2 of 8.
23. 'To RB' (10/XI/1845), *BL*, p. 3 of 8. I have preserved EBB's double point ellipsis.
24. 'To RB' ([2–3/VII/1845]), *BL*, p. 5 of 12.
25. Ibid., p. 5 of 12.
26. Alfred Tennyson, 'The Lady of Shalott' (1832), in *The Poems of Tennyson*, ed. by Christopher Ricks, 3 vols, 2nd edn (Harlow: Longman, 1987), I, pp. 387–95; Euripedes, *The Bacchae* (Harvard: Harvard University Press / Loeb Classical Library, 2002), p. 135. See Andromache Karankia, *Voices at Work: Women and Labor in Ancient Greece* (Baltimore: Johns Hopkins, 2014), p. 188.
27. 'To RB' ([2–3/VII/1845]), *BL*, p. 5 and p. 6 of 12.
28. Ibid., p. 6 of 12.
29. 'To RB' (17/II/1845), *BL*, p. 2 of 18.
30. EBB, *Poems*, 2 vols (London: Edward Moxon, 1844), I, p. xiii.
31. 'To RB' (20–23/VIII/1845), *BL*, pp. 5–6.
32. Catherine Hall, Keith McClelland, Nick Draper, Kate Donington, Rachel Lang, *Legacies of British Slave-Ownership: Colonial Slavery and the Formation of Victorian Britain* (Cambridge: Cambridge University Press, 2016), pp. 192–96.
33. 'To RB' (20/XII/1845), *BL*, p. 4 of 6.
34. Marjorie Stone, 'Browning [*née* Moulton Barrett], Elizabeth Barrett (1806–61), *Oxford Dictionary of National Biography* <https://www.oxforddnb.com> p. 2.
35. EBB, 'The Runaway Slave at Pilgrim's Point', in *The Liberty Bell by Friends of Freedom* (Boston: National Anti-Slavery Bazaar, 1848), pp. 29–44.
36. EBB, 'A Curse for a Nation', in *The Liberty Bell* (Boston, 1855), pp. 1–9.
37. See Denae Dyck, 'From Denunciation to Dialogue: Redefining Prophetic Authority in Elizabeth Barrett Browning's "A Curse for a Nation"', *Victorian Review*, 46.1 (Spring 2020), 67–82 (p. 69).
38. Marjorie Stone, 'Cursing as One of the Fine Arts: Elizabeth Barrett Browning's Political Poems', *Dalhousie Review*, 66.1/2 (1986), 155–173 (p. 168).
39. 'To RB' (17/II/1845), *BL*, p. 12 of 18.
40. Ibid., p. 12 of 18.
41. Ibid., p. 12 of 18.

42. Ibid., p. 13 of 18.
43. Stone, *Elizabeth Barrett Browning*, p. 138.
44. 'To RB' (17/II/1845), *BL*, p. 12 of 18.
45. 'To RB' (9/IX/1845), *BL*, p. 8 of 14.
46. 'To RB' (17/II/1845), *BL*, p. 13 of 18.
47. 'To RB' (27/II/1845), *BL*, p. 2 of 10.
48. Daniel Karlin, 'The Figure of the Singer', *Essays in Criticism*, 50.2 (April 2000), 99–124, p. 114.
49. 'To RB' (31/I/1846–1/II/1846), *BL*, p. 5 of 8.
50. Ibid., p. 7 of 8.
51. Ibid., p. 7 of 8.
52. 'To RB' (17/II/1845), *BL*, p. 2 of 18.
53. Ibid., p. 2 of 18.
54. 'To RB' (15/I/1845), *BL*, p. 3 and p. 4 of 10.
55. 'To RB' (10/XI/1845), *BL*, p. 2 of 8.
56. Ibid., p. 2 of 8.
57. 'To Mary Russell Mitford' (20/IX/1843), *BL*, p. 12 of 12.
58. Ibid., p. 12.
59. Carlyle, *Two Notebooks*, p. 188.
60. Taylor, 'Carlyle, Barrett Browning, and the Victorian Poet', in *On Heroes, Hero-Worship, and the Heroic in History*, p. 236.
61. Caroline Norton (pseud. Pearce Stevenson, Esq.), *Plain Letter to the Lord Chancellor on the Infant Custody Bill* (London: James Ridgeway, 1839), p. 7.
62. Anna Jameson, *Sisters of Charity Catholic and Protestant, Abroad and at Home* (London: Longman, Brown, Green, and Longmans, 1855); Anna Jameson, *The Communion of Labour: A Second Lecture on the Social Employments of Women* (London: Longman, Brown, Green, Longmans, and Roberts, 1856).
63. Jameson, *Sisters of Charity*, p. 3.
64. Ibid., p. 3.
65. Linda H. Peterson, *Becoming a Woman of Letters*, p. 45.
66. Jameson, *Sisters of Charity*, pp. 4–5.
67. Ibid., pp. 9–10.
68. Ibid., p. 12.
69. Ibid., p. 56.
70. Ibid., p. 45.
71. Jameson, *The Communion of Labour*, p. 136.
72. Barbara Leigh Smith, *Women and Work* (London: Bosworth and Harrison, 1857), p. 7.
73. Ibid., p. 7.
74. Jennie Batchelor, *Women's Work: Labour, Gender, Authorship, 1750–1830* (Manchester: Manchester University Press, 2010), p. 93, p. 135.
75. Ibid, p. 93, p. 135.
76. EBB, 'II. Glimpses into My Own Life and Literary Character' (1820), in 'Two Autobiographical Essays by Elizabeth Barrett', *Browning Institute Studies*, 2 (1974), 119–34 (p. 132).
77. Ibid., p. 60.

78. William Morris's allusion to 'male men' in *News from Nowhere* introduces further complication (16:4).

79. 'To RB' (30/XII/1845), *BL*, p. 4 of 10.

80. Sanders Pollock, *Elizabeth Barrett Browning and Robert Browning*, pp. 29–30, p. 33.

81. Matthew Campbell, *Rhythm and Will in Victorian Poetry* (Cambridge: Cambridge University Press, 1999), p. 45.

82. 'To RB' (11/I/1845), *BL*, p. 4 and p. 5 of 10.

83. Ibid., p. 4 of 10.

84. See 'Introduction: Thinkers, Thinking, Style, Stylists', in *Thinking through Style: Non-Fiction Prose of the Long Nineteenth Century*, ed. by Michael D. Hurley and Marcus Waithe (Oxford: Oxford University Press, 2018), pp. 1–10 (p. 3).

85. 'To RB' (31/I/1846–1/II/1846), *BL*, p. 5 of 10.

86. 'To RB' (11/I/1845), *BL*, p. 6 and p. 7 of 10.

87. 'To RB (31/I/1846–1/II/1846), *BL*, p. 5 of 10.

88. Campbell, *Rhythm and Will in Victorian Poetry*, p. 45.

89. EBB, *Aurora Leigh*, ed. by Kerry McSweeney (Oxford: Oxford University Press, 1998), p. 44. Book and line numbers are given in the text.

90. Ibid., p. 41.

91. Ibid., p. 52.

92. Ibid., p. 74.

93. Olive Schreiner, *Woman and Labour* (London: Adelphi Terrace, 1911), p. 50, p. 169.

94. 'To RB' ([2–3/VII/1845]), *BL*, p. 3 of 12.

95. Ibid., p. 3 of 12.

96. An earlier version of this discussion was published in *Letter Writing Among Poets: From William Wordsworth to Elizabeth Bishop*, ed. by Jonathan Ellis (Edinburgh: Edinburgh University Press, 2015), pp. 126–40.

97. Harriet Martineau ['by An Invalid'], *Life in the Sick-Room. Essays*, 2nd edn (London: Edward Moxon, 1844), p. 89.

98. 'To RB' (3/II/1845), *BL*, p. 1 and p. 2 of 18.

99. 'To RB' ([17/IV/1845]), *BL*, p. 3 of 6.

100. Ibid., p. 3 of 6 (45087–00, Wellesley College, Margaret Clapp Library, Special Collections).

101. Elizabeth Berridge, *The Barretts at Hope End: The Early Diary of Elizabeth Barrett Browning*, (London: John Murray, 1974), p. 150.

102. Dennis, *Elizabeth Barrett Browning*, p. 43, p. 260.

103. Frawley, *Invalidism and Identity*, p. 4.

104. Dennis, *Elizabeth Barrett Browning*, p. 45.

105. Berridge, *The Barretts at Hope End*, p. 18.

106. 'To RB' (15/V/1845), *BL*, p. 1 of 10.

107. 'To RB' (11/II/1845), *BL*, p. 6 of 10.

108. 'To RB' (20/III/1845), *BL*, p. 3 and p. 6 of 10.

109. Ibid., p. 3 of 10.

110. Martineau, *Life in the Sick-Room*, pp. 197–221.

111. Peterson, *Becoming a Woman of Letters*, p. 19.
112. For the connection between invalidism and authorship, see Frawley, *Invalidism and Identity*, pp. 11–12.
113. 'Miss E. B. Barrett and Mrs Norton', in Horne, *A New Spirit of the Age*, II, pp. 129–140 (p. 134).
114. Ibid., p. 135.
115. 'To RB' ([10/XI/1845]), *BL*, p. 1 of 8.
116. Frawley, *Invalidism and Identity*, p. 33.
117. Ibid., p. 39.
118. Horne, *A New Spirit of the Age*, II, p. 135.
119. 'To Mary Moulton-Barrett' (n.d./VI/1821), in *The Brownings' Correspondence*, ed. by Philip Kelley and Ronald Hudson (Winfield: Wedgestone Press, 1984), I, pp. 127–28 (p. 128).
120 'To RB' (9/XII/1845), *BL*, p. 4 of 6.
121. 'To RB' (8/VIII/1845), *BL*, p. 3 of 8.
122. Ibid., p. 4 of 8.
123. 'To RB' (17/II/1845), *BL*, p. 12 of 18.
124. Elizabeth K. Helsinger, *Ruskin and the Art of the Beholder* (Cambridge: Harvard University Press, 1982), pp. 138–9; Anne D. Wallace, *Walking, Literature, and English Culture* (Oxford: Clarendon Press, 1993), pp. 52–53.
125. Martineau, *Life in the Sick-Room*, p. 49.
126. 'To RB' (4/II/1846), *BL*, p. 3 of 8.
127. Ibid., p. 4 of 8.
128. Ibid., p. 4 of 8.
129. 'To RB' (20/III/1845), *BL*, p. 7 of 10.
130. 'To RB' ([15/V/1845]), *BL*, p. 2 of 10.
131. 'To RB' ([1/V/1845]), *BL*, p. 4 of 6.
132. 'To EBB' ([15/IV/1845]), *BL*, p. 4 of 6.
133. Ralph Waldo Emerson, 'Self-Reliance', in *The Annotated Emerson*, ed. by David Mikics (Cambridge: Harvard University Press, 2012), p. 180.
134. 'To EBB' ([15/IV/1845]), *BL*, p. 4 of 6.
135. Arthur Hugh Clough, *Amours de Voyage*, in *The Poems of Arthur Hugh Clough*, ed. by F. L. Mulhauser, 2nd edn (Oxford: Clarendon Press, 1974), pp. 94–133 (p. 94).
136. 'To EBB' (3/II/1845), *BL*, p. 13 of 18.
137. 'To RB' ([18–19/II/1845]), *BL*, p. 3 of 8.
138. G. H. Treitel, *The Law of Contract*, 11th edn (London: Sweet & Maxwell, 2003), pp. 24–30.
139. 'To RB' (27/II/1845), *BL*, p. 1 of 10.
140. Herman Melville, 'Bartleby, the Scrivener: A Story of Wall Street', in *The Piazza Tales* (New York: Sampson Low, Son & Co., 1856), pp. 32–108 (p. 107).
141. 'To EBB' ([6–7/I/1846]), *BL*, p. 1 of 10.
142. Dante Gabriel Rossetti, 'To Walter Howell Deverell' ([30/VIII/1851]), in *The Correspondence of Dante Gabriel Rossetti*, ed. by William E. Fredeman, 10 vols (Cambridge: D. S. Brewer, 2002), I, pp. 181–2 (p. 181).

143. 'To Mary Russell Mitford' (1/IV/1842) in *The Letters of Elizabeth Barrett Browning to Mary Russell Mitford 1836–1854*, I, pp. 383–87 (p. 386).

144. Cf Eric Griffiths's critique of Jacques Derrida in *The Printed Voice of Victorian Poetry* (Oxford: Clarendon Press, 1989). Griffiths's title recasts lines from Browning's *The Ring and the Book* (1868–69): '(and since he only spoke in print | The printed voice of him lives now as then)' (I, 165–67).

145. Cf Isaac D'Israeli: 'We converse with the absent by Letters, and with ourselves by Diaries', *Curiosities of Literature*, 3 vols (London: Routledge, Warne & Routledge, 1863), II, p. 206.

146. 'To RB' (10/I/1845), *BL*, p. 3 of 6.

147. 'To RB' (11/I/1845), *BL*, p. 6 of 10.

148. Samuel Taylor Coleridge, 'To William Godwin' (22/IX/1800), *Collected Letters of Samuel Taylor Coleridge*, ed. by Earl Leslie Griggs, 6 vols (Oxford: Clarendon Press, 1956), I, pp. 625–26 (p. 625).

149. 'To RB' ([19/II/1846]), *BL*, p. 1 of 8.

150. Ibid., p. 1 of 8.

151. 'To EBB' ([16/V/1845]), *BL*, p. 4 of 6.

152. 'To RB' ([24/III/1846]), *BL*, p. 2 of 6.

153. 'To RB' (3/II/1845), *BL*, p. 1 of 18.

154. 'To RB' (17/II/1845), *BL*, p. 5 of 18.

155. 'To RB' (27/II/1845), *BL*, p. 7 of 10.

156. Henry David Thoreau, *The Journal 1837–1861* (New York: New York Review of Books, 2009), p. 25.

157. 'To RB' (3/II/1845), *BL*, p. 3 of 18.

158. Ibid., p. 5 of 18.

159. Ibid., p. 4 of 18.

160. 'To RB' (20/III/1845), *BL*, p. 4 of 10.

161. Leighton, *Elizabeth Barrett Browning*, p. 4.

162. 'To RB' (24/XI/1845), *BL*, p. 3 of 6.

163. 'To RB' (20/III/1845), *BL*, p. 4 of 10.

164. 'To Mary Russell Mitford' ([4]/VI/1842), in *The Letters of Elizabeth Barrett Browning to Mary Russell Mitford 1836–1854*, I, pp. 420–22 (p. 422).

Chapter 4

1. Siskin, *The Work of Writing*, p. 120.

2. Ibid., p. 119.

3. Ibid., p. 120.

4. See Archibald Maclaren ('The Gymnasium, Oxford'), *A System of Physical Education: Theoretical and Practical* (Oxford: Clarendon Press, 1869); see also J. A. Mangan, *Athleticism in the Victorian and Edwardian Public School: The Emergence and Consolidation of an Educational Ideology*, 3rd edn (Abingdon: Routledge, 2000), p. 54; and Eric Chaline, *The Temple of Perfection: A History of the Gym* (London: Reaktion Books, 2015), p. 105.

5. Charles Kingsley, *The Water-Babies*, ed. by Brian Alderson (Oxford: Oxford University Press, 1995), p. 165.

6. Henry D. Thoreau, *A Week on the Concord and Merrimack Rivers*, in *Writings*, ed. by Carl F. Hovde (Princeton: Princeton University Press, 1980), p. 106.

7. See, for instance, Ilya Repin, *Portrait of Lev Tolstoy as a Ploughman on a Field*, oil on board, 1887, The State Tretyakov Gallery, Moscow. See Stuart Eagles, *Ruskin and Tolstoy* (Benbridge, Isle of Wight: Guild of St George, 2010); see also Tolstoy, 'An Introduction to Ruskin's Works' (1899), in *Recollections and Essays by Leo Tolstoy*, trans. by Aylmer Maude (London: Oxford University Press, 1937), p. 188.

8. See Herbert Sussman, *Victorian Masculinities*.

9. See Norman Vance, *The Sinews of the Spirit: The Ideal of Christian Manliness in Victorian Literature and Religious Thought* (Cambridge: Cambridge University Press, 1985).

10. See Agatha Romm, 'Gladstone as Man of Letters', *Nineteenth-Century Prose*, 17 (1989–90), 1–29.

11. See also Gladstone, 'A Maker of Verses', in *The Gladstone Papers* (London: Cassell, 1930), p. 34. Apart from founding St Deniol's Library (now, Gladstone's Library), Gladstone was also on the founding committee of the London Library.

12. One admirer observed that Gladstone was 'devoted as ardently to scholarship as to politics' ('Mr Gladstone and the Classics', in *Mr Gladstone in Scotland* (Edinburgh, [1890]), p. 35. Quoted in David Bebbington, *The Mind of Gladstone: Religion, Homer, and Politics* (Oxford: Oxford University Press, 2004), pp. 1–2). His son-in-law, Edward Wickham, confirms that 'His heart was more in his books' (E. C. Wickham, 'Mr Gladstone as seen from Near at Hand', *Good Words* (July 1898), p. 482. Quoted in Bebbington, *The Mind of Gladstone*, p. 2).

13. John Morley, *The Life of William Ewart Gladstone*, 3 vols (London: Macmillan, 1903), I, p. 3.

14. Gladstone was admitted to the Worshipful Order of Turners in 1876. See Peter Sewter, 'Gladstone as Woodsman', in *William Gladstone: New Studies and Perspectives*, ed. by Roland Quinault, Roger Swift and Ruth Clayton Windscheffel (Ashgate, 2012), pp. 155–75 (p. 157).

15. '31/VII/1858', *The Gladstone Diaries* [hereafter, *GD*], ed. by H. C. G. Matthew, et al., 14 vols (Oxford: Oxford University Press, 1990), V, p. 315. This entry is preceded by an allusion to the 'Felling of the three Beeches', on 29/X/1852 (*GD*, IV, p. 464).

16. Sewter, 'Gladstone as Woodsman', in *William Gladstone*, p. 158.

17. Ibid., p. 160.

18. *Speeches of Lord Randolph Churchill*, ed by Henry W. Lucy (London: Routledge, 1885), p. 53.

19. Roy Jenkins, *Gladstone* (London: Pan Books, 2002), p. 396. See also Simon Peaple and John Vincent, 'Gladstone and the Working Man', in *Gladstone*, ed. by Peter J. Jagger (London: The Hambledon Press, 1998), pp. 71–83 (p. 78).

20. Peter Thomas and John Packham, *Ecology of Woodlands and Forests: Description, Dynamics, Diversity* (Cambridge: Cambridge University Press, 2003), p. 417.

21. Sewter, 'Gladstone as Woodsman', in *William Gladstone*, p. 158.

22. E.g. Jacob George Strutt, *Sylva Britannica: or, Portraits of Forest Trees* (London, 1830); Batty Langley, *A Sure Method of Improving Estates, by Plantations of Oak, Elm, Ash, Beech and Other Timber-Trees, Coppice-Woods* (London: Francis Clay and Daniel Browne, 1728) (includes corrective annotations by Gladstone on tree measurements); Christopher Young Michie, *The Larch: A Practical Treatise on its Culture and General Management* (Edinburgh: William Blackwood and Sons, 1882) (gift of the author); Charles Whitehead, *Hints on Vegetable and Fruit Farming* (London: John Murray, 1893) (gift of the author); J. J. Black, *Cultivation of the Peach and the Pear* (Wilmington, 1886) (gift of the author); and Edward Brown, *Poultry Keeping as an Industry for Farmers and Cottagers* (London, 1891) (gift of the author).

23. See GG/1736 (among which, a paper on the removal of tree stumps), Glynne-Gladstone MSS Papers, Gladstone's Library, Hawarden.

24. Bebbington, *The Mind of Gladstone*, pp. 4–5.

25. Peter J. Jagger, *Gladstone: The Making of a Christian Politician. The Personal Religious Life and Development of William Ewart Gladstone 1809–1832* (Alison Park: Pickwick Publications, 1991), p. 68. See also H. C. G. Matthew, *Gladstone 1809–1898* (Oxford: Oxford University Press, 1997), p. 94.

26. S. G. Checkland, *The Gladstones: A Family Biography 1764–1851* (Cambridge: Cambridge University Press, 1971), p. 31.

27. '29/XII/1826', *GD*, I, p. 91.

28. Ibid., p. 155.

29. Ibid., p. 595.

30. '19/II/1830', *GD*, I, p. 285.

31. '26/X/1845', *GD*, III, pp. 491–93.

32. '19/VII/1848', *GD*, IV, p. 54.

33. Anthony Horneck, *The Happy Ascetick; or, The Best Exercise, Together with Prayers Suitable to Each Exercise*, 6th edn (London: Samuel Chapman, 1724), p. 325 (copy in Gladstone's Library, Hawarden).

34. Ibid., p. 388.

35. Ibid., p. 71.

36. George S. Barrett, *Religion in Daily Life* (London: Elliott Stock, 1893) (copy in Gladstone's Library, Hawarden).

37. 'To Alexander Carlyle', (19/IV/1820), in *Early Letters of Thomas Carlyle*, ed. by Charles Eliot Norton, 2 vols (London: Macmillan and Co., 1886), p. 288 (copy in Gladstone's Library, Hawarden).

38. Peter Stansky, *Gladstone: A Progress in Politics* (London: W. W. Norton & Co., 1979), p. 14. E. J. Feuchtwanger similarly connects Gladstone's 'constant wrestling with himself and his sense of sin and weakness' to his having 'stuck firmly to his evangelical roots' (*Gladstone* (London: Allen Lane, 1975), p. 11.

39. Ian Gibson, *The English Vice: Beating, Sex, and Shame in Victorian England and After* (London: Duckworth, 1978), pp. 99–143 (fn. 45, p. 143).
40. See Mario Praz, 'Swinburne and "Le Vice Anglais"', in *The Romantic Agony*, trans. by Angus Davidson (London: Collins, 1960), pp. 461–81; see also [Algernon Charles Swinburne], *The Whippingham Papers* (Ware: Wordsworth Editions, 1995).
41. W. H. Hudson, *A Crystal Age* (London: Duckworth & Co., 1913), pp. 150–51.
42. Ibid., p. 223.
43. Quoted in Sewter, 'Gladstone as Woodsman', in *William Gladstone*, p. 173.
44. ph-28(a)-0010-w, Flintshire Record Office.
45. Rt. Hon. The Viscount Gladstone, *After Thirty Years* (London: Macmillan and Co., 1928), p. 61.
46. *The Times*, 6/VIII/1877, p. 7.
47. Gladstone Papers, British Library Add MS 44747, f. 184.
48. Danahay, *Gender at Work in Victorian Culture*, p. 74.
49. Vance, *The Sinews of the Spirit*, p. 1.
50. Ibid., p. 26.
51. Thomas Hughes, *The Manliness of Christ* (London: Macmillan, 1879).
52. Bebbington, *The Mind of Gladstone*, p. 104.
53. *The Benedictine Lay Brother: A Manual of Instruction and Devotion for the Use of Brothers and Sisters of the Order of St. Benedict*, adapted from the German of Rev. Dom Dudger Leonard, O.S.B. of the Reuron Congregation (Fort-Augustus: Abbey Press, 1888) (copy in Gladstone's Library, Hawarden).
54. *The Benedictine Lay Brother*, p. 9, p. 93 (copy in Gladstone's Library, Hawarden).
55. Ibid., p. 93.
56. *The Rule of Our Most Holy Father Saint Benedict*, ed. by A Monk of St Benedict's Abbey, Fort-Augustus (London: Burns and Oates) (copy in Gladstone's Library, Hawarden).
57. '1/VII/1843', *GD*, III, p. 293.
58. See multiple references across April and May 1839, *GD*, II.
59. Gladstone, 'A Fragment on Carlyle', *The Gladstone Papers*, p. 46.
60. Watkins, *Life, Poetry, and Letters of Ebenezer Elliott, The Corn-Law Rhymer, with an Abstraction of his Politics* (London: John Mortimer, 1850) (copy in Gladstone's Library, Hawarden).
61. Thomas Carlyle, *On Heroes, Hero-Worship, & The Heroic in History* (London: James Fraser, 1841), p. 53 (copy in Gladstone's Library, Hawarden).
62. Matthew, *Gladstone 1809–1898*, p. 316.
63. *The Times*, 24/X/1890, p. 4.
64. Thomas Carlyle, *Reminiscences*, ed. by James Anthony Froude, 2 vols (London: Longmans, Green, and Co., 1881), I, p. 15 (copy in Gladstone's Library, Hawarden).
65. Bebbington, *The Mind of Gladstone*, p. 292.
66. Simon Peaple and John Vincent, 'Gladstone and the Working Man', in *Gladstone*, p. 73.

67. A. Geoffrey Veysey, *Mr Gladstone and Hawarden* (Hawarden, Deeside: Clwyd Record Office, 1982), p. 17; the family later re-founded this institution to supply 'adequate opportunities for literary study, mental refreshment and social intercourse, side by side with those given for physical exercise' (p. 18).
68. '5/VIII/1858', *GD*, IV, p. 316.
69. '29/X/1852', *GD*, IV, p. 464.
70. Carlyle, *On Heroes*, p. 132 (copy in Gladstone's Library, Hawarden).
71. '21/VIII/1878', *GD*, IX, p. 339.
72. '9/I/1868', *GD*, VI, p. 568.
73. '12/IX/1868', *GD*, VI, p. 622.
74. '30/X/1868', *GD*, VI, p. 632.
75. '14/IX/1872', *GD*, VIII, p. 210.
76. '29/X/1852', *GD*, IV, p. 464.
77. '28/XII/1867', *GD*, VI, p. 565.
78. '21/XII/1867', *GD*, VI, p. 564.
79. Ibid., p. 564.
80. Ibid., p. 564.
81. Carlyle, *On Heroes*, p. 146 (copy in Gladstone's Library, Hawarden).
82. '20/IV/1876', *GD*, IX, p. 119.
83. '2/IX/1877', *GD*, IX, p. 254.
84. According to Hugh Lloyd Jones, Gladstone went through *The Odyssey* and *The Iliad* 'about thirty times' ('Gladstone on Homer', *TLS*, 3/I/1975, pp. 15–17).
85. W. E. Gladstone, *Studies on Homer and the Homeric Age* [hereafter, *SHHA*], 3 vols (Oxford: Oxford University Press, 1858); W. E. Gladstone, *Juventus Mundi. The Gods and Men in the Heroic Age* (London: Macmillan & Co., 1869); W. E. Gladstone, *Homeric Synchronism: An Enquiry into the Time and Space of Homer* (London: Macmillan & Co, 1876); W. E. Gladstone, *Homer* (Literature Primers Series) (London: Macmillan & Co., 1878); W. E. Gladstone, *Landmarks of Homeric Study, Together with An Essay on the Points of Contact Between the Assyrian Tablets and the Homeric Text* (London: Macmillan, 1890).
86. Frank M. Turner, 'Gladstone: A Political Not a Cultural Radical', in *William Gladstone*, pp. 15–30 (p. 21); Bebbington, *The Mind of Gladstone*, p. 39, p. 144.
87. Gladstone, *SHHA*, III, p. 141.
88. Ibid., p. 47.
89. Ibid., p. 47.
90. Ibid., p. 71.
91. Ibid., p. 46.
92. Ibid., p. 46.
93. Gladstone, *Juventus Mundi*, p. 424.
94. Ibid., p. 424.
95. Ibid., p. 424.
96. Ibid., p. 444.
97. '23/XII/1867', *GD*, VI, p. 565.

98. '24/XII/1867', *GD*, VI, p. 565.

99. Gladstone, *SHHA*, II, pp. 70–71.

100. Ibid., pp. 70–71.

101. Ibid., p. 72.

102. Gladstone, *Landmarks of Homeric Study*, p. 10.

103. Ibid., p. 53.

104. Ibid., p. 53.

105. Bebbington, *The Mind of Gladstone*, p. 23, p. 36.

106. Aristotle, *The Politics*, trans. by R. F. Stalley (Oxford: Oxford University Press, 1995), p. 270.

107. Gladstone, *SHHA*, III, p. 74.

108. Ibid., pp. 74–75.

109. Ibid., pp. 77.

110. S. G. Checkland, 'John Gladstone as Trader and Planter', *The Economic History Review*, 7.2 (1954), 216–29; S. G. Checkland, *The Gladstones: A Family Biography 1764–1851*.

111. Checkland, *The Gladstones*, p. 321.

112. GG/2796, Inventories: 'Buildings and slaves on plantations Mon Repos, Vredestein, L'Incertitude, Goede Verwagting and Younge Rachel', 1816–17, Glynne-Gladstone MSS Papers, Gladstone's Library, Hawarden.

113. GG/2882, 'Table of compensation rates for slaves in British Guiana', c. 1833, Glynne-Gladstone MSS Papers, Gladstone's Library, Hawarden.

114. John Gladstone, *A Statement of Facts, Connected with the Present State of Slavery in the British Sugar and Coffee Colonies . . .*, 3rd edn (London: Baldwin and Cradock, 1830).

115. Ibid., p. 6.

116. Ibid., pp. 12–13.

117. *Sheffield Independent*, 15/V/1841, pp. 1–2; see also GG/2891 'Case with opinion of counsel (Sir William Follett) concerning a supposed libel of John Gladstone in the *Sheffield Independent*', 1841, Glynne-Gladstone MSS Papers, Gladstone's Library, Hawarden.

118. Relatedly, questions in Parliament obliged John Gladstone to send his son, Robertson, to investigate reports that indentured Indian labourers were being mistreated on his Vreedenhoop estate in Guiana.

119. Ronald Quinault, 'Gladstone and Slavery', *Historical Journal*, 52.2 (2009), 363–83; Richard Huzzey, 'Gladstone and the Suppression of the Slave Trade', in *William Gladstone: New Studies and Perspectives*, ed. by Roland Quinault (Farnham, Surrey: Ashgate, 2012), pp. 253–66; see also Hall and others, *Legacies of British Slave-Ownership*.

120. Quinault, 'Gladstone and Slavery', *Historical Journal*, p. 370, p. 372.

121. Cf Richard B. Sheridan, 'The Condition of the Slaves on the Sugar Plantations of Sir John Gladstone in the Colony of Demerara, 1812–49', *New West Indian Guide*, 76.3/4 (2002), 243–69 (p. 247).

122. Checkland, *The Gladstones*, p. 277.

123. Quinault, 'Gladstone and Slavery', *Historical Journal*, p. 365.

124. Ibid., p. 367.

125. Ibid., p. 368.

126. 'Mr Gladstone at Liverpool', *The Times*, 29/VI/1881, p. 11.

127. *W. E. Gladstone: Autobiographica* ed. by John Brook and Mary Sorensen (H. M. Stationery Office, 1981), p. 41.

128. Morley, *The Life of William Ewart Gladstone*, I, p. 104.

129. Ibid., I, p. 104.

130. GG/719, 'Letters from the General Public to W. E. Gladstone on his view on cottage gardening, and fruit and poultry farming', 1889–94, Gladstone's Library, Hawarden.

131. Gladstone, *SHHA*, II, p. 72.

132. Ibid., p. 72.

133. Theodor W. Adorno and Max Horkheimer, *Dialectic of Enlightenment* (1944; London: Verso, 1973), pp. 60–62.

134. John Henry Newman, *Apologia pro vita sua* (London: Longmans, Green, and Co., 1890), p. xiii.

135. Oscar Wilde, 'The Decay of Lying', in *The Complete Works of Oscar Wilde*, ed. by Merlin Holland (London: Collins, 2003), pp. 1071–92 (p. 1090).

136. Gladstone, *SHHA*, III, p. 522.

137. Ibid., p. 522.

138. W. E. Gladstone, *Homer* (Literature Primers Series) (London: Macmillan & Co., 1878), p. 141.

139. Gladstone, *Landmarks of Homeric Study*, p. 55.

140. Gladstone, *Juventus Mundi*, pp. 388–89.

141. Ibid., pp. 388–89.

142. Ibid., pp. 505–06.

143. Ibid., pp. 505–06.

144. Ibid., pp. 505–06.

145. Ibid., pp. 505–06.

146. Homer, *The Odyssey*, trans. by A. T. Murray, 2 vols (London: William Heinemann, 1960), I, p. 2.

147. Sewter, 'Gladstone as Woodsman', p. 157. An early diary entry shows Gladstone moving between work on 'Euclid & Greek Testament' to 'a lesson in [wood] turning from Powys' (4/II/1828', *GD*, I, p. 163). Entries follow that mention having 'read part of Troilus & Cressida' between 'Frisking on a rope [. . .] & turning in Powy's shop' ('5/II/1828' and '7/II/1828', *GD*, I, p. 163).

148. *The Odyssey of Homer Rendered into English Verse*, trans. by G. A. Schomberg, Books I–XII (London: John Murray, 1879), p. 1.

149. *The Odyssey of Homer: Done into English Prose*, trans. by S. H. Butcher, (London: Macmillan & Co., 1879), p. 1.

150. *A Nearly Literal Translation of Homer's Odyssey into Accentuated Dramatic Verse*, trans. by Rev. Lovelace Bigge-Wither (Oxford and London: James Parker and Co., 1869), p. v, p. 2.

151. Sir Charles Du Cane, *The Odyssey of Homer Books I–XII Translated into English Verse with Notes and Parallel Passages* (Edinburgh and London: William Blackwood and Sons, 1880), p. 3.

152. Pietro Pucci, *Odysseus Polutropos: Intertextual Readings in the Odyssey and the Iliad* (Ithaca: Cornell University Press, 1987), p. 62.

153. Gladstone, *Homer*, p. 130.

154. E. J. Feuchtwanger, *Gladstone* (London: Allen Lane, 1975), p. 121.

155. Cf the dedication 'To the People's William' inscribed on an axe donated by a member of the Skewen and Neath Abbey Liberal Association, South Wales.

156. Gladstone, *Homer*, p. 131.

157. Gladstone, *Juventus Mundi*, pp. 505–06.

158. Matthew notes that 'its employment was a good occasion for bonding with his sons', *Gladstone 1809–1898*, p. 317.

159. '27/XII/1872', *GD*, VIII, p. 263. Similarly, the glossed inclusive pronoun in 'We (three) commenced the cutting of a huge beech' lends significance to the personnel as much as to the act ('17/I/1870', *GD*, VII, p. 222).

160. Tennyson, 'Ulysses', in *The Poems of Tennyson*, I, pp. 613–20 (p. 617).

161. '10/V/1853', *GD*, IV, pp. 524–25 (p. 525).

162. Gladstone, *Homer*, p. 131.

163. S. A. Bent, *Familiar Short Sayings of Great Men, with Historical and Explanatory Notes* (London: Chatto & Windus, 1882), p. 249.

164. Aristotle, *The Nicomachean Ethics*, trans. by H. Rackham (London: William Heinemann, 1968), p. 347.

165. '10/V/1853', *GD*, IV, pp. 524–25 (p. 525).

166. Gladstone, *Homer*, p. 131.

167. Gladstone, *SHHA*, I, p. 7.

168. Cf Mahatma Gandhi reviving the Indian home crafts; also, Winston Churchill as a member of the Guild of Bricklayers; and Mussolini riding a tractor in the 'Battle for Grain'.

169. 'An Unexpected Cut', *Punch*, 21/XI/1874, p. 215. See also Asa Briggs, 'Victorian Images of Gladstone', in *Gladstone*, ed. by Peter J. Jagger (London: The Hambledon Press, 1998), pp. 33-49: 'in a *Punch* cartoon of 26/V/1877 [. . .] Gladstone wields his axe in front of a dying tree called "Turkish Rule", a shocked Disraeli calls out "Woodman, Spare that Tree, I love its every Bough".', p. 42.

170. Matthew, *Gladstone 1809–1898*, p. 317.

171. Peaple and Vincent, 'Gladstone and the Working Man', in *Gladstone*, p. 78.

172. Jagger, *Gladstone: The Making of a Christian Politician*, p. 87.

173. Joseph S. Meisel, 'Gladstone's Visage: Problem and Performance', in *William Gladstone: New Studies and Perspectives*, ed. by Roland Quinault (Farnham, Surrey: Ashgate, 2012), pp. 73–98 (p. 86).

174. Morley, *The Life of William Ewart Gladstone*, II, p. 252.

175. Ibid., p. 252.

176. *The Times*, 6/VIII/1877, p. 7.

177. 'Mr Gladstone at Home', *The Times*, 6/VIII/1877, p. 8.

178. *The Times*, 6/VIII/1877, p. 7.

179. Ibid., p. 7.

180. G. W. F. Hegel, *Phenomenology of Spirit*, trans. by A. V. Miller (Oxford: Oxford University Press, 1977), pp. 111–19.
181. 'To [Sarah] Corlass', 11/II/c.1850, HM 31088, Ruskin Collection, Huntington Library, California.
182. Cf Ruskin's failed erection of a brick column at Oxford's Natural History Museum (16:46).
183. Cicero, *De Officiis* (London: Heinemann / Loeb, 1913), p. 153.
184. Arendt, *The Human Condition*, p. 225.
185. Ralph Waldo Emerson, *The American Scholar*, in *The Collected Works of Ralph Waldo Emerson*, 6 vols (Cambridge: The Belknap Press of Harvard University Press, 1971), I, pp. 52–70 (p. 53).
186. Ibid., p. 427.
187. M. K. Gandhi, *Unto this Last: A Paraphrase*, trans. by Valji Govindji (Ahmedabad: Navajivan Press, 1956), p. v.
188. Sara Atwood, *Ruskin's Educational Ideals* (2011; London: Routledge, 2016); Mark Frost, *The Lost Companions and John Ruskin's Guild of St George: A Revisionary History* (London: Anthem Press, 2014).
189. Hardwicke Rawnsley, 'The Contributors' Club', *The Atlantic Monthly*, 85 (1900), 568–76 (p. 573).
190. Quoted by Tim Hilton from the 'Broadlands Book', *John Ruskin: The Later Years* (New Haven: Yale University Press, 2000), p. 263.
191. Henry W. Acland, 'Mr Ruskin and Oxford Undergraduates', *The Times*, 21/V/1874, p. 12; anon. ('One Who Has Dug'), 'Mr Ruskin's School of Gardening', *Daily News*, 27/V/1874, p. 3; anon. ('One Who Has Rowed'), 'Mr Ruskin's School of Gardening', *Daily News*, 29/V/1874, p. 6; James Reddie Anderson, 'Mr Ruskin's Work at Hinksey', *Daily News*, 30/V/1874, p. 3.
192. '28/X/1874', in *The Diaries of John Ruskin 1874–1889* [hereafter, *DJR*], ed. by Joan Evans and John Howard Whitehouse (Oxford: Clarendon Press, 1959), pp. 819–20 (p. 819).
193. '18/V/1875', in *DJR*, p. 845.
194. Quoted in *The Oxford Book of Oxford*, ed. by Jan Morris (Oxford: Oxford University Press, 1978), p. 233.
195. '3/XII/1874', in *DJR*, p. 829.
196. Rawnsley, 'The Contributors' Club', p. 575. Edward Bagnall Poulton likewise remembers how Ruskin 'asked for a hammer and proceeded to attack a stone of moderate size', *John Viriamu Jones and Other Oxford Memories* (London: Longmans, Green, and Co., 1911), p. 245.
197. More favourably, *Punch* casts Ruskin as a 'Leader of undergraduate thought' ('Hinksey Diggings', *Punch*, 6/VI/1874, p. 236).
198. Douglas Percy Bliss, *John Ruskin and the Hinksey Diggers*, 1863, watercolour and bodycolour over pencil, The Ruskin: Library, Museum and Research Centre, Lancaster University.
199. See, for instance, 'A Lake-Side Home. Brantwood.', *Art Journal*, XII/1881, pp. 353–57 (p. 356).
200. See 'The Study, Hawarden Castle', ph-28(a)-0041-w, Flintshire Record Office; see also 'Gladstone at his Desk', ph-28(a)-0023, Flintshire Record Office; Gladstone reading, ph-28(a)-0028-w.

201. Alexander Wedderburn, 'Celebrities at Home. No. LIX Professor Ruskin at Brantwood', *The World*, 29/VIII/ 1899; accessed as a cutting in the Abercrombie Archive, The Ruskin: Library, Museum and Research Centre, Lancaster University, Lancaster University (p. 1 of 3).
202. Ibid., p. 1 of 3.
203. W. G. Collingwood, *John Ruskin in his Study at Brantwood*, 1882, watercolour, Trustees of the Ruskin Museum, Coniston.
204. Wedderburn, 'Celebrities at Home. No. LIX Professor Ruskin at Brantwood' (p. 2 of 3).
205. W. G. Collingwood, *The Life and Work of John Ruskin*, 2 vols (London: Bury Street, 1893), II, p. 194.
206. Ibid., p. 189.
207. 'To [Susan] Beever', JR 6; typewritten, a corrected proof, with additions in the handwriting of Albert Fleming, Huntington Library, San Marino, CA.
208. '3/VII/1876', *The Brantwood Diary of John Ruskin*, ed. by Helen Gill Viljoen (New Haven and London: Yale University Press, 1971), p. 21; 16/X/1877, p. 56; 2/XI/1877, p. 59.
209. '8/II/1878', *The Brantwood Diary*, p. 89.
210. '28/V/1879', *The Brantwood Diary*, p. 172.
211. 'To [Susan Beever]', JR 209; typewritten; a corrected proof, with additions in the handwriting of Albert Fleming [1878], Huntington Library, San Marino, CA.
212. 'To Joan Severn' ('Darling Pusiky') ([IV(?)]/1873), manuscript letter, The Ruskin: Library, Museum and Research Centre, Lancaster University.
213. In 1881, Ruskin tells John Pincher Faunthorpe that 'My political economy is all in Xenophon and Marmontel' (37:381). In *Deucalion* (1875–83), he speaks of plans for 'a life of Xenophon, with analysis of the general principles of Education, in ten volumes' (26:96).
214. Referring to his 'intimate union of handwork and headwork', Cook and Wedderburn compare Ruskin's labour experiments to those of Philipp Emanuel von Fellenberg, Johann Heinrich Pestalozzi, and Friedrich Froebel (32:65).
215. 'To Joan Severn' ('Di wee pussie') (18/II/[1872]), manuscript letter, The Ruskin: Library, Museum and Research Centre, Lancaster University.
216. For a related account, see Vicky Albritton and Fredrik Albritton Jonsson, *Green Victorians: The Simple Life in John Ruskin's Lake District* (Chicago: University of Chicago Press, 2016), pp. 29–31.
217. 'To Joan Severn' ('My dearest') (20/IV/[1873]), manuscript letter, The Ruskin: Library, Museum and Research Centre, Lancaster University.
218. W. G. Collingwood, *Ruskin Relics* (London: Ibister & Co., 1903), p. 43.
219. Fiona Loynes, 'The Historical Context of Brantwood', unpublished typescript, The Ruskin: Library, Museum and Research Centre, Lancaster University, p. 7.
220. Fiona Loynes, 'Ruskin at Brantwood', unpublished typescript, The Ruskin: Library, Museum and Research Centre, Lancaster University, p. 22.
221. I am grateful to Howard Hull, Director of Brantwood, for drawing my attention to this 'experimental' view of landscape.
222. Collingwood, *Ruskin Relics*, p. 35.

223. Ibid., p. 44.

224. Ibid., pp. 40–43.

225. Ibid., p. 43.

226. Francis O'Gorman, 'Manliness and the History of Ruskin in Love: Writing Ruskin's Masculinity from W. G. Collingwood to Kate Millett', in *Ruskin and Gender* (London: Palgrave, 2002), pp. 10–28 (p. 11).

227. Cf the letter Ruskin wrote as a child to his father, in which he explains that 'I at first intended to make for your Newyears [*sic*] present a small model of any easily done thing' (manuscript letter, 31/XII/1828, Coniston Museum).

228. One digger admits that 'a farmer's cart lost a wheel on our road at the place where my hands had laboured' (L. R. Farnell, *An Oxonian Looks Back* (London: Martin Hopkinson, 1934), p. 61).

229. Poulton, *John Viriamu Jones and Other Oxford Memories*, p. 245.

230. Ibid., p. 246.

231. Quoted from MacEwen's account, published in *The Glasgow Herald*; David Smith Cairns, *Life and Times of Alexander Robertson MacEwen* (London: Hodder and Stoughton, 1925), p. 58.

232. Wilde likewise recalls that 'our friends and our enemies came out and mocked us from the bank', see 'Art and the Handicraftsman', in *The First Collected Edition of the Works of Oscar Wilde, 1908–1922* [hereafter, *WOW*], 'Miscellanies' volume, ed. by Robert Ross (1908; London: Dawsons of Pall Mall, 1968), pp. 291–308 (p. 307)).

233. Wilde, 'Art and the Handicraftsman', *WOW*, p. 307. Cf Marcus Waithe, 'William Morris and the House Beautiful', in *Oscar Wilde in Context*, ed. by Kerry Powell and Peter Raby (Cambridge: Cambridge University Press, 2013), p. 89.

234. Loynes, 'The Historical Context of Brantwood', p. 18.

235. H. W. Taunt, *Ruskin Road-makers at North Hinksey*, June 1874, photograph, in *The Oxford Poems of Matthew Arnold ('The Scholar Gipsy' and 'Thyrsis') Illustrated* (Oxford: Henry W. Taunt & Co., n.d), p. 87; ibid., *Ruskin Road-makers at work, North Hinksey*, 1874, photograph, p. 89.

236. Barringer, *Men at Work: Art and Labour in Victorian Britain*, pp. 72–73.

237. Charles Dickens, *Pickwick Papers*, ed. by James Kinsley (Oxford: Oxford University Press, 1998), p. 81.

238. Frost, *The Lost Companions and John Ruskin's Guild of St George*, p. 208.

239. Henry Holiday, *Reminiscences of My Life* (London: William Heinemann, 1914), p. 177.

240. Hilton, *John Ruskin: The Later Years*, p. 369.

241. Quoted in *Letters of John Ruskin to Charles Eliot Norton*, 2 vols (Boston and New York: Houghton Mifflin and Company, 1904), II, p. 147. See also A. C. Benson on the 'perilous activity of his brain' (A. C. Benson, *Ruskin: A Study in Personality* (London: Smith, Elder & Co., 1911), p. 66).

242. H. Halliday Sparling, *The Kelmscott Press and William Morris Master-Craftsman* (London: Macmillan & Co., 1924), p. 1.

243. This is acknowledged by Sparling's editor, in his Epilogue to Sparling, *The Kelmscott Press and William Morris Master-Craftsman*, p. 132. According to William S. Peterson, Sparling's Arts and Crafts peers thought him 'a weak, unremarkable young man' (*The Kelmscott Press: A History of William Morris's Typographical Adventure* (Berkeley: University of California Press, 1991), p. 167.

244. Sparling, *The Kelmscott Press and William Morris Master-Craftsman*, p. 38.

245. J. W. Mackail, *The Life of William Morris*, 2 vols (London: Longmans, Green, and Co., 1899), I, p. 186.

246. Ibid., p. 186.

247. Ibid., p. 186.

248. Ibid., p. 186.

249. May Morris, 'William Morris as a Writer', in *William Morris: Artist, Writer, Socialist* [hereafter, *WMAWS*], ed. by May Morris and Bernard Shaw, 2 vols (Oxford: Basil Blackwell, 1936), I, pp 373–516 (p. 428).

250. Ibid., p. 428.

251. Ibid., p. 437.

252. Ibid., p. 437. Tellingly, May Morris reports on 'a certain amount of [. . .] work-shop material', repeating the word 'work-shop' several times to bring home the point (*WMAWS*, I, p. 375).

253. May Morris, 'William Morris as a Writer', p. 396.

254. Mackail, *William Morris*, I, p. 190.

255. Walter Pater, 'Style', in *Appreciations, with and Essay on Style* (London: Macmillan, 1889), pp. 1–36 (p. 19).

256. May Morris, 'William Morris as a Writer', p. 428.

257. Ibid., p. 428.

258. Ibid., p. 428.

259. Carlyle alludes to a similar tendency when lamenting the era's lack of true apprenticeship (20:177).

260. This personal motto appears on tiles and glass at Red House, Morris's first family home, built in 1859 at Bexleyheath, Kent.

261. William Morris, 'The Ideal Book. A Paper Read Before the Bibliographical Society, 19/VI/1893', in *WMAWS*, I, pp. 310–18 (p. 311).

262. William Morris, 'The Early Literature of the North – Iceland', in *The Unpublished Lectures of William Morris* [hereafter, *ULWM*], ed. by Eugene D. LeMire (Detroit: Wayne State University Press, 1969), pp. 179–98 (p. 184).

263. Ibid., p. 184.

264. In 'Early England', Morris wrote that 'war brought prisoners sometimes and those prisoners became property and were called thralls', this being a 'blot on the constitution of our forefathers' (*ULWM*, pp. 158–78 (p. 164)).

265. 'To Alice James', (10/III/[1869]–12/III/[1869]), in *The Complete Letters of Henry James, 1855–1872*, ed. by Pierre A. Walker and Greg W. Zacharias, 2 vols (Lincoln and London: University of Nebraska Press, 2006), pp. 233–47 (p. 237).

266. Walter Bagehot, 'To Mrs Russell Barrington' (1874), quoted in Mrs Russell Barrington, *The Life of Walter Bagehot* (London: Longmans, Green, and Co., 1914), p. 442.

267. Sparling, *The Kelmscott Press and William Morris Master-Craftsman*, p. 38.

268. May Morris, 'William Morris as a Writer', p. 494.

269. Dante Gabriel Rossetti, *The Bard and Petty Tradesman*, V/1868, pen and brown ink, British Museum. Two likenesses stand back-to-back, one plucks an Orphic harp, the other rests his fists on a shop counter.

270. Peter Floud, 'The Inconsistencies of William Morris', *The Listener*, 14/X/1954, p. 616. Tanya Harrod observes that 'his designs were carried out by professional craftsmen' (*The Crafts in Britain in the 20th Century* (New Haven: Yale University Press, 1999), p. 16).

271. In *News from Nowhere*, Ellen addresses 'the old grumbler' as 'Grandfather' (16:157), only to call him 'father' later on (16:184).

272. Peter Ackroyd, *Shakespeare: The Biography* (London: Vintage, 2006), pp. 19–20.

273. Morris, 'Some Thoughts on the Ornamented Manuscripts of the Middle Ages: A Fragmentary Essay Never Published by Morris', in *The Ideal Book: Essays and Lectures on the Arts of the Book by William Morris*, ed. by William S. Peterson (Los Angeles: University of California, 1982), pp. 1–6 (p. 4).

274. Morris, 'Early England', in *ULWM*, p. 169.

275. Ibid., p. 169.

276. In Morris's lecture, 'Art: A Serious Thing', he notes that 'the right meaning of the word craft is simply *power*' (*ULWM*, pp. 36–53 (p. 45)).

277. Ian Felce, *William Morris and the Development of a Heroic Ideal: Old Norse Works 1868–1876* (unpublished doctoral thesis, University of Cambridge, 2015), p. 143.

278. Ibid., p. 141; see, also, Ian Felce, 'The Old Norse Sagas and William Morris's Ideal of Literal Translation', *Review of English Studies*, 67.279 (1/IV/2016), 220–36 (p. 232–33); and Ian Felce, *William Morris and the Icelandic Sagas* (Martlesham, Suffolk: D. S. Brewer, 2018).

279. Felce, *William Morris and the Development of a Heroic Ideal*, footnote 378, p. 142.

280. Stephen Arata, 'On Not Paying Attention', *Victorian Studies*, 46.2 (Winter 2004), pp. 193–205 (p. 197, p. 205).

281. Ibid., p. 197.

282. Walter Crane, 'William Morris and his Work', in *William Morris to Whistler: Papers and Addresses on Art and Craft and the Commonweal* (London: G. Bell & Sons, 1911), p. 5.

283. As E. P. Thompson notes, Morris signed his Democratic Federation membership card, 'William Morris, Designer', but when advertising his lectures to comrades preferred 'The Author of the *Earthly Paradise*' (*William Morris: Romantic to Revolutionary*, rev. edn (London: Merlin Press, 1976), p. 110).

284. Dante, *The Divine Comedy I: Inferno*, trans. by R. Kirkpatrick (Harmondsworth: Penguin, 2006), p. lxxxvi.

285. Michael Hurley, 'Interpreting Dante's *Terza Rima*', *Forum for Modern Language Studies*, 41.3 (VII/r2005), 320–31 (p. 329).

286. RB, 'Caliban Upon Setebos', *Browning: Poetical Works*, ed. by Ian Jack (London: Oxford University Press, 1970), pp. 836–44 (p. 841).

287. See Waithe, *William Morris's Utopia of Strangers: Victorian Medievalism and the Ideal of Hospitality* (Cambridge: D. S. Brewer, 2006), pp. 71–90.

288. Carl Jung, 'On the Psychology of the Trickster-Figure', in *Four Archetypes* (Oxford: Routledge, 2003), pp. 159–179 (p. 169).

289. For more on this mythic figure, see Lewis Hyde, *Trickster Makes this World: How Disruptive Imagination Creates Culture* (Edinburgh: Cannongate, 2008).

290. Jung, 'On the Psychology of the Trickster-Figure', in *Four Archetypes*, p. 167.

291. Wilde, 'The Decay of Lying', in *The Complete Works of Oscar Wilde*, p. 1090.

292. In 'Textile Fabrics', Morris refers to 'a Greek vase of about 400 bc', which depicts 'Penelope seated before her famous web, which is being worked in an upright loom' (20:274).

293. Nina Auerbach, *Woman and the Demon: The Life of a Victorian Myth* (Cambridge: Harvard University Press, 1982), p. 4.

294. Morris, 'The Early Literature of the North – Iceland', in *ULWM*, pp. 158–88 (p. 188).

295. Ibid., p. 188.

296. Ibid., p. 188.

297. William Makepeace Thackeray, *Vanity Fair: A Novel without a Hero*, ed. by Helen Small (Oxford: Oxford University Press, 2015), p. 843.

298. A. Welby Pugin, *The True Principles of Pointed or Christian Architecture* (London: John Weale, 1841), p. 21.

299. This occurs, according to Morris, 'when we may limit ourselves to certain heavy, close, and very costly cloths' (22:251).

300. John Henry Dearle, MS of 'Article on Textiles for the Catalogue of the Paris Exhibition', MOR4, Sanford and Helen Berger collection of William Morris, Huntington Library, San Marino, CA.

301. Oscar Wilde, 'The Decay of Lying', in *The Complete Works of Oscar Wilde*, pp. 1071–92.

302. Versions of this perspective emerge later in the century as socialist complaints against 'wage slavery'.

303. Cf the student volunteers who broke the General Strike of 1926 (see Keith Laybourn, *The General Strike of 1926* (Manchester: Manchester University Press, 1993), p. 68); Morag Shiach, *Modernism, Labour and Selfhood in British Literature and Culture, 1890–1930* (Cambridge: Cambridge University Press, 2004), pp. 200–46.

Part III

1. Salmon, *The Formation of the Victorian Literary Profession*, p. 67.

2. David Masson, 'The Three Interests in Old English Literature', *Contemporary Review*, XXI (I/1873), 199–225 (p. 217).

3. Cf William Barnes's *An Outline of English Speech Craft* (London: C. Kegan Paul, 1878) on '*Letter-craft*', 'speech-strain' and 'word-building' (p. 1, p. 3). In a related, but satirical context, Carlyle's coinage 'Novelwright' (28:49) dwells on the incongruity between mere novels and the sedimented meanings of 'wright' (from the Anglo-Saxon 'wyrhta', meaning 'artificer or handicraftsman', 'creator', 'deity' (*OED*)).
4. Pettitt, *Patent Inventions*, p. 159.

Chapter 5

1. Baudrillard, *The Mirror of Production*, pp. 98–99.
2. Walt Whitman, 'Song of Myself', *Leaves of Grass*, in *Walt Whitman: Complete Poetry and Collected Prose* (New York: The Library of America, 1982), pp. 27–247 (p. 198).
3. Edward Carpenter, *Towards Democracy* (Manchester: Labour Press, 1896), 37, p. 57.
4. Carpenter, *Towards Democracy*, 18, p. 29.
5. Ibid., 46, p. 68.
6. The time traveller in Morris's *A Dream of John Ball* happens upon 'a carved niche [. . .] – St Clement to wit, as the dweller in the house was a blacksmith'(16:218).
7. Henry Wadsworth Longfellow, 'The Village Blacksmith', in *The Poetical Works of Henry Wadsworth Longfellow*, 6 vols (New York: AMS Press, 1966), I, pp. 64–66.
8. Longfellow, 'The Village Blacksmith', p. 64.
9. Ibid., p. 65.
10. Herman Melville, *Moby Dick* (Harmondsworth: Penguin Books, 1992), p. 33.
11. Ibid., p. 531.
12. Ibid., p. 6.
13. See Annie Creswick Dawson, with Paul Dawson, *Benjamin Creswick* (York: Guild of St George, 2015), p. 40.
14. David L. McDougall, *The Country Blacksmith* (Oxford: Shire Publications, 2013), p. 39, pp. 44–45.
15. Charles Dickens, *Great Expectations*, ed. by Margaret Cardwell (Oxford: Clarendon Press, 1993). Subsequent references to this edition are given parenthetically in the text.
16. Charles Dickens, *David Copperfield*, ed. by Nina Burgis (Oxford: Clarendon Press, 1981), pp. 26–27.
17. Carlyle, 'To Robert Browning' (16/VII/1856), *CLO* (para. 1 of 1).
18. Louttit, *Dickens's Secular Gospel*, p. 8.
19. William Cohen, 'Manual Conduct in *Great Expectations*', ELH, 60.1 (Spring 1993), 217–59.
20. Siskin, *The Work of Writing*, p. 44.
21. Cohen, 'Manual Conduct in *Great Expectations*', ELH, p. 225.

22. Ibid., p. 225.
23. Louttit, *Dickens's Secular Gospel*, p. 39.
24. Charles Dickens, 'To John Forster' ([X/1860]), *The Letters of Charles Dickens*, ed. by Graham Storey, 12 vols (Oxford: Clarendon Edition, 1997), V, p. 325.
25. Steven Connor, 'Forgeries: The Metallurgy of *Great Expectations*' <www.stevenconnor.com/forgeries/forgeries.pdf> p. 11 [accessed 28 June 2022].
26. Ibid., p. 11.
27. Re 'the nature of professional agency', see Jan-Melissa Schramm, *Testimony and Advocacy in Victorian Law, Literature, and Theology* (Cambridge: Cambridge University Press, 2000), p. 103.
28. Caroline Levine, *Forms: Whole, Rhythm, Hierarchy, Network* (Princeton: Princeton University Press, 2015), p. 51.
29. Ibid., p. 49.
30. Ibid., p. 49.
31. Ibid., p. 49.
32. Richard Sennett, *The Craftsman* (London: Penguin, 2009), p. 62.
33. Iamblichus, *On the Pythagorean Life*, trans. by Gillian Clark (Liverpool: Liverpool University Press, 1989), p. 51.
34. John Butt and Kathleen Tillotson, *Dickens at Work* (London: Methuen, 1957), p. 14.
35. Charles Dickens, *Our Mutual Friend*, ed. by Michael Cotsell (Oxford: Oxford University Press, 2008), p. 39.
36. Anny Sadrin, 'Oedipus and Telemachus', in *Charles Dickens's Great Expectations*, ed. by Harold Bloom (New York: Chelsea House, 2000), pp. 269–86 (p. 280).
37. David Hunter, *The Lives of George Frideric Handel* (Woodbridge: Boydell Press, 2015), p. 201.
38. The triennial London festival crowd 'generally originated in the industrial north and the Midlands' (Introduction, *Words and Notes in the Long Nineteenth Century*, ed. by Phyllis Weliver and Katherine Ellis (Woodbridge: Boydell Press, 2013), p. 1).
39. Charles Dickens, *Dombey and Son*, ed. by Alan Horsman (Oxford: Oxford University Press, 1982), p. 687.
40. Ibid., p. 687.
41. Charles Collins, 'Our Eye-Witness with Handel', *All the Year Round*, 1 (16/VII/1859), pp. 276–79.
42. Richard Clark, *Reminiscences of Handel, His Grace the Duke of Chandos, Powells the Harpers, The Harmonious Blacksmith, and Others* (London, 1836), p. 6.
43. Clark, *Reminiscences of Handel*, p. 6.
44. Iamblichus, *On the Pythagorean Life*, p. 51.
45. Clark, *Reminiscences of Handel*, p. 6.
46. Ibid., p. 6.
47. Ibid., n.p. (appendix).
48. Collins, 'Our Eye-Witness with Handel', *All the Year Round*, p. 276.

49. Tom Paulin, 'The Great Horn-Handled Jack-Knife: *Great Expectations* as Epic Poem', in *Minotaur: Poetry and the Nation State* (Cambridge: Harvard University, 1992), pp. 112–32.

50. Ibid., p. 131.

51. Kathryn Murphy, 'Thomas Traherne, Thomas Hobbes, and the Rhetoric of Realism', *The Seventeenth Century*, 28.4 (2013), 419–39 (p. 428).

52. Ibid., p. 432.

53. Anon. [George Sala], 'Colonel Quagg's Conversion', *Household Words*, 30/XII/1854, 459–65.

54. [Sala], 'Colonel Quagg's Conversion', p. 464.

55. Murphy, 'Thomas Traherne, Thomas Hobbes, and the Rhetoric of Realism', p. 430.

56. Nicholas Shrimpton, '*Great Expectations*: Dickens's Muscular Novel', *Dickens Quarterly* (VI/2012), 29.2, 125–41 (p. 135).

57. Murphy, 'Thomas Traherne, Thomas Hobbes, and the Rhetoric of Realism', p. 430.

58. Paulin, *Minotaur*, p. 114. Relatedly, see Claude Lévi-Strauss, *Tristes Tropiques*, trans. by John Weightman and Doreen Weightman (London: Penguin, 2011).

59. Ibid., p. 116.

60. Claude Lévi-Strauss, *The Savage Mind* (London: Weidenfeld & Nicolson, 1974), p. 17.

61. Robert Browning, *Sordello*, in *The Poetical Works of Robert Browning*, ed. by Ian Jack and Margaret Smith (Oxford: Clarendon Press, 1984), II, pp. 193–498 (p. 273). Cf Ross Wilson, 'Ruskin, Browning / Alpenstock, Hatchet', in *The Labour of Literature*, ed. by Waithe and White, pp. 81–96.

62. Linda M. Austin, 'Labor, Money, and the Currency of Words in *Fors Clavigera*', *ELH*, 56.1 (Spring 1989), 209–27.

63. Ibid., 212.

64. Ibid., 223–24.

65. Ruskin's success in this respect may seem improbable, but the addresses recorded in the visitor book of his St George's Museum in Sheffield confirm at least a local reach into working-class neighbourhoods (Collection of the Guild of St George, Museums Sheffield).

66. Cook and Wedderburn gloss the word 'darg' as '"a day's work," the word being a syncopated form of *daywerk*' (27:599). Ruskin elsewhere defines it simply as 'doing' (27:607).

67. W. B. Yeats, 'Leda and the Swan', in *The Major Works*, ed. by Edward Larrissy (Oxford: Oxford University Press, 2001), p. 112.

68. Cf Murphy's account of Thomas Traherne, where 'Abuse is the power to choose to obey or disobey God, and thus represents human liberty' ('Thomas Traherne, Thomas Hobbes, and the Rhetoric of Realism', p. 430).

69. David Pye, *The Nature and Art of Workmanship*, rev. edn (1971; London: Herbert Press, 1995), p. 20.

70. Cardinal Manning, 'To John Ruskin' (21/X/1873); quoted by Cook and Wedderburn (36:lxxxvi).

71. Austin, 'Labor, Money, and the Currency of Words', p. 225.
72. Ruskin writes that 'One man is made of agate, another of oak; one of slate, another of clay' (11:262).
73. Sara Atwood, *Ruskin's Educational Ideals* (Oxford: Routledge, 2016), p. 86; Plato, *Republic*, trans. by Chris Emlyn-Jones and William Preddy, 2 vols (Cambridge: Harvard University Press / Loeb Classical Library, 2013), I, Book III, p. 333.
74. Dinah Birch, Introduction, in John Ruskin, *Fors Clavigera: Letters to the Workmen and Labourers of Great Britain*, ed. by Dinah Birch (Edinburgh: Edinburgh University Press, 2000), p. xxxiii.
75. Ibid., p. xxxiii.
76. See Canto XLVI: the Bank of England 'hath benefit of interest on all | the moneys, which it, the bank, creates out of nothing' (*The Cantos of Ezra Pound* (London: Faber and Faber, 1981), pp. 431–35 (p. 233)).
77. Frost, *The Lost Companions and John Ruskin's Guild of St George*, p. 208.
78. Birch, Introduction, in Ruskin, *Fors Clavigera*, p. xxxv.
79. Plato, *Phaedrus*, in *Plato I*, trans. by Harold North Fowler (London: William Heineman / Loeb Classial Library, 1966), 405–579 (p. 563).
80. 'To Oxford', in *Poetical Works of Gerard Manley Hopkins* [hereafter *PW*], ed. by Norman H. Mackenzie (Oxford: Clarendon Press, 1990), pp. 71–73 (p. 72).
81. Gerard Manley Hopkins, 'Boughs Being Pruned, birds preened, who more fair', in *PW*, p. 68.
82. S. T. Coleridge, 'To William Godwin' (22/IX/1800), in *Collected Letters of Samuel Taylor Coleridge*, I, pp. 624–26 (p. 625).
83. 'To Robert Bridges' (26–27/IX/1882), in *Gerard Manley Hopkins Correspondence*, in *The Collected Works of Gerard Manley Hopkins* [hereafter *CW*], ed. by R. K. R. Thornton and Catherine Phillips, 8 vols (Oxford: Oxford University Press, 2006–), II, (2013), pp. 537–40 (p. 538). N.B. dates given for Hopkins' poems indicate the time of composition, not publication.
84. G. M. Hopkins, '18 December 1873', in *Gerard Manley Hopkins: Diaries, Journals, Notebooks*, in *CW*, II, pp. 565–66 (p. 565).
85. Ibid., p. 565.
86. 'To Richard Watson Dixon' (30/VI–3/VII/1886), in *CW*, II, pp. 791–97 (p. 792); Hamo Thornycroft, *The Mower* (1888–90), bronze, Tate Gallery, London.
87. Catherine Phillips, *Gerard Manley Hopkins and the Victorian Visual World* (Oxford: Oxford University Press, 2007), p. 240.
88. G. H. Gardner, *Gerard Manley Hopkins (1844–1889): A Study of Poetic Idiosyncrasy in Relation to Poetic Tradition*, 2 vols (London: Martin Secker & Warburg, 1944), II, p. 12.
89. Geoffrey Hill, 'Alienated Majesty: Gerard M. Hopkins', in *Collected Critical Writings*, ed. by Kenneth Haynes (Oxford: Oxford University Press, 2008), pp. 518–31 (p. 528).

90. Hopkins, '—Yes for a time', *Floris in Italy*, in *PW*, pp. 40–41 (p. 41)
91. Ibid., p. 41.
92. Hopkins, 'Fragments of *Floris in Italy*', in *PW*, p. 41.
93. Ibid., p. 43.
94. Ibid., p. 36.
95. Hopkins, 'Felix Randal', in *PW*, p. 165.
96. Hopkins, 'The Alchemist in the City', in *PW*, pp. 75–76 (p. 75).
97. Frederick William Faber, *The Creator and the Creature; or, The Wonders of Divine Love* (London: Thomas Richardson and Son, 1858)
98. Jill Muller, *Gerard Manley Hopkins and Victorian Catholicism: A Heart in Hiding*, 4th edn (London: Routledge, 2003), p. 54.
99. Hopkins, 'The Principle of Foundation', in *The Sermons and Devotional Writings of Gerard Manley Hopkins* [hereafter, *SDW*], ed. by Christopher Delvin (London: Oxford University Press, 1959), pp. 238–41 (p. 238).
100. Ibid., p. 238.
101. Ibid., p. 238.
102. Ibid., p. 239.
103. Ibid., p. 238.
104. Hopkins, 'God's Grandeur', in *PW*, p. 139.
105. Hopkins, 'Hurrahing in Harvest', in *PW*, pp. 148–49 (p. 149).
106. Hopkins, 'In the Valley of the Elwy', in *PW*, p. 143.
107. Hopkins, 'To Robert Bridges' (15/II/1879), in *CW*, I, pp. 333–34 (p. 334).
108. Bernard Bergonzi, *Gerard Manley Hopkins* (London and Basingstoke: Macmillan, 1977), p. 176.
109. Hopkins, 'The Wreck of the Deutschland', in *PW*, pp. 119–28 (p. 119).
110. Ibid., p. 124.
111. Hopkins, 'Henry Purcell', in *PW*, p. 157–58 (p. 157).
112. Hopkins, epigraph to 'Henry Purcell', in *PW*, p. 157.
113. Hopkins, 'Felix Randal', in *PW*, p. 165.
114. Hopkins, 'Harry Ploughman', in *PW*, p. 193.
115. Bergonzi, *Gerard Manley Hopkins*, p. 65.
116. Hopkins, 'No Worst', in *PW*, p. 182.
117. G. K. Chesterton, 'The Hammer of God', in *The Complete Father Brown Stories*, ed. by Michael D. Hurley (London: Penguin Books, 2012), pp. 122–35 (p. 132).
118. Hopkins, 'The Wreck of the Deutschland', in *PW*, p. 119.
119. Ibid., p. 120.
120. Hopkins, 'The Loss of the Eurydice', in *PW*, pp. 149–52 (p. 149).
121. Hopkins, sermon preached at St Francis Xavier's, Liverpool (18/I/1880), in *SDW*, pp. 58–62 (p. 58).
122. Hopkins, 'The Principle of Foundation', in *SDW*, p. 240.
123. Hopkins, 'The Windhover', in *PW*, p. 144.
124. Hopkins, 'Felix Randal', in *PW*, p. 165.
125. Hopkins, 'The Sea and the Skylark', in *PW*, p. 143.
126. Hill, 'Eros in F. H. Bradley and T. S. Eliot', in *Collected Critical Writings*, pp. 548–64 (p. 563).

127. 'To Robert Bridges' (7/VIII/1868), in *CW*, I, pp. 186–87 (p. 186).
128. 'To Robert Bridges' (3/II/1883) in *CW*, II, pp. 568–70 (p. 570).
129. 'To Richard Watson Dixon' (12/V/1879), in *CW*, I, pp. 356–57 (p. 357).
130. 'To Richard Watson Dixon' (1–16/XII/1881), in *CW*, I, p. 503.
131. 'To Richard Watson Dixon' (29/X/1881–2/XI/1881), in *CW*, I, pp. 488–95 (p. 493).
132. 'To Richard Watson Dixon' (1–16/XII/1881), in *CW*, I, p. 502.
133. 'To Bridges' (4–5/I/1883), in *CW*, II, pp. 560–62 (p. 560).
134. John Duns Scotus, 'II. Man's Natural Knowledge of God', in *Philosophical Writings: A Selection*, trans. by Allan Wolter (Indianapolis: Hackett, 1987), pp. 13–33 (pp. 32–33).
135. Muller, *Gerard Manley Hopkins and Victorian Catholicism*, p. 75.
136. 'To Ernest Hartley Coleridge' (22/I/1866), in *CW*, I, pp. 86–87 (p. 86).
137. Ibid., p. 87.
138. Hopkins, 'How all's to one thing wrought!', in *PW*, p. 159.
139. Scotus, 'The Existence of God', in *Philosophical Writings: A Selection*, pp. 34–81 (p. 61).
140. Robert Bridges, *Prometheus The Firegiver* (Oxford: H. Daniel, 1883).
141. Bridges, *Prometheus The Firegiver*, p. 5.
142. Norman H. Mackenzie, 'Hopkins and Science', *Studies in the Literary Imagination*, 21.1 (Spring 1988), 41–56. I am grateful to Michael Hurley for alerting me to this article. See also John Gordon, 'The Electrical Hopkins', *University of Toronto Quarterly*, 65.3 (Summer 1996), 506–22.
143. Mackenzie, 'Hopkins and Science', *Studies in the Literary Imagination*, p. 43.
144. Ibid., p. 43; Hopkins, 'God's Grandeur', in *PW*, p. 139.
145. Hopkins, 'Epithalamion', in *PW*, p. 165.
146. 'To Everard Hopkins' (5–8/XI/1885), in *CW*, II, pp. 745–51 (p. 748).
147. Hopkins, 'The Wreck of the Deutschland', in *PW*, p. 126.
148. Gardner, *Gerard Manley Hopkins*, p. 116.
149. Ibid., p. 116.
150. Richard Chenevix Trench, *On the Study of Words: Lectures Addressed (Originally) to the Pupils at the Diocesan Training School, Winchester*, 6th edn (London: John W. Parker and Son, 1855), p. 16.
151. For further discussion of this effect in metalwork, see Marcus Waithe, *Ruskin and Craftsmanship* (York: Guild of St George, 2015).

Chapter 6

1. Virginia Woolf, 'Craftsmanship' (10/IV/1937), in *The Death of the Moth and other Essays* (London: Hogarth Press, 1942), pp. 126–32 (p. 126).
2. Woolf observes of Arnold Bennett that he wrote a book 'so solid in its craftsmanship that it is difficult [. . .] to see through what chink or crevice decay can creep in.' ('Modern Fiction', in *Collected Essays* (London: The Hogarth Press, 1966), pp. 103–10 (p. 104)).

3. See Donna Elizabeth Rhein, *The Handprinted Books of Leonard and Virginia Woolf at the Hogarth Press, 1917–1932* (Ann Arbor: UMI Research Press, 1985).
4. Woolf, 'Craftsmanship', in *The Death of the Moth and other Essays*, p. 126.
5. Ibid., p. 126.
6. Virginia Woolf, *To the Lighthouse* (Oxford: Oxford University Press, 2006).
7. Virginia Woolf, *The Years*, ed. by Hermione Lee (Oxford: Oxford University Press, 2009), pp. 173–74, p. 179.
8. Wyndham Lewis, 'A Review of Contemporary Art', in *Blast: Review of the Great English Vortex* (London: John Lane, The Bodley Head, July 1915), 2, pp. 33–47 (p. 46).
9. See Heather R. Perry, *Recycling the Disabled: Army, Medicine, and Modernity in WWI Germany* (Manchester: Manchester University Press, 2017).
10. Marianne Brandt, 'Tea and coffee set', 1924, silver, ebony, glass, Bauhaus Archive Berlin; *Bauhaus Archive Berlin: The Collection* (Berlin: Bauhaus Archive Berlin, 1999), p. 112.
11. Pye, *The Nature and Art of Workmanship*, p. 54.
12. Peter Nicholls, 'Preface to the Second Edition', *Modernisms* (Basingstoke: Palgrave Macmillan, 2009), p. viii. See also Tim Armstrong, 'Social Credit Modernism', *Critical Quarterly*, 55.2 (July 2013), 50–65 (p. 50); and *Modernism, Technology and the Body: A Cultural Study* (Cambridge: Cambridge University Press, 1998), p. 2.
13. See Alexandra Harris, *Romantic Moderns: English Writers, Artists and the Imagination from Virginia Woolf to John Piper* (London: Thames and Hudson, 2015).
14. Shiach, *Modernism, Labour and Selfhood*, p. 63.
15. A recent exception is Hope Wolf's exhibition and catalogue, *Sussex Modernism: Retreat and Rebellion* (London: Two Temple Place, 2017).
16. Dieter Meindl, *American Fiction and the Metaphysics of the Grotesque* (Columbia: University of Missouri Press, 1996), p. 134.
17. Marcus Waithe, 'Strenuous Minds: Walter Pater and the Labour of Aestheticism', in *The Labour of Literature*, ed. by Waithe and White, pp. 147–66.
18. Henry James, 'To W. D. Howells' (I/1895), in *The Letters of Henry James: 1883–1895*, ed. by Leon Edel, 4 vols (London: Macmillan, 1981), III, p. 512.
19. Percy Lubbock, *The Craft of Fiction* (London: Jonathan Cape, 1960), p. 19.
20. Percy Lubbock, 'Introduction', in *The Letters of Henry James*, ed. by Percy Lubbock (New York: Charles Scribner's Sons, 1920), pp. i–xxxi (p. xix).
21. Linda Merrill, *A Pot of Paint: Aesthetics on Trial in Whistler v. Ruskin* (Washington and London: Smithsonian Institution Press, 1992), pp. 147–48; for Whistler's recorded version, see J. M. Whistler, *The Gentle Art of Making Enemies* (London: Heinemann, 1890), p. 5.
22. Frances Spalding, *Whistler* (Oxford: Phaidon, 1979), p. 7.
23. Whistler, *The Gentle Art of Making Enemies*, p. 8.
24. Ibid., p. 8.
25. Meindl, *American Fiction and the Metaphysics of the Grotesque*, p. 134.

26. Pater, 'The Beginnings of Greek Sculpture', in *Greek Studies: A Series of Essays* (London: Macmillan and Co., 1910), pp. 187–250.
27. Ibid., p. 198.
28. Ibid., p. 198.
29. Ibid., p. 188.
30. Ibid., p. 193.
31. James Joyce, *A Portrait of the Artist as a Young Man* (Oxford: Oxford University Press, 2000), p. 213.
32. Ibid., p. 233.
33. Cf Gustave Flaubert, 'To Mme De Chantepie' (18 March 1857), in *Selected Letters of Gustave Flaubert*, trans. by Francis Steegmüller (London: Farrar, Straus and Young, 1954), p. 186: '*L'artiste doit être dans son oeuvre comme Dieu dans la Création, invisible et tout-puissant*' ('An artist must be in his work like god in creation, invisible, and all powerful').
34. See Sidney Feshbach, 'Joyce Read Ruskin', *James Joyce Quarterly (JJQ)*, 10.3 (Spring 1973), 333–36; see also Harold I. Shapiro, 'Ruskin and Joyce's *Portrait*', *JJQ*, 14.1 (Fall 1976), 92–93; and Fred Radford, 'The Nautilus and the Tower: John Ruskin and the Victorian Medievalism of James Joyce', *JJQ*, 28.3 (Spring 1991), 595–615; See also, 'Introduction', *Ruskin and Modernism*, ed. by Giovanni Cianci and Peter Nicholls (Palgrave, 2001), p. xi, p. xvi.
35. A poem 'comes right', remarks Yeats, 'with a click like a closing box' (W. B. Yeats, 'To Dorothy Wellesley', (8/IX/1935), in *Letters on Poetry from W. B. Yeats to Dorothy Wellesley* (London: Oxford University Press, 1940), p. 24–25 (p. 24)).
36. W. B. Yeats, 'Byzantium', in *The Collected Poems of W. B. Yeats* (London: Macmillan, 1961), pp. 280–81 (p. 280).
37. Yeats, 'Sailing to Byzantium', in *The Collected Poems of W. B. Yeats*, pp. 217–18.
38. Olive Schreiner, 'To Havelock Ellis', (7/VIII/1912), Letters/506, NLSA Cape Town, *Olive Schreiner Letters Project* [hereafter, *OSLP*], <https://www.oliveschreiner.org>, 57. When dealing with letters transcribed by Cronwright-Schreiner, an editorial disclaimer applies that he 'often changed or even bowdlerised' Schreiner's text.
39. Liz Stanley, *Imperialism, Labour and the New Woman* (2002; London: Routledge, 2013), p. 12.
40. Vernon Lee, *The Handling of Words and Other Studies in Literary Psychology* (London: John Lane, The Bodley Head, 1923), p. 21.
41. See Catherine Maxwell, 'Vernon Lee's *Handling of Words*', in *Thinking through Style*, ed. by Hurley and Waithe, pp. 282–97 (p. 291).
42. See, for instance, Arnold Bennett, *How to Become an Author: A Practical Guide* (London: C. Arthur Pearson, 1903); see also Philip Waller's discussion of 'Literary Advice and Advisers' in *Writers, Readers, and Reputations*, pp. 68–115.
43. Lee, *The Handling of Words*, p. 41.
44. Ibid., p. 36.

45. Ruth Livesey, *Socialism, Sex, and the Culture of Aestheticism in Britain, 1880–1914* (Oxford: Oxford University Press, 2007), p. 165.
46. Ibid., p. 165.
47. Quoted in Giovanni Cianci, 'Tradition, Architecture and *Rappel à l'Ordre*: Ruskin and Eliot (1917–21)', in *Ruskin and Modernism*, pp. 133–54 (p. 142).
48. Sennett, *The Craftsman*, p. 50.
49. Fiona MacCarthy, *Eric Gill* (London: Faber and Faber, 1990).
50. The first book edition – which was published by the Hogarth Press in 1923 – lacks the dedication that Eliot wrote in the Boni & Liveright edition given to Pound, and which was subsequently included in *Poems, 1909–1925* (London: Faber and Gwyer, 1925).
51. Virginia Woolf, 'Professions for Women', in *The Death of the Moth and other Essays*, pp. 149–54 (p. 149).
52. Ibid., p. 149.
53. Maria Antonietta Saracino, 'The Diamond and the Flaw', in *The Flawed Diamond: Essays on Olive Schreiner*, ed. by Itala Vivan (Sydney: Dangaroo Press, 1883), pp. 146–59 (p. 148).
54. Virginia Woolf, 'Olive Schreiner', in *Women and Writing*, ed. by Michèle Barrett (Orlando: Harcourt, 1979), pp. 180–83 (p. 181).
55. Ibid., p. 182.
56. Ibid., p. 181.
57. Cf Zoë Thomas, 'At Home with the Women's Guild of Arts: Gender and Professional Identity in London Studios, c. 1880–1925', *Women's History Review*, 24.6 (2/VI/2015), 938–64 (p. 940).
58. In *Women and Socialism* (1879), August Bebel describes the 'Rise of the Patriarchate', and its displacement of the 'Matriarchate' (trans. by Meta L. Stern (New York: Socialist Literature, 1910), p. 28). See also Friedrich Engels on the matriarchal institutions of Germanic tribes (*The Origin of the Family, Private Property and the State, in the Light of Researches by Lewis H. Morgan*, trans. by Alick West (London: Lawrence & Wishart, 1940)).
59. Eleanor Marx and Edward Aveling, 'The Woman Question: From a Socialist Point of View', *Westminster Review*, 125 (I/1886), 207–22 (p. 217).
60. Livesey, *Socialism, Sex, and the Culture of Aestheticism in Britain, 1880–1914*, pp. 129–30 (p. 51).
61. Olive Schreiner, *Woman and Labour* (London: T. Fisher Unwin, 1911), p. 167.
62. Joseph Bristow, 'Introduction', in Olive Schreiner *'The Story of an African Farm*, ed. by Joseph Bristow (Oxford: Oxford University Press, 2008), pp. i–xxix (p. xxvii).
63. 'To Miss Louis Ellis', (7/III/1894), Letters/430, NLSA Cape Town, *OSLP*, 16.
64. 'To S. C. Cronwright-Schreiner', (5/III/1907), MSC 26/2.16/351, NLSA Cape Town, *OSLP*, 4–5.
65. Schreiner, 'Reminiscences', quoted in S. C. Cronwright-Schreiner, *The Life of Olive Schreiner*, p. 14.
66. 'To Adela Villiers Smith', (27/VIII/1912), Letters/509, NLSA Cape Town, *OSLP*, 74–5.

67. 'To Havelock Ellis', (19/III/1890), HRC/CAT/OS-4b-xiv, Harry Ransom Research Center, University of Texas at Austin, *OSLP* transcription, <https://www.oliveschreiner.org>, 34–35.
68. 'To William Thomas Stead', (12/VII/1890), T120 (M722), National Archives Depot, Pretoria, *OSLP*, 16–17; 21–2.
69. Schreiner, *Woman and Labour*, p. 140.
70. 'To Havelock Ellis', (1/XII/1885), NLSA Cape Town, *OSLP*, 4–6.
71. 'To S. C. Cronwright-Schreiner', (25/III/1908), NLSA Cape Town, *OSLP*, 2–3.
72. Olive Schreiner, *From Man to Man (or PERHAPS ONLY . . .)* (London: Adelphi Terrace, 1926), p. 58.
73. Schreiner, *From Man to Man*, p. 58.
74. Schreiner, *Woman and Labour*, p. 33.
75. Ibid., p. 195.
76. Ibid., pp. 200–01.
77. Ibid., p. 34.
78. Ibid., p. 34.
79. Ibid., p. 50.
80. Ibid., pp. 83–84.
81. Schreiner, 'Reminiscences', quoted in S. C. Cronwright-Schreiner, *The Life of Olive Schreiner*, p. 10.
82. 'To Havelock Ellis', (2/V/1884), Harry Ransom Research Center, University of Texas at Austin, *OSLP*, 50–52.
83. Ibid., 47–48.
84. 'To Edward Carpenter', 1908, National English Literary Museum, Grahamstown, *OSLP*, 4–16.
85. Edward Carpenter, *Days with Walt Whitman* (London: George Allen, 1906), p. 105.
86. Ibid., pp. 114–15.
87. Schreiner, *From Man to Man*, p. 181.
88. 'To Havelock Ellis', (9/IV/1885), NLSA Cape Town, *OSLP*, 4–5.
89. 'To Havelock Ellis', (5/IV/1885), NLSA Cape Town, *OSLP*, 4.
90. 'To Havelock Ellis', (5/II/1889), NLSA Cape Town, *OSLP*, 19–21.
91. 'To Isaline Philpot', (18/II/1888), NLSA Cape Town, *OSLP*, 4–5.
92. *The Letters of Olive Schreiner 1876–1920*, ed. by S. C. Cronwright-Schreiner (London: T. Fisher Unwin, 1924), p. v.
93. Cronwright-Schreiner, *The Life of Olive Schreiner*, p. 356.
94. *The Letters of Olive Schreiner*, p. vi.
95. Schreiner, *Woman and Labour*, p. 61.
96. Ibid., p. 174.
97. Ibid., p. 169.
98. Ibid., p. 173.
99. Ibid., p. 129.
100. Ibid., pp. 129–30.
101. Ibid., p. 130.
102. Ibid., p. 132.

103. Ibid., p. 31.

104. Ibid., p. 223.

105. 'Enclosure in No. 17', from *Rand Daily Mail*, 6 June 1903, in *South Africa. Further Correspondence Relating to the Affairs of the Transvaal and Orange River Colony*, Command Paper 1895 (Houses of Parliament, 1904), LXI, pp. 36–44 (p. 42).

106. Saul Dubow, 'South Africa's Racist Founding Father was also a Human Rights Pioneer', *New York Times*, 18 May 2019, https://www.nytimes.com/2019/05/18/opinion/jan-smuts-south-africa.html [accessed 28 June 2022].

107. Jan Smuts, *Holism and Evolution* (London: Macmillan and Co., 1927), p. 270.

108. Smuts, *Holism and Evolution*, p. 229.

109. Ibid., p. 100.

110. Ibid., p. 187.

111. Stanley, *Imperialism, Labour and the New Woman*, p. 157.

112. Schreiner, *Woman and Labour*, p. 142.

113. Olive Schreiner, 'To Havelock Ellis', ([?]/VI/1911), NLSA Cape Town, *OSLP*, 5–6.

114. Schreiner, *The Story of An African Farm*, p. 55–57.

115. Schreiner, *Woman and Labour*, p. 77.

116. Saracino, 'The Diamond and the Flaw', p. 155.

117. Schreiner, *Woman and Labour*, p. 81.

118. Ibid., p. 82.

119. Ibid., pp. 97–98.

120. Ibid., p. 84.

121. 'To William Philip Schreiner', (24/IV/1909), UCT Manuscripts & Archives, *OSLP*, 11–12.

122. Schreiner, *From Man to Man*, p. 435.

123. Anna Snaith, *Modernist Voyages: Colonial Women Writers in London, 1890–1945* (Cambridge: Cambridge University Press, 2014), p. 55.

124. Schreiner, *Thoughts on South Africa* (London: T. Fisher Unwin, 1923), p. 61.

125. Ibid., p. 98.

126. Ibid., p. 98.

127. Schreiner, *Thoughts on South Africa*, p. 73.

128. Schreiner, *Woman and Labour*, p. 92.

129. Schreiner, *Thoughts on South Africa*, p. 106, p. 117.

130. J. A. Hobson, *The War in South Africa: Its Causes and Effects* (London: James Nisbet & Co., 1900), p. 226.

131. Cronwright-Schreiner, *The Life of Olive Schreiner*, pp. 6–7.

132. Olive Schreiner, 'A Letter on the Jew', in *The Letters of Olive Schreiner*, pp. 392–95 (p. 393).

133. Schreiner, *From Man to Man*, p. 328.

134. Schreiner, 'A Letter on the Jew', p. 393.

135. Ibid., p. 395.

136. Schreiner, *Thoughts on South Africa*, p. 51.
137. Schreiner, *Woman and Labour*, p. 158.
138. Schreiner, 'Three Dreams in a Desert', in *Dreams* (Boston: Little, Brown, and Co., 1915), pp. 51–70 (p. 57).
139. 'To Henrietta ('Ettie') Schreiner', (22/VI/1904), UCT Manuscripts & Archives, *OSLP*, 22–23.
140. 'To Betty Molteno', (27/VII/1902), UCT Manuscripts & Archives, *OSLP*, 74–79.
141. 'To Betty Molteno', (15/VI/1902), UCT Manuscripts & Archives, *OSLP*, 18–20.
142. Wanne Mendonck, PhD draft, (University of Cambridge, 2019).
143. Schreiner, 'To William Philip Schreiner', ([?]/I/1919), UCT Manuscripts & Archives, *OSLP*, 31.
144. 'To Havelock Ellis', (14/IV/1885), Harry Ransom Research Center, University of Texas at Austin, *OSLP*, 6–8.
145. 'To Havelock Ellis', (5/IV/1885), NLSA Cape Town, *OSLP*, 10–11.
146. Cronwright-Schreiner, *The Life of Olive Schreiner*, p. 229.
147. Ibid., p. 231.
148. Ibid., p. 269. She was, he claimed, 'as ill-qualified for the work-a-day world as almost anyone could be' (p. 100).
149. Ibid., p. 251.
150. Schreiner, *The Story of An African Farm*, pp. 101–18.
151. Bristow, 'Introduction', in *The Story of an African Farm*, p. xxviii; Jane Marcus, *Virginia Woolf and the Languages of Patriarchy* (Bloomington: Indiana University Press, 1987), p. 63.
152. Eric Gill, 'Idiocy or Ill-Will', in *In A Strange Land: Essays by Eric Gill* [hereafter, *ISL*] (London: Jonathan Cape, 1944), p. 58.
153. Ibid., p. 58.
154. Ibid., p. 59.
155. Ibid., p. 59.
156. Eric Gill, 'The Failure of the Arts and Crafts Movement: A Lesson for Trade Unionists', *Socialist Review*, 4 (December 1909), 289–300.
157. MacCarthy, *Eric Gill*, p. 252.
158. Eric Gill, 'Art-Nonsense', in *Art-Nonsense and Other Essays* [hereafter, *ANOE*] (London: Cassell & Co., 1929), pp. 310–24 (p. 323).
159. Eric Gill, *Autobiography* (London: Jonathan Cape, 1940), pp. 136–37.
160. Ibid., pp. 136–37.
161. Gill quoted in Malcolm Yorke, *Eric Gill: Man of Flesh and Spirit* (London: Constable, 1981), p. 258.
162. Gill, *Autobiography*, p. 74.
163. Ibid., p. 115.
164. Ibid., p. 270.
165. MacCarthy, *Eric Gill*, p. 42.
166. Ibid., pp. 51–52.
167. Ibid., p. 65.
168. Gill, *Autobiography*, p. 162.

169. Ruth Cribb, 'Eric Gill (1882–1940)', in Ruth Cribb and Joe Cribb, *Eric Gill and Ditchling: The Workshop Tradition* (Ditchling: Ditchling Museum, 2007), pp. 11–17 (p. 14).

170. Gill, 'A Grammar of Industry', in *ANOE*, pp. 6–14 (p. 12).

171. Gill, *Autobiography*, pp. 57–58.

172. Ibid., p. 57.

173. Ibid., p. 110.

174. Gill, 'John Ruskin (*An address to the English Speaking Union, 8 Feb. 1934*)', in *ISL*, p. 85.

175. Gill, *Autobiography*, p. 112.

176. MacCarthy, *Eric Gill*, p. vii.

177. Constitution of the Guild of St Joseph and St Dominic, in Cribb and Cribb, *Eric Gill and Ditchling*, pp. 27–28 (p. 27).

178. Cribb and Cribb, *Eric Gill and Ditchling*, p. 27.

179. Ibid., p. 27.

180. Gill, 'A Grammar of Industry', in *ANOE*, p. 13.

181. MacCarthy, *Eric Gill*, p. 78.

182. Holbrook Jackson, *William Morris: Craftsman-Socialist* (London: A. C. Fifield, 1908).

183. A. J. Penty, *The Restoration of the Gild System* (London: Swan Sonnenschein & Co, 1906).

184. Pope Leo XIII, *Rerum Novarum: Encyclical Letter of Pope Leo XIII on the Condition of the Working Classes*, trans. by Joseph Kirwan (London: Catholic Truth Society, 1983), p. 27.

185. Gill, 'Quae ex veritate et bono', in *ANOE*, pp. 65–79 (p. 71). Gill argues likewise that '[A]ll men who make things are artists' ('The Criterion in Art', in *ANOE*, pp. 276–98 (p. 276–77)).

186. Epigraph to Gill, *ANOE*, p. iv.

187. Cf David Jones in 'The Utile': 'We were then *homo faber, homo sapiens* before Lascaux and we shall be *homo faber, homo sapiens* after the last atomic bomb has fallen' (*Epoch and Artist: Selected Writings of David Jones* [hereafter, *EA*], ed. by Harmon Grisewood (London: Faber and Faber, 1959), pp. 180–85 (p. 184)).

188. Gill, 'Essential Perfection', in *ANOE*, pp. 3–5 (p. 5).

189. Gill, 'Stone-Carving', in *ANOE*, pp. 80–95 (p. 82).

190. Jacques Maritain, *The Philosophy of Art: Being 'Art et scolastique' by Jacques Maritain, translated by the Rev. John O'Connor, S. T. P. with an introduction by Eric Gill O.S.D.* (Ditchling, Sussex: St Dominic's Press, 1923).

191. Jacques Maritain, *Art and Scholasticism*, trans. by J. F. Scanlan (London: Sheed & Ward, 1930), p. 63.

192. Gill, 'The Lord's Song: A Sermon', in *ISL*, pp. 9–17 (p. 9).

193. Gill, 'Essential Perfection', p. 5.

194. Gill, 'The Future of Sculpture', in *ANOE*, pp. 299–309 (p. 299).

195. Ibid., p. 301.

196. Gill, 'The Criterion in Art', in *ANOE*, pp. 276–98 (p. 293).

197. Gill, 'Christianity and Art', in *ANOE*, pp. 232–49 (p. 232).

198. Gill, 'The Future of Sculpture', p. 301.
199. Gill, 'Stone-Carving', p. 82.
200. Gill, 'Christianity and Art', p. 232.
201. Gill, 'Sculpture on Machine-Made Buildings', in *ISL*, p. 112.
202. Rowan Williams, *Grace and Necessity: Reflections on Art and Love* (London: Continuum, 2005), p. 5.
203. Williams, *Grace and Necessity*, pp. 18–19.
204. Ibid., pp. 15–16.
205. Ibid., p. 164.
206. Ibid., p. 165.
207. *The Philosophy of Art: Being 'Art et scolastique' by Jacques Maritain*, p. 91, p. 92.
208. Ibid., p. 93.
209. Ibid., p. 92.
210. Jacques Maritain, *'Art et scolastique'* (Paris, 1927), p. 103.
211. Ibid., p. 104.
212. Ibid., p. 92.
213. Ibid., p. 91.
214. Gill's diaries and other personal papers (MS Gill) are held at the William Andrews Clark Memorial Library, University of Los Angeles, California.
215. MacCarthy, *Eric Gill*, p. viii.
216. *The Philosophy of Art: Being "Art et Scolastique" by Jacques Maritain*, p. 51, p. 95.
217. Ibid., p. 95.
218. Ibid., p. 30, p. 10; Maritain, *Art and Scholasticism*, trans. by J. F. Scanlan, p. 7.
219. David Jones, 'Art and Sacrament' (1955), in *EA*, p. 174.
220. Jacques Maritain, *Art and Scholasticism, with Other Essays by Jacques Maritain*, trans. by J. F. Scanlan (London: Sheed & Ward, 1930), pp. 4–5.
221. *Conversations with Flannery O'Connor*, ed. by Rosemary M. Magee, (Jackson and London: University Press of Mississippi, 1987), p. 39. Quoted in Brian Barbour, 'Introduction', *Art and Scholasticism* (Tacoma: Cluny Media, 2016), pp. i–xvii (p. viii).
222. David Jones, 'Art and Sacrament', p. 172.
223. Eric Gill, *An Essay on Typography* (1931; London: Penguin Books, 2013), p. 23.
224. Ibid., p. 23.
225. Ibid., p. 119.
226. Ibid., p. 119.
227. David Jones, 'Eric Gill' (1940), in *EA*, pp. 296–302 (p. 301).
228. MacCarthy, *Eric Gill*, p. 14.
229. Eric Gill, *Autobiography*, p. 26.
230. Jones, 'Art and Sacrament', in *EA*, pp. 143–79 (p. 167).
231. 'Sculpture on Machine-Made Buildings', in *ISL*, p. 132.
232. Gill, *Autobiography*, p. 120.
233. Williams, *Grace and Necessity*, p. 2.

234. Jones, 'The Viae', in *EA*, pp. 189–95 (p. 194).
235. See Lida Lopes Cardozo Kindersley and Marcus Waithe, *Words Made Stone: The Craft and Philosophy of Letter Cutting* (Cambridge: Cardozo Kindersley, 2022), p. 142.
236. Jones, 'Preface, *The Anathemata: Fragments of an Attempted Writing* (1952) (London: Faber and Faber, 1972), p. 21.
237. Ibid., p. 12.
238. Jones, 'Art and Sacrament', in *EA*, p. 158.
239. Robert Casillo, *The Genealogy of Demons* (Evanston: Northwestern University Press, 1986), p. 36.
240. Ibid., p. 8.
241. Tim Redman, *Ezra Pound and Italian Fascism* (Cambridge: Cambridge University Press, 1991), p. 65.
242. Serenella Zanotti, 'Fascism', in *Ezra Pound in Context*, ed. by Ira B. Nadel (Cambridge: Cambridge University Press, 2010), pp. 376–90 (p. 386).
243. Pound, 'Ecclesiastical History', *The New English Weekly*, 5 July 1934, in *Ezra Pound: Selected Prose 1909–1965* [hereafter, *SP*], ed. by William Cookson (London: Faber and Faber, 1973), pp. 61–63 (p. 61).
244. Aaron Jaffe, *Modernism and the Culture of Celebrity* (Cambridge: Cambridge University Press, 2005), p. 132.
245. Michael Alexander, *Medievalism: The Middle Ages in Modern England* (New Haven and London: Yale University Press, 2007), p. 229.
246. T. S. Eliot, 'On a Recent Piece of Criticism', *Purpose*, 10.2 (April–June 1938), 90–94 (pp. 92–93); Pound asserts the primacy of Arnaut in *The Spirit of Romance*, using Dante's words as a chapter heading (*The Spirit of Romance* (1910; London: Peter Owen, 1970), p. 22).
247. Eliot, 'On a Recent Piece of Criticism', 90–94 (pp. 92–93).
248. Ezra Pound, *ABC of Reading* (London: Faber and Faber, 1963), p. 53.
249. A. J. Penty, 'Aestheticism and History', *The New Age*, 2 April 1914, 683–84.
250. Pound, 'The City', in *SP*, ed. by William Cookson (London: Faber and Faber, 1973), pp. 194–96 (pp. 194–95).
251. Pound, 'Yeux Glauques', *Hugh Selwyn Mauberley* (London: Faber and Faber, 1975), pp. 98–112 (p. 101)
252. Cianci and Nicholls , 'Introduction', in *Ruskin and Modernism*, p. xv.
253. Eliot, 'A Commentary', *The Criterion*, 10.39 (January 1931), pp. 309–10.
254. Casillo, *The Genealogy of Demons*, p. 50.
255. Pound, 'The Jefferson-Adams Letters as a Shrine and a Monument', *North American Review* (Winter 1937–38), in *SP*, pp. 117–130 (p. 127).
256. Pound, 'Immediate Need of Confucious', *Aryan Path*, August 1937, in *SP*, pp. 89–94 (p. 92).
257. Pound, 'Treatise on Metre', in *ABC of Reading*, pp. 195–206 (p. 197).
258. Pound, 'The Serious Artist', in *Literary Essays of Ezra Pound* [hereafter, *LEEP*], ed. by T. S. Eliot (New York: New Directions, 1968), pp. 41–57 (p. 55).
259. Pound, *Hugh Selwyn Mauberley*, p. 98.
260. Redman, *Ezra Pound and Italian Fascism*, p. 28.

261. Pound, 'How to Read', in *LEEP*, pp. 15–40 (p. 21)
262. Ibid., p. 21.
263. Ezra Pound, 'An Introduction to the Economic Nature of the United States' (1944, in Italian), in *SP*, pp. 137–55 (p. 148).
264. Redman, *Ezra Pound and Italian Fascism*, p. 28.
265. Ibid., p. 28.
266. Pound, 'The State', in *SP*, pp. 184–85 (p. 185).
267. Ibid., p. 185.
268. Cf Clive Wilmer 'Sculpture and Economics in Pound and Ruskin', *P. N. Review*, VII–VIII/1998, 43–50 (p. 43).
269. Ezra Pound, 'Musicians: God Help 'Em', in *Pavannes and Divagations* (1958) (New York: New Directions, 1975), pp. 217–20 (p. 219).
270. Ezra Pound, *I gather the Limbs of Osiris*, in *SP*, pp. 21–43 (p. 42).
271. Pound, 'A Retrospect', in *LEEP*, p. 9.
272. Pound, *I gather the Limbs of Osiris*, p. 34.
273. Hugh Kenner, *The Pound Era* (London: Faber and Faber, 1975), p. 27.
274. Pound, 'A Retrospect', in *LEEP*, p. 3.
275. Donald Davie, 'The Poet as Sculptor', in *New Approaches to Ezra Pound: A Co-ordinated Investigation of Pound's Poetry and Ideas* (London: Faber and Faber, 1969), pp. 198–214 (p. 214).
276. Davie, 'The Poet as Sculptor', p. 214.
277. Pound, *ABC of Reading*, p. 198.
278. Ibid., p. 32.
279. Denise Riley, 'On the Lapidary Style', *differences: A Journal of Feminist Cultural Studies*, 28.1 (2017), 17–36 (p. 26).
280. Pound, '*Dubliners* and Mr Joyce', in *LEEP*, pp. 399–402 (p. 399).
281. Pound, 'Cavalcanti: Medievalism', in *LEEP*, pp. 149–200 (p. 154).
282. Pound, 'A Retrospect', in *LEEP*, p. 10.
283. Ibid., p. 10.
284. Ibid., p. 12.
285. Louis B. Salomon, understands this 'instinct for teaching' as the chief link between the two men: 'The Pound-Ruskin Axis', *College English*, 16.5 (February 1955), 270–76 (p. 271).
286. Pound, 'A Retrospect', p. 5.
287. Pound, 'How to Read', *LEEP*, pp. 15–40 (p. 21).
288. Pound, 'A Retrospect', p. 6.
289. 'To Isabel W. Pound' (XI/1913), in *The Selected Letters of Ezra Pound, 1907–1941* (New York: New Directions, 1971), pp. 25–26 (p. 26).
290. T. S. Eliot, 'Ezra Pound' (1946), in *Ezra Pound: A Collection of Essays edited by Peter Russell to be Presented to Ezra Pound on his Sixty-fifth Birthday* (London: Peter Nevill Ltd, 1950), pp. 25–36 (p. 35).
291. Sennett, *The Craftsman*, p. 27.
292. Ibid., p. 27.
293. 'CANTO 46' (12/II/1942), in *"Ezra Pound Speaking": Radio Speeches of World War II* [hereafter, *EPS*], ed. by Leonard W. Doob (Westport: Greenwood Press, 1978), p. 37.

294. Clive Wilmer, 'Sculpture and Economics in Pound and Ruskin', *P. N. Review*, (VII–VIII/1998), 43–50 (p. 47).
295. Pound, 'Canto XLV', *The Cantos of Ezra Pound* [hereafter, *CEP*] (New York: New Direction Books, 1996) p. 230.
296. Kenner, *The Pound Era*, p. 325; Hugh Witemeyer, 'Ruskin and the Signed Capital in Canto 45', *Paideuma*, 4.1 (1975), 58–88.
297. 'WITH PHANTOMS' (18/V/1942), in *EPS*, pp. 137–40 (pp. 137–8).
298. Major C. H. Douglas, *Social Credit* (London: Cecil Palmer, 1924), p. 207.
299. Pound, 'HOW COME' (10/VII/1942), in *EPS*, p. 196.
300. Ibid., p. 196.
301. Ibid., p. 196.
302. Ibid., p. 196.
303. Ibid., p. 196.
304. T. S. Eliot, 'Tradition and the Individual Talent', *The Sacred Wood: Essays on Poetry and Criticism* (London: Faber and Faber, 1997), pp. 39–49.
305. Giovanni Cianci, 'Tradition, Architecture and *Rappel à l'Ordre*: Ruskin and Eliot (1917–21)', in *Ruskin and Modernism*, pp. 133–54 (p. 137).
306. Cf Hargrave's Morrisian concern with the Teutonic and Icelandic institutions of 'folkmoot' and 'Althing'. Hargrave's stipulation that his male followers wear 'Men's Habit' also recalls Gill's fondness for monastic dress. See also Hargrave's *The Pfenniger Failing* (London: Duckworth, 1927), a novel about a stonemason resembling Gill.
307. Armstrong, 'Social Credit Modernism', p. 50.
308. Maj. C. H. Douglas, *Social Credit* (London: Cecil Palmer, 1924), p. 63.
309. Cf Marx in *The German Ideology*, in *Marx / Engels Collected Works*, 50 vols (London: Lawrence & Wishart, 1976), V: 'in communistic society [. . .] it is possible for me [. . .] to hunt in the morning, fish in the afternoon, rear cattle in the evening, criticise after dinner' (p. 47).
310. Pound, 'For a New Paideuma' (*The Criterion*, January 1938), in *SP*, pp. 254–59 (p. 258–59).
311. Ibid., pp. 258–59.
312. A. H. Mackmurdo, *The Immorality of Lending for Payment of Interest, or for any Usurious Gain* (London: C. Watts, 1978); Ruskin, 'Letter 24' (December 1872), *Fors*, in *Works*, XXVII; and R. G. Sillar, *Usury, its Pernicious Effects on English Agriculture and Commerce*, introduction by Ruskin (London: A. Southey, 1885) [this work has a different cover title to that given on its title page].
313. Jeremy Bentham, *A Defence of Usury* (1787; Cambridge: Cambridge University Press, 2014), p. 2.
314. Gill, 'Sculpture on Machine-Made Buildings', *ISL*, pp. 103–36 (p. 105).
315. Ibid., p. 107.
316. Gill, 'The Revival of Handicraft', in *ANOE*, p. 117.
317. Gill, *Autobiography*, p. 249.
318. Anthony Julius, *T. S. Eliot, Anti-Semitism, and Literary Form* (Cambridge: Cambridge University Press, 1995).
319. Dan Stone, *Responses to Nazism in Britain, 1933–1939: Before War and Holocaust* (Basingstoke: Palgrave, 2003), p. 131.

320. Armstrong, 'Social Credit Modernism', p. 54.
321. Edith Hope Scott, *Ruskin's Guild of St George* (London: Methuen & Co., 1931), p. 19.
322. Pound, 'HOW COME' (10/VII/1942), in *EPS*, pp. 195–97 (p. 197).
323. Ibid., p. 197.
324. Gervase Rosser, *The Art of Solidarity in the Middle Ages: Guilds in England 1250–1550* (Oxford: Oxford University Press, 2015), p. 25.
325. Ibid., p. 8.
326. Ibid., p. 8, p. 223.
327. Ibid., p. 25.
328. H. D., *End to Torment, With the Poems from 'Hilda's Book' by Ezra Pound*, ed. by Norman Holmes Pearson and Michael King (New York: New Directions, 1979), p. 22.
329. Redman, *Ezra Pound and Italian Fascism*, p. 18.
330. See also, Waithe, *William Morris's Utopia of Strangers*, p. 117–37.
331. E. T. Kemble, *The Saxons in England: A History of the English Common-wealth till the Period of the Norman Conquest*, 2 vols (London: Longman, Brown, Green, and Longmans, 1849), 2, 310–11.
332. Edward A. Freeman, *The Growth of the English Constitution from the Earliest Times* (London: Macmillan and Co., 1872), p. viii; Morris acknowledges Freeman's influence in 'The Revival of Architecture' (22:319).
333. Rosser, *The Art of Solidarity in the Middle Ages*, p. 8, p. 20, p. 22; Joshua Toulmin Smith, *Local Self-Government and Centralization* (London: John Chapman, 1851), p. 13.
334. G. D. H. Cole, *Social Theory* (London: Methuen, 1920), p. 183, p. 209.
335. Bernard Leach, *A Potter's Book* (London: Faber and Faber, 1940), p. 10.
336. MacCarthy, *Eric Gill*, p. 278.
337. Peter Makin, *Bunting: The Shaping of his Verse* (Oxford: Clarendon Press, 1991), p. 114.
338. Aldritt, *The Poet as Spy*, p. 94.
339. Leon Surette, *Pound in Purgatory: From Economic Radicalism to Anti-Semitism* (Urbana: University of Illinois Press, 2003), p. 89.
340. Alex Houen, 'Anti-Semitism', in *Ezra Pound in Context*, pp. 391–401 (p. 394).
341. Ibid., p. 395.
342. Pound, 'Gists', in *SP*, p. 325.
343. Pound, 'Ecclesiastical History', p. 61.
344. Ibid., p. 61.
345. 'What is money for?', in *SP*, pp. 260–72 (p. 260).
346. John Palmer, *Parmenides and Presocratic Philosophy* (Oxford: Oxford University Press, 2013), p. 271.
347. William Shakespeare, *King Lear*, ed. by R. A. Foakes (Walton-on-Thames: Arden / Thomas Nelson and Sons, 1997), p. 164.
348. William Patterson and Michael Godfrey, *A Brief Account of the Intended Bank of England* (London: Randal Taylor, 1694).
349. Desai, *The Route of All Evil: The Political Economy of Ezra Pound* (London: Faber and Faber, 2006), p. 68. Pound may have been drawn to

Hollis by a discussion of usury on the same page as the Paterson quotation (Christopher Hollis, *The Two Nations: A Financial Study of English History* (London: G. Routledge and Sons, 1935), p. 36). I am grateful to the Bank of England Archive, and to Claire Wilkinson, for discussions and clues that may assist further investigation.

350. Pound, 'Canto XLV', *CEP*, pp. 229–30 (p. 229).
351. Ibid., p. 230.
352. Pound, 'Canto XLII', *CEP*, pp. 209–14 (p. 209).
353. Pound, 'Canto XLIII', *CEP*, pp. 215–22 (p. 219)
354. Pound, 'Canto XLIV', *CEP*, pp. 223–28 (p. 228).
355. Thoreau, 'Thomas Carlyle and his Works', in *The Writings of Henry D. Thoreau*, p. 228.
356. Pound, 'An Introduction to the Economic Nature of the United States' (1944, in Italian), in *SP*, p. 143. A modern statue in Philadelphia of another Founding Father, Benjamin Franklin, commemorates him as 'CRAFTSMAN'.
357. 'There is no gold sproutin' up in England', he proclaims, because of 'usury against every man who does a day's work, physical or with his mind' (Pound, 'GOLD: ENGLAND' (8/III/1942), in *EPS*, pp. 55–58 (p. 55); 'BUT HOW? SECOND ITEM' (23/III/1942), in *EPS*, pp. 70–73 (p. 73)).
358. Pound, 'BUT HOW? SECOND ITEM' (23/III/1942), in *EPS*, p. 73.
359. Pound, 'PERFECT PHRASING' (17/VII/1942), in *EPS*, p. 206.
360. Pound, 'THE KEYS OF HEAVEN' (8/VI/1942), in *EPS*, pp. 162–65 (p. 162).
361. Casillo, *The Genealogy of Demons*, pp. 33–34.
362. Ibid., pp. 33–34.
363. Pound, 'Demarcations', *British Union Quarterly*, 1 (I–IV/1937), p. 37.
364. Pound, 'Immediate Need of Confucious', *Aryan Path*, August 1937; *SP*, pp. 89–94 (p. 90).
365. Casillo, *The Genealogy of Demons*, p. 237; Plato, *Phaedrus*, in *Plato I*, p. 563.
366. Pound, 'Canto XLV', *CEP*, pp. 229–30 (p. 229).
367. Ibid., p. 229.
368. Ibid., p. 330.
369. Ibid., p. 229.
370. Ibid., p. 230.
371. Hyde, *Trickster Makes this World*, p. 10.
372. Ibid., p. 257.
373. Pound, 'CANTO 46' (12/II/1942), in *EPS*, p. 34.
374. Ibid., p. 36. Cf 'And the earth was without form, and void [. . .] And God said, Let there be light'.
375. Ibid., p. 34.
376. Ibid., p. 34.
377. Casillo, *The Genealogy of Demons*, p. 237.
378. Ibid., p. 237.
379. Riley, 'On the Lapidary Style', *differences: A Journal of Feminist Cultural Studies*, p. 30.

380. K. L. Goodwin, *The Influence of Ezra Pound* (London: Oxford University Press, 1966), p. 35.
381. Morris draws on anti-Semitic caricature in portraying the merchant, 'Penny-thumb' (15:62). See Waithe, *William Morris's Utopia of Strangers*, pp. 166–68.

Conclusion

1. Epigraph to Gill, *ANOE*, p. iv.
2. Pater, 'Style', in *Appreciations*, p. 14.
3. Houen, 'Anti-Semitism', in *Ezra Pound in Context*, p. 395.
4. See, for instance, Fredric Jameson, *Postmodernism, or, the Cultural Logic of Late Capitalism* (Durham, NC: Duke University Press, 1991).
5. Zygmunt Bauman, *Liquid Modernity* (Cambridge: Polity, 2000).
6. Peter C. Dooley, *The Labour Theory of Value* (Oxford: Routledge, 2005), p. 226.
7. The Crafts Council reports that 'In six years, 2007–2013, student participation in craft-related GSCEs fell 25%', while in 'higher education, the number of craft courses fell 46%'; Anon., 'Our Future is in the Making' (Crafts Council Education Manifesto) (London: Crafts Council, 2014) <http://www.craftscouncil.org.uk/content/files/7822_Education_manifesto%4014FINAL.PDF> [accessed 16 April 2018].
8. Leadbeater, *Living on Thin Air: The New Economy*, p. vii.
9. Peter Dormer, *The Art of the Maker: Skill and its Meaning in Art, Craft and Design* (London: Thames and Hudson, 1994), p. 7.
10. Dormer, *The Art of the Maker*, p. 13.
11. David Pye, *The Nature and Art of Workmanship,* rev. edn (1971; London: Herbert Press, 1995). For more on this tradition, see Marcus Waithe, *Ruskin and Craftsmanship* (York: Guild of St George, 2015).
12. I. A. Richards, *Practical Criticism: A Study of Literary Judgment* (1929) (London: Kegan Paul, Trench, Tubner & Co., 1930), p. 344.
13. Bunting, 'What the Chairman Told Tom', *Complete Poems*.
14. Bunting, *Briggflatts* (Tarset, Northumberland: Bloodaxe, 2009), p. 15.
15. Yael Zarhy-Levo, *The Making of Theatrical Reputations* (Iowa City: University of Iowa Press, 2008), p. 35.
16. Leslie Paul, *Angry Young Man* (London: Faber and Faber, 1951).
17. Ibid., p. 60.
18. Ibid., p. 29.
19. Ibid., p. 55.
20. Thom Gunn, *The Sense of Movement* (London: Faber and Faber, 1968).
21. Richard Hoggart, *The Uses of Literacy: Aspects of Working-Class Life with Special Reference to Publications and Entertainments* (London: Chatto & Windus, 1959), pp. 238–49 (p. 247).
22. Hoggart, *The Uses of Literacy*, p. 246.
23. Seamus Heaney, 'Digging', in *New Selected Poems*, 2 vols (London: Faber and Faber, 2014), I, pp. 1–2 (p. 1).

24. Ibid., p. 2.
25. Tony Harrison, 'v.', in *Selected Poems* (London: Penguin, 1987), p. 236.
26. Ibid., p. 236.
27. Geoffrey Hill, *Mercian Hymns* (XXV), in *Broken Hierarchies: Poems 1952–2012*, ed. by Kenneth Haynes (Oxford: Oxford University Press, 2013), p. 107.
28. Hill, 'Poetry and Value', *Geoffrey Hill: Collected Critical Writings*, ed. by Kenneth Haynes (Oxford: Oxford University Press, 2008), pp. 485–86 (pp. 478–89). See also Marcus Waithe, 'Hill, Ruskin, and Intrinsic Value', in *Geoffrey Hill and his Contexts* (Oxford: Peter Lang, 2011) pp. 133–49.
29. Geoffrey Hill, 'Improvisation on "Warum ist uns das Licht gegeben?"', *Without Title* (London: Penguin, 2006), p. 519.
30. Hill, dedication, *Broken Hierarchies*, n.p.; see also Marcus Waithe, '"Dense Settling": Geoffrey Hill's *Broken Hierarchies*', *P. N. Review*, 219 (September–October 2014), pp. 14–18.
31. Riley, 'On the Lapidary Style', *differences: A Journal of Feminist Cultural Studies*, p. 35.
32. Alice Oswald, *The Thing in the Gap-Stone Stile* (London: Faber, 1996).
33. Alice Oswald, *Memorial: An Excavation of the Iliad* (London: Faber, 2012).
34. 'Germany Exports its Apprenticeship Model', *Financial Times*, 24 January 2014 <https://www.ft.com/content/b9008b70-68cf-11e3-bb3e-00144feabdc0> [accessed 17 April 2018]; 'Switzerland Thrives on Apprenticeship Tradition', *Financial Times*, 14 December 2017 <https://www.ft.com/content/98e06036-d99b-11e7-a039-c64b1c09b482> [accessed 17 April 2018].
35. Schaffer, *Novel Craft: Victorian Domestic Handicraft and Nineteenth-Century Fiction*; Sennett, *The Craftsman*.
36. D'Israeli, *The Literary Character; or, The History of Men of Genius, Drawn from Their Own Feelings and Confessions*, I, p. 238.
37. Michael Polanyi, *The Tacit Dimension* (1966; Chicago: Chicago University, 2009), p. 7.
38. Pye, *The Nature and Art of Workmanship*, p. 20.

Index

Note: page numbers in *italics* indicate figures.

EU representative:
Easy Access System Europe
Mustamäe tee 50, 10621 Tallinn, Estonia
Gpsr.requests@easproject.com

www.ingramcontent.com/pod-product-compliance
Lightning Source LLC
Chambersburg PA
CBHW051101030726
47504CB00006B/1727